LETTERS TO GRACE

One Family's First-Hand Accounts of World Events from 1912 – 1970

CURATED BY BETSY CHRISTENSEN

bookhouse
PUBLISHING

bookhouse
PUBLISHING

2950 Newmarket St., Suite 101-358, Bellingham, WA 98226
www.bookhouserules.com

Library of Congress Control Number: 2026910974

ISBN: 978-1-967874-05-7 (Paperback)
ISBN: 978-1-967874-43-9 (Hardcover)

Editing: Julie Scandora
Book design: Scott Book & Melissa Vail Coffman

Contents

INTRODUCTION

READING AN OLD LETTER is a form of time travel, placing us in the middle of a conversation from another era. We no longer live in an age of letters, and I think that fact makes the existence of old letters all the more interesting.

This is a collection of family letters written primarily to one person, my grandmother Grace Salisbury Ingles. The letters span six decades—starting in 1912 with a letter from her father and ending in 1970 with a series of letters from her daughter, my aunt. There is also a series of letters from her son, my father, in the 1940s. Although Grace is the recipient of these letters, she is a silent character in the dramas the letters portray. Other than the occasional note scrolled on the bottom of one of the letters, Grace's voice is not present in these conversations and has to be inferred from context. And yet, she is also the central character of these everyday stories. Her influence on the letter writers is evident, as is the love they all shared for her.

Though mostly silent in this collection of letters, Grace was anything but timid in life. She earned a bachelor's degree from the University of Nebraska at a time when only 2.5 percent of women in the United States attended college. Upon graduation, she traveled to Puerto Rico to work as a teacher, a journey that would have required train travel to a port city and then passage on an ocean liner. The trip was facilitated by a church, but when things didn't go as promised, Grace left the organized group and found her own placement at an orphanage. She returned to the States to marry her high school sweetheart Hal Ingles on December 26, 1914.

Family lore is full of stories of Grace's audacity. When dating and engaged to Hal, Grace would have dinners with the Ingles family. Hal's father, John W. Ingles (1842-1917), was in the habit of retreating to his study to read. Grace would invite herself to join the senior Ingles for conversation, much to the chagrin of Hal's older sisters who would never include themselves in their father's ritual. Once married to Hal, now a young officer in the army, the couple was expected to entertain. During prohibition it would have been inappropriate for a military officer to be seen at a speakeasy to acquire alcohol, so Grace would go instead. When women won the vote in 1920, they had to become registered to exercise this right. According to the family stories, when Grace went to register, she was requested to take a literacy test. She refused to do so because she had informed the staff she was a college graduate and that fact demonstrated she could read. The staff member insisted on the requirement, and Grace left the registration office only to return the next day with her diploma. Apparently, the staff completed Grace's registration without requiring she take the literacy test.

One of the best stories of Grace's audacity revolves around her age. She was born in 1887. Hal was born in 1888. At the time, there was a stigma of marrying a younger man. Grace married Hal anyway but was bothered by the age difference. At Grace's birth, no birth certificate was submitted, a practice common with rural, home births. In order to get a birth certificate, someone who was present at your birth had to appear with you to apply at the state's Division of Vital Records. On June 8, 1936, Grace and her mother, Jessie Osborn Salisbury, applied for a birth certificate from the state of Nebraska stating that Grace had been born in 1889, thus making her a year younger than Hal. This bold act, on the part of both mother and daughter, has caused the genealogists and family historians grief ever since, including a heated family debate about what date should appear on Grace's headstone in Arlington National Cemetery.

From these stories, Grace can be viewed as either pompous or pragmatic. Perhaps she was a little of both. It is said that she didn't "suffer fools well," and if the solution to a problem was a little unconventional, well, so be it. Unfortunately, I never heard any of these stories directly from Grace; they were only retold primarily by my father, Grace's son. Dad always told these stories in the spirit of admiration, clear evidence of the love he had for her. I can see how Grace could be accused of being domineering, but I have always been inspired by her determination.

About the Letters Themselves

The collection is divided into three parts, based on the writer of the letters. It is happenstance that the dates of the letters do not overlap. The first section, letters written by Grace's father, Stephen Olin Salisbury, begins in 1912 when Grace, in her mid-twenties, travels to Puerto Rico on a mission trip. This section ends in 1928 on the event of Stephen and Jessie Osborn Salisbury's fiftieth wedding anniversary. The second section, letters written by Grace's son (my father), John Stephen Ingles, spans the years of 1940–45 and includes firsthand accounts of Officer's Training School and life as a lieutenant in WWII. The third and final section is the longest. This section contains letters written to Grace by her daughter (my aunt), Mary Osborn Ingles, who worked as a social worker for the American Red Cross. The letters are from Mary's overseas assignments in Germany, Japan, Korea, and Vietnam, covering the years of 1950–1970.

It is a mystery to me why some letters have survived and why others were destroyed. I can't believe that the curation of them was accidental. For the first set of letters, those from Grace's father, obviously these were precious artifacts to her. From the thousands of letters that must have been written by Stephen Salisbury to Grace, the fact that only four remain indicates the significance of the events they chronicle.

In the case of my father's letters to his mother, these may have been returned to him not too long after they were written. It appears the full set was preserved and passed back to Dad. His parents (my grandparents) moved from a large house in Washington, DC, to an apartment sometime in the late 1960s, and I suspect the letters were turned over to my father during the move.

The mystery behind Mary's letters looms larger. Someone—Grace or Mary—went through and selected which to keep and which to throw out. I don't know when this process happened. Who purged these documents, and why did some make the cut and others disappear? What was in the missing letters? What was the criteria for getting rid of them? Were they just boring ones, or did they contain information that Mary or Grace didn't want anyone to ever see again? Sometimes there are hints in the surviving letters about the missing ones, but still a lot of speculation remains.

In fact, with Mary's letters, I'm surprised any survived. I can remember, when she lived in her apartment in Alexandria and I was living in the DC area, her telling me one day that she took "boxes of photos from her travels" and threw them into the trash chute. Had the letters already been culled at this time, or did some go out along with the photos? Why save the words but destroy the images?

Another mystery that struck me as I transcribed Mary's letters was why didn't I know all this before? I have traveled quite a bit in both Europe and Japan. By the time I was in high school, Mary lived a few miles away from my family, and we socialized with her sevcral times a year. Why didn't she tell me about her experiences when I was getting ready to launch on my journeys? I would have enjoyed hearing about the places she had gone, and as I read the letters, I regret that I can't ask her questions. Mary was not shy about sharing her opinions. Why was she so reserved about sharing her experiences? I knew she had traveled a lot, but as a teen and in my early twenties, I didn't really piece together that I was going to places she had been. I wonder if her silence had something to do with her strained relationship with my mother. Or did she just believe that I wouldn't have cared to hear her tales? As I ponder the way things played out, I can't help but mourn a missed opportunity. I was lucky enough to transcribe my father's letters while he was still alive, and he and I had many conversations about the events. He even self-published a book, *A Soldier's Passage*, about his military experiences that leaned heavily on information from the letters his mother had saved.

My regret at not knowing the stories of my relatives is driving me to complete this project. My children and their cousins are not so far removed from these letter writers, and yet if I don't liberate the stories from the fragile paper and fading ink, they will be lost forever. The people revealed in these letters are far from perfect. They made mistakes, they had self-doubts, they had prejudices, they were sometimes cuttingly judgmental. But none of us are saints, and I think it is a worthy cause to see the realness of those on whose shoulders we stand.

Letters have been transcribed as they were written—with the capitalization and punctuation that may not conform to today's standards. Any changes made to the letters are presented in brackets, [ ].

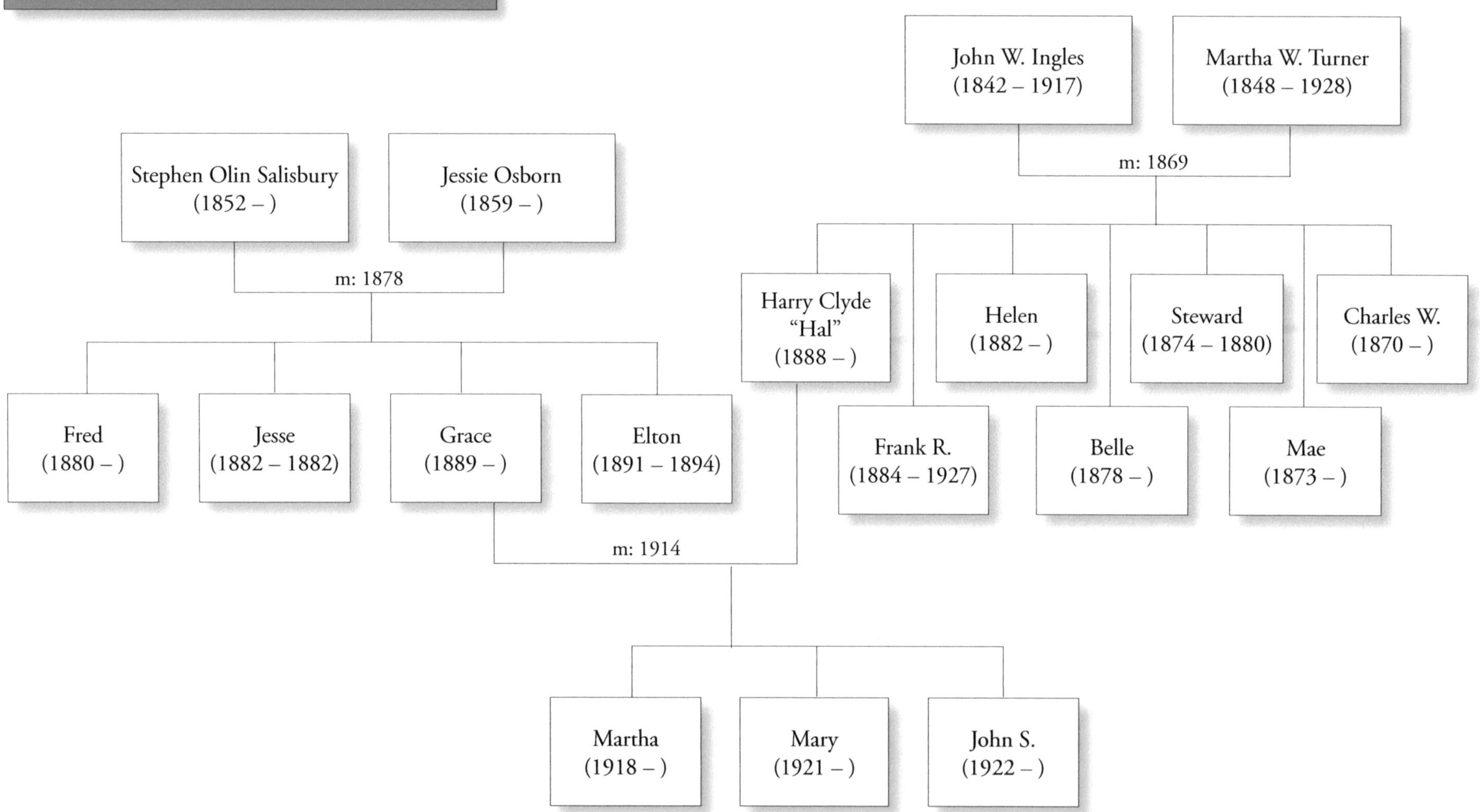

— FAMILY TREE —
CIRCA 1928

John W. Ingles
(1842 – 1917)

Martha W. Turner
(1848 – 1928)

m: 1869

Stephen Olin Salisbury
(1852 –)

Jessie Osborn
(1859 –)

m: 1878

Harry Clyde
"Hal"
(1888 –)

Helen
(1882 –)

Steward
(1874 – 1880)

Charles W.
(1870 –)

Fred
(1880 –)

Jesse
(1882 – 1882)

Grace
(1889 –)

Elton
(1891 – 1894)

Frank R.
(1884 – 1927)

Belle
(1878 –)

Mae
(1873 –)

m: 1914

Martha
(1918 –)

Mary
(1921 –)

John S.
(1922 –)

Section One: The Letters of Stephen Olin Salisbury, 1912–1928

Historical and Cultural Context

Stephen Olin Salisbury (1852-1930) was born in Norway, New York, and moved to Nebraska in 1871. There he met Jessie Osborn (1859-1941), whom he married in 1878. Nebraska was still considered a frontier state during the life of their daughter, Grace (1889-1977), and her brother, Fred (1880-1948), when they lived in Lincoln. Stephen had "read the law" and was practicing law when Grace was born. As such, the family would have been one of the wealthier and more influential in town.

The world that Grace was born into was one where most women in the United States did not attend college. Few colleges admitted women, and the women's colleges that did exist were all located in the East. However, many land-grant universities, like the University of Nebraska, did allow female students. Grace attended her state university and graduated in 1912 with a degree in education, one of the only degrees allowed for women.

Harry Clyde ("Hal") Ingles (1888-1976) had grown up on a farm in Pleasant Hill, Nebraska, and moved to Lincoln to stay with his older sister to attend high school and, after that, the University of Nebraska. We know Hal and Grace met in high school but are not sure when they began dating. We do know they were engaged by 1912.

Hal had no intention to return to the farm after university, but finances for his education were a burden. According to family lore, Hal had completed three years at the University of Nebraska when one of his fraternity brothers said there was chance to apply to West Point. Hal leapt at the opportunity because admission to West Point meant he

Stephen O. Salisbury as young man

did not have to pay for his education, and he would have a job upon completion. It did mean, however, that his eventual degree would take seven years as he had to enter West Point as a freshman. It seemed to be a tradeoff that served him well. He excelled at West Point and went on to have an illustrious career in the US Army.

PERSONAL REFLECTIONS ON THE LETTERS FROM 1912

WHEN GRACE GRADUATED FROM the University of Nebraska in 1912, she was engaged to Hal, who was at West Point and would not be finished until 1914. Regulations at the military academy required them to wait until Hal graduated to be married. I guess staying at home, waiting, didn't appeal to Grace, so she went to teach in Puerto Rico. I have always marveled at what would have been involved to simply get to Puerto Rico from Nebraska in 1912. We know that at least one friend went with Grace, but beyond that, there is no documentation of the journey. The trip was organized through a church, but apparently the program was not all that had been promised. The oral history is a little sketchy, but we know Grace left the organized trip for some reason and managed to independently arrange for work at an orphanage in Puerto Rico. The letter from September 1912 is a beautiful fatherly message to a brave young woman off on a grand adventure. The long letter from November of the same year has some references to the difficulties Grace encountered and her apparent aplomb in solving them.

* * *

Sept 8 – 1912

Dear Grace,

You will not maybe appreciate how hard it is to have you go away for so long. I wish you to go, for you wish to, but you were all we had. Fred being away so much and it is mighty hard to give you up. There is no one in the world to take your place to me. No one I love more and am more proud of. You may not think it but I['m] crying like a child as I write and you have very seldom seen me cry. Be careful of the friends you make and don't take to[o] much on trust. I mean be always on your guard with strangers particularly men. You are not a child and have had some experiences with the world but you cannot be too careful. I know, Grace, you will make good wherever you are. You have it in you to mix well, much better than Fred. I am sure you will enjoy your trip and don't think you will get very lonesome having so many of your friends with you. We shall look forward to your letters and begin to plan your coming home. Be a good girl. I know you will be. May God bless and protect you.

Lovingly,
Father

* * *

Nov. 19, 1912

Miss Grace Salisbury,
San Juan, Porto Rico. [*sic*]
Box. 966.

Dear Grace,

Your letter of Nov. 9th received, also one from Dr. Murray. I replied to him yesterday and you told me he was a pretty good joker, so I guess he will take what I said in the spirit in which it was written.

I am enclosing you a clipping from the Journal regarding the Kansas-Nebraska Game. Fred and I went. It was quite thrilling but the facts were that Kansas had the best of it all the way through until about ten minutes before the close of the last quarter. I wouldn't have given a penny for Nebraska's chances before that time.

I think you do just fine Grace, to write such nice long letters as you do for I know you have more cares and worries than ever before. I don't believe I would have consented to you going at all if I hadn't thought it would give you an experience that would help you. I hardly thought the experience would come in as large doses as they have to you, but "keep a stiff upper lip" put up a good fight and you will be all the better for it when your year is over, I am sure.

The work you are doing gives you a new view on life entirely. Don't let it get on your heart too much for there are many things that you have written us that are depressing.

The trip to Porto Rico [*sic*] alone would be worth the while even to have the love and confidence of the little girl Josephine. Poor little kiddie, I hope she will get better and not droop and die, as you seem to think she will.

I am sorry that Miss (Dis-) Comfort is doing things so unpleasant there, but that is just one more experience in self-control and gives you an insight as to characters such as hers and how unworthy she is to be doing it in Christ's name.

There are three classes of people whom I utterly detest, first a hypocrite, next a dead-beat and finally a snob. I am perhaps a little too democratic myself, but I have always had a great deal of sympathy for the under dog and you are coming in contact with it at first hands there. You say that skies seem bluer, and the stars and moon brighter there, and I believe you have a clearer conception of what it means to be a Christian than ever before. It is the pearl of the Great Price.

I think separation is beneficial to us all. When you were home, of course you came and went and I am sure we didn't appreciate you as fully as we should have. We have always been proud of you, but never as much as now. Hereafter we will be better pals than we have before. While I may not always have done my full duty to my family, I believe I can honestly say that I have tried to, and I am glad that you do appreciate me. There has never been one thing that we have deprived ourselves for the benefit of our children that hasn't been done by both your Mother and myself gladly and our regret has always been that we couldn't do more, and as you say if we haven't pilled [*sic*] up very much, I believe I can always say I have played the game square.

I am afraid from the tone of your letters Grace, that you have a pretty good case of homesickness on your hands, and I know just how it is. You will remember that I left home when I was only nineteen years old, and a good home too, to come out into Nebraska when it was all new and crude and everybody poor, without any experience and not very much education, but you never knew until now what I endured in homesickness then.

Take the sunny view of it. It won't be very long and that lonesome feeling will wear away as time goes by. I hope it will never be gone entirely.

Well, enough of this.

You spoke of Floyd and ask me whether or not I thought he could break Uncle Than's Will. As you know Fred and I made the draft of the Will here and it was gone over carefully after we had finished it by a good lawyer who pronounced it unbreakable in Nebraska. The Will was later made up and signed in Kansas and by a Kansas lawyer, who ought to have known whether or not it was good in Kansas. I don't know what the Kansas Statutes are governing trusts. In this State, as I said before, the Will would be good and if there is nothing in the Kansas Statutes that prohibits the making of a trust, he can't break it. Whether there is or not, I don't know.

Regarding the letter which I asked you to write for the Journal. I don't want to impose on you to do that thing. If you were to try a year, you never could write a nicer letter for publication than the one you wrote describing your trip to Ann's. By cutting out a few little references as to home matters, it would be ideal. Mr. and Mrs. Frank Harris were over and read it and Frank said at once, "That letter ought to be printed," and I would be glad to do so if you are willing, but won't think of doing so without consulting you.

You certainly did have an exciting time on election day going into Porto Rico [*sic*] and it does seem you are the most unlucky kid about getting into scrapes of that kind in the world. As you say, all of these experiences help you and to be able to think in a crisis where one person has the advantage over the crowd, and your ordering the motorman to go ahead was exactly the right thing to do.

You have before this read all of the dope on the election [and] know, that the entire State ticket was elected excepting Mr. Shellenbarger. There were many things that entered into his defeat. Not however, by the people he thought were his enemies. He was turned down by the liquor crowd as against the Bryan people.

We are going to get our Christmas boxes off this week. Will add about ten more dolls to the collection since receiving your letter.

I am going to write Harry a letter today. I will do that when I finish this. Should have done so before.

I told your Mother yesterday that I thought we had better invite Mr. and Mrs. Ingles up over Sunday while the weather is nice. I am sure they will be glad to read your letters and see the pictures and we have the dining room in shape now so we can entertain them nicely.

Fred went out Sunday night for a trip to Iowa. Will probably not bc back until nearly Christmas times. We have decided to go ahead without putting out an extra man, as the office work is all I can handle without more help, as it is.

I don't intend to miss writing you on every boat but sometimes I can't get to it, so please take the will for the deed and I will get to it as often as I can.

Pearl Fee came up and called yesterday evening. We prevailed on her to stay to dinner. Had a very nice visit with her. She isn't looking very well but I think she is better than she was earlier in the Fall. She is just as nice as she can be and we enjoyed having her very much.

Eula called Sunday and stayed a few minutes. She wants us to come over this Fall and if we can get away, we will do so.

Mother will write you the local news. I can't think of anything just now that is of especial interest. You say in your letter that you are not only teaching school, but have entered for a good, stiff course for yourself. I appreciate it and the education you are getting will be well worth the while. Experience is the best teacher and I will admit it is pretty tough while you are learning. You are a good "sport" Grace. Keep your courage, your health and if you don't make any money, when the time comes you will have things for your [trousseau].

With dearest love,
I am, as ever,
Your Father.

PERSONAL REFLECTIONS ON THE LETTERS FROM 1916 AND 1928

THOUGH IT NEVER MENTIONS it directly, the letter in 1916 is written to Grace and Hal ("Dear Children"), now married, after Grace has suffered a miscarriage. Pregnancy was a much riskier business than it is now, and the event of the miscarriage clearly distressed Grace's father.

The final letter, written on the day of Grace's parents' fiftieth wedding anniversary is a capsule of joy and shows the success her father must have enjoyed financially. They are traveling, dining, and playing golf—it is a picture of the Roaring Twenties about a year before the financial crash that would change so many lives.

* * *

2/21 – 16

Dear Children,

    We sent a [?] letter which you received by this time. It was a shock to us and you know how sorry we are for you but it is such a relief to know our own little girl is safe and I hope when this reaches you will be well on the way to recovery. If you need any financial aid you know I am sure how glad I shall be to help you. It is very hard to hear such high hopes shattered in a few hours. I know you will be [?] and reconcile yourselves to it. There are <u>many</u> <u>many</u> things we cannot understand but surely our Heavenly Father knows best and sometimes we shall know and understand. How or when I cannot tell but it will be so. I cannot write any more now.

Lovingly
Daddy

* * *

STEPHEN O. SALISBURY PLAYING GOLF

Los Angeles
3/17 – 28

Dear Children,

We arc vcry happy this bright beautiful day. We have received a great many letters—cards/telegrams with Congratulations on our 50th Wedding Anniversary. We are both very thankful for so many blessings. Of good health good children good friends and so many blessings that we enjoy. "Surely goodness and mercy hath followed us all the days of our lives and we will dwell in the House of the Lord forever." Mr. and Mrs. Calhouse are coming about noon. We are going for a ride—will go to Hollywood. To the Chinese Theater there. Go to some nice place for dinner. We read your letter yesterday. So glad to get it to know Mary was getting along so well and to get the picture of my <u>big</u> Pal. He is growing so fast. We look for Fred in about two weeks. I wish you could be with us. We shall go to San Francisco about April 15th. After a few days there I am going to Seattle [and then] Spokane to see Grace Van Patten and Fred and Jessie are going home over the Union Pacific. So we will not see you on our way home but hope to see you soon after we do get home. We are both real well and having a very pleasant winter. Very little rain much sunshine. I play golf three days a week on a very good course. Play with Mr. Leach most of the time and play about 100 for 18 holes. We go a good deal. We are going with Louis Clark and wife tomorrow for a ride and to dinner. Tuesday next at the Helborn at Long Beach etc.

With much love to you all
Your Father S O Salisbury

* * *

Stephen Olin Salisbury died in 1930. Undoubtedly many, many more letters were written to Grace during his life, but no others were saved.

CHRISTMAS CARD FROM 1928 FROM STEPHEN AND JESSIE SALISBURY

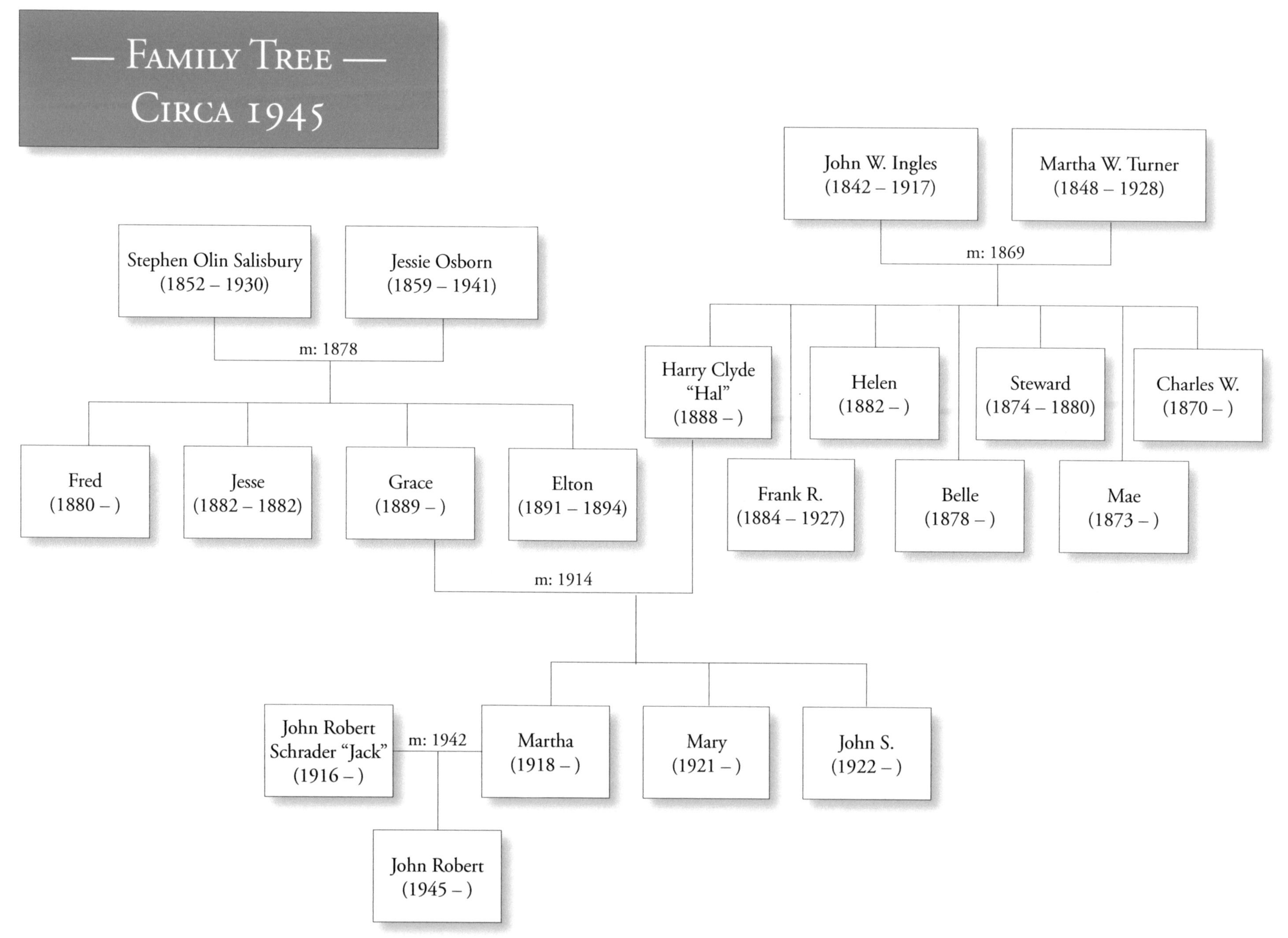

Family Tree — Circa 1945
John W. Ingles (1842 – 1917)
Martha W. Turner (1848 – 1928)
m: 1869
Stephen Olin Salisbury (1852 – 1930)
Jessie Osborn (1859 – 1941)
m: 1878
Harry Clyde "Hal" (1888 –)
Helen (1882 –)
Steward (1874 – 1880)
Charles W. (1870 –)
Fred (1880 –)
Jesse (1882 – 1882)
Grace (1889 –)
Elton (1891 – 1894)
Frank R. (1884 – 1927)
Belle (1878 –)
Mae (1873 –)
m: 1914
John Robert Schrader "Jack" (1916 –)
m: 1942
Martha (1918 –)
Mary (1921 –)
John S. (1922 –)
John Robert (1945 –)

Section Two: The Letters of John Stephen Ingles, 1940–1945

<hr>

Historical and Cultural Context

JOHN STEPHEN INGLES WAS the youngest of Grace's three children. He was born in Manila, Philippines, in 1922 when Grace and Hal were stationed there.

The Great Depression was ushered in by the stock market crash of 1929. John would have been seven at the time, and as a result, most of his childhood was during the Depression. Although conditions were often rugged by today's standards, the family never seemed to want. Being in the army and moving from base to base meant that housing and transportation were never in question.

The Ingles family—Grace, Hal, and their three children, Martha, Mary, and John—moved frequently as Hal's career in the army demanded. Making friends was something that seemed easy enough for the transients. But keeping those friends over the years was difficult for the youngsters. Grace and Hal, however, seemed to excel at that skill. In many ways, the army was a small world with people reappearing in lives at different times due to changes in postings and advancements in careers. The Ingles's army

friends were friends for life. The nuclear family was extremely close since often the children had only each other to play with. This closeness is reflected not only through the terms of endearment frequently used in the letters but also in the level of detail shared.

The five years between 1940 and 1945 were transformative for the nation and, indeed, the world. WWII was well underway, but until 1941 the United States had been primarily a spectator. That ended with the bombing of Pearl Harbor, and the nation that had been sitting on

JOHN STEPHEN INGLES
– HIGH SCHOOL AGED

the edge of the war was suddenly in the center of it. All families were upturned, and none more so than military families.

PERSONAL REFLECTIONS ON THE LETTER FROM 1940

IN 1940, MY FATHER, John Stephen Ingles, was finishing high school in Washington, DC. His parents had been stationed in Ft. Sam Houston, San Antonio, Texas, but it was decided that John should stay in DC to complete his schooling at Western High School (now the Duke Ellington School of the Arts). He was boarding at the house of a classmate, and the mother provided only one meal a day for John—breakfast. He was on his own for lunch, usually at school, and dinner, which he usually got at one of the many diners that were open at the time. The first lengthy letter recounts events from his final weeks in DC before graduation. It covers the momentous ROTC [Reserve Officers' Training Corps] drill competition, as well as details of a youth enjoying the recreations in Washington, DC, including going to Glen Echo Park and playing baseball on the grounds of the Mall.

* * *

[May 19, 1940]

Dear Mother,

It is about 12:15 Sunday afternoon, and I finally have time to write you all about the Competitive. The best place to start is a week ago last Friday when we started in on our cleaning. We worked for a couple of hours that afternoon, and then really put in a big day, about nine hours Saturday. Nine more hours Sunday finished the job. Almost all of the boys came and worked on Saturday, and certain ones came on Sunday. On the whole, they cooperated very well. Sunday night, we all met up at school at 7:30, and then went down into Rock Creek for our company rally. Jack,

JOHN IN ROTC UNIFORM, WESTERN HIGH SCHOOL

Charley and I had gotten a permit for one of the picnic grounds. We had a good rally, with some food, and a lot of talk. The fellows seemed to have a good time, and showed good spirit. After the rally was over, we took the company out to the A&W to put the finishing touches on the food proposition. The whole thing came off in good order, and broke up a little before 11:00. I came home and went right to bed, but didn't sleep awfully well. In the morning, Monday, I went up to school at about 7:30, and with Charley, Al, and a couple of others put the finishing touches on the uniforms. We went on the field at 11:00 and the fellows were excused from school at 9:15. They got into their uniforms, got shoes shined, etc. and we got on the bus to go over to the stadium. L Co. was on the field when we arrived. I asked Mr. Hawkins how they were doing, and he said that George had left out four commands, and made another mistake, all told costing himself about 4 points. Poor George! We went on the field then and it was quite an experience. I wasn't at all nervous, really disgustingly calm. I left out two commands which cost us 1⅓ points. I never had any idea they were even there. It was a halt and then a forward which I left out. I had never practiced them, and I had no idea that I was supposed to give them. Mr. Hawkins said that, as many times as he had seen us go through the drill program, he never realized I was leaving out those commands. If I had gone on the field a million times, I would have left them out every time, because I didn't know they were there. The boys really drilled awfully well, and Jack, Charley and Al did a swell job in their part of the drill, especially Jack. Mr. Hawkins said, "That Pixton looked like a million dollars on that field." After we came off the field, we put the fellows on the bus to go back to school and then went back to watch the other companies drill. H was just finishing their drill and, as I told you Monday night, Mr. Hawkins told me that they had beaten us by a long way. I didn't see enough of their drill to really tell, but you know they always looked like a million bucks from the stands, and I was plenty worried. We stayed at the stadium and watched the other companies drill that afternoon, and didn't see any good companies. Tuesday morning we went out to the stadium and watched Tech and

John, center, with Western High School ROTC at competition

Western High School ROTC in parade formation

Central drill. We didn't think Central was any good, but Tech really looked good. K was our exhibition company and they drilled very well. This Anacostia Company that won also drilled that afternoon, and although we thought they were a pretty good company, they didn't look like the best we had seen by any means. As the day went by, Mr. Hawkins began to qualify his statement that H had beaten us badly, and told me we might possibly have beaten them, but he doubted it. He thought that they would get 1st and that we might place up to the very end. That's what I thought when we formed on the field. When they took the first place to Anacostia, we all almost dropped dead. So did everyone in Anacostia's winning company. The captain was so shocked he didn't know what was happening. They pretty much messed it up going up to get their awards. When they came to Western for 2nd I thought it was surely H. When, however, it came to our Battalion, I felt sure it was G. Dickson Jewell, our Battalion Adjutant got the slip, and just stood there looking at Arthur and [me]. I said, "Come here with that damned thing!" and over he came. Big moment! The company put on about the best drill they have ever done going out to get the ribbons. Mr. Hawkins said they really looked good. When we came back to our positions, I didn't pay much attention to who got third place. We hadn't been impressed with the Central co. that got it. I got just about the biggest thrill of all when we passed by the Western stands on the pass in review. Everyone was standing up, hollering and cheering. Gee, it was wonderful! But, after all, we had kept the record going. When we went outside, everyone like Charley Harrison and Charley Asbertson was waiting to congratulate us. That's when they took the terrible picture that's in the Breeze I'm sending you. They printed the thing backwards. You'll see that it looks as if we were carrying our sabres in our left hands. I have some good pictures that were taken while we were actually drilling on the field. I'm having enlargements made of them. – Sunday Evening now – In the evening, i.e. just after drill we came back to school and I tried to get you long distance, but you weren't home, so I sent a telegram. When I got up to school, Al had formed the company, and gave me my present, a 17-Jewell, Shockproof, Benevues wrist-watch. It is really beautiful. We then had our banquet at school. After dinner, we went out to Glen Echo where we got free tickets on the amusements. Surprisingly enough, I came home early, and got a good night's sleep for a change. Wednesday was a wonderful day. In the morning, we had our big assembly. That was a thrill too, when, after everyone was in the assembly hall, G Co. marched in and everyone stood up and cheered. I had to give a speech which everyone says was very good. There were quite a few speeches, and a lot of nice things about G Co. (and also its Captain). Then medals were given out, and we did pretty well there too. Jack got the prize-lieutenant medal with Charley runner-up. Al won the prize 1st Sergeant medal. After the assembly, they took a picture of the company to hang in the hall at Western. After that, G Co. together with the band and the staff checked out, and marched down-town. We got in all the movies free. We saw "One Million BC", "Rebecca", "Forty Little Mothers", and "Saturday's Children." Also two stage shows. Thursday was spent in recuperating, although we were in school. We are getting down to ground now. Some of the fellows are getting a bit hard to live with around school, they are so proud of themselves. We really had a swell time though. Friday afternoon, Mr. Hawkins took George, Charley and [me] over to the stadium and we watched the competition of the colored high schools. It was really a scream some of the movements they did, and we enjoyed ourselves a lot. Yesterday morning, I went out to

Walter Reed to get my V.M.I. [Virginia Military Institute] physical. I registered at 9:15, got to a doctor at 11:40 and got away at 12:25. Same old dispensary. Yesterday afternoon Mr. H took George, Johnny D. and [me] out to the U. of Maryland, where we saw a very good lacrosse game. This afternoon, George and I played some baseball together down at the Washington Monument. This evening I have studied hard for a Physics test tomorrow. I almost forgot to mention that H Co. came in fourth and K fifth. George was 13th. You can see by the scores in the Breeze that if George hadn't thrown away about 4 points, he would really have been right up near the top. The cup for the highest Regimental average came to Western for the third time since they started awarding it 4 years ago. If I had given my halt and forward, G would have won by more than a point. IF!! It seems too bad to have to close this letter with very sad news. All through last week, Jack's mother was dying of cancer. He didn't take part in hardly any of our celebrations. When he was absent on Friday, I figured it was just about the end. Mrs. Pixton died Saturday morning. They are going to Florida for the funeral this week. Jack called me this evening. He said they were leaving right away, and that he will be gone all week. He is coming back next Saturday, but his father won't be back for a week after that. Jack wants me to come over and stay with him until his father comes back. Naturally I told him I would come. It's the least I can do. I know you will want me to do it. Poor Jack, I feel so sorry for him. Even with all this tragedy hanging over him, he did a marvelous job on the field last week. Jack's such a swell kid, I hate to see this happen to him. Well, I won't dwell on it. I'll send you the Pixton's address tomorrow so you can write me there while I'm staying with Jack. Good-night now.

Love,

John

Personal Reflections on the Letters from VMI, December 1941–January 1944

The letter of December 7, 1941, is significant because it is written the day Pearl Harbor was bombed. With a husband in the military and a son attending a military school, Grace especially felt the impact of this event, as did the rest of the family and so many other families across the United States. At the time of the bombing, Grace, Hal, and John's eldest sister, Martha, were living in Panama.

In the next twenty-five months, several significant events would happen in the Ingles family. Grace and Martha would be relocated to Texas. Hal would be promoted to major general and sent overseas. And for John and the rest of his classmates at VMI, their education would be interrupted, and their military careers fast-tracked so they could also see action in WWII. Martha would marry Jack Schrader, an army captain, in July 1942.

In this section, we have several entries from Martha's journal, where she lovingly references her little brother as "Johnny."

* * *

[December 7, 1941]

VMI

Dear Mother,

Naturally my mind tonight is taken up with the news of the Japanese attacks on Pearl Harbor, Guam and Manilla. It looks like the attacks on Hawaii caught everyone unprepared and apparently the loses were quite severe. Everyone here is quite shocked by the news, and there is a great deal of enthusiasm for a declaration of war, which we expect for tomorrow. I don't know what affect [sic] the entrance of the United States into war will have on life in the Canal Zone. I'll just wait until I hear from you or Daddy.

I'll discuss my Christmas plans. I looked at overcoats

JOHN AT VMI

uptown yesterday. I can get a topcoat for $26.00, which I think is pretty reasonable. If you will send me the money, I will be able to buy the coat before I leave here on the 20th. Mary and I have not yet made our different arrangements. I planned to write her tonight, but I don't know if I'll get it done now or not. Reports are coming in that the Canal Zone is blacked-out and on the alert against attacks. I know you aren't frightened, but I wish I weren't so far away from you. Don't you worry about Daddy. He is fully

trained to carry out his part in any emergency. I feel, as I know you do, proud that he is in a position where he can best serve the country.

All this news has made it pretty hard to study tonight. Life goes on here as usual though. Please write and send me the money to buy the overcoat right away.

Love to all,
John

* * *

December 1941
VMI

Dear Mother,

I received your letters via Mary and successfully unraveled your very clever code. Since you are leaving about nine days before Mary's birthday, I will take time right away to write you in the hope you will get it before you leave.

I heartily approve of all your plans. I think you are very wise not to try to buck the system and fight for a few extra days or weeks. You can leave more comfortably now, and I feel that the sooner the inevitable situation is dealt with, the happier both you and Daddy will be. It is far worse for you to continue in a state of "suspended animation" as it were, than for you to leave now and get comfortably settled in Texas as soon as possible. I know that I can have no appreciation of what it means to you to have to leave Daddy at this time. But I know you will be brave and steady and make the separation easier for both of you. We shall all be called upon to make sacrifices before the world is made free for democracy again, and I know I can be very proud of the manner in which you are making your sacrifice. Even if we can't all be together, we know that we are all backing each other up. Although I wish I could be nearer and of some material help to you, I know that Martha will help you and that you will manage everything splendidly. Unless I hear otherwise, I'll send my next letter to the St. Charles Hotel, N.O.

All my love,
John

* * *

WESTERN UNION TELEGRAM

THE MESSAGE TO GRACE indicates Hal's promotion from brigadier general to major general when he was stationed in Panama

1942 DEC 14 AM 12 30
NSA2 CABLE=CD AMEHIF 14 NFD
LC MRS H C INGLES =
126 CANTERBURY SANANTONIO (TEX)=
:PROMTED DECEMBER SECOND=
HARRY C INGLES.
126.

Official Letter from VMI

VIRGINIA MILITARY INSTITUTE
Lexington, Virginia
December 21, 1942

Memorandum to Parents and Guardians of Cadets:

1. The following information regarding the status of members of the Corps of Cadets has been received from the War Department Bureau of Public Relations:

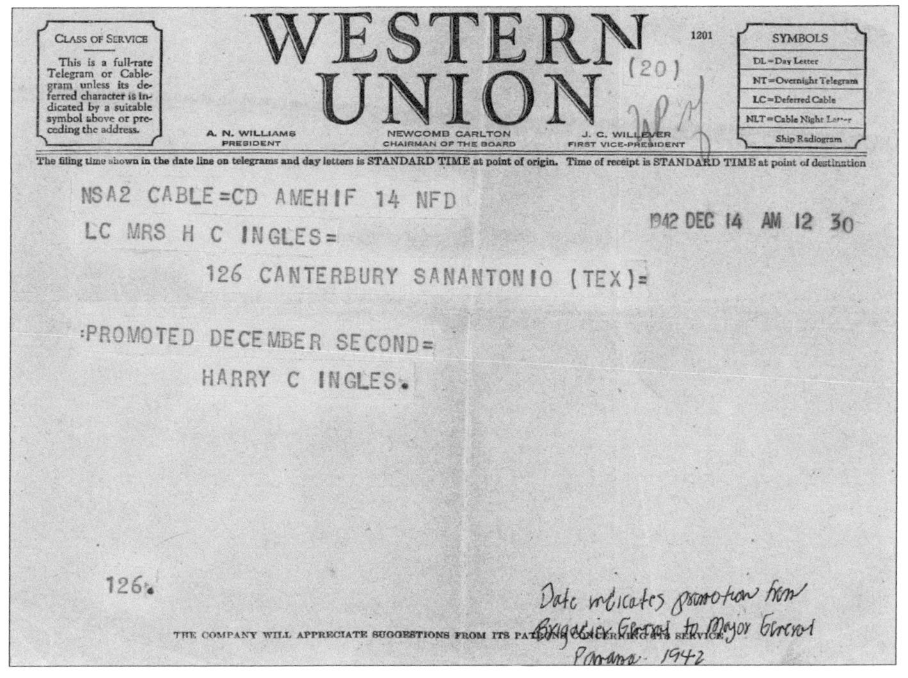

ORIGINAL TELEGRAM

(a) Those taking the pre-medical course, who are in the Enlisted Reserve Corps, or inducted prior to June 30, 1943 taking approved courses, will continue in an inactive status until the end of this academic year and then will be called to active duty. Those selected for further medical or pre-medical training will be detailed for such instruction under the Army Specialized Training Program. It is believed that this will not affect members of the First Class, or those members of the Second Class who are not enlisted in the Army Enlisted Reserve Corps.

(b) Members of the First Class, taking advanced R.O.T.C. training, will be ordered to active duty upon graduation, or upon completion of this academic year. Upon entering an active duty, they will be ordered to their respective branch schools and

HC INGLES RECEIVING SECOND STAR AND BEING PROMOTED TO MAJOR GENERAL

commissioned upon successful completion of the course.

(c) Members of the Second Class, who are in the Enlisted Reserve Corps, or inducted before June 30, 1943, will continue in an inactive status until the end of this academic year and will then be called to active duty. Those selected at the completion of their basic military training for further technical training, will be detailed for such instruction under the Army Specialized Training Program.

(d) Members of the Third and Fourth Classes, who are members of the Enlisted Reserve Corps, will be called to active duty at the end of the current semester (January 27th), and upon completion of basic training will be eligible for selection for training under this program or other military duty.

At the completion of any phase of specialized training, under this Program, the soldiers will be selected for,

1. Further training in Officers' Candidate School;

2. Recommended for a technical non-commissioned officer;

3. Returned to troops;

4. In exceptional cases, detailed for very advanced technical training;

5. In very exceptional cases, be made available for very technical work to be done out of the army, but deemed to be highly important to the war effort.

With references to cadets not in the Enlisted Reserve Corps, those taking Engineering or Chemistry or preparing therefor will be deferred to the end of the year, by Selective Services Headquarters; it is possible that the War Department may give similar considerations to those in the Enlisted Reserve.

Parents and guardians of members of the Third and Fourth Classes are urged to have their sons or wards return at the end of the Christmas furlough and remain through the midyear examinations in order that credit may be obtained for work of the first semester. If the examinations are not taken, no credit can be given for the half-year's work.

Deposits should be made in accordance with statements that have been sent out by the Treasurer, and, in event of withdrawal at the end of the examination period, refunds, accompanied by detail statements of accounts, will be made on the basis of what has been furnished.

C. E. Kilbourne
Superintendent

* * *

Journal Entries from Martha Ingles Schrader

Tuesday—Jan–4–1944

I got the sweetest letter from Johnny today. He was writing to thank me for my Christmas present and also for a long birthday letter I had written him. I remember very well the day I wrote that letter. I started thinking about him, for some reason, and it suddenly came over me in a great wave how very very much I loved him, and what a wonderful brother he was, and always had been in every way. And so I just sat down, while the mood was on me, and wrote and told him all the loving things I was thinking of him. This was his answer, and it was so sweet, it warmed my heart. Johnny and I are, basically, very much alike. We have always understood each other perfectly. He said, in this letter, "I want to thank you for the Christmas book, and also for the very dear long letter you wrote me. Of the two, I hope you will not mind if I prize the <u>letter</u> most!"

Johnny is in my prayers so much—So often I think, in thinking of him—"God love him and keep him!"

Jack and Daddy and Johnny—what a wonderful threesome of men I have to love and pray for in this war.

* * *

Wed. Jan. 12 – 1944

Today something happened that made me happier than any "event" has made me in <u>months</u>. I had a telegram from mother saying that Johnny has gotten orders to report to Officer Candidate School at Ft. Sill, the 28th of this month!! I can't remember when <u>pure joy</u> over a thing has leapt up in me like it did when I read those words in the Telegram! It is so <u>wonderful</u> for Johnny, God love him! It has been his heart's dream, his one desire—ever since the war started two years ago. First he was too young, and then, when he was ready for it, they had cut down the candidate schools until they were practically non-existent. It seemed that he hadn't a chance in the world to go—and now, I just put my head down on my arms and cried real tears—I was so happy for him. He's waited so long for his break and he is so deserving of it.

I guess I must not be a completely selfish person, after all. I've often worried that I was too selfish – but I <u>couldn't</u> be entirely so, when things good and bad that happen to people that I love affect me so genuinely and acutely.

Personal Reflections on the Letters from Officer Candidate School (OCS), Fort Sill, Oklahoma, January 1944–May 1944

The letters from OCS paint a detailed picture of the training received by the young men, preparing them to go to war. John, having grown up in the military and having already completed several years at VMI, reports on the drills, tests, demerits, and challenges in the tone of a news reporter. Grace, as an army wife, would have been very familiar with the lifestyle and curriculum that John was recounting. These letters also show some of the challenges John felt from being "the General's son." And the letter from General Ward to Grace indicates that John's father was trying to be sensitive to the situation.

These letters also reflect some of the mundane activities that occur even during the most historic events. Banks still have inconvenient hours, items from home need to be sent, paperwork for personal affairs gets lost, mothers and sons calculate the number of days before they will see each other again. The multiple comments on the "receipt" and "Mr. Springer" obviously reference some sort of banking complication that had to be resolved. I asked my father if he remembered what that was about. My father's memory of this time period was extraordinarily sharp, but he had no idea what all the fuss was about.

Also reflected in the letters is the comfort brought by simple gifts from home: a box of gumdrops, clipping of a favorite comic strip (*Terry and the Pirates*). Grace must have sent thousands of small, thoughtful gifts over the generations of correspondences. And it is a practice that John learned well from his mother. My father wrote me weekly until a few years before his death when Parkinson's disease made it too difficult for him to write. He lovingly clipped and enclosed articles and comics from the newspaper that he thought I would enjoy. Knowing that someone is thinking about you, even when you are separated by hundreds or thousands of miles, is a powerful thing.

Because my father was writing his mother weekly, many of the letters from Fort Sill were originally dated with only the day of the week. In later years, my father clarified the dates. These dates have been indicated with brackets [ ].

* * *

January 30, 1944

Dear Mother,

I hope that you received my telegram from Oklahoma City and that that satisfied your worries about my getting here on time. My trip was very unusual in the fact that all the trains ran right on schedule from the start. We arrived in St. Louis, Oklahoma City and Ft. Sill right on time. They picked us up at the station in trucks and brought us up here to the O.C.S. area. We have been assigned temporarily to huts here, with four men in a hut. We were just assigned as we came in, and we won't get our permanent huts or roommates until we start our course. A new class of about 75 men or so starts the course every week. My class which is class 111 will start two weeks from tomorrow, which is Monday. Our class will run 17 weeks and ends June 10. We have found a great many boys that we took basic with at Bragg, boys from Harvard and Yale, are in the classes a week or so ahead of us. That should be a help, as they can give us a line on what to expect. The general opinion seems to be that the academic work is not too difficult, but the military system and the demerit system are the hardest part. Of course, they are terrifically strict about personnel appearance and hut cleanliness, and more boys are kicked out for demerits than any other thing. It seems to be run something like the rat system, with the tactical officers playing the part of the upper classmen. All candidates have to brace or "fin out" in V.M.I. language and that sort of thing. Yesterday at dinner they started working on us, and it seemed very familiar to hear "pull your chin in, Mister!" and "Get those shoulders back!" again. Of course, that part of the system doesn't phase [*sic*] the V.M.I. boys very much, as you can imagine. So far, we haven't done anything except get some equipment and take a little arithmetic test yesterday. I really don't know what we do for the

John during OCS

next two weeks. I guess we have drills and orientations and so forth. I will be able to give you more information about that next week.

Daddy wanted to know who was in charge down here. We are part of the Field Artillery School, which is commanded by Maj. Gen. Orlando Ward, who, if I remember correctly, is a classmate of Daddy's. Brigadier General J. D. Balmer is commandant of the F.A. School. Just who is in direct charge of the O.C.S. I don't know yet.

Yesterday Lonas and I walked all around the post, which is tremendous. It has an old and a new part and reminded me a lot of Ft. Sam Houston, although it is much larger in area and not quite so new. It is really very nice, but it doesn't have anywhere near as good facilities for Enlisted men, i.e., with regard to theaters and service clubs as we enjoyed at Bragg. But we soon won't have time for much recreation anyway so it won't make much difference. I think we will go into Lawton and see what it's like next weekend. We went to the movies last night and saw "Lifeboat" and again today to see "A Guy Named Joe" with Spencer Tracy and Irene Dunn. The latter was <u>very</u> good, and I am sure you and Mary would enjoy it, and I know Daddy would if it comes around when he gets back.

I am afraid that I must ask you to send me a couple of things. First, my bathrobe, which I can use here, since we have to go out to the latrine. Second, my flashlight, which I left with you, but which I can use. Last, my alarm clock, which is the Big Ben that Mary has been using. As I remember, there are a couple around the house, so I guess you can spare it. Please send mine, because it is quiet and keeps good time. Sorry to ask you for this stuff, but I need it, particularly the alarm clock.

Well, that's about all for now. Let me know what you hear from Daddy. This may arrive before he leaves. I hope so.

All my love,
John

* * *

OFFICER CANDIDATE SCHOOL
FORT SILL, OKLAHOMA

[February 5, 1944]

Dear Mother,

Well, a whole week passed here at Ft. Sill, and it won't be much longer until we get down to work. This past week has been one of the laziest I have spent in the army. I have caught a couple of work details (cleaning windows or sweeping out buildings around here) and we had a physical exam and a night-blindness test, but that just about sums up the week. We have been having an hour of drill every morning, but, once that is over, we have nothing to do for the rest of the day. The gunnery classes that we were supposed to have had didn't materialize. So we just lie around on our bunks, read and sleep, play a little touch-football and engage in "bull sessions." It is all very pleasant, but we all have a feeling that it is the lull before the storm, and we are anxious to get started. We actually start our course this Thursday, although don't start until a week from Monday.

I know you will be glad to know that I came through O.K. on my physical. I read 20/70 with my left eye, which is slightly better than usual. Of course, I knew what the chart was before I went in there, which made it easier. Everything else was O.K. and the dentist even complimented me on my teeth. This wasn't the final physical, although it was pretty thorough. We take one more exam near the end of the course, which is the important one. If they don't change the eye chart between now and then, I won't have any trouble, and even if they do, I will be O.K. I think. The night-blindness test was a new one for me. It wasn't official, but they were just using us as guinea pigs for a new type of test that has been devised. We were first put in a dark room for 30 minutes to accustom our eyes to the darkness. We then went into another dark room where we sat at a table. Across the room there was a small cross which was placed against a very dim background. The light on this background could be varied through 6 stages of darkness. The operator turned the cross around so that it pointed in different directions. If we could see it, we indicated the direction it was pointing by operating a dial that was on the table in front of us. We had ten trials at each stage of darkness. I scored 45 out of 60, which was slightly above average, but I used my glasses. It was an interesting test, and one which they told us may soon be widely adopted. You will be glad to know that I weighed 163 pounds on my physical which, as far as I know, is the most I have ever weighed.

Right now, I am on a detail up at the Headquarters of the Student Officers Regiment. It is an easy detail, but, unfortunately it came on Saturday night, and kept me from going into Lawton or to a movie. I have been on since 7:00pm and go off duty at midnight. There is another fellow up here, one of the enlisted personnel here, who knows what the score is. I just have to deliver any telegrams or phone messages that come in. So far, I haven't had much business.

I received a letter from Daddy the other day, and I assume that he is on his way by now. I hope that he is able to write you while he is away, although I doubt if you can write him. I see by the papers that "Uncle Pete" Corlett is in the midst of things in the Marshalls.

Well, I'll close now.

All my love,
John

* * *

OFFICER CANDIDATE SCHOOL
FORT SILL, OKLAHOMA

[February 13, 1944]

Dear Mother,

I'm afraid this won't be much of a letter, since, for the first time since I have been here, I am a little rushed. Tomorrow we start our course, and we have a lot of last-minute cleaning up to do. We have had a very easy week for the most part. I have been on duty in the mess-hall serving food all week. That didn't take too much of my time. We had to report to the mess hall 15 minutes before each meal, serve the meal (cafeteria style), eat and then leave. We have had a couple of gunnery classes, some orientation lectures, and a lot of sleep. We have spent several hours cleaning up our hut and getting things arranged according to the regulations. We are still in our temporary area and we don't move to our permanent area until about Wednesday. We hope to get off to a good start and not run up too many demerits the firsts week or so. We start our academic work tomorrow, so I must study a little tonight. If I get a moment, I'll write you a note later in the week. The weather here has been very cold here the last couple of days, and it is snowing tonight. I received the candy, the clock, robe etc. Many thanks. All for now.

All my love,
John

* * *

OFFICER CANDIDATE SCHOOL
FORT SILL, OKLAHOMA

Tucsday P.M.
[February 15, 1944]

Dear Mother,

I must admit that, when I spoke in my last letter of writing you during the week, I didn't really expect to have the time. But we do have a little time this afternoon, so I will tell you a little about our first couple of days of the course. We started our course yesterday morning with talks by General Ward and Colonel Turner, who is in charge of the O.C.S. We were all, I think, very favorably impressed with General Ward and quite the opposite with Colonel Turner. Colonel Turner seemed to be more interested in telling us how easy it would be for him to throw us out for any little thing, and I didn't feel that a threatening attitude was quite right for the occasion. Perhaps he annoyed me a little more than the others because he devoted about 15 minutes to telling us that he didn't give a damn how much "influence" we had, he would kick us out if we didn't stack up, How [sic] he had kicked out the nephew of the Assistant Secretary of War, how we couldn't bring any pressure on him, etc. All very true, of course, but quite unnecessary. Of course, all the fellows kidded me about it, which I took in good nature, but didn't appreciate.

So after a none too pleasant start, we got into our classes. We had mostly lectures on leadership and morale, administration and methods of instruction. In the afternoon, we had a three hour Chemical Warfare Demonstration, which was pretty interesting, and a quiz on the demonstration. This morning, we had administration (with a quiz), Training Management, and 2 hours of Tactics. In that we studied the organization of the Army, and of every organization from The Army right on down to the Battery. Quite a dose for two hours. We got a break this afternoon. We had classification interviews scheduled for all afternoon, but it only took about two hours. You can already tell that it is going to be a very intensive course, but we have all been very pleasantly surprised with the uniformly good quality of the instructors.

We move into our permanent huts tomorrow. I came out pretty well on the hut assignment. I am with 2 V.M.I boys (Jack King and Joe Jones) and 2 Duquesne boys. Your roommates aren't as important here as at V.M.I., because you spend very little time in your huts.

Well, I just wanted to sort of bring you up to date. Mr. Springer sent me some more stuff to get signed, and I will get it done when I can, although it couldn't be more inconvenient. I can't possibly get to a Notary Public, but Mr. Springer said my commanding officer could serve. So I will have to go to the tactical officer of our class, which I don't like to do. Mr. Springer was a little nasty about it, said everything was in order before and he didn't understand Daddy's action. Goodness knows, I don't know what it's all about, but I'll take care of it in a few days. I haven't gotten a letter yet this week from you, but expect I will get one in a day or so.

Well, all for now. Give my love to Mary.

Love,
John

* * *

OFFICER CANDIDATE SCHOOL
FORT SILL, OKLAHOMA

[February 20, 1944]

Dear Mother,

Well, I can finally write you a letter and say that we have done something. We have one week behind us, which is at least something. It hasn't been a very hard one, but we have been kept very busy. We find that eight hours of class every day is quite a grind. We have breakfast at 7:00 and drill from 8 to 9 in the morning. From 9 until 1:00 we have classes, and then again from 2:00 to 6:00. This even includes Saturday, which doesn't give us much of a week-end. I went over to the regular post last night, and got a steak dinner at the post cafeteria and went to the movie. This afternoon, we went to the early show and then spent a couple of hours cleaning up our hut. We have been inspected this last week, but our demerits don't start counting until tomorrow. I was hut orderly this past week and would have picked up a number of demerits had we been playing for keeps. It really couldn't be helped, for we had just moved into our new huts, and they were in pretty sad condition. But we have ours pretty well cleaned up now, and I hope to get off to a good start.

The academic work hasn't been too hard, but I find it impossible to give the work adequate preparation. Our assignments are supposed to require three hours, but I never get to do them all. I find we only have about two hours to study, and even if we had three hours, I could never get it all done. They get a grade or two from us every day. So far, I haven't gotten any "U"s. I hope I can keep it up. We finish up our administration, Methods of Instruction and Mapping courses with exams on Friday. We then start two weeks of motors.

I got a lot of mail this week, two letters and a telegram from you, Daddy's letters and letters from Jimmy Irwin at Ft. Knox and Bob Weadock down at Florida. Weadock says that some of the Florida boys are coming out here the 28th of this month, but that he is staying for seven more weeks to get his degree. Jimmy reports that all the boys at Knox are getting along O.K.

I will sign the papers you sent and send them on and will enclose the check. I can't get it cashed here, but will endorse it and send it to you. I will try to get the papers notarized when I can. I don't think I can get the papers notarized up town, since we don't get away from here before about 6:30 Saturday evening. I will take it up to the tac officer in a week or so. I don't want to rush up there until he gets to know us all. With our demerits just starting, I don't want to be the first one they get their eyes on.

I am glad that Daddy's trip seems to be going well and that you are getting frequent news of him. Pretty soon now he will be on his way home.

All my love,
John

P.S. We don't get "Terry and the Pirates" in the paper around here. I wonder if you could tear the strips out of the Post each day and enclose a few when you send my letters.

Love,
John

* * *

OFFICER CANDIDATE SCHOOL
FORT SILL, OKLAHOMA

[February 27, 1944]

Dear Mother,

Well, another week gone by, and my first series of classes over with. We had exams on Administration, Military Law, and Mapping on Friday, and on Saturday we started our Motors Course. They use the "block" system from here on in, and for the two weeks we are taking motors, we take motors and nothing else. Since the motors area is nearly a mile from our area, that is a good thing. Walking out there and back twice a day at attention will be plenty. So far, the academic work has been pretty easy. We got our grades (S or U) on the mapping exam, but haven't heard from the others yet. I thought they were pretty easy though, and am not worried about them. This was our first week of demerits, and I came through O.K. I got two demerits on Tuesday, but that is all so far. Of course, I wasn't hut orderly, so I didn't have to do anything except keep my own equipment in order. Some of the boys ran in a little bad luck, however. One of the Duquesne boys got 19, and several other fellows got 10 or over. They set you back a few classes when you get 34 demerits. Of course, they were stricter the first week than they are later on, or so we are told.

We are finding the grind a little trying already. Nothing that we do is individually very hard, but we keep awfully busy, and never really have any time to relax from one weekend to the next. We each had an interview with the tactical officer last week. They went over our college courses and asked us a lot of questions. He asked me some questions about Algebra and Calculus, some of which I could answer and some of which I couldn't. Then he asked me if I wanted to stay in the Army, what job in the Artillery I wanted to do, what I thought of the instruction and discipline in the school, etc. I was very pleased that he didn't mention the general once, although I am inclined to think that he just doesn't know about it yet. Anyway, it was a much more satisfactory interview than the one I had before the O.C.S. board at Fort Bragg.

I haven't heard from you since the first of the week, but I expect I will get a letter tomorrow or the next day. I hope you hear from Daddy now.

> All my love,
> John

P.S. We got some of our travel pay this week. We thought we would get 5 cents a mile but apparently we are only going to get 3 cents a mile. I will send you the check as part of what I owe you. I will send you the rest when I can.

> Love,
> John

* * *

OFFICER CANDIDATE SCHOOL
FORT SILL, OKLAHOMA

[March 5, 1944]

Dear Mother,

I received your letters and the funny papers this week. Thank you for sending them. I am glad that you have had some news of Daddy. I hope that, by the time you get this letter, you will have some news that he is on the way home. I know that you will be mighty glad to have him back again. I would certainly like to talk to him about it, and I hope that he will find time to write me all about it.

Well, another week has gone by. We had our first week

of motors. We have gotten along pretty well. They concentrated on driving and technique of conducting motor marches mostly. This is the way they taught us to drive. The first hour they taught us elementary driving. The second hour we learned how to turn, back, park, etc. The third hour they took us over a difficult driving course. Then on Thursday, we went on a twelve-hour road march including two hours of black-out driving. As one of the boys said, I'd hate to see them give a course in surgery out here. But we all got through O.K. with no crack-ups. I drove a ¾ ton most of the time and did all right. This next week we do a lot of mechanics work. It has been a good course, and I have been learning a lot. They give us an awful lot, but they have very good methods of instruction, and I think that they get a surprising amount of it across.

It seems like we have been here a long time to only have three weeks of the course behind us. But three weeks is something, and the time is going by. I don't believe I have ever looked forward to anything as much as I do to coming home an officer. Maybe the fact that I am so anxious to get through makes the time go slowly.

Well, I'll close now. Give my love to Mary and say "Hello" to Daddy when he gets back.

All my love,
John

* * *

OFFICER CANDIDATE SCHOOL
FORT SILL, OKLAHOMA

[March 12, 1944]

Dear Mother,

I received two letters from you this week, and was glad for the news that Daddy has returned home safely. I am glad that he got home in time for his birthday, and I hope that your plans for a little birthday party for him went through O.K. I know that he is glad to be home, although I know he had a good trip. Before he left, he promised to write me all about it when he returned, and I hope he will get the time soon.

First I'll tell you about the business with Mr. Springer. The day before I got your letter, I got one from Mr. Springer telling me to take care of the check and the receipt right away. Well, as you know, I have already taken care of the check. But the receipt was a new one on me. So I checked through all the stuff he has sent me and didn't find any trace of it or any reference to it in any way in his letters. I still have all the stuff he sent me with the bonds, but no receipt. So I wrote him Friday and told him to send me the receipt and I would sign it. I don't know what the slip up has been, whether he meant to enclose it in one of his letters and didn't or whether he sent it separately and I didn't get it. All this stuff has been going to Lexington and then back here, so the latter is possible. I sent him my new address Friday. So I hope we will get it all straightened out. Saturday, we got through about 5:00 P.M. and I went right into town in the hope that the banks might still be open and I could get the bonds signed. But the banks close at 3:00 P.M. on Saturday so I didn't have any luck. The reason that I haven't taken the bonds to Lt. Smith, my tactical officer, is not because I mind reporting to him, because I have already done that several time[s]. But right on the bonds, where I have to sign and he would have to sign it says "John Ingles, c/o Major General H. C. Ingles, 3133 Conn. Ave etc." So far as I know, he doesn't know about Daddy, and I would very much prefer to leave it that way, or, if he has to find out sooner or later, I would rather he find out by some other means than my going up there and sticking it in his face. I plan now to wait until the week-end after next, which will be March 25th, to get it done. That is the week-end before we start gunnery, and we get off at noon on Saturday that day and I can get up to Lawton before the banks close. That is our only afternoon off in the course. If you or Daddy think I should get them signed before then, just let me know and I will. I will be glad when the whole matter is finished up.

We finished up out Motors course last week and started in on Material Friday. We have 10 days of that, in which we study all the weapons of the F. A. I enjoyed the Motors very much and really learned a lot. It is rather unfortunate that we have to go so fast, since we just scratch the surface enough to see how little we know about any one subject. It is quite a revelation to compare the instruction methods down here with the way we were taught at V.M.I. I think that all educators would do well to study the Army's methods, since they could really learn a lot.

I think I have been getting along pretty well, but it's hard to tell down here. I haven't gotten any more demerits since the 2 I got the first week, but I have been unusually lucky on that score. Also, I haven't been hut orderly (the boys call it "hut slut") yet. We don't have any very hard academics until we hit gunnery, which lasts 6 weeks and is reportedly pretty tough. We all pretty much loafed through motors, with not much study going on in the evenings. Of course, you hardly loaf when you go to classes eight hours a day.

I had to go up to the personnel office a while back, and, since I was born in the Philippines, they want a copy of my birth certificate to prove my citizenship. They said there wouldn't be any hurry, just get it to them before I graduate, which, believe me, isn't very soon. So, I will ask you to send me a copy sometime when it is convenient. I am enclosing a money order for $60. I still owe you $40 for my ticket and trip out here, since I already sent you $40. The Army sure did us dirt on that deal. We only got $39.95 for the whole trip, and it cost most of the boys about $80.

Well, this letter has been full of finances, never a pleasant subject. Say "Hello" to Daddy and Mary for me. Today is Daddy's birthday, March 12th. With good luck and good traveling time, I might be home three months from tonight. Is that a date?

All my love,
John

* * *

OFFICER CANDIDATE SCHOOL
FORT SILL, OKLAHOMA

[March 19, 1944]

Dear Mother,

I didn't get a letter from you this week, and I hope that it doesn't mean that you have been sick with a cold or something. However, I did get your box of gum-drops and also Daddy's grand letter about his trip. Thank you for the candy and please thank Daddy for his letter. He certainly gave me all the details of his trip, and I very much appreciate his taking the time to write me. I would certainly like to see him and talk to him, and I hope it won't be too long before I will.

We have five weeks down with twelve to go, which is getting along. We had Material all last week and got along pretty easily. We have been pretty much coasting for the last three weeks, but I'm afraid the vacation is just about over. We start gunnery this Friday, and, from all reports, that is a mighty tough course. It lasts for six weeks and is by far the most important course we have. Almost everybody that bills out of here does so during gunnery. Not that I'm expecting to bill out, but I am expecting a lot of hard work. I may have been wrong to have taken things pretty easy these first few weeks, as I could undoubtedly have learned more if I had worked a little harder. But I like to think that I have saved a little reserve that will help me later on. As one of the officers told us at the start of the course, this is not a 100 yard dash that we are running here. He said that you have to set a pace that you can keep up. I have passed all my work so far without finding it too difficult. It's a pretty hard place to figure out. I don't exactly trust the "tac" officers. One of ours seems to be a pretty level headed fellow, but I sure don't think much of the other one. You like to feel that the men that are making the decisions about you and your friends are good men, and it is a little disconcerting not to have any confidence in one of them. I hope they don't get any ideas about me. They had Leonard Lonas up there this week for acting "immature" and he is one of the most sophisticated, serious boys in the whole bunch. I sure hope they know what they're doing. At any rate, our class hasn't had any casualties yet. Speaking of "casualties" I heard a rather round-about rumor that Ross Walker had washed out of his pilot training. I sure hope there is nothing to that one.

I want to ask Daddy something about the boys who want to get in the Signal Corps. There are a couple, including Cliff Bain, here and three or four more, including Jimmy Irwin and Tom Peyton, with the Armored Force at Fort Knox. Jimmy wrote me a few weeks ago, and I told him I would find out when Daddy got back from the Pacific. They want to know what procedure they should go through, etc. If Daddy wants their names and serial numbers or other data such as their class numbers and when they will graduate, I will write and get that information.

Tell Daddy that I'll bet he is really looking like a Christmas tree these days, as I guess that he has rearranged his ribbons to make a place for his Pacific ribbon and his Venezuelan ribbon. I sure wish that, between the three of us, we could figure out some slick way to get them to give him his D.S.M. [Distinguished Service Medal]. I still think that the best way is to figure out some way, either direct or indirect, of telling General Somervell about it. I'll bet that he could get them to give Daddy the medal, in spite of their practice of not giving medals to people in Washington. And since we are talking about ornamenting the old general, I think that they most certainly ought to give him another star. I see by <u>Time</u> that the Navy department in Washington got a bunch of promotions, with the Chiefs of the Medical, Personnel, and Yard and Docks sections made three-star admirals. And when they make Jimmy Doolittle and Dick Sutherland (also your heel-clicking friend J. C. H. Lee) Lt. Generals, the time has come for the Signal Corps to get its first Lt. General. Anyway, if you and I were running things, we would take good care of him. We would probably hide him behind his array of ornaments.

Well, I am still going along on my 2 demerits, but I hardly expect to get through this coming week unscathed. I am on hut orderly this week, and for any dust, etc. they find around the room, I get not one but two demerits. I expect to get a few, but hope to keep it under five by Thursday. If I don't, I will be confined for the week-end. It's a hard life.

I received your telegram, but couldn't find the receipt. I found a note from you saying you were sending it. So I guess that the only conclusion is that I lost it. I have no recollection of having either received it or signing it, and I guess I fouled things up somewhere along the line. I have written Mr. Springer again and asked him for instructions. Other than that, I don't know what to do about it.

Well, I must close now. Say "Hello" to Mary for me.

All my love,
John

* * *

LETTER FROM MAJ. GEN. ORLANDO WARD TO MAJ. GEN. INGLES, WRITTEN ON FIELD ARTILLERY SCHOOL LETTERHEAD.

HAL INGLES WAS THE oldest classmate in his West Point class. This fact earned him the nickname of "Dad" by his fellow members of the Long Gray Line.

FIELD ARTILLERY SCHOOL
OFFICE OF THE COMMANDANT

FORT SILL, OKLAHOMA
22 March 1944

Major General H. C. Ingles
Chief Signal Officer
Army Service Forces
War Department
Washington, D. C.

Dear Dad:

Here is a copy of a current report on your youngster. It is a very good one. You might say it is a sort of a work sheet which of course changes from day to day. I have noted that there is a tendency to mark "Satisfactory" on these boys when they don't know much about them. Compared to the others, this is very fine.

I will continue to keep an eye on him but will not ask him to dinner as you have suggested that I do not. On the other hand, I would like very much to have him meet my youngster.

Sincerely,
(signed) Pinky
ORLANDO WARD,
Major General, U. S. A.,
Commandant.

* * *

OFFICER CANDIDATE SCHOOL
FORT SILL, OKLAHOMA

[March 26, 1944]

Dear Mother,

Well, Mr. Springer came through with another receipt, and I signed it and sent it right back to him, so I hope that will take care of that. I didn't get the bonds signed, because instead of getting Saturday afternoon off as I had thought, we went to a Demonstration which lasted until after 6:00. I'm hoping for better luck this week. The Demonstration was really a good one. They worked out a defensive problem with an infantry battalion and three artillery battalions. At one point, they brought some P-39's and B-52's in for some strafing and low level bombings. I guess nearly 5,000 officers, officer candidates, and trainers were there to watch it. I guess they fired a good 500 rounds of artillery, plus all the infantry weapons. Quite a show.

We finished our sixth week this week and started

FIELD ARTILLERY SCHOOL
STUDENT REGIMENT
Fort Sill, Oklahoma.

RATING & OBSERVATION REPORT ON OFFICER CANDIDATE

Officer Candidate _Ingles, J.S._ (Name)   OCS No. _111_ (Class)   _End of 5th week_ (Date)

Submitted by _Class Tactical Off. (Lt Smith)_ (Print Name)

1. MANNER
commanding
convincing
alert
animated
receptive
retiring
timid
blunt

2. PRESENCE
impressive
attractive
neat
sober
unattractive
colorless
untidy
slovenly

3. RESULTS
excellent
decisive
dependable
questionable
faulty
unreliable
poor
unsatisfactory

4. CHARACTER
aggressive
determined
trustworthy
self-reliant
cautious
unstable
superficial
negative

5. MENTALITY
imaginative
quick-witted
able
versatile
practical
mediocre
inept
dull

6. DISPOSITION
cooperative
cheerful
adaptable
tactful
excitable
complaining
faultfinding

7. APPLICATION
enthusiastic
resourceful
thorough
industrious
persistent
slow
indifferent
careless

8. KNOWLEDGE
accomplished
informed
well-grounded
unconversant
uninformed
shallow
dabbler
dense

9. ATTRIBUTES
Use check list on reverse side of sheet.

10. LEADERSHIP
(Check One)
Unsatisfactory
Satisfactory
Very Satisfactory
Excellent
Superior

RECOMMENDATION: (retain)   turnback   drop   watch   board-int.

REMARKS: _As cadet Btry Comdr: Excellent job — In control of unit at all times. An outstanding candidate. All academic grades thus far "Excellent"_

NOTES: *a.* Place check mark alongside word (words) in each category which most aptly describes or fits the Officer Candidate under observation.

b. Comments on voice, posture and other related officer qualifications to be written under "Remarks".

(OVER)

ATTRIBUTES

PLACE check mark alongside each numbered category which describes or fits Officer Candidate under observation. Line out words under the checked number which do not apply to Candidate.

Positive, or active, attributes

1. Active, Energetic, Quick and fiery. Restless. Athletic.
2. Bold, Aggressive. Firm. Just. Positive type. Forceful.
3. Vain, Cocksure. Proud. Argumentative. Insistent on "rights".
4. Optimistic.
5. Impatient, Intolerant. Stubborn. Prejudiced. Exacting.
6. Self-confident. Intuitive. Poised. No waste motion. Courage of convictions. Power of decision.
7. Talkative. Nervous.
8. Radical. Original. Unorthodox. Resourceful. Ingenious. Imaginative. Experimenter.
9. Brusque. Abrupt. Hot tempered. Outspoken.
10. Grasps essentials. Not especially interested in petty details. Will accept 80% of a job.
11. Mentally alert. Reasonable. A good thinker. Well balanced. Mentally coordinated. Intelligent. Thinks ahead.
12. Interested in nonprofessional matters. Observant.
13. Inspires respect of his subordinates.
14. Works well under pressure.
15. Good sense of humor.
16. Willing to assume responsibility.

Negative, or passive, attributes

1. Inactive, Passive, Slow and sure. Steady, Studious.
2. Weak. Reserved. Negative Type.
3. Unassuming. Taciturn.
4. Pessimistic.
5. Patient. Tolerant. Pliable. Easily turned. Ability to admit his own errors. Lenient.
6. Lacks confidence. Inclined to putter. Becomes rattled. Becomes confused. Hesitant.
7. Quiet. Calm. Lethargic.
8. Conservative. Orthodox. Conventional. Painstaking. Lacks imagination.
9. Courteous. Considerate.
10. Slow to grasp essentials. Falls back on details as a refuge. Careful. Particular about details.
11. Not an ordered thinker. Jumps to conclusions. Lacks mental coordination. Learns slowly.
12. A "wheel-horse". A plodder. One track mentality. Unobservant.
13. Does not inspire confidence in subordinates.
14. May burn out, or crack, under pressure.
15. Lacking in humor. Matter of fact. Serious type.
16. Avoids, or is unwilling to assume, responsibility.

(Place an X in the appropriate column)	UNSATIS-FACTORY	SATIS-FACTORY	VERY SATIS-FACTORY	EXCELLENT	SUPERIOR	UNKNOWN
Military Bearing and Neatness			X			
Intelligence				X		
Attention to Duty				X		
Leadership				X		
Handling men				X		
As an instructor						X
Cooperation			X			
Initiative			X			
Force			X			
Judgement and Common Sense			X			

FAS, Fort Sill, Okla., (9-16-43—20,000)—28036

Weekly report from OCS sent by General Ward

gunnery on Friday. The gunnery course promises to be pretty strenuous. I was very fortunate to get through my week on hut orderly without any demerits, but I'm glad I won't have to worry about keeping the room clean for a while again. This week was a fairly slow one academically. We did some firing with the carbine, 45 Pistol, Thompson Sub-Machine Gun, and M-3 sub-machine gun on Saturday. Tuesday we did some anti-aircraft firing with the 30 and 50 caliber machine guns. We each fire about 180 rounds at balloons and radio-controlled target planes. It would have been a lot of fun if the weather hadn't been so cold. The weather here is completely unpredictable. Yesterday morning it was cold and raw. But today it is a beautiful, warm day. This afternoon we saw "Up In Arms" with Danny Kaye and Dinah Shore. It was very good, and I'm sure you all would enjoy it. Tomorrow we start on a new schedule. Everything is just moved up an hour. We go to bed at 9:30 and have breakfast at 6:00. This week we have to rate the other members of our platoon. It's a pretty hard job. I find that I can easily pick the first five and the last five, but rating the ones in the middle is pretty hard. I think that the work in gunnery is going to be a little harder than the things we have been doing. I am very anxious to learn all about it, however. Learning to handle the guns is about the most important thing for an artilleryman to do.

Well, I'll close now. I'm sure I told you that I got your candy and thanked you for it. I got your letters and the funnies this week. I am always very glad for your letters and all the news. Give my love to Mary and Daddy. Please send me some stamps. Incidentally, I have sent you $100, about $80 of which I owed you. I will ask you to save the remainder for me, as well as any other money that I send home when I get paid. I don't spend all of my pay each month, and I don't have any place here to keep my money. Well, that's all for now.

Love,

John

* * *

OFFICER CANDIDATE SCHOOL
FORT SILL, OKLAHOMA

Saturday, April 1 [1944]

Dear Mother,

Well, 7 weeks down and 10 to go, which is pretty close to the half-way mark. This last week has been a hard one, our first in gunnery. The vacation that we enjoyed through Motors and Material is definitely over. They worked us mighty hard this week, and we were all ready for a week-end rest. We finished up at noon today, which was a pleasant change. Unfortunately, however, it was just my luck to get Charge of Quarters today, so I have had to hang around. However, I haven't had any duties to speak of, so I have just been sitting around all afternoon, reading <u>Time</u> and generally doing nothing. I go off duty at taps tonight, so it hasn't been much of a detail. Had I gone on during the week, I would have had quite a number of duties to perform.

I am very sorry to hear that Martha isn't well, and I certainly hope she responds to her treatment O.K. I had a letter from her this week, but she didn't mention any of her troubles, just wrote me a sweet letter. I am glad that Daddy is in good spirits and that things are going well at the office. This must be a very busy time for him, with the Spring Offensive Operation imminent. The Italian campaign certainly has gone sour. I don't think that they should have taken General Eisenhower from that Theater. He was doing pretty well down there, and I think Marshal would have been the best man for the Cross-Channel Operation. But, then, I'm not running the war. It looks like General Patton will get one of the armies in the cross-channel operation. Well, he's got plenty of drive, and that will be very tough going. I wouldn't mind going that way when I get through here. The boys that have been graduating from here in the last few classes seem to go to one of three places. Some are assigned to various courses here (Executive Course, Survey Course, Communications, etc), some go to the pool at Bragg and some go to the pool at Camp Roberts, California. Nobody seems to be getting unit assignments these days. Of course, the situation may change completely by the time I get out of here. We won't start worrying about what happens to me after I become a 2nd Lt. until I have become one. One thing is pretty sure though, I will get some time at home on my way to my new station. That is really something to look forward to, and that will be a very proud day for me. I think of it often.

It is really a God-send for all of us to be together down here. It's a mighty tough grind, but we all manage to have a lot of laughs together. All of the boys have been doing very well, and so far we haven't lost any V.M.I. boys from our class yet. I don't imagine we will come through gunnery with everybody, but I don't think we will lose many. Cliff is doing fine. He had his 20th birthday last week. Nobody down here has heard whether the rumor about Ross was true or not. Word comes from Fort Knox that some of the boys are finding the Armored Force course pretty tough. However, failing a couple of courses isn't usually fatal for an R.O.T.C. man. If they feel that he is any good at all, they just drop him back a few classes and let him try again. One boy has been dropped back to our class and is getting his third try at gunnery. I sure hope that I go straight through. Seventeen weeks in this course is plenty.

Thank you for sending the funnies so regularly. I enjoy them very much. Give my love to Daddy and Mary.

Love,
John

P.S. I got 2 demerits this week, giving me a total of 4.

* * *

OFFICER CANDIDATE SCHOOL
FORT SILL, OKLAHOMA

[April 9, 1944]

Dear Mother,

I had two letters this week, one from you and one from Daddy. I was very glad for both of them. Please tell Daddy to put my class number on my address. I have been getting his letters O.K., but they have to be sent over to the headquarters here to get my class number from the records there, and it delays delivery a little. I haven't received the candy yet, but I imagine it will arrive tomorrow.

Today is Easter and I have thought of you all. A bunch of us went into town to church this morning. We went to the Methodist Church for some reason. I didn't care much for the service, it didn't seem like church at all. I guess I am too used to an Episcopal service. I guess you all went to church too.

We have finished our second week of gunnery, and it has been a pretty interesting one. We had three periods of firing problems, and I found that a lot of fun. Of course, the problems we fired this week were pretty elementary, and they were easier than later problems will be. It sure puts you on the spot, though, when the instructor points out the target somewhere out there on the range and says, "Your problem, Mr. Ingles." It's really up to you, then, and you have to get your adjustment without anybody else's help. I fired two problems, and although neither of them were perfect, I got a couple of "S's" out of it. It really is a good feeling to fire a good problem, and it make you feel that the Artillery is the only thing. Of course, after I have fired a "U" or so, I probably won't think it is so much fun. We were adjusting 75's this week, and that is a good accurate gun, although it is too small for combat work these days. In fact, I see in <u>Time</u> that they think the 105 is too small in Italy. Most of the new outfits being activated these days are big stuff, 8 inch and 240 howitzers. A lot of the V.M.I. boys that we see around here in 8 inch outfits. I don't know whether I would like being in one of those outfits or not. I don't know anything about them.

This week the class elected an honor committee of six

men, two from each section. I was one of the men elected from our section. All six members are V.M.I. boys, Cliff Bain, Albert Cooper, Billy Lawson, August Mueller, and Houston Smith and I. We don't have any very important duties, although we would have to report any irregularities that we saw. Wednesday night Lt. Smith, our Class tac [tactical officer], had all of us up there and spent about two hours about this candidate and that candidate. It wasn't very easy to talk about our classmates, but we all did the best we could to be frank and also fair. Lt. Smith is a pretty smart fellow, and it was quite amazing to me to see how well he has the class sized up. We haven't lost any men so far except for sickness. I'm afraid, however, that the ax is going to fall on some of the men pretty soon. The fourth week in gunnery is a week for clipping a few men out of each class and I guess our class won't be any exception. I am not much worried about myself, but I would feel badly if any of my brother rats failed out or were put back. As things stand out here, we will be one of the last classes to go through out here. Some of the Florida boys who passed up their first chance to come out here to stay in the ASTP [Army Specialized Training Program] seven weeks longer and get their college degrees, are now out here and aren't going to get in the course. The have about 350 R.O.T.C. men out here now who aren't going to go to O.C.S. out here. About 300 are being sent to the Infantry at Fort Benning and about 50, including most of my Florida friends, are going to the Armored Force at Fort Knox.

Incidentally, I wish you would remind Daddy to send me some dope about the men who want to transfer to the Signal Corps after they are commissioned. He didn't mention in in his last letter, and I don't know what to tell them to do. I hope he can find time to write me again soon and give me dope.

Well, we go over the hump next week, since we will be half way through the course by the middle of next week. Class 102 graduated this week, and from now on there is a class graduating every week. So it won't take long for 111's turn to come up.

All my love,
John

* * *

OFFICER CANDIDATE SCHOOL
FORT SILL, OKLAHOMA

Monday, April 10

Dear Daddy,

I am taking time to write you a short note because I would like to ask your help in a matter that came up today. As you may recall, all the members of my class out here took a physical exam in a week or so before we started our course. Well, two of my V.M.I. classmates who are down here in my class received word today that they were being dropped from the course for physical defects that came up on that exam. It seems that their defects are not of a very serious nature, since, although they do disqualify them for O.C.S., they are not serious enough to necessitate a discharge. Therefore, they are to be sent to a line outfit. Naturally, we were all rather upset about it. The boys in question went to Col. Turner. He was very nice about it and told them that he would do what he could to get them sent to Quartermaster or Finance O.C.S. I don't know how the physical qualifications for commission in those branches differ from the Artillery requirements, but Col. Turner apparently has some reason for thinking they are somewhat lower. One of the boys is being disqualified for weak eyes, and the other for a football shoulder injury. Both of these men have been getting along fine out here and would, I am sure, have passed the O.C.S. course without any difficulty. They have the same background that I have, one year advanced R.O.T.C. at V.M.I. One had three years of civil engineering and the other three years of electrical engineering.

I don't know just how you can help, but I thought that, if you were to call the matter to General Gregory's attention, he might be able to use them in the Quartermaster Corps. I would like to emphasize again that they are both good men, with clear records at V.M.I. and also out here. I am sure they will make good officers if they are not disqualified physically. Their names are Burton P. Short (ASN 13063918) and Warren L. Overstreet (ASN 13063908). Short took Civil Engineering at school and Overstreet took Electrical.

I always feel very hesitant about writing you about such a matter, because I realize how very busy you are and how trivial the troubles of my little group are. But I do feel that this is a very worthy case, and that these men are capable of rendering very good service as officers if they get the chance. I hope that you will be able to help them in some way.

Love,
John

* * *

OFFICER CANDIDATE SCHOOL
FORT SILL, OKLAHOMA

[April 16, 1944]

Dear Mother,

I see by your letter that you are planning to go to Florida on Thursday, but I will send this on to Washington in the hope that it will arrive before you leave. First on the list is some good news. We had Saturday afternoon off this week, and I went uptown to the bank and got my bonds signed and properly witnessed at the bank. I am sending them on to Washington with the evening mail tonight. You and Daddy have been very patient with me on this subject, and I have appreciated it. I have had to wait a long time to get uptown before 3:00 p.m. on Saturday, but I feel that it is better to have had it done at the bank. Incidentally, with regard to Daddy's last letter: I very much appreciate General Ward's wanting to have me to dinner, but I don't think it would be such a good idea while I am in the course out here. This is a pretty competitive system out here, and it would be rather embarrassing to me to be trotting over to have dinner with the commanding general. I hope that General Ward will understand, as it is very kind of him to think of me.

We went over the hump this week out here, and now have nine weeks behind us with eight to go. We are really beginning to feel that the end is in sight. This last week was just about our hardest so far, since the gunnery department really kept us on the ball. I saw my first time problem fired this week. Who was firing it? Well, I was. I caught the first problem in our first time fire shoot Tuesday. I did well enough to get an "S" which is O.K. by me. We are not studying lateral conduct of fire and had our first [The rest of the letter is missing].

* * *

OFFICER CANDIDATE SCHOOL
FORT SILL, OKLAHOMA

[April 23, 1944]

Dear Mother,

Only time for a very hurried note tonight. From your schedule, I think that you will be with Martha this week and so I will send this letter to Florida. Please thank her for her sweet letter that I got this week and give her my love.

This last week has been a very busy one for us. We fired problems on the range five times and had at least one unit on exam each day. I fired three more problems this week and came through O.K. We also spent two mornings actually firing the guns ourselves. I enjoyed that, as I always do. We worked on the 105's and the gun I worked Friday morning fired 88 rounds, which was considerably more than I had ever fired at one service practice before. We rotated through all the positions on the gun crew during the morning, so we got some good practice on everything. We had an "exciting" little diversion this afternoon. Our tac officer decided that we hadn't been showing enough proficiency in close order drill, so he trotted us out for an extra drill period from 1:00 to 2:30 Sunday afternoon. One would think that, after three years of drilling in high school, three at V.M.I. and one in the Army, I ought to be getting proficient pretty soon. However, after the drill, we went to the movies and then uptown for a steak.

Well, we have 10 weeks down and 7 to go, which is beginning to put a pretty substantial balance in our favor. It won't be too long now. Please say "Hello" to Martha and Jack for me.

All my love,
John

* * *

OFFICER CANDIDATE SCHOOL
FORT SILL, OKLAHOMA

[April 30, 1944]

Dear Mother,

I received your letter written from Orlando, and I am glad that you found things well with Martha. I am glad that the treatments they are giving her now seem to be doing some good. I know that you will feel easier about her now. I am sorry that Jack's status seems to be rather unstable again. I hope that everything works out O.K.

We finished up our 11th week this week and only have six weeks to go. It won't be long now. Bud Harvey, Bill Haley and Bill Lawson and I wrote in to American Airlines in Dallas and were fortunate enough to get reservations on a plane for June 10th. We will leave Dallas at 7:53 P.M. and get into Washington at 5:30 A.M. the next morning, Sunday the 11th. It will cost us $78.95, which isn't but $20 more than my Pullman ticket down here cost me. It saves me quite a bit of time, since it gets me home at least 24 hours and probably 36 hours before I could get home on the train. I have invited the boys to have breakfast with me Sunday morning if you can feed four hungry boys. Preferences for breakfast seem to run to Orange Juice, Fried eggs and bacon, hot buttered toast and milk. Of course, there are only about ten thousand things that could happen between now and June 11th to interfere with our plans, but we will keep on hoping. I wish that, when you get a chance, you would take some of the money I have sent you and make out a money order to $78.95 to the American Airlines and sent it to me. I will send it in to Dallas. Of course, we may lose our reservations, but there are pretty good railroad connections between Dallas and Washington.

We finished our fifth week of gunnery this week and it was a pretty strenuous one. I fired two more problems this week and kept up my "S's." I think I will be picking up a "U" or so pretty soon though. They are really trying to give the few of us that haven't any firing "U's" yet the tough targets. I fired on a target Friday that was way off on the right flank so that angle between the guns, the target and my position was about 1200 mils (around 70 degrees). In addition to that, he told me that my front lines were about 50 yards in front of my target, so that any short rounds would be in my own line (an automatic "U"). I was pretty lucky to pull it off.

We heard some pretty bad news from the V.M.I. boys down at the Fort Knox Armored Force O.C.S. this week. They have had a lot of hard luck down there. One of our boys got shot with a 50 caliber machine gun, another was injured in a tank accident. And now comes word that Jim Irwin and [indecipherable first name] MacIntyre bulled out at the end of the 13th week. We haven't heard the details yet, but that is pretty discouraging news. We have been very lucky down here.

Short and Overstreet came back from their furlough, and they are getting pretty good treatment. The school here contacted the Quartermaster Corps. They are now working on a play to let them complete their O.C.S. here and then transfer them to Q.M.C. They are now waiting for a ruling on their case from the Army Ground Forces. I will let you know about them. They are both very appreciative of Daddy's help, and I think his talking to General [undecipherable] helped a lot.

Well, I'll close now. Thank Mary for the cookies and note from N.Y.

All my love,
John

* * *

OFFICER CANDIDATE SCHOOL
FORT SILL, OKLAHOMA

[May 7, 1944]

Dear Mother,

I received your letter written last Saturday sending me the money for my plane ticket and also one from Daddy. You have asked me several times if I have received a book from Mrs. Lattin. As yet, I haven't received any book from her. I have been anxiously waiting [for] your letter written after you got my letter of last week-end, since I am very interested in what Daddy has to say with regard to my uniforms. They have given us the go-ahead sign on buying our uniforms, what with gunnery behind us. I haven't done anything yet, since I plan to buy only the minimum requirement here and fill in with a little shopping in Washington while I am home. I wish you would send my suitcase out here, since, if I'm going to be an officer, I won't be carrying my stuff around in a barracks bag. If you send me out a uniform, you could send them together.

Well, we finished our 13th week and also our gunnery course this week. We are now studying communications. We started last Thursday, and the course runs through Thursday this week. We then have three weeks of tactics. Two weeks from Wednesday our class has to act as officers in a regimental parade. They made me regimental commander, and I have to organize the whole thing, appointing all the other officers, drill the officers, get the other classes notified, etc. Fortunately, since I have marched in a couple of thousand parades, I guess it will all come off O.K.

Daddy wrote me about my assignment after I leave here. I would very much like to get assigned to a 105 Bn

[Battalion] in some Division Artillery, but I doubt if anybody in this class will get that assignment. I have put in for both the Survey Course and the Battery Executive's Course here at the F.A.S. Both courses are four-week courses and are considered pretty desirable. If I get sent to one of those courses, I figure that I would be in pretty good shape as far as getting a good assignment is concerned when I finish. The Survey work is pretty interesting and important and, since I had some Civil Engineering, I have some qualification for it. I would also be very interested in the Exec. Course. Our recommendations for those courses come from the gunnery department and I should have a pretty good chance. Incidentally, I fired one more problem this week, a Large T Bracket problem and came through O.K.

Cliff is thinking for spending a couple of days in Washington on his furlough. I asked him to come up and we could see some ball games. Do you think there is any way we could work it for him to stay either with us or in the Kennedy-Warren [an apartment complex in DC]? I seem to remember Mrs. Coleman saying she had a few rooms there. Cliff hasn't much at home now with his father at sea and his brother in Annapolis. What do you think about his spending a couple of days with us?

Well, that about all. We have written to Dallas to see about train reservations to supplement our plane reservations.

All my love,
John

Written in Grace's handwriting at the bottom of the page:
Please send this back—as I've saved the O.C.S. letters.

* * *

OFFICER CANDIDATE SCHOOL
FORT SILL, OKLAHOMA

[May 14, 1944]

Dear Mother,

First to acknowledge your nice long letter and Daddy's informative one about the uniforms and the boys who want to get in the Signal Corps. I have given the dope he sent to Cliff here and will sent it on to the boys at Knox. Please thank him for me. Tell him that I think Mr. Dondero has a good offer and to go ahead and get the uniform from him. I will be about to pay you for it when I get home. It will be two weeks before I need it here so any time that you can send it will be O.K. If he can't have it ready by then, just send me a receipt or something to show that I have one ordered. Also, please remember to send my suitcase. Incidentally, since we won't get paid this month, I could use about 24$ [*sic*] if you could send it to me. I will have plenty to travel with, since we will get paid when we graduate. I did quite a bit of shopping last night. I bought a short overcoat, some shirts, insignia, and some other things we are required to have. We can sign for such stuff now and pay when we get our uniform money upon graduation. I plan to buy a summer uniform, but it is not required for graduation and I will wait till I get home, since I feel I can do better in Washington.

We finished our communications course O.K. and have now started our combined arms or tactics course. After we finish that, there "ain't no more." It will be some relief to have it all over with. I sure hope our plane reservations work out O.K. If they do, I'll be home three weeks from this very minute.

We had a very interesting experience this week. Friday night they had an optional lecture given by two boys who were forward observers in Africa, one with the 9th Division and one with the 1st. They had both been wounded in action and sent home and are on duty here at the FAS. They were both very interesting and gave us a lot of practical stuff. One of them was a Lt. Lippencott. When he got up I had the feeling that I had seen him before. After the lecture, several of us were up talking to him and he said to me, "Where have I seen you before?" The strangest part is that neither of us could remember where we had seen each other. I didn't get much chance to talk to him, but he said he didn't go to school in Washington, so that eliminates Western. I didn't talk to him much, since there was quite a crowd and I didn't want to monopolize the conversation. He said he was at Bragg for a couple of weeks while I was there last summer but he was in a different regiment. I still haven't placed him. It was very interesting to talk to them since they had a very interesting outlook on combat. They both said they had enjoyed it tremendously and had gotten a lot of laughs out of it. We hear so much talk about our men developing neurotic conditions in combat and coming back nervous wrecks. Well, there was nothing wrong with these boys and they seemed pretty damn normal in spite of having been through it all and come out seriously wounded. Lippencott said it was "the greatest sport I've ever seen" and he was crazy to go back. They both were just as enthusiastic as Daddy was when he went over to England. I found it quite refreshing to talk to them.

I got a book of Cartoons this week sent from New York. Did you send it or was it from Mrs. Lattin? There was no card with it.

All my love to all of you. Did you get my last letter with the information Daddy requested about my assignment?

All my love,
John

* * *

OFFICER CANDIDATE SCHOOL
FORT SILL, OKLAHOMA

[May 21, 1944]

Dear Mother,

I received your letter and Mary's this week and was very glad to hear from you. Also, thanks for the check. I am going to ask you for more money and here is why. I have a chance to get a ride down to Dallas with A. B. Horn, who has his car here. However, he is planning to leave here right after graduation and doesn't want to wait for us to settle up our bills. So I am asking you to send me about $125 if you can. That way I can settle up my bills and catch a ride with A.B. I realize that you have sent me an awful lot of money, $80 for my plane ticket, $25 in your last check and almost $70 for my blouse. With this, it will make about $300. But I will be able to pay you back when I get some pay.

You will be glad to know that Short and Overstreet have been admitted to the school here again. They will get limited service commissions and may be transferred to another branch, but they are very happy to get back in under any conditions.

This has been a very busy week. We have been very busy with our tactics course. Also we [had] two practices for our parade, which comes off this Wednesday. I will be glad when it is over, since it has kept me pretty busy. In addition, I was Charge of Quarters one day and platoon leader another day. Friday night we had some more lectures by officers back from combat. This time we had two officers, both of whom had been decorated for gallantry, who had served as liaison officers with the infantry, one with the 1st Armored Division in Tunisia and the other with the 3rd Division in Sicily and Italy. The latter had been in 4 landings. North Africa, Sicily, Salerno and Anzio. It was very interesting to listen to them.

Wednesday, General Ward had me over to dinner. I took Jack King with me and we had a very pleasant evening, a very good family dinner and a very relaxed evening. General and Mrs. Ward were very nice to us, and wanted to be remembered to you and Daddy. General Ward said that he had received Daddy's letter suggesting that he not invite me, but he said that, since I had gotten this far without getting in any trouble, he figured it would be O.K. I was very happy to go and had a fine time.

By this time next week, I should have gotten my assignment and can tell you where I will be going after my leave. Incidentally, I should have about 10 days leave, depending on where I am sent. Mary seemed worried that I might be sent to the Infantry. Several classes were sent there a couple of months ago, but the last few classes have either been sent to school here or to big gun outfits. I would be pleased with either of those assignments, although I don't know the first thing about big guns. There is a big trend towards big guns in the artillery now. General Ward told us that a great many A-A Battalions were to be converted to heavy artillery. I hope that Jack doesn't get converted to artillery, since I imagine he would be very displeased.

Well, I will close now and send you all my love. I hope you are getting along O.K. with the dentist. You have certainly had a siege.

All my love,
John

When I reviewed the OCS letters with my father in 2012, he shared two stories about them. The first concerned the "little diversion" on April 23, 1944, when the tac officer ordered the 111th class to do an extra close order drill, or a parade formation. My father said that since so many of the men in the 111th were VMI students, they had extensive parade experience. Dad was put in charge of the formation, and he was able to place other VMI men in critical positions to ensure the successful execution of the parade. When the parade was conducted, Dad watched from the viewing platform along with his tac officer, Lt. Smith, and Col. Turner. The parade went off flawlessly. Upon completion, Col. Turner said to Lt. Smith, "That was the best damn parade I've ever seen." My dad caught the eye of Lt. Smith and just winked.

The second story dealt with the outcome of the 111th class. Dad reported that all the men in class 111 successfully completed the course. Some had to be moved to other classes primarily due to becoming sick during their time at Ft. Sill and not being able to maintain the rigorous schedule. But eventually all graduated as officers. Of the men in class 111, 50 percent were from VMI. As a group, they decided to make sure everyone would make it through. At OCS, which had a system of success designed around competition, this type of cooperation was unusual. The demerit system was the primary way candidates were "bulled out," so the 111th class devised a system to spread out demerits rather than let one candidate accrue too many. My dad admitted had it not been for the fact that their tac officer, Lt. Smith, seemed amused by the approach of the class, the whole thing could have backfired. I think it is an extraordinary example of how collaboration and community strengthen the men facing such challenging times.

PERSONAL REFLECTIONS ON THE LETTERS FROM WWII

THIS SECTION BEGINS WITH a journal entry by Martha Ingles written on D-Day. Upon completion of OCS, John was sent to Europe to do his part under the command of General Patton. He was only twenty-one when he was sent overseas. During his tour of duty, he participated in the Battle of the Bulge, witnessed concentration camps firsthand, and was involved with the complicated job of repatriating POWs. He was proud of his service, but

JOHN AND MARY INGLES OUTSIDE THE KENNEDY-WARREN APARTMENTS, 1944

he suffered from violent nightmares about these years for the rest of his life.

The last correspondences in this section were written after censorship of soldiers' letters was lifted and include more detail than earlier ones. His letter of May 23, 1945, is an extensive recap of his combat experiences. A lengthy letter of December 30, 1945, recounts his leave over the Christmas holiday with his GI [Ground Infantry soldier] buddy Zeke. This is the last letter in the set and ends with the poignant summary:

> Happy New Year Honey to you and all the family. As you said in your letter it has been a good year for us in that it is safely past and everybody is well. It is my dearest hope that I will be home before 1946 is too far gone but at least we know now that I will be home sooner or later and I don't have to worry as I did many times about never getting home again. One of these fine days I will be knocking at your door and then we can start being together all over again.
>
> All my love,
> John

My family, indeed, was among the lucky ones.

Journal Entry from Martha Ingles Schrader

Tues – June 6 [1944]

This morning I turned on the radio at about 8 o'clock—and discovered that the Invasion had begun. It had been going on since 12:30 am. "The Invasion of Europe by the Democracies"—the thing that we have all been waiting for, holding our breaths for, for weeks. It was in progress.

I remember, along about the first of this year, I had quite a battle with myself—a battle to squelch down the fear that possessed me that Jack would be in Europe for the Invasion. I was sure that he would be there, taking part in it, and the thought gave me many very real nightmares.

I cannot thank God enough that he is not there. He will be in this war before it is through—but I thank God, with my whole heart and soul, that he was not there for this part of it. I sat there in my chair, and thanked Him the Invasion had started without my Jack and then I sat there and listened to the dramatic story of how 8,000 ships and landing boats, protected in the skies by 14,000 air planes, ploughed across the English Channel and landed great armies of our men, and great masses of equipment on the northern coast of France. The greatest operation of its type ever undertaken in the history of the world. I sat there, and the goose flesh came out all over me, and wouldn't go away. I listened to how General Eisenhower, their supreme commander, had spent the whole evening before visiting the troupes personally and encouraging them—and the tears began to roll down my face and they wouldn't stop. The tremendousness of it—and the terrible death-toll that there will be—just took hold of my emotions and shook them good. I am sure the same thoughts did just that to the emotions of every Englishman and every American living. It is too big a thing, almost, even to talk about. The hearts of all the people in the land are full to overflowing today, I know.

Letter from John in London

Written on a small note pad (3.5" x 5.5") from London where John was briefly stationed before going to France.

London, Oct 4 [1944]

Dear Mother,

Just a note while I am killing a little time. I am fine,

and things are going pretty well. I am comfortably billeted, although my room is quite a distance from the mess where the officers eat. Of course, I can eat anywhere I choose, but they say that the food is better at the officers' mess than almost any other place in town. The food is very cheap at the officers' mess, and also, since it is an American place, I can figure out what is going on. I am sure Daddy knows the place well, since he probably ate all of his meals there when he was here. The junior officers get their meals cafeteria style. It is a very large place, very highly organized, and is commonly known as "Willow Run."

Last night I got a cab which took me down to my hotel. It was too late when I got settled to come to the officers' mess, so I went to a hotel a few blocks from mine and got my supper. I had my choice of partridge or fish, and, as you may guess, I chose the partridge, which wasn't bad. When I left, I had my first experience finding my way home in the blackout. I made it OK, but I don't know just how well I could do if I had very far to go. Tonight, I hope to get home before dark.

Since I started this letter, I have been interrupted and my affairs seem to be straightening out OK. I delivered Ed Clewell's overcoat liner as per Daddy's instructions.

I don't know just when I shall mail this, since I don't have an envelope now, and I must find an APO [American Post Office] in order to mail it. I don't imagine that I will get it mailed until tomorrow. I hope that you don't mind getting a letter written on this funny paper, but I don't really think that you will.

All my love,
John

* * *

PAGE ONE FROM LONDON LETTER

LETTERS FROM JOHN IN FRANCE

France, Sunday Oct. 15 [1944]

Dear Mother,

Well, to you it must seem like things are pretty ordinary with me sitting down to write you on a Sunday night. But it is actually pretty much of a coincidence that I have time to write you on Sunday. Actually, I practically had to look at my little calendar to see that today is Sunday. The fact that every day is pretty much like every other one is one of the hardest things to get used to over here. Also, it is difficult to get used to not working on a schedule, you know "training starts at 0715, one hour out for lunch, retreat at 1725, etc." Now we just work all the time except when you take time to eat and sleep. I am very well situated with regard to eating and sleeping, as we have been very comfortably situated. Not comfortable by home standards, but comfortable by standards over here.

I hope that you heard about my assignment before this, and I assume that you did. Of course I haven't received any mail yet, but I hope that maybe I will get some this week. I am certainly looking forward to getting some. I can tell you that it will certainly mean a lot to be getting mail.

I know that you are interested in my trip over here. It was very comfortable and very pleasant. I saw practically nothing in London, since I was only there one and a half days, and spent most of that time sitting around one office or another. Except for what I could see walking from my billet to the headquarters, I didn't see any sights. In Paris, however, I did much better. I was there for three days, most of which I had to myself. I walked a good many miles around the city trying to see as many of the points of interest as I could. It was very interesting, but I wished all the time that the family could have been there to share it with me. Paris is as beautiful as I had expected, although it is quite run down now. However, I can imagine that, in better days, it is really lovely.

I have been getting along very well here. They have been breaking me in rather slowly. So far, I have been doing the type of work I studied particularly in Oklahoma and have been able to handle it OK. I am working with a very fine bunch of people here, and everybody has been very nice to me.

Well, I'll close now. I am looking forward to news from you.

All my love,
John

* * *

France, Sunday Oct. 22 [1944]

Dear Mother,

Well, another week has gone by, and a very busy one at that. Still no mail from you, but I know that you have written if you have learned of my address. Most of the mail, in fact, as far as I know all of it, that has been arriving up here is dated at a time when I was still in the states. I hope that you have heard from me in one manner or another, since I know you will be worried about me if you have not received any letters. Incidentally, this is the third letter I have written you since I left home.

This is a pretty small world. The other day I ran into a boy I knew at V.M.I. He wasn't anyone you would know. He was in my company but a class ahead of me. I ran into him up on a hill a few thousand yards from the front lines. I was running a survey and he was putting in a telephone line. We just had time to exchange a few brief "What the hell are you doing here's" and then we both went our way. I often wonder just where and when I will meet some [of] my friends again. I don't expect to meet many of them around here for a while, since I was probably the first of my particular group that came this way.

I am pretty well pleased with my job here so far. I don't like being around a headquarters since there is too much rank around. On the other hand, I am out all over the division sector every day, and have probably seen as much of the big picture in such a short time as is possible for a young officer.

Well, I must close now. I send all my love to each of the family. I will send a request. How about sending me a heavy O.D. scarf?

All my love,
John

* * *

France, Oct. 29, 1944

Dear Mother,

Another week without mail, but I am not discouraged about not hearing from you. Everyone here assures me that the mail is slow coming at first, and I expect that I will get a bunch of mail one of these days. I imagine that the first letters you wrote were sent before you received my specific address, and so those letters may be a little late in reaching me.

This has been quite a red letter week for me. I had a shower, my first bath since London. At that, I imagine that it will be at least that long before I get another one. In addition to that, I have seen three movies, imagine that. I had seen them all in the States, but I enjoyed seeing them again. We had "The Mask of Dimitrious" "And the Angels Sing" and tonight "Two Girls and a Sailor." This made the third time I had seen the last one, but I enjoyed it very much just the same. It is a good picture with a lot of my favorite music.

It must look like I have been having a veritable vacation over here. But I have been very busy too, and have had a lot to do. Any job is one that is continuous, since you never get finished in any one area. We are really quite comfortable here, and we have been eating very well and regularly. I don't get as much sleep as I would like, but I am feeling fine.

Well, all my love to everyone. I feel that I am getting way behind on family news, and I hope everything is OK at home.

All my love,
John

* * *

France, Nov. 6 [1944]

Dear Mother,

It seems that each week I start by saying "another week without mail" and this week is no exception. I am hopeful, however, that I will come through with some mail any day now. We are pretty near the end of the line here, and can't expect to get the service that we enjoyed when Daddy was in England. I only hope that my letters have been coming through to you in good time, because if you haven't heard from me as of this date, I guess you must be quite worried. Once the mail starts coming, it will probably come with some semblance of regularity, and we won't notice so much that it is a few weeks late. I know for sure that you have been writing me regularly, and I will probably get a batch when it finally arrives.

I received my pay for September and October, plus a little travel pay. I am enclosing money orders for the amount of $280 for you to deposit for me. I am taking out an allotment for $75 which will be sent to you each month, starting with November's pay.

You will be glad to know that I am keeping up with "Terry and the Pirates" over here. It appears in <u>The Stars and Stripes,</u> which we see quite regularly.

Well, all my love to everyone.

Love,
John

* * *

France, Nov. 15 [1944]

Dear Mother,

I have lapsed a little in my letter writing, it having been about 10 days since I wrote. During the interim I have finally heard from home, a letter from Daddy, a Halloween Card from Martha and a cablegram from you. I am very distressed that you didn't hear any news from me until General Rumbough's letter. I have written you regularly ever since I left home, the first being mailed in England. I hope it will all catch up with you. If Daddy didn't hear about my assignment he can only blame "the greatest communication system in the world." Col. Hammond was out when I left his headquarters, but I left a note telling him where I was assigned and asking him to send Daddy a radio message. I know he knows where I am, since he has mentioned my name to several people coming up here. I don't know why he didn't notify Daddy. I hope that, since I have heard from you, some of my mail may have reached home. I am sure that the delay has been a cause of much worry to you, but it hasn't been because I haven't written. Daddy writes that Martha is home. I hope that she is well, and I hope that she will be able to move into the Kennedy-Warren near you.

It is, of course, not possible for me to write much of what is going on here. It is now permitted for us to say that our division is part of the 12th Corps, Third Army. I am enclosing a snapshot one of the boys in the section took of me.

All my love,
John

* * *

France, Nov. 21 [1944]

Dear Mother,

Well, I have received a lot of mail since I wrote you last, which was only a few days ago. I have received two letters from you, one from Mary, a V-Mail from Martha, and three letters containing funnies, clippings, etc. Thank you all for writing. I hope that my mail has also been reaching you now. You can't expect to get the kind of mail service that people whose husbands are in Paris and London get. It probably takes longer, even twice as long, for the mail to get home from Paris up to here as it does for mail to get from Washington to Paris. And, of course, the same applies going back. But, once things get started, maybe the flow will be fairly regular.

I am glad that you and Daddy had such a nice weekend in New York with the Paitzolds and the Lattins. It was a good break for both of you. I haven't seen Bob Matteson yet, but have tracked him down sufficiently to find out what office he works in. I will go and see him if I get back to Hqs. However, I haven't had any time for visiting recently.

I have added some equipment to my stuff since coming here. I bought some overshoes, which are an essential item, and also some combat pants. The latter are made of the same stuff as a field-jacket (a bit heavier stuff) and are like overalls. You put them over everything. They are very helpful in keeping warm and dry. I am often cold and wet, but I have the tremendous advantage of sleeping inside. I don't see how the infantry stands weather like we've had.

Well, all my love.
John

The V-mail mentioned in the letter above refers to Victory Mail, which was a secure and preferred method for correspondence with American soldiers during World War II. It was written on a small sheet of paper, 7" by

V-Mail service provides a most rapid means of communication. If addressed to a place where photographing service is not available the original letter will be dispatched by the most expeditious means.

INSTRUCTIONS

(1) Write the entire message plainly on the other side within marginal lines.

(2) Print the name and address in the two spaces provided. Addresses of members of the Armed Forces should show full name, complete military or naval address, including grade or rank, serial number, unit to which assigned or attached and army post office in care of the appropriate postmaster or appropriate fleet post office.

(3) Fold, seal, and deposit in any post office letter drop or street letter box.

(4) Enclosures must not be placed in this envelope.

(5) V-Mail letters may be sent free of postage by members of the Armed Forces. When sent by others postage must be prepaid at domestic rates (3c ordinary mail, 6c if domestic air mail service is desired when mailed in the U. S.)

POST OFFICE DEPARTMENT PERMIT NO. 1

Instructions for V-Mail included on the back of paper used by sender

9 1/8". After being censored, the letter was copied to microfilm and, once at its destination, was printed back onto a smaller sheet of paper, 4¼" by 5¼". The military preferred V-mail since transportation of the mail on film saved shipping space for war materiel.

* * *

Nov. 21, 1944

Dear Daddy,

This is just a short note, a sort of continuation of one I am writing to Mother at the same sitting. I am sending this to your office because the bit of news it contains might upset Mother. You can tell her about it in such a way that she won't be worried.

I was wounded in action a couple of weeks ago, but

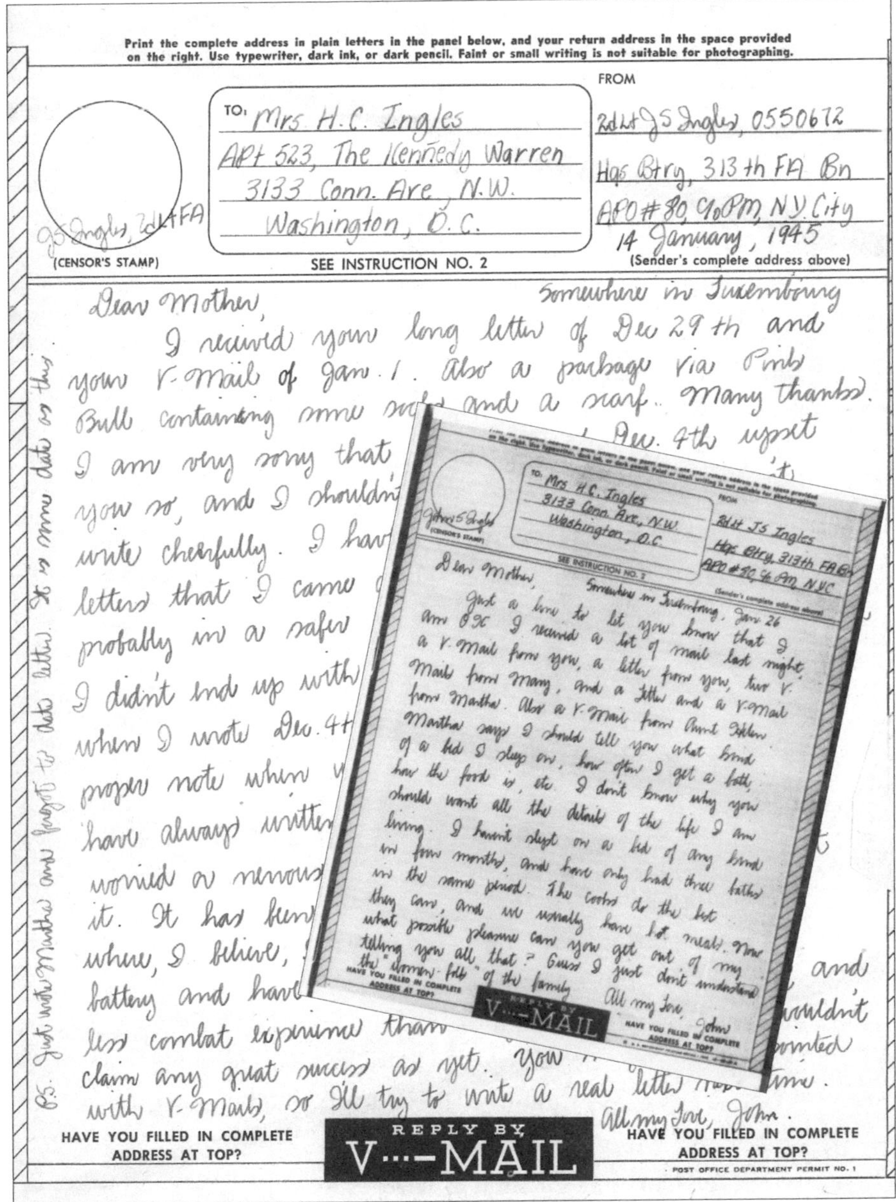

V-mail as written in the background. Original would be 7" x 9 1/8", and in the foreground, the V-mail as received. Original would be 4 1/4" x 5 1/4"

fortunately, not seriously so. We were running a survey up close to the infantry front lines and ran into some German artillery fire. I was hit with the first volley, just as I was in the act of hitting the ground. A small fragment passed across my left leg, where it just broke the skin, and struck my right thigh about eight inches above my knee. It made what the Doctor called a "puncture", a small hole less than 1/8 of an inch across. He probed in about an inch and a half looking for the fragment. However, he couldn't find it and didn't try to take it out. I wasn't laid up at all by it, and haven't missed any duty. It is nicely healed by now and I don't even have a bandage on anymore. So you can see that I was very fortunate and that I am perfectly all right. I was given the Purple Heart for "wounds received in action."

Well, that's all there is to it. I am writing Mother at this same time, so I will close now.

Love,
John

* * *

27 Nov. 1944

Dear Mother,

I am getting into the habit of writing you every six days or so while I am on duty during the early morning hours. It sort of reminds me of the times I used to write you during the "wee small hours" when I was on guard back at VMI. It is a good time to write, since I usually have some spare time. Most of my daylight hours are pretty full, and I would be hard put for time to write to you if I didn't catch a late shift every so often.

I haven't received any mail since I wrote you last, which is very disappointing. I think that it would be wise to start mixing in a few V-Mails with the Air-Mail letters you have

been sending. Although the V-Mails aren't as satisfying as a regular letter, they seem to come through more quickly. I am pretty disgusted about the whole mail situation and I guess you are too, since my letters don't seem to have been reaching you any better than yours have been reaching me. Maybe it won't be too long before we won't be so many miles apart. Although I haven't even been over here for two months yet, it sure seems like it has been a long time. As a rule, when you are busy, the time seems to fly. But I guess we are too busy over here for that rule to hold true.

It will be Martha's birthday very shortly, and, although I haven't a card or a present to send to her, I will be thinking of her and wishing her a very happy birthday. I feel sure that the coming year will be one that is full of happiness and joy for her. I am very hopeful that she can get an apartment in the K-W so that she can be comfortably fixed up near to you.

Well, I guess that's about all for now.

All my love,
John

* * *

Letter from Georgina Hammond

Her husband, Col. Elton Hammond, was General Patton's signal officer. The V-mail that follows this was attached to the letter.

Dear Grace,

I know you will enjoy reading this brief bit about John, and no doubt you will read it over and over again until at least John's letters catch up to the date of this one – Do keep the letter, Grace. Little snatches of news about your son do mean much to you – I'm so glad Elton saw him and that he is doing so well.

Could you and Martha come over for luncheon next Friday or Saturday? Either day—and there will be only us—

Our best to you all—
Affectionately—
Georgina—

Sat. PM
Attached V-Mail:
To:
Mrs. Elton F. Hammond
2800[?] Old Dominion Blvd
Alexandria, Virginia
U.S.A.

From:
Col. Elton F. Hammond
[?] Third Army, Signal [?]
APO [undecipherable] c/o Postmaster, NW
28 November 1944

Dearest Sweetheart,

Visited the unit in which Lt. John Ingles is serving today. He is in the Artillery Section, is doing fine, likes his work, and seems happy at it. He is well liked, particularly because he is standing on his own feet and not asking for favors of any sort. His connections remained unknown until the story was let out by someone else. His C.O. likes him, and likes his work. Apparently he is working very hard and to good purpose. He told me that he was writing home regularly, and is receiving his mail. In other words,

JOHN IN ST AVOLD, FRANCE

he is proving himself a man, and a son of whom his mother and dad should be very proud. He is in a fine outfit, which is, and has been doing, excellent work. Be sure to tell his folks when you can. His address is 80th Infantry Division, A.P.O #80.

All my love to my sweetheart and to our wonderful daughters. Countless hugs and kisses. I love you! Your own loving husband,

Elton

* * *

Dec. 4, 1944

Dear Mother,

I guess that the first thing you will notice is the change in address, which in itself indicates a considerable change in my duties. I haven't moved very far, however, from the Headquarters where I was formerly assigned and

Daddy can understand my present status merely from the address. When I was sent up here I was told that I had been doing O.K. in my job, and that I wasn't being transferred because my work wasn't satisfactory. Some people back there told me that the request for my transfer came from higher up, which is quite possible. Of course, I am not too happy about it all right at the moment, since I was well broken in at the job I was doing and felt that I was doing O.K. I haven't had any previous experience whatsoever in the type of unit I am in now, and I feel very much at sea. Time will probably solve that problem, and I guess I will be able to do my job here once I find out what the score is. At least I'll try hard to do a good job. I don't believe that Daddy had anything to do with the latest change in my status, but, if he did, let's leave well enough alone. I'll do my job as best I can and go through what's necessary to get the job done. But I am also very interested in living through this war. All of which may seem like strange talk, but it's hard not to be concerned about yourself after you have had a few close calls. You've got to accept what fate has in store for you, but it doesn't make much sense to give fate too much help.

No mail from home in two weeks now. I think that I've made every conceivable comment on that subject before, so I won't try to think of anything new to say. I only hope that the letters I have written have been reaching you. I tried to see Bob Matteson but didn't have any way of getting over to his place, although we were in the same town. My chances of seeing him now are not very good, but I will take advantage of an opportunity I get.

Well, all for now.

All my love,
John

* * *

France, 6 December [1944]

Dear Mother,

I am writing you tonight, not because I have any news to report, but because I want to acknowledge a grand bunch of mail I got a couple of days ago. A lot of it was old mail which you had mailed when you first received my APO, but some of the V-Mails were written around the 20th of November. Included was a cable which you sent when you received a letter from me, which should give you some idea of the relative value of sending me a cable. It may give you the feeling that you are communicating with me by the quickest way, but actually it reaches me slower than a V-Mail. The V-Mails seem to come quickest of all, as the air-mail is very irregular. Of course the air-mails are more welcome because you can write so much more, but if you have anything you want me to know quickly, the V-Mail seems to be the best. In the bunch of mail I received there were letters from everyone in the family, three weeks of <u>Terry and the Pirates</u>, and clippings about the World Series. It marked the third time I have received mail, and it was by far the largest amount I have ever received. I enjoyed each letter and you are all very good to write me so often. I was particularly glad to learn that Martha has an apartment in the Kennedy-Warren. I know that you are glad to have her well-situated and it sounds like a good situation all around. I think of her very often.

I was interested in the letter Daddy received saying that I would be given a job for which I was suited. I haven't had [incomplete]

* * *

JOHN WITH HIS FATHER HAL IN EUROPE, 1944

France, Dec. 14 [1944]

Dear Mother,

Just a note while I am enclosing a money order for $70.00. I am very pleased that I have been able to save so much of my pay while I have been over here. Maybe when I get back where there is something worth spending money on I will have some to spend. I wrote at long length last night, so I won't write any more than to say that I am fine.

All my love,

John

* * *

France, December 15 [1944]

Dear Mother,

You must be quite astonished to be getting such a deluge of mail from me, since this is the third letter in four nights. But I am thinking of all of you and I figure that, as long as I have the time, I am happy to write. Maybe this will help tide you over future periods when I am not able to write so frequently. If my mail is any indication, you will receive these letters over a period of a month. I received a lot of mail today, with letters from you, Martha and Daddy, a cable from you (sent I don't know when), a Christmas card and note from Mrs. Peck, some funnies and some football clippings. Everyone has been grand about writing, and I have never appreciated my mail more. The only drawback is that all the mail was sent in early November, and, since I have received letters sent in December, this "news" didn't seem very new. But that's the way the mail runs, and since I am always happy to receive any mail at all, I certainly don't complain about a little matter such as that.

I am sending home my Purple Heart Medal. I don't know why you should want it, but I have no place to carry it and would probably lose it eventually. I am keeping the ribbon in case I should ever put on a blouse over here, but am sending the rest of it home. Lest you are picturing me receiving my "decorations" from the commanding general with flags flying and bands playing, I shall describe the impressive ceremony at which I received it. After the doctor finished dressing my leg he told me to go over to my room and lie down. I was sitting on my bed-roll removing my shoes when a medic private (name unknown) came in and said "Lt. Ingles?" I said, "Yes." He said, "Here" gave me my medal and departed. All of which shows the importance attached to such a medal in a combat division. However, I am glad to have it, since I fulfilled all the requirements and in future years, can dream up more impressive details to tell my children (and nephew or nieces—Martha please note).

You have expressed considerable interest in my living conditions. I have been super fortunate so far in that I have slept in a building of some kind every night. Don't know how long that streak will last, however. When I was running Survey for Div. Arty I was, of course, out in the open all day. But I had the great advantage of returning to a dry place to sleep every night. That was particularly gratifying during the terrible weather which you read about in middle of November. That was just about the worst weather I have ever seen. The weather has been bad ever since I came over here, with a clear day an unusual occurrence. Lately the weather has been improved, definitely colder but not so much rain. I guess that we can expect a lot of nasty weather all winter, however. I wear a lot of warm clothes though. My usual uniform consists of something like this: First, long underwear and wool socks. Next my sleeveless sweater and over that, a GI long sleeved sweater. Next—my shirt and pants and combat boots. Then combat pants, Field Jacket and over-shoes. And, if it is real nasty, I have my overcoat to put on over everything. It must sound like all that would be too much to carry, and, if I were marching with the dough-boys, I probably wouldn't wear that much. I don't notice the weight unless I am wearing my overcoat, but in any case I guess I keep about as warm as possible. I had to laugh at myself the other day when I was peeling down to take a shower. It took considerable undressing to get down to me.

Will close now. Am glad Daddy could help Sanford.

All my love,

John

* * *

Dec. 25, 1944—Merry Christmas

Dear Mother,

Haven't written for several days due to having been very busy, but I did want to make a special effort and get a letter off today, to send you all my love and let you know that I am O.K. I received one of the Christmas packages, the one from Martha and Jack. I enjoyed every little gift and everything was so nicely wrapped. Tell her that I received it and how much I appreciated it. I guess that I will be receiving the other packages shortly. I also received the scarf you sent and am putting it to good use. One major news item is that yesterday I received a V-Mail from you written Dec. 15. Only 9 days, imagine! That was the only letter I have received in about a week, however. You said that you had received my letter of Nov 27th, but apparently you hadn't heard about my being wounded yet. I hope that that letter didn't get lost, since I have sent my Purple Heart home, and if you receive that without any warning, you will be upset. My leg is perfectly O.K. now, and I won't even have a scar to show you when I come home.

I am glad that Daddy is able to get news of the movements of the Division, since then you are able to know where I am, if that is any comfort to you. I have finally been assigned to a regular job here, since I am motor officer in this headquarters battery. My duties, which, in addition to trying to keep our vehicles moving, include being censor, mess officer, supply officer, etc, are not very spectacular, but I am glad to have a regular job. Particularly so since I thought that I had come up here destined to be a forward observer. As it is, I guess I am in less danger in this job than when I was out running survey every day. I guess that it sounds funny to talk about your own

John in battle gear

safety, but anyone who says he doesn't worry about his own safety is a liar.

We had a good Christmas dinner today. I literally slept in a manger on Christmas Eve, very appropriate don't you think? The war goes on today as usual. I guess that the news of late came as quite a shock to most people at home. But it simply confirms what most of us over here have felt for a long time. Those who are actually doing the fighting know that the German Army is still strong and well-equipped. No gains for months have been made without overcoming strong resistance. If the news will serve to put people back to work and help us get the stuff we need, maybe the Germans will have done us a service. As you may recall, even before I came over here, I wasn't one to believe in an early end to the war over here. I would guess that American ground operations in this theater, which began on D-Day, have by now about reached the half-way mark. I guess that everyone is entitled to a prediction, just for a record.

I will make a request for some food. I think I would like some cans of fruit and orange juice. We sometimes get grapefruit juice, but some orange juice and some cans of fruit would be quite a treat.

Will close now.

All my love,
John

* * *

Somewhere in Luxembourg
Sunday, Dec 31, 1944

Dear Mother,

Not much news tonight, and I am wondering how you are spending New Year's Eve at home. I imagine that you are celebrating quietly, since tomorrow will be another day for Daddy, as it will be for us here. I don't remember any very riotous New Year's Eves in our family. I remember how, at Monmouth we used to sit up and listen to the New Year's Eve radio programs. They used to have a series of 15 minute programs from all the night clubs and all the "name" bands would be on. The program used to go on all night. At midnight, they would describe the scene at Times Square in New York. And you and Daddy [would] call home from the club right after midnight and wish us a "Happy New Year." I remember the last two New Year's Eves which I spent at VMI and weren't very happy ones either. The last one doesn't seem to have left much of an impression, but I remember the one before that. Cliff started out early in the evening to drink the new year in. He passed out very amiably about 10 o'clock, we put him to bed, and he didn't know it was 1943 until the next morning. So we are used to being apart on New Year's Eve, as we weren't used to being apart on Christmas. I have high hopes for the New Year of 1945. I think it will see an end to the war over here, and maybe I will be home for a while anyway. I guess the latter part is just "pipe dreaming" and not based on any facts.

No letters from you since I wrote you on Christmas. I did receive another of the Christmas packages, this one from you with some good food in it. Thank you kindly. I am expecting one more, since I recall that you mentioned three being sent, and I received Martha's about a week before Christmas.

A day or so ago a couple of fellows from Bob Matteson's section were up here on a job. I asked if they knew him and told them I had been trying to contact him. They said they would tell him where I was located. Today he was around this way and stopped by. We talked for a few minutes. I thought he was a very nice fellow and I was glad that we finally met each other.

Well, all for now.

Love,
John

P.S. Received a V-Mail from Aunt Helen. I will try to answer it if I have time. If you are writing you might tell her I got her letter and thank her for it.

* * *

Somewhere in Luxembourg,
Jan. 6 [1945]

Dear Mother,

I am afraid that I have been neglecting you lately. But we are busy and the time seems to slip away. I have been with this division just about three months now, during which we have seen some hard fighting. I expect that we have a good bit of the same ahead of us. The outfit I am with now is a very good one, and has a very fine record of achievement behind it. I find that things are a lot different in a battery which has had as much combat experience as this one than they were in training in the U.S. I remember that there were nine officers in my battery at Camp Butner and we had to supervise every move that was made. Here, where the batteries are consistently under-strength the non-coms and men pretty much run themselves. Not that the officers don't do anything, but once a decision has been made and a plan laid out, you aren't worried much with the details of execution. I think that an officer's biggest job is in training and once his outfit is committed to action, the control he exerts is very limited. It is then up to each individual to know his job and take it upon himself to see it through to completion in spite of the difficulties or hardships. The credit for the success of this battalion certainly belongs not to the officers that are here now and have come in as replacements, but to the officers who trained it in the States and, above all, to the men themselves. The details that are emphasized so much in the States, such as a snappy appearance at parade, a spotless barracks at inspection, or a shiny bunch of vehicles, are not the things that are the pay-off in combat. The good soldier over here is the soldier who knows his job and has guts enough to stay with it and do it in spite of what may be going on. We had a transit operator on the survey crew when I was working with them who could handle a transit better than any man I ever saw. He could set up his instrument and measure his angles about four times as fast as I could do the same job. But I have seen him panic under fire, and when the time came to go out into an area that was under fire, I would take one of the other boys to handle the instrument because I knew that, although it might take him a little longer, he would stay with the job until it was finished.

Well, here I am writing away and it must all be of very little interest to you. The only mail I have received in the last two weeks was a V-Mail from Aunt Helen, one from Mary, and another from Martha. Please thank the girls for writing. I am, of course, expecting quite a bit of mail eventually, since I know that you have written. I am wondering if the creation of the new "five-star" rank will eventually mean another star for Daddy. I read over here that his boss Bill was considered for another star and I guess that, if he gets another, Daddy might get another also. At least, you and I think he should, don't we? Let me know if there are any rumors along those lines.

Well, guess I'll close now. All my love to everyone at

home. If this should arrive sometime around Mary's birthday, please wish her a very happy birthday for me.

Love,
John

* * *

Letter Transmitted via V-Mail

To: Mrs HC Ingles
Apt. 523, The Kennedy Warren
3133 Con. Ave., N.W.
Washington, DC

From: 2dLt JS Ingles 0550672
Hqs. Btry, 313 FA Bn
APO # 80 C/O PM, NY, NY
Jan. 11, 1945

Censor's Stamp:
Signed JS Ingles, 2dLt FA

Somewhere in Luxembourg

Dear Mother,

The fact that I have received nothing but V-Mails from home for three weeks makes me wonder if the air-mails I have been sending have been meeting with similar difficulty. Hence, I am writing a V-Mail. Yesterday I received four V-Mails from you (complete with funny printing) and a cable saying "Parcel received, etc." I am glad that my letter about being wounded finally reached you, and I am sure glad that it beat the parcel home. I can assure you that I didn't make light of it and it never bothered me very much. I have only a small scar now and I expect that will

be gone before I get home. I was very lucky. One of the boys received a clipping from a Philadelphia paper which described rather accurately our part in the present operations. I hope you saw the same story. The papers tell you a lot of things that I cannot write. Many thanks for the mail. All my love, John.

PS—Finally received the third Christmas box—from Mary. Many Thanks and Happy Birthday to her!

* * *

Letter Transmitted via V-Mail

To: Mrs HC Ingles
Apt. 523, The Kennedy Warren
3133 Con. Ave., N.W.
Washington, DC

From: 2dLt JS Ingles 0550672
Hqs. Btry, 313 FA Bn
APO # 80 C/O PM, NY, NY
Somewhere in Luxembourg
Jan. 14, 1945

Censor's Stamp:
Signed JS Ingles, 2dLt FA

Dear Mother,

I received your long letter of Dec 29th and your V-Mail of Jan. 1. Also a package via Pink Bull containing some socks and a scarf. Many thanks. I am very sorry that my letter of Dec. 4th upset you so, and I shouldn't write home when I can't write cheerfully. I have tried to indicate in later letters that I came out OK on the change, and am probably in a safer position than I was before. Obviously, I didn't end up with the job I had been led to expect when I wrote Dec. 4th. It is difficult to strike the proper note when writing home, particularly since I have always written home so frankly. When I am worried or nervous, I feel sure that my letters reflect it. It has been difficult for me to take over here, where, I believe, I am the youngest man in the battery and have had less service, less time overseas, and less combat experience than any of the men. I wouldn't claim any great success as yet. You may be disappointed with V-Mails, so I'll try to write a real letter next time. All my love, John. P.S. Just wrote Martha and forgot to date the letter. It is the same date as this.

* * *

Somewhere in Luxembourg
Jan. 17, 1945

Dear Daddy,

Yesterday I received your letter of Jan 5th, and it came, incidentally, in record time—11 days. I am sorry that you thought it necessary to, as you put it, "square yourself with me." I have never blamed you for anything that has happened to me in coming over here. You knew that I wanted to come overseas, and, for all the reasons that you mentioned, you did what you thought was best. And, although you know that I have never wanted your position to influence what I was doing in the Army, I am glad that I came over. Although I know that I have made a very small contribution, I am proud to have taken some part in what has gone on over here. I did feel that it was possible, at the time of my transfer over to this Bn [battalion], that you had had something to do with it. I knew that, when I came overseas,

the understanding was that I was to go to a battery. And so I thought it possible that, when I was assigned to the Div Arty staff, you were not pleased about it. However, I am glad that you didn't have anything to do with it. When I came up to this Bn, I was led to believe that I would be assigned as a Forward Observer. I was, and I admit it freely, scared as hell of that prospect. However, it was decided to assign me in my present position, and the officer I replaced took over the forward observer position. I assume that the fact that I have had so little commissioned experience was the factor that influenced the decision. As I see it, however, it was simply a case of postponing the inevitable. There is only one artillery job for a young officer in my position, and that is forward observer. Barring the possibility that someone might need a survey officer sometime, the next time that I change jobs, that is the one I will get. But I will worry about that when the time comes, and am well satisfied with my present job. I know that all the "interest" in what I am doing is coming from topside, but it would have been the same if I had stayed with the 89th. It is an unfortunate situation, but I certainly don't blame you for it. But I was very worried and confused by it all when I first came up to this Bn, and I guess I took it out on the family in my letters, since I have no other outlet or nobody here to blow off steam to.

The operation you referred to in your letter was a tough one for these units that participated in it, but I wasn't involved. We have seen some hard fighting since we moved up here, and the intense cold has been more of a bother than the Germans. I have said it before but it can bear repetition the infantry really has it tough. It is with them that the war is fought.

Love to all,
John

OBERFEULEN, LUXEMBOURG, JANUARY 1945, JOHN (STANDING) WITH PFC. ELDEN K. FREEMAN, PFC. LEONARD L. KRYLL AND T/5 RAYMOND A. STRAYTON

* * *

Somewhere in Luxembourg
20 Jan., 1945

Dear Mother,

Not much news tonight, but I will send a line along to let you know I am O.K. The mail situation mystifies me. The other day I received an air mail from Daddy (written Jan 5th) in 11 days. Tonight I received an Air Mail from Martha, the letter Sanford sent me and a Christmas Card from Mrs. Sherrill (both Air Mail)—all three mailed around Nov. 23, almost two months ago. They must have been routed through the Philippines! But I am always glad to receive any mail, no matter how old it is. Incidentally I wish you would have <u>Time</u> start sending me their "Pony Express" specially printed for overseas. I should have some left on my subscription, I don't know. I am always very hungry for reading material over here. The Army sends us up some books and magazines, but we go through them very quickly. When we are not moving, we have time to read. I recently finished "A Tree Grows in Brooklyn."

We were recently issued sleeping bags and I got one of them. I haven't needed one as long as I have been sleeping inside, but I can't be sure how long my luck will last. I now have a sleeping bag and four blankets in my bed-roll, so I should be able to keep warm at night. The weather has been very severe. We have had snow on the ground since before Christmas and the temperature has dropped to 0° on occasion.

Well, I'll close now and send my love to all.

Love,
John

* * *

Letter Transmitted via V-Mail

To: Mrs HC Ingles
3133 Con. Ave., N.W.
Washington, DC

From: 2dLt JS Ingles 0550672
Hqs. Btry, 313 FA Bn
APO # 80 C/O PM, NY, NY

Censor's Stamp:
Signed John S Ingles

Somewhere in Luxembourg,
Jan 26 [1945]

Dear Mother,

Just a line to let you know that I am O.K. I received a lot of mail last night, a V-Mail from you, a letter from you, two V-Mails from Mary, and a letter and a V-Mail from Martha. Also a V-Mail from Aunt Helen. Martha says I should tell you what kind of bed I sleep on, how often I get a bath, how the food is, etc. I don't know why you should want all the details of the life I am living. I haven't slept on a bed of any kind in four months, and have only had three baths in the same period. The cooks do the best they can, and we usually have hot meals. Now what possible pleasure can you get out of my telling you all that? Guess I just don't understand the "women-folk" of the family. All my Love, John

* * *

Somewhere in Luxembourg,
Jan 30 [1945]

Dear Mother,

I received a V-Mail from you and one from Mary, also a note in an air-mail with a bunch of clippings. You are all grand about writing and your letters are about the only thing I have to look forward to from day to day. It is rather discouraging to have you getting the wrong idea about what I am doing. I just happened to be in the message center when Bob Matteson came around, and I am certainly not "the officer in message center." As Daddy knows from the TO, there is no such animal. The Battery Commander and I run the Hqs. Btry and handle the communications. At least that is the way it is supposed to work. I have many duties, none of which the BC seems to think I do very satisfactorily. Of course, it would be quite a bit of help if I knew what the whole business was all about. I am very rapidly approaching the point that I don't give much of a damn. I am willing to do anything that is required tactically, but I am about through trying to keep everything smooth and satisfactory, since it is impossible in the first place. I just wish the whole mess was over with and everybody could be home where he belongs. I have been doing a lot of thinking lately about what I will do when the war is over. Of course, I know that I am not going to get out of the army for several years anyway. But, as you must have realized by now, I am not thinking about the Army as a career any more. I have been in the Army for about 20 months now and I have never been happy or satisfied with it, particularly since I have been commissioned. I wasn't happy with the ways things were going at Camp Butner, and, from the very beginning, my whole service overseas has been impossible. The obvious handicaps of coming as I did, and the

lack of age, knowledge, or ability, have been so aggravated by personalities here, that my whole reaction is just to want to get as far from the entire business as possible. I got along fairly well as long as I was doing technical work with a small section where I could do most of the job myself and all that was required was a willingness to do the job. But I find that I don't have the personality or leadership to work with the troops successfully, and I certainly am not doing any good now. But I am glad that I came overseas, since it is everybody's duty to do his part in this great catastrophe. Also, I could never have been able to make a good decision about staying in the Army if I hadn't had combat service overseas. This is supposed to be the climax of an Army career, the thing you are trained for, the experience that the professional soldier wants most of all. I remember how excited Daddy was and still is about going overseas, and how disappointed he was about coming home. If I can't realize any satisfaction out of combat service, then what satisfaction could I get out of the Army as a career? I can just picture Daddy saying, "Well, if you don't want to stay in the Army, what do you want to do?" And I wish I had the answer to that one in my own mind. I certainly can't see my way clear at the moment. I have misdirected my effort all my life. All through school I just worked my head off for grades, like a kind of perpetual contest against myself. I didn't relax and have fun and acquire the social graces and ability to get along with all kinds of people that are so much more important than any scholastic attainments that it is pathetic. I remember the night before I went to VMI when Martha came to my room at Monmouth and talked to me a long time about the way I was and how she hoped VMI would improve things. It seems funny now, after three years at VMI, although she meant it so sweetly.

Right now I am 22, and will be older before I get home to stay. Except for my wonderful family, who have always been so sweet and understanding and comforting to me, I have nobody in the world. I have friends, yes, who are scattered all over the country and whom I would probably never see. Nobody except the family, nobody here or anyplace else, would give a damn if I pulled through all this or not. Not much of an accomplishment in 22 years. Well, I'll keep on working on things mentally on this end, and maybe I'll come out with a good answer. Anyway, as always, I send all my love.

John

* * *

March 7, 1945
Somewhere in Germany

Dear Mother,

I have received a stack of mail in the past few days—Air Mail of Feb. 21 from Martha, V-Mail Feb 25 from Mary, V-Mail Feb 27 from Martha, V-Mail Feb 22 from Daddy and V-Mails from you Feb 17, 22, 24 and one undated. Your idea of sending me a sort of continued V-Mail, #1, #2, etc is a good one except that they don't arrive together or sometimes within a week of one another. But it doesn't make much difference and I enjoy every tid-bit of news. Everybody is wonderful about writing me.

Have two big events to report, a move and a shower in the past couple of days. Sure is a tough war.

You all occasionally drop some remark about asking me to tell you something and saying "that won't violate security regulations." I guess I am a little conservative about what I write, probably because I do so much censoring myself—better than 1000 letters per week. But there isn't much about what I do that would make very interesting reading. I am usually pretty busy doing my job and trying to appear busy.

I expect that I will be packing my bags pretty soon and moving to another job. I ran into my artillery commander this afternoon—through no fault of my own—and he wanted to know what my job was. I told him that I was Asst. Communications Officer in Hqs. Btry. So he told my Bn commander that I should be in a firing battery. So here we go again. I said my little piece last time I changed jobs, so I will let this go without biting comments. As you know, I haven't been too happy with my present battery commander, but at least I am getting used to this job and am finding out what I am supposed to do. I have never had a chance from the start over here and as I have said before, just don't give a damn any more. I hope the whole thing is forgotten, but doubt that it will be. At least, changing batteries in the Bn. won't interfere with my mail, which is really about all that matters greatly to me.

I guess I gave you all the wrong impressions about the reading material, since I haven't even taken time to read the Stars and Stripes in the last month, or since the B.C. decided he didn't like to see me sitting down. But I will enjoy Time and I won't have any trouble dispensing of the books you send.

Well, that's about all for now. The war news looks good and I hope it will soon be over. I will be thinking of Daddy on his birthday and will wish him "Happy Birthday" now. I think of you all often and of the day when I can come home again.

All my love,
John

* * *

JOHN (FRONT) SHARING A PITCHER OF BEER WITH SGT. FEAGANS (LEFT)
AND SGT. BRINKER (CENTER)

Letter transmitted via V-Mail.

To: Mrs HC Ingles
3133 Con. Ave., N.W.
Washington, DC

From: 2dLt JS Ingles 0550672
Hqs. Btry, 313 FA Bn
APO # 80 C/O PM, NY, NY

Censor's Stamp:
Signed John S Ingles

Somewhere in Austria, 8 May [1945]

Dear Mother,

Since this has been officially announced as V-E day, I am making sure to write you a letter tonight, as I know that, when you receive it, you will be somewhat relieved. I am, as you can see "somewhere in Austria." We have sure moved a lot in the past two months. This country is really beautiful if you go for spectacular scenery – snow capped mountains etc. I have received two letters in the last two days – I sure wish that would keep up, but our mail is very irregular. Your letters were April 25th from home and April 22, mailed over here by Col Taltin. I am very distressed that you waited for four weeks without mail. I have written at least once a week, and you will get all my letters eventually.

All my love,
John

* * *

Letter transmitted via V-Mail.

To: Mrs HC Ingles
3133 Con. Ave., N.W.
Washington, DC

From: 2dLt JS Ingles 0550672
Hqs. Btry, 313 FA Bn
APO # 80 C/O PM, NY, NY

Censor's Stamp:
Signed John S Ingles

Somewhere in Austria, 11 May [1945]

Dear Mother,

I received your letter and the picture you sent, and, believe me, I am crazy about the picture. I have already placed it in my little picture album, and it is, I think, much nicer than the other one I have. I certainly have enjoyed all of my pictures and I have carried them with me all the time. I am glad to hear that Martha and the baby are doing so nicely. I am certainly looking forward to seeing them both. I received a V-Mail from Mary (April 23) today. She has certainly been good about writing to me. Please send me a box, since you say you have some goodies saved up. Saw a movie today Kay Kyser in "Carolina Moon" [*Carolina Blues*]. I enjoyed it very much. The main topic of discussion now concerns guessing what will happen to us now.

Love, John

* * *

John in Austria

Austria, May 23 [1945]

Dear Mother,

Since I am away from the battery in charge of a 48 hour guard, I have time for some writing. In view of the relaxed censorship regulation, which permit[s] us to tell you something of our combat experiences, I will try to give you some of the details of the months that I have been overseas.

I left Washington, you remember, just after midnight on October 1. The trip was very much like a long trip on a day-coach. The plane flew smoothly along—hour after hour—high above the clouds. I soon tired of looking out of the window, and spent my time reading magazines and dosing [sic] off. We stopped once in Newfoundland for breakfast, but were soon in the air once again. We arrived in Scotland after about 16 hours in the air. Immediately after landing we were hustled off to an old country house which the ATC used as a hotel. The house, I discovered the next morning, was just what I had imagined an English country home would be like. There were big high-ceilinged rooms, wide stair cases, gravel driveways and beautifully kept grounds with big shade-trees and neatly trimmed hedges. It was also cold and drafty inside and the "hot" water in the bathroom was cold. I took off again about noon for London, about a three-hour trip.

Once I reported at headquarters in London, I discovered that my trip was a kind of a "treasure hunt." The "secret orders" which Daddy was so concerned that I get in Washington turned out to be nothing more than a note, written by the girl at the ATC desk in Washington, which directed me to report to headquarters in London. In London they had nothing for me, so I got a billet and came back the next day. The next morning I received more "secret orders"—this time to report to headquarters in Paris. We took off about 1300 and arrived in Paris late in the afternoon. Headquarters in Paris had nothing for me. But I was learning fast, and, instead of sitting in their office, I adopted a policy of checking in about three times a day. This worked out very well, and during the two days I was in Paris, I really saw something of the town. I walked and walked and walked, seeing all the places I had read about— Notre Dame, the Eiffel Tower, the Place de la Concorde, the Champs-Elysees, the Arc de Triomphe, Tombe de Napoleon, etc. The weather was clear and cool, and I really enjoyed the outing. I finally received orders to report to Third Army Hqs. (which is where I had known all along that I was going). I drew some field equipment and complete with carbine and steel helmet, set out for the front. I went on a truck with several other officers. Our route took us along the famous Red Ball highway to Soissons, Rheims, and finally to Etaine [sic]—where Third Army Hqs. was then located. We arrived about supper time, and, after supper Col. Hammond and Col. Mathews took me in tow. We went over to the General's [Patton's] home to find out if the General wanted to see me. While we were waiting around, I heard the officers talking about an attack the 80th Division had made that day and commenting on how well the job had been pulled off. We finally learned that the General would "like very much to see me but in the morning." His aide took me into town and arranged a very nice billet for me—the last time I was to sleep on a bed for many months. The next morning, after breakfast, I went back to Hqs. and, in due time, over to meet the General. He was standing outside his trailer. His aide and I saluted, and, after the aide had introduced me, he shook my hand and said "Glad to have you with us, Boy." The rest of the interview consisted of his telling the aide what was to be done with me. Then he wished me luck and the aide and I departed. The General was very pleasant to me and I was rather surprised to find that his voice was high-pitched and rather soft. He is about my height but rather heavy-set. He was not as big a man as I had expected him to be.

Right after lunch I was provided with a jeep and a driver, a map, and orders to report to the 80th Division Artillery at Belleville, France. About half way to our destination the jeep broke down and we limped into an Ordnance Company. There I talked a nice, southern, ordnance captain into fixing my jeep and lending me one to complete my journey with. We reached Belleville without mishap and I reported in as ordered. There were some more hours of waiting to see if the General wanted to see me. The General did, and, about 2200 I went in for a talk. He asked about Daddy, about what experience I had had, and seemed particularly interested in my survey experience. The next morning the S-1 gave me orders to report to one of the battalions. I was loading my equipment on a jeep when the General passed by. He asked me where I was going and I told him. But the General, it seemed, had other ideas. So I unloaded my equipment and became Asst. Div. Arty. Survey Officer. The date was October 9th—eight days after I had left home.

Lt. Jameson was (and is) Div. Arty. Survey Officer, and I went out with him and his crew the next morning. We struck it off fine from the start, and (after we had shared the same ditch during a few shellings and received a few reprimands together for not doing this or for doing that) we soon became good friends. The Division was then holding a defensive position while building up for a general offensive. We surveyed and surveyed and, during the next four weeks, I got to know the area between the Moselle and Seille Rivers southwest of Pont-a-Mousson better than I have ever known another area in Europe. I learned a lot about the Germans then too. I learned that when you

stuck your neck out, the Krauts usually shot at you, and I found out personally, on November 4, that they don't always miss. But my wound was very slight, and I was out with the survey crew again when the 80th Division jumped off on November 8th. The preparation laid down by the artillery to support the Seille River crossing was the biggest I ever saw, before or since. The weather was unbelievably bad—cold and raw with rain almost all of every day and night. The armor operating with us was completely road-bound, since every field was a lake or a quagmire. The Seille River, normally about thirty yards wide, was about 200 yards wide when we crossed it, and even the Moselle bridges were temporarily washed out. But the offensive gained momentum and finally broke through. The next month brought the toughest fighting that I was to see. The Krauts had plenty of infantry and artillery, and our survey crew was fired on almost every day and sometimes several times a day. Somehow we all came through O.K. I was pretty miserable myself, since my leg bothered me considerably and the mud made it necessary to walk everywhere. We had not been issued overshoes, and the constant soaking of our feet soon gave most of us a mild case of trench foot. Finally the doctor put the entire crew to bed for a day and, with the simultaneous arrival of overshoes, our foot trouble soon disappeared. The offensive ground slowly ahead and we took Falquemont [sic], pierced the Maginot line—which existed mostly in the newspapers—and took St. Avold. While we were in St. Avold, I received a short visit from Col. Hammond, and the next day, the General called me in and told me he was sending me to the 313th. I reported in the next morning and was assigned to Hqs [Headquarters] Btry. At that time Lt. Pettingill was BC [battalion commander] and Lt. Hostetler was the only other officer in the battery. I became motor officer. A couple of days later, Captain Dudman, who had been wounded in September, returned and took over the battery. About two days after that the 80th Division was pulled out for a rest. We weren't pulled out, actually, but we merely stayed where we were while another division passed through and took over. The 313th immediately packed up and moved about 50 miles to the rear where we spent about two days preparing for and firing a special demonstration. We then returned to St. Avold for our rest. I use the word "rest" loosely, since, as during such periods, the men were required to spend most of their time cleaning and repairing their equipment, with the result that more work is usually done during a "rest" than when we are in contact. But there are showers and a few shows and the freedom from enemy fire is very welcome.

After about a week we were on the move again, South to the sector around Bitche, where a new offensive was planned. We moved down on Dec. 17th, and reconnaissance was made for firing positions to be occupied the next day. That night we heard rumors of a Kraut counterattack up North. The next morning we were alerted for a long move, and about noon we hit the road. Our destination was a town near the French-Luxembourg border. We had plenty of gas, but only a few of the more far-sighted boys provided themselves with emergency rations. We passed back through St. Avold, West to Metz, and then North towards Luxembourg. It was bitter cold and one of those typical road marches in which we would move a ways – stop for twenty minutes – move on – stop, etc. Our destination was changed several times while we were on the road—and we moved on North—through Esche and Luxembourg City. One of the boys had a radio and during one stop I remember that we listened to Jimmy Durante saying "There are a million good-lookin' guys, but I'm a

novelty." We finally stopped at Ernster, a small town north of Luxembourg City. We arrived about 0300 on the 19th, after 150 miles and 15 hours on the road. We got a laugh later when you sent the clippings telling how the 80th Division had "dashed North at breakneck speed." The next day we moved West, contacted the Krauts and attacked to the North. During the next four or five days we advanced about 15 miles against mounting resistance until we were stopped along a general line of the Sauer River. This was on Christmas Day. In the meantime, one combat team of the 80th had been with the 4th Armored in the attack to relieve Bastogne in Belgium, drawing down some well-deserved press notices, and giving you the impression that I was in Belgium.

The division then went on the defensive and we stayed in one place, Oberfeulen for 28 days—a record for the 313th. During this period we received a good bit of shelling, and the Krauts attacked several times. But the guns fired day and night and every attack was held. Lt. Hostetler had left the battery while we were resting at St. Avold, and while we were at Oberfeulen Lt. Pettingill returned to his Battalion—leaving only Captain Dudman and [me] in Hqs. Btry. Finally—late in January—we attacked again and pushed the Germans back through Wiltz and to within a mile or so of the German border when we were again relieved. We moved directly South again and relieved another division in positions along the Our River between Diekirch and Echternach. After about a week of preparation—we jumped off again on a major attack—this time to cross the Our River into Germany and break the Seigfried Line. The attacks went slowly at first, then gained momentum, and finally, after the breakthrough was made, the armor passed through and went all the way to the Rhine. When we lost contact we stopped as another division chased the armor and we rested for about four days.

On March 10th we received a new mission and things swung into high gear again. We moved out at 0200 on the 11th, traveled back almost to Luxembourg City then swung down to the southern tip of Luxembourg—within sight of France. We crossed the Moselle into Germany again, crossed the Saar at Saarburg and moved into the line on a small sector east of Isch. We launched a strong attack on the 12th, this time to break through the Siegfried Line again. We met very heavy resistance at first, as the Krauts "shot the works" with mortars, rockets, and artillery. But the breakthrough was made and the armor and infantry took off. We moved very fast, changing positions three or four times a day. We swept through Kaiserlautern [*sic*] and on to Bad Durkheim. During that drive we saw the German army destroyed, as General Eisenhower had said it would be, West of the Rhine. Their losses in men were very heavy, but the losses in equipment were the death blow to the German Army. During one move one of the boys started out to count the number of destroyed trucks and similar vehicles he saw along the road. Within a few miles he had counted 400 and—as we picked up speed—he soon lost track completely. The 80th stopped just beyond Bad Durkheim as other units moved on to the Rhine and the 7th and 3rd Army units were unscrambled. We moved North to the vicinity of Rockenhausen where we went into a rest period of about four days. The 313th was set up in a little town named St. Alban. During this period Captain Dudman went on a pass to Paris, leaving me in charge of the battery. The day that he left we got another mission— to establish a bridgehead over the Rhine at Mainz.

The German Army was now on the ropes—and we felt that if we could keep pushing them it would soon be over. The Rhine is, I guess, some 500 yards wide at Mainz. The crossing met considerable resistance for a few hours, but the bridgehead was made and a bridge soon completed. The 313th crossed on about the 28th of March. It was really a thrill to cross a river of that size. We really began to move after the Rhine crossing. Wiesbaden fell with almost no resistance and we turned Northeast to drive on Kassel. We advanced some 90 miles the first day, driving up the great super-highway that linked Frankfurt to Kassel and the interior. As we skirted the airfield at Frankfurt, three C-47 transport planes circled and landed. They were immediately followed by many others. As we sat on the side of the road for a half-hour at noon to eat our K-rations— more than 100 C-47's landed on the field—a magnificent sight. The resistance around Kassel was very strong and the infantry had a terrific fight clearing out the town. The city itself was completely leveled—a mass of ruins and rubble that surpassed anything I had seen at that time. I saw almost all of it thanks to getting lost in the town a couple of times. After we had moved several miles past Kassel we were relieved by a First Army Division. We moved South and East to a position just beyond Gotha—from which position we opened an attack on Erfurt. Here again we met strong initial resistance and the artillery did a lot of shooting. But, after several days, Erfurt was encircled and the armor passed through and took off to the East. The 80th followed close behind the armor, and together we drove straight down the super-highway toward Chemnitz. Erfurt, Weiman, Gera, Jena, Limbach fell in rapid succession. On April 13th, I was ordered to report back to Div. Arty Hqs. (Captain Dudman had returned when we were just outside of Kassel.) The Asst. Comm. O at Div Arty had gone to the hospital, and the General wanted me to replace him. Lt. Hostetler came back to Hqs Btry 313th to take my place. I was only at Div Arty three days before the Asst. Comm.

O returned, and I in turn returned to Hqs Btry 313th. I enjoyed the time, although I worked hard and wished that I had my own battery to do the job with. It was a pleasure to work with Lt. Pettigill again. The only change that resulted from it all was that Lt. Hostetler remained on in Hqs Btry as Asst. Comm. O, and I became Motor Officer again. But I feel that the change worked to my advantage. Our Communications Chief in 313th, Sgt. MacDonald, told me that the Captain didn't appreciate what I had been doing until I was gone. Whether that is true or not, the Captain has been more friendly since I came back and, although he didn't recommend my promotion, he O.K.'d it. And I am, of course, glad to have Lt. Hostetler around.

When I returned to the 313th, our guns were firing on Chemnitz. The city was given an ultimatum, which was refused, and we prepared to make an attack. But, all of a sudden, the 80th was again relieved by a First Army Division and went into reserve. We moved clear back to Erfurt and then moved South to Nurenburg. We rested in Nurenburg for about a week.

Nurenburg stands in my mind as the most completely destroyed city I have ever seen. The city was a shrine to Nazidom—and the site of the famous stadium where Hitler held his Nazi rallies. The old part of the city was, in prewar days, the most perfectly preserved example of a medieval city. But it all looks the same now, a great mass of rubble and burned buildings. We sent a couple of trucks into the town each day to take the boys in to see the stadium and ruins. After a week at Nurenburg, the 80th hit the road again. We moved down to the Danube, crossed the river at Regensburg and went into action once again. Our mission—to establish contact with the Russian forces in Austria. It was another fast drive, since resistance was now weak and disorganized. We reached the Austrian border in

three days, and crossed on May 1, to the accompaniment of a sharp snow-storm. A couple of days later, the division was split into combat teams and task forces and seemed to be pushing in about six different directions at once. The contact with the Russians was made, and the 313th swung back and turned south-east into the Alps. One of the division task-forces did turn North into Czecho-Slavkia [*sic*] where, according to the papers, the last shot was fired. I have heard it claimed that the 313th fired the last round in the 80th Div. Arty, which should have been close to the last artillery fired in the war. We were deep in the Alps at Windishgarsten [*sic*] when the end came on May 9.

Well, I have been working on this, off and on, all day and I guess it is time to quit. I haven't received any mail recently, but I received another box yesterday. Many thanks.

All my love,
John

* * *

July 22, 1945
Germany

Dear Mother,

No letters from home all week for some reason. So I am deprived of my usual opening sentence of acknowledgement of the letters I have received. But nobody has received much mail the past three or four days, and I expect that, today or tomorrow, I will receive several letters.

The only big news of the week is that Capt. Dudman has left us. He was transferred to another division, along with quite a number of officers who had more than 85 points. In the entire battery, I haven't heard one man express regret over his leaving. Lt. Hostetler was in command of the battery for a couple of days, but that was too good to be true. A new captain was transferred in (along with a number of new officers) and he has taken over. His name is Magnuson. It is a little early to tell what he will be like, but I am confident that <u>anybody</u> would be easier to work with than Dudman. We have also lost several EM [eligible men] already under the point system, but so far we have been able to fill in our vacancies with capable men. Our 1st Sgt. left Saturday. His name was Moore. We always hit it off fine, and he almost broke down when he came in to say goodbye to me. He said that, if he goes through Washington, he will call you. So, if he does, you will know who he is and I know you will be nice to him.

We put on a review for General Patton last week and he gave a very colorful speech. Our division was with him from the start, and, we like to think, was his best Infantry division. I would like to see him get a Pacific command because I don't think there are very many better Army commanders around.

Well, all for now Honey. I'll be seeing you around Christmas time.

All my love,
John

* * *

Germany, Aug 15, 1945

Dear Mother,

Well, I don't have any particular news today, except that tremendous news that everybody is celebrating. It is certainly a breathtaking surprise—not that it hadn't been expected for several days—but just to think that the war is finally over. I can remember when it all really started for us—1939 when I was still in Western. And ever since then the world has looked forward to peace. And now—after six years—the war is over. It was a strange day for such great news. We had all been listening for every bit of news all week—making wise cracks about the slowness of the diplomatic exchange of notes. The official announcement came through late last night, and I heard about it at breakfast when some officer I never saw before said casually, "Well, it's all over." And then we went right through the day's routine of classes, studying aerial photos of Japanese airfields and gun emplacements as if nothing had happened. You know how immobile the Army is—business as usual "by order of G-2." This afternoon we listened to a rebroadcast of the victory celebrations at Times Square, Independence Hall and 14th and F in Washington. It all seemed very far away to us, as all we could see around us was the same group of GI's going about the same jobs and the same sullen Germans going about their business and talking to one another in a language we don't understand. But I'm sure we were all thinking thoughts of home and of the past and of the future—not bothering with the rather drab present. I thought of the family and gave thanks that we had all come through O.K. How lucky we are that our small family group was untouched. And I thought of coming home and how happy I will be and how lucky I am to have so much to come home to. And I thought of the men I have seen die over here and I wonder if they knew that the day of victory and peace had finally come. And I thought of turning to the ways of peace—how strange they will be—and I wonder what I will be doing a few years from now. But I am sure of one thing—that, whatever I am doing, I will look back on this day with a certain amount of personal satisfaction. For I am proud that I was able to serve my country and my family when the war came and I know that I made some contribution to the final victory that is being celebrated today. And in the years to come I will be able to look anybody in the eye and say that I did my part. But I think that—most of all—each of us is, within his heart, giving thanks to God that the end has come and that He has given us victory.

All my love,
John

In Grace's handwriting on the envelope:
Miss Horner -

> *Will you or Mrs. Messinger please make me six copies of this letter. Thank you.*

Grace S Ingles

I don't know who those copies were sent to, but it doesn't surprise me that Grace would want to share such a beautiful and joyful letter. It was still several months before John would be home with his mother, but with the arrival of VJ Day, his safe return home was finally a sure thing.

* * *

Letter Typed on 80th Infantry Division, 315th Field Artillery BN. Letterhead

30 December, 1945

Dear Mother,

Well long time no letter, but during that time I have of course talked to you and you know where I have been and that I have been well. You will no doubt notice the fancy stationery again, this time borrowed from Lt. Cameron, who was as you might guess a former member of A Btry, 315th. But I guess that you are most interested in my trip to Switzerland. So I will try to tell you something about it. I am enclosing a map of the country and I hope that you will understand the little notes that I have made on it and

that you will be able to follow my route. I will explain a little in this letter, too.

We started our trip by going to Munich and taking a train to Strassburg [*sic*]. This was a full days trip but not too uncomfortable, since the train service has improved quite a bit since my last trips that I took in September. (I have just gotten another typewriter since the ribbon on the last one was worn out.) But—to continue—we spent one night in Strassburg [*sic*] and went to the Swiss leave center the next day, the Swiss leave center being located at Mulhouse. There we were assigned to our tours, had our money changed, received some orienting on what to expect and what to do in Switzerland. There are several different tours that one can take and we got tour 8, which was about our third choice. When I say "We" I mean Lt. Kimberlin and [me] since we were together all the time. We spent the night in Mulhouse and saw a very good show at the theater there. The movie was "Her Highness and the Bellboy" which I had seen at the post under very adverse conditions before and which I enjoyed very much. There was also a very good stage show imported—they said—from Holland. At any rate it was a first class show. We went into Switzerland the next morning. The tour itself cost us 35 Dollars and they let you take 200 Swiss francs with you—about 41 Dollars. That is a ridiculously small amount for 8 days of shopping and entertainment, so the first of the GIs who went into Switzerland made up for their cash shortages by selling everything under the sun. Even now you can sell anything in the world in Switzerland. They don't give black-market prices, but will buy anything in the way of clothes, candy, cigarettes, that you will sell. The result is that they limit everything that you can take in to the country with you—down to the last pr of socks and handkerchief. As it is the GIs still sell plenty but they are holding it down quite a bit. So, after quite a time getting through customs at Basle, we entered Switzerland. Lt. Kimberlin (who is called Zeke as a tribute to his middle initial which is Z—for Zay) remarked that he never had so much trouble crossing a border before, since when we entered Germany the customs officials seemed to be taking the day off. At any rate, we made it and they rushed us right on a bus for a sightseeing tour of Basle. We were quite fascinated by our first look at Switzerland. The nicest thing was the sight of shop windows full of food, automobiles, clothes, or whatever the shop specialized in. We spent a good part of the time during the whole tour just gaping at the shop windows and wishing that we had enough francs to buy and buy. The town itself is nice and clean as are all Swiss towns but you could still see some of the damage that had been done to some of the buildings by a couple of the Air Corps "precision" attacks on the German border towns a few miles away. We crossed the Rhine a couple of times and finally went to a nice café for a lunch of steak and French Fried potatoes. By this time we had just about decided that Switzerland was OK. There was one girl on our tour—a civilian who was from some government agency in Frankfurt. As everybody had gotten on the Sightseeing bus, the conductor had given her a present and an invitation to spend Christmas eve with them in their home in Basle. Since we weren't going to be in Basle on Christmas eve she wanted to go out and see the people and thank them and express her regrets. So Helga, Zeke and I went calling on this family after dinner. We found the house after a while, and found everybody at home. These people turned out to be a young couple with two young boys about 7 & 9. They spoke pretty good English and were very cordial to us and very interesting to talk to. After a while we said goodbye and went Downtown for a little window shopping. We soon found out after pricing a few items that our money wasn't going to go very far but we started a habit that

we continued right through our stay in Switzerland. We succumbed to the charm of a particularly attractive tea shop and went in for tea. We got some very nice pastries and some coffee. The pastries were what attracted us particularly and they were certainly good. We left Basle at about 1600 and went on to Langenthal where we spent the first night. Langenthal is a pretty small town, but the hotel was OK. We had our supper and went out to one of the local cheese warehouses where they showed us all the cheese and fed us some of it. The also served some wine and sang some Swiss songs—yodeling and all. We had a good enough time but one had the feeling all the time that they were trying to build up their American markets after the war. The next day we moved on and stopped early in the afternoon at Fribourg which was a very beautiful town and the site of one of the Swiss universities. We went out to the university and found it very new—it was completed during the war—and very modernistic and really exceptionally beautiful. The town itself was very lovely, small and clean, situated on the crest of a great river canyon. After a couple of hours there we moved on again to Bulle. We spent the night there and went sightseeing the next morning to Gruyere, which is the site of an old castle in perfect state of preservation. That is another big cheese center and we had to try the cheese there and promise never to buy anything else when we get home. (If those people knew how little cheese is served in our house, they could have saved themselves a lot of trouble.) From Bulle we moved on to Vevey, which is a fair sized town located on Lake Geneva. We did most of our shopping in Vevey and I was there when I received your telephone call. It came at about 1700 for me and it came right through soon after they alerted me. You sounded fine and I had no trouble understanding you. You sounded very far away and a little like I would imagine that you would sound on a phonograph record but it was very clear. It made me so happy to be able to call you right around Christmas time. I knew that you would be worried about me on Christmas and wondering what I was doing. I didn't try to plan things and don't even think that I wished everybody a happy New Year and a Merry Christmas. But you know that that was in my heart. After two days in Vevey we moved on to Geneva. We stayed at a very nice hotel there and found the city very much alive and interesting. The two big drawbacks by this time were that we had spent all of our money and we had two days of rain and very nasty weather in Geneva. But even so we got to see something of the town and enjoyed seeing city life going on without the complete devastation that we associate with city life in Germany. I completed my shopping in Geneva and left that city without a single franc in my pocket. You know how you have always taught us to travel with some money in our pockets and I don't ever recall a time in my life when I was completely without money. But that was the way it was and I can't say that I enjoyed it. We traveled back from Geneva on the day before Christmas and stayed overnight in Olten. All of the people on the tour were invited out to spend Christmas Eve with some Swiss family. Zeke and I went out to a family that included Mother and father and three grown children—two boys that were in college and an older sister who was married. They didn't talk much English and I found myself in the unfamiliar role of interpreter with my pretty poor French. But everybody got along OK and the family couldn't have been nicer to us. We had a very good dinner and afterwards sat around while they all opened their presents. They had little presents for us too, cigarettes, chocolate and a very fancy undershirt for both of us. They kept pouring out wine or cherry brandy for themselves and us until the party became very jovial and my French got better and better. We left just before midnight as the family all went to church and

we went back to the hotel because Zeke was expecting his phone call. It came through on Christmas morning for us, and Zeke said that the connection was not very good but that they understood most of it. At any rate the best thing was for them to just talk to one another and just know that they were well. So that just about completed our Swiss tour. We got up early Christmas morning and went to Basel and subsequently to Mulhouse. We had our Christmas dinner at Mulhouse and went to a movie there—"Christmas in Connecticut"—and spent the day there. The next morning we started the long trip back to Munich, which we made all in one jump of about twenty hours. And so back home to Bad Aibling once again.

We really enjoyed our trip very much. The country was very beautiful and the people very nice to us. Zeke and I, who are probably pretty suspicious of people after so much time in Germany, tried to figure out just what different individuals were interested in by treating the "brave Americans" so nicely. Of course, the people who were showing us their cheese cellars were interested in building up some markets in the States for their product. Sometimes some one would drop a remark about being glad that Switzerland and America were such good friends since America was so strong and Russia is such a menace, as bad as the Nazis, etc. That kind of talk is one of the things that I dislike the most at the present time. We sometimes "amuse" ourselves down here in Bavaria by wondering just what action we would take in case of trouble with the Russians. Since we have a pretty good idea of what the US Army in Germany now is like, we estimate that the Russians could run us out of Europe in about a week. There are a lot of people in the States who also talk about war with Russia, but from what I can gather those people are not the ones who are going to have to fight in case there were to be a war. But except for some of the people who were interested in business or politics, the average Swiss treated us well I thought because they were genuinely pro-american [*sic*] and very thankful that the war is over and that we had beaten the Germans. It was a very interesting trip and I am very glad that I got to call you and that I could buy some nice Christmas presents for the family. I bought presents for you and the girls. I had already sent Daddy's present home. I will send Martha's present to you since you will probably be interested in seeing it and you can send it on to here when you are sending something on to her. I think that you will realize that Mary's present is the nicest of all but I didn't mean to slight the rest of you. But Mary's present is meant for both Christmas and Birthday and besides that Mary is so good to me and I don't have much chance to show her that I appreciate it. I am very happy about all the presents though, since I feel that they are very nice and that you will all be interested and pleased with them. They would probably be pretty expensive in the States but were not very expensive in Switzerland. Speaking of sending things to Martha, I wonder if Daddy remembers that the P-38 German pistol that he brought home for me in July was a present for Jack. I know that it is kind of hard to send that kind of stuff around but I don't believe that he ever got it to Jack since I have never heard that Jack had received it. Martha once wrote to me that Jack was interested in the P-38 that Daddy brought home from France when he was over here in 1944, and since I had more pistols than I could use I intended the P-38 for Jack. The small Mauser that he brought home for me I had intended for my own. I would be interested in hearing about what he did with the pistols. It isn't very important but I just happened to wonder about it.

I see by the papers that the Army will promote all Lts who have been in grade for 18 months when they go on terminal leave. I may have to wait over here so long that I will be eligible for that myself. Since overseas time counts time and a half on that deal, I would be eligible if I am still in the states by May 15, 1946. But I sure hope that is one promotion that I don't get since it is my hope that I will be home by that date. But it wouldn't surprise me much if I am still overseas in May since I haven't heard anything that would lead me to believe that I will be home that soon. We received several letters from Lt. Nichols who left here on Thanksgiving. He had the usual 6 weeks in the various staging areas and is probably on the boat now. We thought when he left that he would be home by Christmas but he was still in France or just getting on the boat. It just seems to take about four weeks to get on a boat once you leave here. Speaking of promotions I think that Cliff will probably get a captaincy about in February. He will have been in a captain's job 6 months by that time and since he has only 57 points he will be over here the required 90 days after his promotion. His colonel has asked him about his status with regard to a promotion and said that he wanted to promote Cliff if he will be eligible. I am in a captain's job now too, but like the other way of getting it, I hope that I will be on my way home before I am eligible for the promotion. I would be very glad to see Cliff get it though since he might as well get the extra pay to save while he is over here. Cliff may still get his Bronze Star and he would much prefer the extra 5 points to a promotion.

When I got back from my trip to Switzerland, I found ten letters waiting for me—only two real letters and the rest Christmas cards. But it was nice to get so much mail and I have received two more Christmas cards since then. The real letters were from you—Dec 9—and Martha—Dec 4. It is the last word that I have had from you, except for the phone call. You asked for a request so "Please send me a box of food and reading material." I seem to feel from your letters that you are more relaxed and rested these days but I am sorry that Daddy has to continue working so hard. I have said it all before, but I really feel that he should try to get away for a rest. I also received the program from the Army+Navy game. You are very good about sending me things to read and I am always very glad to get them.

Well Honey I have certainly rambled on and this has turned into quite a long letter. I haven't written this all at one sitting by any means since it is now New Year's Eve and this letter has been on the typewriter for more than a day and I have stopped for a few minutes now and then to add a few words to it. I was on guard the 30th but I am off now and am enjoying the New Year's Eve programs on the radio. I have a very good radio that Lt. Nichols gave me when he went home and I enjoy and use it all the time. The job at the Btry seems to be going along OK and so far it has kept me busy but I have been pretty much on my own and I realize now that I was having a lot of headaches down there at Post Utilities that I am well rid of. The Lt. who took the job is fresh from the States and I guess that he is having his troubles. I have been dropping in on him almost every day since I got back—not to try to run his business for him but to give him any help that I can and fill him in on the background of the work that is being done. I will close this out now. I am enclosing the map of Switzerland with my route marked on it and also a card given me by the family who gave Zeke and [me] our Christmas party. The arrow marks the house and the foolish little note was put on when I thought that the people were going to mail the card but they just put a stamp on it and gave it to me not realizing that the stamp wouldn't do me any good. But anyway there it is. I am having a box made and will send

the presents along to you. I will insure the box and please be sure and tell me if arrives OK!

Happy New Year Honey to you and all the family. As you said in your letter it has been a good year for us in that it is safely past and everybody is well. It is my dearest hope that I will be home before 1946 is too far gone but at least we know now that I will be home sooner or later and I don't have to worry as I did many times about never getting home again. One of these fine days I will be knocking at your door and then we can start being together all over again.

All my love,
John

PS Please note that my APO is changed to <u>150</u>. This is the branch of APO 403—Third Army APO—that serves our BN, and we have been ordered to start using 150 as our APO. Any letters that you have sent to 403 will, of course, reach me OK but sending them to 150 will just eliminate a step and make the letters arrive a day or so quicker. To make sure this is clear I will write the complete address below—

1st Lt John S. Ingles, 0-550672
Hqs Btry, 243 FA Bn
APO 150, c/o PM, NYC

[Handwritten on bottom of page:]
I just read this over and found that I have made even more mistakes than usual. I hope that you can follow it. Love, John

* * *

John was able to knock on Grace's door in the spring of 1946. He and many of his fellow VMI rats soon returned to Lexington to complete

JOHN AND AUDREY INGLES AT VMI LIBRARY WITH JOHN'S BOOK, "A SOLDIER'S PASSAGE" CIRCA 1990

their degrees. He graduated in 1947 with a BA in civil engineering. After his experiences in WWII, he decided not to continue as a career soldier. Upon graduating from VMI, he began a thirty-five-year career with the Chesapeake and Potomac Telephone Company. We will continue to learn some of his life's stories in the next section where he is mentioned in letters written by his sister, Mary.

Although there are no additional letters to Grace from John, he continued to be a devoted letter writer. When his three children went to college, he wrote each of them once a week. This practice continued until the last two years of his life, when Parkinson's disease robbed him of the ability to write.

John lived to be ninety-three and passed away surrounded by his family on July 6, 2016.

— Family Tree — Circa 1952

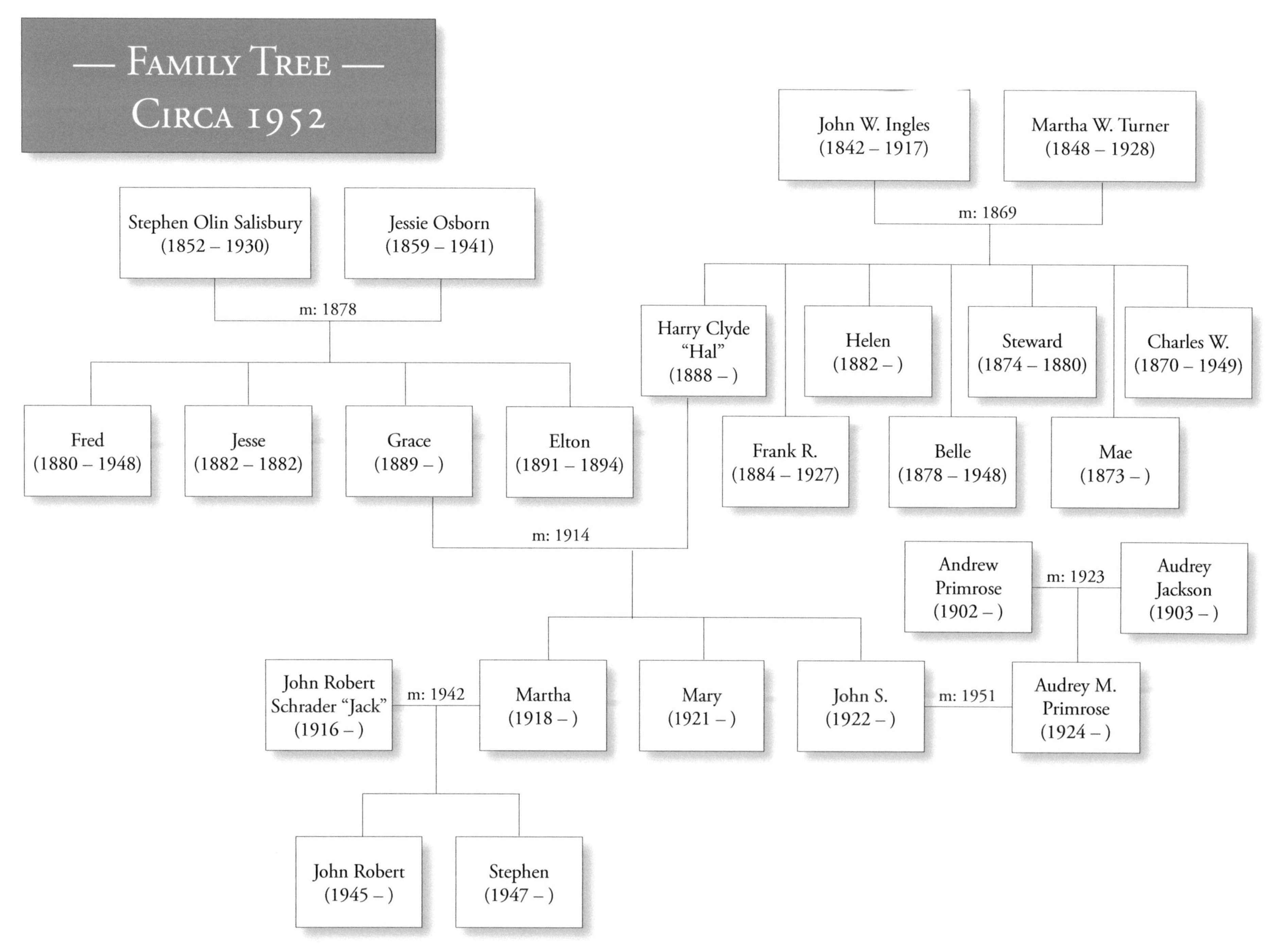

Section Three: The Letters of Mary Osborn Ingles, 1950-1970

THE LETTERS FROM MARY INGLES are from four very distinct parts of her life. Mary's entire career was with the American Red Cross (ARC). The letters presented here are from four different postings: Germany (1950-52), Japan (1956-57), Korea (1957-58), and Vietnam (1969-70). Due to the volume of letters, 421 total, only excerpts are printed here. These excerpts are arranged by themes that became apparent with each set of letters.

As in the letters from Stephen Salisbury and John Ingles, there are frequent references to work colleagues and friends in Mary's letters. To the extent possible, based on my ability to decipher her handwriting, I used the names Mary wrote. In a few cases, where I thought there was a need to protect possible living relatives, I used pseudonyms. Mary used a variety of nicknames for family members, so for the ease of the reader, I have standardized family names consistent with family trees at the beginning of each set of letters.

Mary consistently dated her letters, but she did not always use the same format. I have standardized the format for dates. She generally included her location in the letters, but sometimes if she was in one location for several days or was at her "home" location, she did not include that information. I have added all locations to help the reader place the letter.

I transcribed the letters as accurately as I possibly could, including Mary's use of dashes and other unique punctuation. To maintain the tone of the letters, as little editing as possible has been done and only when absolutely necessary to provide clarity.

GERMANY

Historical and Cultural Context for the Germany Letters (1950–52)

IN THE YEARS OF Mary's first overseas assignment, post–WWII Europe was trying to get back on its feet. The United States still had a strong military presence in several countries, including Germany. Many resources, particularly petrol, were still rationed. During the time Mary was in Germany, the Korean war, and US involvement in it, escalated. However, Europe on the whole felt like a safe and recovering place to be.

MARY'S PASSPORT (1950 – 1952)

PERSONAL REFLECTIONS ON THE GERMANY LETTERS

BY 1950, MARY HAD graduated from Smith College with a BA and had a master's degree in social work from Catholic University. Having grown up an army brat, she had lived all over the United States, in Manila, Philippines, and in Panama. She once told me that when she turned thirty (in 1951) she knew she would never marry, so therefore she could not rely on a man to show her the world or take care of her. The American Red Cross seemed to be her ticket to world travel. She had been with the ARC for approximately five years by 1950, and we believe Germany was her first overseas assignment.

It is clear from her letters that Mary planned to take full advantage of her time in Europe to do the "grand tour" of old. No steamer trunks and linen table clothes needed, she took her car to Germany and for the first year drove herself just about everywhere. The fact that she even owned a car, as a woman, was unusual for the times. Generally, she had a female companion with her on her adventures—in the American Red Cross, there seemed to be a bevy of willing travelers. It still would have been unusual for women to travel alone, but the war began to crack the glass ceiling socially as well as professionally. The shortage of men due to the horrific casualty count was one reason women began to be seen out and about on their own. These letters beam with tales of adventure and grand sights. There is a sense of being carefree and competent.

Weekends were spent going to different locations and week-long or even two-week-long trips were meticulously researched and scheduled. There were many descriptions of lodgings stayed in, ranging from "truly awful" to "luxurious." She reported on tours taken in various cities. And as happens during many travels, she included the occasional mishap, as well. In the two years abroad, she traveled to over seventy-eight cities in a dozen countries and cataloged her journey in great detail. In contrast, she made only forty-five references to work in the same two years, and in many cases, those references are as vague as "I worked late today."

Beginning with these letters and continuing through all the rest, I am struck by the level of detail that Mary knew about the lives of her family so many miles away. Clearly Grace was the primary conduit of these facets of life, but Mary was also getting information from her sister, Martha, about the likes and challenges of Martha's children. It also became clear that Gracie was sharing more than just facts and sometimes some rather negative opinions, which Mary generally adopted.

The Grand Tour

Mary's journey began with nine days on a ship crossing the Atlantic Ocean. She was no stranger to long overseas travel, having made an infamous trip from Panama to the United States a few years earlier. That trip's claim to fame was the fact that it was carrying bananas as well as passengers and took a longer, slower route through a storm to protect the produce. Mary claimed to have never eaten a banana after the journey. The trip to Europe went slightly better.

At the time of Mary's travel, it was known by the family that her sister, Martha, brother-in-law, Jack, and two nephews, John Robert and Stephen, would likely be making the same journey in a few months. Jack, a captain in the US military, was to be stationed in Germany shortly after Mary's arrival. Mary passed along some advice to Martha about the passage.

Below are excerpts from the fourteen-page letter Mary wrote while aboard the ship.

* * *

While on the ship to Europe
Sat, Jun 17, 1950
I'll start a sort of log and add to it every day or so.
So far, everything has gone OK, and the Dramamine seems to be doing its work. After you left yesterday, I unpacked and got settled. We were given our "sittings", and I was happy to get the second. That means breakfast at 8:30, lunch 12:30, dinner 5:30. The food so far is fair, but at least it is edible. I am trying to eat a lot so as not to get sick.

. . . This morning we had a lifeboat drill complete with life jackets and the rest of the time I sat in a deck chair and read or dozed. It is not a pretty day—very overcast, and the sea is getting rougher.

Mon, Jun 19, 1950
. . . I went to the Church services yesterday morning and saw Bob Hope in "The Great Lover" in the evening. In between, I just endured. I have finished the book Martha gave me. Last night was the first night I got any sleep, so I feel much better today.

. . . I thought everything on shipboard would be very clean. However, the smokestack puts out soot constantly and it gets on everything. You can see how dirty this paper is. There is also a lot of spray which leaves salt all over you. I don't see why people take cruises for pleasure. As of noon yesterday, we had gone 579 miles, and had 3100 more to go. Ugh!

Wed, Jun 21, 1950
I certainly guessed wrong about what to wear on shipboard. I'll never take another trip without a pair of slacks and a long coat. The last two days have been clear enough to sit on deck, but too cool for a cotton dress and sweater. I don't want to get my red jacket all dirty, so consequently I have to spend most of the time indoors. I put my uniform on for dinner, mainly because it is wool.

The sea has been calm for a couple of days and I have stopped taking Dramamine. It is a relief because it gives you the most awful taste in your mouth all the time. They don't sell any gum on board which you sorely crave. I had one package with me, and am using it a third of a stick at a time. PX [Post Exchange] is out of life savers, too.

This letter sounds full of gripes. Actually, I can't ever remember enduring such a dreary set of days unless it was my trip back from Panama. The best thing about the 2 year assignment will be that I can postpone the return boat ride that long.

I have thought so often of Martha and Jack on this trip, and of the trip they will eventually have to take with the children. There are millions of children—mostly under 10—and they are so pathetically cooped up. Whenever they do take the trip, they must be sure to pack plenty of blue jeans and warm sweaters and coats for the boys—regardless of the time of year—and a whole suitcase of things to amuse them.

. . . Sat, Jun 24, 1950

Received your cable today and it was wonderful to have it. I feel so completely cut off from everything and everybody. Tonight, we have a meeting to receive our debarkment [*sic*] instructions. We have seen land off and on today—southern coast of England. It is too far away to be more than a blue line on the horizon. I am afraid we will go thru the Channel tonight, so I'll miss seeing the White Cliffs of Dover.

. . . Sun Eve, Jun 25, 1950

Time has caught up with me, so I'll have to end this. We dock at 8:30 and will all be debarked by noon. Then go directly by train to Frankfurt and change for Esslingen.

* * *

Mary spent three days in Stuttgart before moving to her first assignment in Munich. It is at this time she first discussed her plans to travel the Continent. She also referenced having her car sent over on a separate ship.

* * *

Stuttgart, Germany
Tues, Jun 27, 1950

I realize you may be a little confused by the two cables I have sent the last two days, but I'll try to straighten things out here. Actually, so much has happened I am a bit confused. That is complicated by the fact that everything is still going up and down like a ship.

Anyway—to go back—we docked at Bremerhaven at 8:30 am yesterday (Monday). The Red Cross man there, Mr. Southgate, came on board and literally led us around by the hand all day. Before we left the ship, we converted our money into script +$1.55 worth of deutsche marks (6 marks) to be used for tipping porters. We debarked about 10:30 and went by army bus to the Dependents Hotel. We checked our luggage there, and then Mr. Southgate took us all to lunch at one of the Officers' Clubs—The Casino Club. Then he drove us around Bremerhaven a little, introduced us to the Red Cross staff etc. The day was lovely—sunny and it was good to be off the ship. Bremerhaven isn't much of a place—quite a bit of damage.

Before we left the boat, we were given train tickets and berth reservations on the train to Frankfurt. It was free and was part of our transportation over. We were picked up by bus at the hotel at 5:45 and taken to our trains. It was all systematic and organized. The sleepers were quite nice, and Trudy and I were in one compartment. We had dinner on the train (very poor)—40 cents. It is an Army train and food is Army food.

I didn't sleep a wink on the train to my sorrow. We had to get up at 6:00 and change trains at Frankfurt at 6:45. We got in the train for Stuttgart and had breakfast on it—again 40 cents. We left Frankfurt at 7:37 and reached Stuttgart at

11:45. All trains are exclusively for American people traveling in connection with the Army—no Germans allowed. The train crew is German but each of the trains carries an army staff to sort of run things.

Did I tell you that there were 199 children under 10 on our ship? I knew there were a lot, but I didn't count them until I saw it in the ship's paper.

. . . ARC Hqrs are at Esslingen which is about 20 minutes from here by car. This is the nearest point on the railroad, so we are housed here in the Gray Zeppelin Hotel. It is a hotel just for military personnel. They turned us loose this afternoon, but tomorrow and Thurs we will be "processing" at Esslingen. None of the rest of our group know his or her assignment yet.

. . . The short distances here amaze me. We went nearly the whole length of Germany in about 15 hours. Frankfurt is only 8 hours by train from Munich and even shorter by car. It is about 3 hours from here to Munich. Bremerhaven is only 300 miles from Frankfurt. You will just have to get a good map of Germany so all these places and distances will mean something to you.

. . . No word on the car, but I am sending them my permanent address today so that they can notify me.

*　*　*

Stuttgart
Wed, Jun 28, 1950
. . . This evening T and I went to a German restaurant for dinner. We had the most expensive dinner on the menu—filet mignon—and it was 5½ mark which included the tip. That is about $1.35. There is about 4.2 marks to a dollar. It is not hard to pick up individual words in German, but their sentence structure looks impossible.

We had another beautiful sunny day. If it is nice tomorrow, we are going to the streetcar to the edge of town and see the Stuttgart Flower Show after work. It is supposed to be world famous. American personnel can ride street cars free by showing your AGO [Adjutant General's Office] card. Also, when you travel on orders, your train and berth is free. I'll have orders to go to Munich. They also tell me that when I go to Bremerhaven to get my car, I'll be given temporary duty orders so that I can travel on the train free and it won't be charged against my annual leave. Also, when you are traveling on orders you can stay at these military hotels like the one I am in. The only charge is 15 cents a night service charge which you can put on your voucher and ARC reimburses. The allowances for laundry and dry cleaning have been discontinued—tough!! I certainly can see why people don't want to go back to the States. If you didn't travel on leave, you never would spend money. Don't worry—I'll travel.

I must get to bed. It doesn't get dark here until about 10:30 and the sun comes up at 3:30 am. I am getting very anxious to get mail. I should have had you send some here—everyone else did. However, I followed orders.

*　*　*

Stuttgart
Thurs, Jun 29, 1950
. . . This will be the last epistle from Stuttgart as I leave for Munich tomorrow at 11:55. I have to make a brief trip to Esslingen in the morning to get my voucher settled. Then I'll be off. My trunks will go with me, and Miss Henry will meet me at 4:00.

. . . You'll be glad to know, I'm sure, that I have been very happy I came over since I hit Germany. The boat trip was such a nightmare, but here the sun is shining, and I feel good. . . . The way I feel now is that I am already hating the thought that I will have to leave when I go back to the States. That is silly after four days, I know. Maybe I'll be fed up at the end of another four.

Well, I must stop and get ready for bed. I hope that I'll have some mail from you about Monday. It seems a long time—two weeks tomorrow.

Did I write you how pretty you looked standing at the dock, looking up at me?

* * *

Munich would serve as Mary's home base for the next eleven months. During this time, she rarely wrote about her job but instead sent home reports of her various excursions with an occasional mention of her living situation and attempts at making her quarters a home away from home. Mail from home was also carefully tracked and answered.

Munich
Sun, Jul 2, 1950

This is a "red letter" day as letter number one arrived. We stopped and picked up the mail on the way to church, and I had to wait all through church and dinner afterward before I could read it. It is postmarked June 28th, so that is really quite quick. You must have been on the way to the mailbox when my cable with the address arrived. It is so wonderful to have it as it made me feel so close again. Two weeks with only one cable is a long time. You should be getting my letters by now, so all should be well from now on.

. . . On weekends here, everyone who is not on duty takes off. Thus, only Rae and I and the three recreation workers on duty are here. It is quiet and peaceful, and I am glad for the rest.

. . . They have just reduced the gas ration to 100 gallons a month. That should be plenty, however, since there will be no need to do much driving except on weekends.

Will you please ask Daddy to write to the National Geographic and have them send me the very excellent map of Germany which they put out? It has the zones marked and is very complete. I want to put it on the wall in my room or office so I can get very familiar with the locations, etc. Why don't you get one too, so you can see the places I will write about. I don't imagine they cost very much.

* * *

Less than two months after arriving in Munich, Mary claimed her car and took off for the first of many multi-country trips. From August 21 until September 6, Mary and an ARC friend, Billie, traveled to England and Scotland. Most of the letters were a simple travelog—"we went to the Cathedral . . . we were able to find a nice hotel . . . we ate at a pub . . . the food was awful . . . British hotels do not have many bathrooms en-suite." However, the beginning and ending of the trip were a little more noteworthy, as the letters below demonstrate.

Mon, Aug 21, 1950
London

This won't be much of a letter, but will be a line to let you know how we are coming.

We are at Saint Ermin's Hotel and so happy to be here. We have really had a very strenuous and exhausting trip. We were delayed starting as we wanted to wait until American Express opened so we could cash our maintenance checks dated 19 August and put the money into travelers checks for our kitty. So it was 9:30 before we were underway and we didn't get to Nancy until 7:30 that night. After trying three hotels, we got a very satisfactory room at Hotel de

Palais de La Bier (The Beer Palace Hotel). We both slept well and got off about 9:00. We reached Reims by noon and had a nice lunch. We went to the cathedral, which is magnificent.

Then we went to Calais and didn't get there until 8:30. The only hotel we could find was God awful. We had a room with one three quarter sized bed on the 4th floor. We had trains outside and mosquitoes inside. I don't believe I slept two hours, as tired as I was. We drank two bottles of wine for dinner in order to knock ourselves out, but it didn't help.

We've really planned it all wrong. The boat didn't go until 2:45 and we should have spent the night somewhere else and just arrived for the boat. We had been told that there was a morning boat. Anyway we were able to use the morning alright as we had to see to shipping the car and ourselves, buy 1100 francs, (about $30) for the purpose, etc. Actually, the business of getting across the channel took all day. We didn't get away from Dover until after 6:00. You never saw so much red tape. All British. I had to get British license plates, and Billie and I both had to get British drivers licenses. Having the carnet helped but much more was needed. The crossing itself was moderately smooth and I took some Dramamine and stayed on deck, so all was well. They load the cars into the hold of the ship, just like it was a transatlantic voyage.

Anyway, we finally drove the 70 miles to London and had no trouble finding a hotel, although it was nearly 9:00 when we arrived. We have had dinner (only fair), baths and now are about ready to hit the bed. This hotel is old and full of elderly people, but clean, comfortable and well located I think. It is in Westminster section of London. I'll be able to tell more tomorrow.

I'm not making up my mind on France on what we saw, but it was surely run down and dirty. I will wait until I can make a pilgrimage to Paris. But it is wonderful to be in a country where you can speak the language, even if they do have a lot of red tape and drive on the left. First thing tomorrow we are going to inquire about changing of the guard at Buckingham Palace and plan our itinerary around that. I think it is tomorrow. I'm too tired to write more to night. I'll write again when I can.

* * *

Mon, Sep 4, 1950
Canterbury

I am sure you will be as surprised to learn that I was still in England on this date as I am to be here. When trouble set in, it really did it all at once.

I think I wrote you that after Billie got sick, I changed all our reservations until Monday.

(Today—ha ha). We were to leave London Sunday afternoon and spend the night in Canterbury. Then we were to cross the Channel Monday and spend the night in Ostend (Belgium). I had hotel reservations in all of the appropriate places.

Well, Sunday morning we packed our bags and at 11:00 I went to the garage to get the car. The only one in the garage was a young attendant. When he went to get the car, he discovered that some damn fool had left the ignition turned on for two days and the battery was completely dead. Of course, it was impossible to have a battery recharged in London on Sunday. The boy said it would probably take 6-8 hours to recharge it fully and they could start it at 8:00 AM on Monday. Well, you can imagine the way I felt. However, I was completely helpless. I had had such a time getting everything changed once and here I had to do it all over again. While I was in the garage I went to get my camera, which I had inadvertently left in the glove compartment and of course someone had stolen it. Cameras are very critical items in England as import duties are terrific. I reported it to the manager of the garage, but "they are not responsible for items left in the cars etc."

Back I went to Saint Ermin's and on bended knee begged them to keep us another night. They finally said "yes," but we had to move to another room. Then I telephoned Canterbury Hotel and was able to cancel last night's reservation and make one for tonight.

At 8:00 AM. This morning I was at the garage to see that they fixed to the battery and give them a piece of my mind. Then when the doors opened at 9:00, I was at the booking office for Channel Crossings. The gods were good and I was able to get a crossing to Ostend at 12:20 tomorrow. I then called Pier Bussati (Travel Agency) and had them telephone the hotel in Ostend and change our reservation. That cost 10 shillings, but my French wasn't up to that. So all has turned out all right. I picked the car up at 3:00 and we took off about 3:30. We got to Canterbury about six. It has been a beautiful day today. We checked into the hotel and then dashed off to see the cathedral.

I'll go back and pick up the pieces in between Sunday AM and this AM. I had planned to see the Guard Change Sunday, but it was pouring so I gave that up. Billie was better—no temperature—so we called Maggie to come have dinner with us at St. E's. She came at 12 noon. After dinner we sat around a bit and at 4:30 we went to see the White Tower. Not very good. We had supper afterwards at her hotel. This AM after coping with my chores B and I went shopping on Bond Street for shoes. I wanted some low-heeled walking shoes for trips and sightseeing. I had a terrible time getting fitted as most shoes didn't come narrower

than a B width. I finally found some Brevite shoes in grey suede, moccasins with white stitching, lacings and leather soles—flat heel. They really are very smart looking, beautifully made and wonderfully comfortable. They were 3 pounds and 19 shillings—about $11. I'm real pleased with them and have worn them already today. Well, I guess that brings me up to date. Oh, yes. Maggie met us for lunch at the Cumberland today. Being Labor Day, she was off.

Now my prayers are that the car will start in the morning and that we will have no more trouble. All this delay is eating into my annual leave and probably writ fines [Latin: final word] to my plans to go to Switzerland next month for four or five days.

Well, B has lost her fountain pen and wants to borrow mine to write a letter, so I'll stop. Also, I lost your collapsible umbrella in a London taxi the first time we were there so this has proved an expensive trip. Our hotel bill this AM was about 20 dollars. I am really going to be broke when I get back.

Well, I am really not bitter and I did have a good time. I'll be awfully glad to get my mail.

* * *

Munich
Thurs, Sep 7, 1950

Just a note to report us safely back in Munich. I have much mail here from you to answer. I won't try to do that tonight, however.

. . . As you know, I am all involved in going to Oberammergau this weekend. It should be a nice weekend, but I wish it didn't come so soon on the heels of our trip.

This morning we took our time and got away from Frankfurt about 10:00. Our trip—Autobahn all the way—was uneventful and took about 6 ½ hours. One event was that I got a ticket on the Autobahn—seems to be getting to be a habit. In typical army fashion, the MP [military police] took down my license number, etc, and then told me to go on. When I asked him what would happen, he didn't know. All he knew was that he would report it to his CO. So in due course I shall hear about it through channels no doubt. I don't know what the penalties are.

Well, I have to finish unpacking and I want to get to bed. From what the girls tell me, there is much work piled up for me at the office. And I'll only have one day to get it whipped into line before I go away again.

* * *

Back in Germany, Mary took advantage of local cultural activities. She reported on concerts and performances that she attended. Some of these were specifically for the troops stationed in Munich, but many were shows by local talents, including the renowned Oberammergau passion play, which she traveled to see with several other ARC staff.

Oberammergau
Sun, Sep 10, 1950

I'll start a slight letter to you while I have a moment, and I'll probably have to finish it later today. Our weekend has gone very well in spite of the rain all day yesterday. I met Rae and her sister and friend at their hotel and we had lunch. We left about 2:30 and came down via Garmisch. We stopped there for gas and to look around the PX. Whenever you go any place, you always look in the PX to see if they have anything yours doesn't.

We got here about 6:00. All our arrangements were made by American Express, and this is a lovely place. I have some pictures. We have a sort of little wing with two rooms and a private toilet—no bath—basins in the room. The place has apparently been fixed up, almost new for the Passion Play year. And it's clean, fresh. The food is also very good.

After dinner last night. We went down to the town and shopped. All the stores were open. It was pouring rain, but we didn't let that deter us. This place is world famous for its wood carving. I got your birthday present, which I shall send when I can. I also got a couple of little things to put in the Christmas box for Martha and Jack. I spent all the marks I had and ten of Rae's. Actually only about $10. We finished up the evening with a bottle of red Tyrolean wine.

This morning, of course, we were up and at it early as the play started at 8:30, we found it was a beautiful day. We went armed with air cushions, blankets, candy bars, opera glasses, and copies of the text in English. The play runs from 8:30 to noon and from 2:00 to 6:00. There are no intermissions during either the morning or the afternoon sessions. It had warmed up enough so that we could leave coats and blankets home for the afternoon session.

The place where they have the play is a huge auditorium open at the stage and the stage is out of doors. I really can't describe it, but it is terribly effective. The stage is huge and at times there were a couple of 100 people on the stage at once. They had it all worked out to handle them, however. The audience was about four to 5000.

The prologue of the acts was sung by a chorus of 80. They had gorgeous tableau during the prologue and then of course the whole story was acted out. I think I'll send you the book so you can get some idea of the scope of the thing. Save the book for me.

The play was extremely impressive, even though it was all in German. All of the actors are the townspeople and of course, amateurs. The men and boys have all let their hair and beards grow long, and you see them all over town in their everyday clothes. The play is only given every 10 years and because of the war this is the first time since 1933. Although it was exhausting, it was really an experience. I believe it would have been even more moving if you could understand the German. People all around us were in tears at the end.

Since I didn't have my camera, I bought some pictures of Oberammergau to send to you. They did not allow any photography during the play itself.

After the play, we had dinner at our pension and drove back to Munich, arrived about 9:30. I'm enclosing a money order for $100, which is another payment on the car balance equal $800. I made it out to mother as I thought it would be easy for her to cash it at the new branch offices on Mamaroneck Ave.

I got my pictures from the trip and they are no good. It makes me sick that after finding a camera I could take good pictures with I had to have it stolen. All for now.

* * *

Munich

Tues, Sep 19, 1950

. . . Everyone over here is crazy about Italy. Pier Busetli has a wonderful 13 day tour which I am tentatively planning to take next spring. You pay a flat rate—under $300—and that includes everything hotels, meals, sightseeing trips, porters, etcetera. It goes every place—Florence, Rome, Naples, Venice, and other places that I can't think of.

* * *

Munich

Wed, Sep 27, 1950

. . . My plans for going to Berchtesgaden are about jelled. Friday I'm going to do errands in Munich and at 3:00 Aileen and I will take off. It is only about a 2½ hour drive, so we will be there in time for dinner. We have made a reservation through Special Services. On Saturday morning we will go to Salzburg to shop. The shops are only open in the mornings on Saturday.

. . . I took the car out today for the 5000-mile service. I am not at all satisfied with the PX garage. I'm going to investigate the German Opel place which is supposed to service General Motors cars. The service today cost me $10.55, of which $6.75 was a labor charge. That seems very high to me.

* * *

Munich

Sun, Oct 22, 1950

. . . Thursday will be four months since I landed in Germany. I must say the time has gone quickly. Of course I get very homesick at times and much of the time am not too thrilled with my job. But on the whole I think I have made a pretty good adjustment. The time ahead seems very long, but at this point I don't want to come home until I have seen everything I want to see here. Also, the future back home is pretty questionable, especially if I have to start job hunting. If it just works out so that you and Daddy can come over while I am here, I think I'll make it all right (barring world events, of course). I should think that by spring they would have let us know whether the casework program is going out on schedule. However, knowing Red Cross as I do, I won't be surprised if we hear nothing until the 11th hour.

* * *

Munich

Sat, Nov 4, 1950

. . . Thursday evening, Frances, our head recreation worker asked Bess and me in for cocktails to meet a German woman doctor who is a friend of hers. The doctor was in her late 30s, lovely looking, utterly charming. I enjoyed meeting her very much. Then last night I went with them to the opera. They had been invited by a Colonel and his wife to go and sit in the general's box. Then one of the Colonel's children got sick, so they gave Frances the tickets and she asked me. The opera was Wagner's The Flying Dutchman. Although I was unfamiliar with the music, I really enjoyed it very much. The singers were excellent and the music beautiful.

Tonight, Helen Murray's sister invited me to dinner at their apartment. They are such a nice couple and I really enjoyed the evening very much. I don't know if I wrote you about his job. You know he speaks Russian. He is over here on a Howard University project under the auspices of the Air Force interviewing Russian refugees to get information about what is going on back of the curtain.

* * *

Munich

Tues, Dec 5, 50

It's been quite a while since I have written, but I guess you know that I have been off on another weekend jaunt. I found two letters from you, one from Martha and one from John when I got back. I'll not answer them immediately as I want to give you a report on my weekend first.

As I wrote you, we were a little uncertain about snow conditions, but we took off complete with skiing equipment. We got away around 10:00 AM Saturday and drove to Berchtesgaden. It was 90 miles from here. The weather was quite cold and the day rather overcast. The drive down was beautiful as always.

In B, we checked our reservation which was for the Berg Hotel on the Predigtstuhl above Bad Reichenhall about 15 miles from B. Then we brought some mittens in the PX, had a sandwich at one of the hotels, and decided to take a tour of the castle in Berchtesgaden. We still didn't think there would be much snow as there was none in B. The castle proved quite interesting. It was formerly a monastery, but for many years belonged to the Wittelsbach family, the royal family of Bavaria. It is primarily a museum now and has some wonderful pieces of china and porcelain. I have a booklet which I will send you.

We finally decided to head for the hotel. You park your car in Bad Reichenhall and proceed to the hotel by cable car. The hotel is 5326 feet up and the cable car ride takes about 10 minutes. You really feel on top of the world up there. As we went up, we could see all the lights of the town and those of Salzburg in the far distance.

The hotel is one of the military hotels and is run as a ski lodge. It takes both enlisted, officer and civilian personnel. We had an adequate double room but no view. The meals were also adequate but no choice. We paid $1.50 a night each for the room and $0.50 a meal upon arrival. We cleaned up, had a drink and dinner. Then I listened to the Army Navy game over the shortwave. It was quite a sensation to sit on the top of a mountain in Germany and hear the game. I won't say anything about the game—it was too painful.

Sunday morning. We had breakfast in our rooms and were on the ski slopes before 10:00. They had had a good bit of snow some time ago and it was all right, but sort of hard.

We rented skis and poles for $0.50 and signed up for lessons also for $0.50. It was a beautiful sunny day. They have ski tow but it wasn't running, which meant a lot of climbing.

I had decided I shall abandon my instruction in the French method skiing, which I started last year. All the instructors here naturally teach the Arlberg method, which was what I was taught in college. One is about as good as the other, so I am working on this now. I ski better than Aileen, but I'm not really much good. We skied about four hours on Sunday, 2 in the am and 2 in the pm. As always, I enjoyed it very much, although I certainly wish I had my own skis over here.

Sunday evening we rode the cable car down and drove to Berchtesgaden. We had a very good steak dinner at the Berchtesgadener Hoff where I had stayed before. We saw a poor movie at the theatre in B. It was raining down there, but when we got back up to the mountain it was snowing. It snowed all night and nearly all day Monday and again today.

As the result of the snow, the skiing conditions were really perfect and we have skied again most all day Monday. I don't see much improvement in my skiing ability, but I keep trying. Monday night they showed a 16 millimeter movie at the hotel which of course we went to.

We skied again this morning but stopped early enough to have lunch and catch the 12:30 cable car down. We found that there had been snow in the lower region. There were some pretty bad spots on the road coming back, but we made it fine. We got back around 4:00 PM. I immediately called for an appointment for my hair and went about 5:00. Now I've eaten a snack, will write to you and then must study my German lesson.

I was very pleased with all my new ski clothes. The weather was really not very cold. All I needed each day was one sweater and my parka. I'm so glad I have the right things to wear.

I'm enclosing 3 postcards of the hotel. They didn't have any winter scenes, but they will give you some idea. Honey, I'll stop now and answer your letters tomorrow. I'm kind of stiff and sore, but nothing I won't live through.

* * *

Munich
Wed, Dec 6, 1950

. . . Don't take any blame onto yourself for my spending habits. I know I ought to save, but I don't think I will unless I stay over here for two years. I'm determined to take as many trips as I can and travel costs. Also I will be at least until June getting the car paid for. However, I'll do the best I can.

* * *

Munich
Sat, Jan 6, 1951

. . . I have no plans for this weekend, except I'm going to hear Jose Iturbi tonight and for free. He is giving a series of concerts for the "boys" in Europe. Tonight he is at one of the service clubs. They allotted 50 tickets for to hospital personnel. All interested put their names in a pot and I was lucky enough to be a winner. I certainly am having some wonderful "cultural" opportunities over here.

Aside from that, I will devote myself to chores I think. Although the weather is nice today, the roads are too slippery to do any driving out of the city.

I have a folder on the Italian trip which I am going to take in April, which I will send you. It is really a marvelous trip for $200. There are several possibilities of who may go with me, but if they don't work out, I'll go alone. There are always big groups on these tours, so I won't actually be alone.

Aileen and I may go to Bad Gastein in Austria skiing the last weekend in January. It is a wonderful winter resort, about two hours by train from Salzburg. Unless you go to the Army places, Austria is one of the cheapest places to go.

* * *

Munich
Sun, Apr 1, 1951

Sometimes it comes over me with a start, "What am I doing here?" This is one of those times, because here I sit in the lobby of the Carlton Hotel in Frankfurt, Germany, waiting for a train to take me to Munich. And in spite of it all, I really feel quite at home and secure. I have just seen Mary Liz off on a train to Bremerhaven and have three hours to kill, so I'll use the time to catch you up on my doings.

As I always do when I am with Mary Liz, I have had such a good time. Actually, we don't do anything exciting. We just seem to have fun doing nothing together.

Aileen and Bess took me to the train Friday evening. I got in at 10:30 and the train left at 11. I was lucky to have a double compartment to myself and I hope I'll be as lucky tonight. I never can sleep much on trains and the German trains are worse than ever. We used to complain about the rough roadbed of the Pennsylvania. But compared to the ones over here, theirs is like a ride on cotton. In addition, you ride sideways to the train like you do in a bedroom on US trains, which I do not like. Add to that the three-piece

MARY SKIING

German mattress and you have the picture. The train got in at 6:40 AM and the porter called me at 6:15.

Mary Liz's train got in at almost the same time, so we met in the station. After getting our return reservations, we checked our bags and came across the street to the Carlton for a big breakfast. The Carlton is a military hotel, but you can't stay here unless you are on orders. A friend of Mary Liz's had made a reservation for us at the Frankfurter Hoff—a German hotel. It is very plush and we had the nicest room and bath (private!!) I have had since I left the US. It was very luxurious and we really enjoyed it. The room with breakfast came to 45 marks, about $10.50, which is a lot for Germany, but we felt it was well worth it.

After unpacking and getting settled, we decided to go look in some of the shops. Mary Liz had the address of a shop where you can get clothes imported from the US. We mostly window shopped, except she bought a summer dress for $16.50 when we finally found the place. The weather was nice in the morning so we enjoyed walking around.

We had lunch at the Casino Club, which is a very nice officers club. When we finished it was raining so we took a cab out to the 97th General Hospital. Mary Liz wanted to see some of the people she knew there. On the way back, we stopped at the PX. Whenever you go anyplace, you always look over the PX to see if they have anything your own PX doesn't. We got a couple of pairs of socks some [?] and some film.

We got back to the hotel about 4:00 and took naps until 6:00. Then we talked and dressed and went to the French Club for a delicious dinner. It is really French—run by French people but open to all Allied personnel. We had onion soup, chateaubriand and wine. We came back to our hotel, had a liquor in the bar and were in bed by 10:00. We needed it as neither of us had slept on the train.

This morning we got up around 9:30 and had breakfast, coffee and rolls—continental style—in our room. Then we really got down to the business of planning our trip. Of course, we had been talking about it all the time, but we sat down with calendar and maps and really settled it.

We left the hotel at 11:30 and took a cab out to the Casino Club. I waited there and read some of the paper while Mary Liz went across the street to church. When she got back, we had a second breakfast—eggs, ham, etc. Then we walked over to where the ARC girls from the 97th live as Mary Liz wanted to see a couple of them we didn't see Saturday.

We got back to the hotel about 4:00. Checked out and took our bags to the station. Then, since it was raining, we came across to the Carlton had drinks and an early dinner. Mary Liz's train left at 7:05.

I haven't the exact time schedule for our trip with me— it is in my suitcase. However, we decided to go to Paris first. We felt our clothes would look better and we would feel fresher if we hadn't already been on the road for two weeks. We will take the same itinerary I wrote you about, only in reverse. I can't start my leave on Friday, May 11th, but I can get started about 2:30 or 3:00 that afternoon. I'll drive to Frankfurt and spend the night here. Mary Liz will take the night train down from B and I will meet her Saturday morning. We'll have breakfast and take off immediately, spending the first night in Luxembourg. The second night will be in Paris.

Mary Liz seems to be very content in Bremerhaven. The job is practically nothing, but she has a lot of social life. She doesn't expect to be there much longer as she has been told she will be transferred, probably to a bigger hospital.

Well, I guess that brings you up to date as of tonight. I will sit here and read a magazine until I can get on my train. I'll get to Munich about 6:30 tomorrow morning. Before I go to work I am going to have my car inspected and re registered. It has to be done before 20 April and I want to get it done before I go to Italy on Friday. I am going tomorrow so in case it doesn't pass inspection, I can have any needed work done on it this week.

Don't try to write me in Italy, but keep writing so I'll have lots of letters when I get back.

* * *

Munich

Thurs, Apr 5, 1951

. . . I'm home now [from the hairdresser] and will finish this before I pitch into my packing. I've done so much traveling since I have been over here that packing begins to come sort of naturally. I'm not taking a great deal. A couple of suits, black dress, blouse, etc.

. . . I was disappointed not to get a letter from you today, as I hoped to hear from you again before I started out. I had a lovely note from Betty Smith yesterday inviting me to stay with them in Paris. Of course I won't do that, but we'll love seeing them. She offered her services as sightseeing guide, which should be a real help. I'll write her as soon as I can.

I guess I had better stop now as my mind is more on getting ready to go procedures than the letter I am writing. I'm taking $220 in travelers checks and I'll be ready to shoot myself if I spend all of that. I'll be writing to you as I go along. I'll be in Bolzano tomorrow night and Rome Saturday night. I can't believe it.

* * *

Mary wrote seven letters during her trip to Italy, recounting the travel arrangements, the meals, the lodgings, an audience with the pope, and all the sights seen. Overall, she was very pleased with the tour and seemed to be very impressed with Italy.

She also spoke of traveling with Tom, who has not been referenced in any letters prior to the Italy trip. While in Rome, she wrote about being able to see some of the night life and said, "It is wonderful to travel with a man because otherwise I wouldn't get to do this sort of thing at all."

Upon returning to Munich, she concluded the story of her trip with the following letter, which captured both the highs and lows of travel.

* * *

Munich

Thurs, Apr 19, 1951

It is a bit difficult to settle down to work today. Since I haven't really picked up the reins again, I'll start a letter to you.

I'm a little hazy as to when I last wrote, but I believe it was about noon on Monday. Anyway, we went off for an hour's gondola ride. A "floating" photographer in a boat took our pictures. We got copies, so I have one which I'll send on later. Later that afternoon we shopped, although I didn't buy anything. In the evening, we all turned in early.

Tuesday we had a lovely carefree day with gorgeous weather. We rode up to the top of the campanile for a lovely view of the city, shopped for a little. I bought a lovely watercolor of Venice, then sat in the sun on Saint Marks Square over tea and rolls for an hour and a half. The afternoon passed calmly, mostly spent on the terrace of the hotel in the sun. I have a little sunburn to show for all the "sun sitting," but it was very relaxing.

We left Venice at 6:15 on a crowded train and endured until reaching below Bolzano at 10:30. They had a hot dinner waiting for us at the hotel. Yesterday we left Bolzano at 9 and didn't get to Munich until 6:15. It was a long, boring, tiresome trip. I was very glad to get back. I had a bath, a light supper, unpacked, talked to the girls and finally got into bed at 10:00 to read my mail. It took me nearly 1½ hours. I'll not try to answer it now as I need to reread it all again. Anyway, I was so glad to have it all as I have felt sort of cut off from home for so long.

. . . Well, honey, I may write again tonight and answer all of your wonderful letters—tomorrow anyway. I did want to finish up my report on Italy. I didn't write to anyone else while I was away, so you might send my letters on to Lincoln after you have finished them. Please have them returned to you for safekeeping for me.

It was a wonderful trip and I enjoyed it completely—every minute.

* * *

Prior to the Italy trip, Mary had received information that she would be restationed to Berlin in early June. She already had a trip scheduled with her friend Mary Liz to drive to Paris, which she took, even though it left her very little time to prepare for the new assignment. She also did a trip to Vienna, chronicled below.

Munich
Fri, Apr 27, 1951

. . . As you know, I am leaving tonight for a weekend in Vienna, so probably won't have another chance to write you until Monday.

. . . I took my car out to the garage yesterday for a motor tune up. I wanted to get it done before Aileen left so that she could bring me back and forth to the garage. It is a ways out. I got 7 quarts of oil to take on the trip, so feel the car is now all ready to go. That car has certainly been a pleasure up to now. I have almost 9000 miles on it. I expect to put 3-4000 more on it on this trip. I'll have the 10,000 mile checkup when I get back. I've never had to use the GM oil in it as up to now I have been able to get Sinclair oil.

Well, there was no stateside mail today, so I'll get this one on its way.

* * *

Vienna
Sat, Apr 28, 1951

. . . I find I have a little free time to write you after all. This is certainly a beautiful city and I am so glad not to miss it. It has a real air about it. It is so open—full of trees and parks. Right now, all the lilacs are in bloom everywhere.

As usual, I had a bad night on the train. I never sleep well on the darn things. We got off the train at 6:30 this morning and came to the Regina Hotel—Army billeting. We have a large room with three beds, adequate certainly for $1.00 a night. After breakfast, we took off for an hour's shopping. I wanted to get Steven a sleeveless sweater like the one I sent John. I ended up with two, just alike for both of them. Quite different style, but very handsome, I think.

At 10:00, we reached the Special Services Club and went on a 2½ hour city tour. We got back to the club in time for a quick snack before another tour at one. We had signed for a Vienna Woods tour, but a thunderstorm came up. So we went to Schonbrunn Castle—summer palace of the Habsburgs. It cleared in a couple of hours and we ended up at a sidewalk cafe over tea and cakes.

Now we are relaxing for a while. Later we will go out to a Hungarian restaurant I was told about for a leisurely dinner. Tomorrow we have tickets to hear the Vienna Boys Choir at 10:00 Mass, and in the afternoon we'll take the Vienna Woods tour.

Here I can get a taste of what Berlin will be like. The city is divided into sections and there are many parts you have to avoid. I guess you just get used to it. We see Russian soldiers about and of course many buildings have Stalin's "handsome" face on them. You are strictly forbidden to photograph any Russian buildings.

I forgot to say that this morning the tour included a ride on the Ferris wheel, which was in "Third Man."

Sunday afternoon

This has been another lovely day. We got up about 8, had breakfast, and got to the church a little past nine. We had asked the desk clerk to get us tickets, but he had only gotten two, so we had to get there early to get a third. The church is the chapel of the city palace of the royal families. It was quite small but very beautifully decorated. The Vienna Boys Choir has sung there since 1485. The choir was way up at the back so we couldn't see them, although our seats were in the third row. They were accompanied by an orchestra and also some adult male voices. They sang the whole Mass, but we never learned who composed the music. I think it was Beethoven. There were three priests, and their vestments were magnificent—white satin lined with red embroidered with flowers and heavy with gold embroidery. It was a high Mass, of course. Much incense etcetera—four altar boys. Really most mysterious and lovely.

After church, we went to Hoch Haus, which is a restaurant on top of the highest building in Vienna, 16 stories. It was a fairly clear day, so we had a good view of the city. We had a good lunch of Wienerschnitzel, salad, pastry and white wine. At one we took a three-hour bus

tour of the Vienna Woods. The woods cover a tremendous acreage and all over hills out from the town. Very lovely with lovely views. We got our only sight of the Danube from there, as it is in the Russian sector. We stopped for tea at a nice place with a lovely view. The day was clear—slightly hazy.

Now we are back at the hotel and in a little while we go down to the station to see if we have to set up all night. We made our reservations the moment we got off the train, but were told there was little likelihood of our getting a sleeper. If it were a civilian train, they would put on an extra sleeper, but the Army doesn't care. There was only one sleeper on the train we came down on and many people set up on the wooden benches all night. Well, we had a good night's sleep last night.

I guess I'll end this so I can mail it in the morning. I have really liked Vienna, it is a lovely city. It would be a wonderful place to live in, if you know what I mean.

PS Aren't I a lucky girl to be able to see so much?

* * *

Munich
Tues, May 1, 1951

Today is a big German holiday, their Labor Day and of course has great communist significance. So we are restricted to our quarters, to which we must repair immediately at 5:00 PM. It is OK with me as I have a lot of things to do tonight anyway.

Our worries over having to sit up all night coming back from Vienna were promptly dispelled when we reached the station. We had good accommodations on the nicest sleeper I have ever seen in Germany. I even slept pretty well.

Yesterday, of course, I went home from the station and changed my clothes and went right to work. The nicest thing that happened yesterday was that when we got our checks so all received a cost of living increase, which for me amounted to $24—$18 actually after increased tax deductions etc. My salary is now $348 a month and as of 1 July I should receive another increase, as I will then be reclassified to Assistant Field Director, which is a grade higher than my present grade. I don't think I'll be able to afford to resign from Red Cross as I could never approach these good salaries starting out new in another agency. All of this plus approximately $70 a month for maintenance with all my leave. I am losing on maintenance as it's not paid when you are on leave.

On the strength of the raise, I went right to finance and bought enough marks to finish paying for my Oberammergau bookends. I picked them up last night and I'm so happy with them. Bess and I had an early dinner last night at the Hans de Kunst. When we got home, Billie had just arrived back from leave, so we had to hear all about it. She and another girl had been on a three-week trip by car through Italy and Switzerland. After hearing about all of her difficulties in Italy with her car, eating, language trouble etc., I was more glad than ever that I toured Italy as I did. I don't anticipate similar difficulties on my trip, but at least in France I can get by with the language. My car is much better than hers. She has an English Morris and it is a real lemon.

For our last meal in Vienna, we went to a very ancient restaurant. It was typical Viennese—good food, wonderful wine and zither music. I have a folder on it which I will send. We rode the Vienna subway to get there. It was quite an experience. In Vienna we rode everything from a Ferris wheel to the subway. I loved Vienna. After I get to Paris

and Berlin, I will have been in all of the most famous world capitals: London, Rome, Vienna, Paris, Berlin, of course Berne in Switzerland too. Also Edinburgh. I've also been through Brussels and we will go to Luxembourg en route to Paris. Aren't I a lucky girl?

. . . I have only 6½ more days to work at the 98th. May 8th—VE Day—is a holiday and I have a day off next week compensating time for working weekends. I have to work this weekend. If May 8th is nice, I think I'll make the last pilgrimage to the mountains that I have loved so much. All for tonight.

* * *

Mary wrote to her father during her time in Germany, but one of the only letters saved was one she wrote to explain an unexpected wire correspondence before she was to leave on her car trip with Mary Liz to Paris. The letter was sent to her father so as to not upset her mother, although I know he would have shared the contents of it with Grace.

Munich
Fri, May 4, 1951

Dear Daddy,

I hope you and Mother weren't upset today by my wire for money. I believe I had written previously about being concerned over whether I had enough money for my trip and hoped you would think that was what it was for.

Actually it is. However, the necessity for cabling for money was forced on me because my wallet was stolen today. I had $70 in it because I was going to Swiss Leave Center to pay for the Swiss part of our trip. With that money gone, I had to ask for some. I decided I would ask for 200 instead of 100 so that I would feel comfortable on the trip. I hate to travel without plenty of money. I have every expectation of returning at least 100 immediately after my trip is over and the rest when I can.

The wallet business is particularly upsetting since it contained my AGO card, driver's license, PX card, gas coupon book, ARC identification plus $70 and 20 Deutschmarks. I really don't know if I can go on leave if I don't get my AGO card back. I cannot get out or into Germany without it. And it takes several weeks to get a new one if it isn't found. I hope I can get some sort of identification letter to act in place of it. Without it, I won't be able to get the gas coupons for France either.

I missed the wallet first about 11:30 when I was getting it out to go to lunch. It was in my purse in a drawer of my desk. Desk was unlocked, although I was in my office for about two hours continually from 9:30 to 11:30. Before that I was in another office across the hall and my office was unlocked. Of course I reported it to the Provost Marshall immediately. When the MP's came up to check, they caught our German handyman with two cartons of Red Cross cigarettes. They caught him in the latrine, taking the seals off the packages. He finally admitted to stealing them from Bess's office after removing with a screwdriver the clasp from her cigarette cupboard which is padlocked. He denied taking my wallet, of course, and it wasn't found on him or anywhere in the Red Cross area. The hard part is that Bess's wallet was stolen from her desk about a month ago, exactly as mine was—out of her purse. She got the wallet back with the cards, etc. but no money. It was picked up on the grounds of the hospital about a week later. So you see that it has been an upsetting day and one which will inconvenience me to no end.

Even without proving he took Bess's and my wallets, Warner has had it. The least that will happen to him is that he will be fired and will never be able to work for the Americans again. He can be tried in a German court too. I really feel badly about him. He has worked for the Red Cross at the hospital for five years. He is a hard worker, always willing and very capable. I think the temptation of seeing all those cigarettes within reach—and possibly the wallets too—was just too much for him. Just catching him with the cigarettes is very serious as they are very valuable item over here.

Well that is enough of that. We have also had another problem in that Billie came in the other night with her hands full and left her keys hanging in the lock of the door. When she remembered them, they were gone from the lock, so we have had to have the lock changed on the door. Yesterday was a German holiday so no one was working and the maid wasn't here, so Billie and I had to take turns staying home all day so that the apartment wouldn't be empty until we could get the lock changed. That is taken care of now. Always something.

Last night I went to supper for the Episcopalians in Munich. It was just a social gathering and about 35 people were there. So you see, I am trying hard to live up to having a vestryman in the family. There is no Episcopalian chaplain in Berlin but I think I shall try and go to see some of the Church of England services the British are bound to be having.

Well, I hope you can spare me the $200 and have no trouble sending it to me through American Express. I put the date in there as I start to leave on the 11th. It certainly is wonderful to have a family like mine to fall back on when you get into trouble. It is one of my greatest comforts.

* * *

Munich

Sat, May 5, 1951

I wrote Daddy a long letter last night explaining all my troubles, so I won't go into them again. As of this morning. Nothing has been found of my wallet, however.

. . . I am going downtown after I finish my stint at noon and pay Swiss Leave Center for our reservations in Switzerland. I have enough money left for that, so I won't have to cash any travelers' checks I already have.

Monday I'm going to have to start out and get a new driver's license, AGO card, etcetera. It's all a d- nuisance.

I had a typhoid booster today, so I'll be safe for my trip. I was due for one this month, anyway. I decided to do it today so that if I have a reaction, I can have the weekend to recuperate.

Tuesday is a holiday and my original plan was to take a last trip to the mountains. However, I have decided instead to go to Rothenberg. It is about 3 hours from here and is one of the least altered of the medieval walled towns. Everyone raves about it and I have been wanting to go for a long time. I've invited Florence, a new recreation worker, to go with me. I hope we have a nice day.

* * *

Munich

Sun, May 6, 1951

Well, the big news is that I've got my wallet back without money, gas coupon, book or postage stamps, of course. However, AGO card, PX card, driver's license, etc. were all intact.

The MPs at the hospital called me yesterday afternoon and said they had it. The story of its recovery is that one of the MPs happened to go into a latrine at the front part of the hospital—far from the Red Cross area—and saw someone standing on one of the bowls reaching up on the top of the box holding plumbing. It was a patient, and when he emerged with my wallet in his hand, the MP was standing there. The patient claimed he saw something at top of the box and just reached up to see what it was. However, in these old buildings, the plumbing boxes are at least nine feet off the floor and it would be impossible to see anything up there unless you knew it was there and went looking. However, the patient did not have the money on him. There are a couple of possibilities. Either he stole it from my office Friday, took the money out and hid the wallet in the latrine, then went back later for the wallet, possibly planning to drop it somewhere where it would be picked up and returned to me. Or someone else hid it in there and told him it was there. Anyway I haven't much hope of getting the money back, but I am so relieved to get all the necessary cards etc. It sort of throws suspicion off of Werner, too. The Provost Marshall told me that the fact that they caught Werner with the cigarettes while looking for my wallet sort of threw them off the track. They had been concentrating their search efforts in the Red Cross area, however, Warner could have hidden it in the other latrine. And maybe was seen by the patient who later went back to get the wallet. Anyway, that is really the MP's problem now. I don't know who the patient was, although I think tomorrow they will ask me to see him and state whether I had ever seen him in my office. He isn't on the ward I cover.

Well, it has been a mess, but I feel it has had some happy conclusion as far as I am concerned. It has been an expensive lesson to me not to be casual about leaving my desk unlocked.

American Express called me yesterday morning that

the money you cabled was there. I couldn't get there before they closed at noon, but will get it tomorrow. Now that I have my AGO card back identification will be no problem. That was certainly wonderful cooperation from my family. I didn't send Daddy my cable until about 3:00 Friday afternoon, and they called me from the American Express about 11:00 AM Saturday. It is a wonderful feeling to have such a family back of you.

I've had a lovely, relaxed weekend, especially since yesterday afternoon when I got my wallet back after work. I went down to the Swiss Leave Center and got that taken care of. We are going to stay at the Bellevue Palace in Berne, which I believe is where you stayed.

* * *

Munich

Thurs, May 10, 1951

I've had a very busy day. Even though I was off all day, I really kept on the run. I spent the better part of the morning going through stacks of letters and throwing them out. You know how I feel about throwing letters away and I still had every one I had received since I left home. I didn't allow myself to read them or it would have been a three-week job. As I tore up letter after letter of yours, I realized how really marvelous you have been about writing me all these months. Your letters are really the most important thing in my life. As I have often said to you, when I am home, I really miss getting your letters.

Speaking of that, I hadn't had any mail all week and certainly hope I get some tomorrow before I start out.

I packed 1½ foot lockers today. Preparatory to going to Berlin, one has winter clothes complete with moth flakes. I don't expect to open it until fall.

I had $30 cash which I hadn't put into travelers' checks, so I went to American Express today and got $20 worth of French francs and $7.20 worth of Luxembourg francs. The latter odd amount was because that was all the Luxembourg money they had. I always like to have some currency when I hit a country. Now I have script, $20 in greenbacks, deutschmarks, French, Luxembourg and Swiss francs and Italian lira. Isn't it a mess?

I think I am ready to start except for putting suits, dresses and blouses in my bag which must be left for morning. I will put everything in the car when I go to work. It has rained all day today, but I hope I will have better luck tomorrow. I think tomorrow will be my hardest day as I will have to do at least seven hours drive all alone and I can't start before 2:30 or so. Well I guess this is it for now. I'll keep you posted as I go along.

* * *

From May 11 to 31, Mary and Mary Liz traveled by car through mostly France and Switzerland and but also other major locations. They went to Luxembourg, Paris, Toulouse, Limoges, Montpellier, Nimes, Avignon, Marseilles, Monte Carlo, Nice, Milan, Genoa, Berne, Montreux, and Lucerne before they returned to Munich on June 3. Mary wrote at least every other day, chronicling their hotels (a wide range from luxurious to "truly dreadful"), meals, the weather, and experiences with sightseeing. For the most part, the trip was a great success, with a few typical tourist problems. For this reason the bulk of the letters are not transcribed.

There are two notable exceptions in the text, which are transcribed below. The first is when Mary and Mary Liz picked up a set of hitchhikers. The second is when Mary was in Nice and received a letter from her mother containing some important family news.

Antibes, France
Thurs, May 24, 1951

. . . As we were driving out of Lourdes we spotted girls by thc roadside "thumbing." We decided they looked like Americans and thought they might be in some trouble, so we stopped. They were American exchange students at the University of Zurich from, of all places, the University of Nebraska. They said they came from a small town between Omaha and Sioux City but I never pinned them down on where. Anyway, we took them with us to Toulouse. Those crazy kids were seeing Europe by hitchhiking when we picked them up. They were on their way back from Spain. I think they have rocks in their heads. They admitted they had been questioned many times by the police, who assumed they were prostitutes. They said we were the first American ride they have had—have ridden in trucks, etc. They also admitted their families didn't know they were hitchhiking around. I can imagine that their families would have a fit if they knew. We didn't say much as it wasn't our business, but I feel sure they realized we didn't approve. Isn't that a terrible thing for two 21 year olds (at most!) to be doing? People just don't hitchhike over here, not even the natives. At least they were safe with us for one afternoon. We left them at the railroad station, but I am sure they started thumbing as soon as we pulled away.

* * *

Antibes, France
Fri, May 25, 1951

My heart leapt today when I asked for mail at American Express in Nice and the girl handed me your letter. I had hardly dared hope there would be one.

So much news! I'm so very sorry that your trip turned out so badly. It just seemed unnecessary. I suppose actually you were tired from the wedding excitement before you started and just ripe for a bug. I am glad you turned around and came home. Surely by now you were "all better" again. I sincerely hope so. Do try and take it easy for a while.

Of course, I am very delighted that the Schraders are coming to Germany. I hope they can stay in Germany and not have to go to France or England later, where living is so terrible. Living in Germany is comfortable and they will have nice quarters, maid, etc. It is infuriating that I'll be stuck in Berlin with no leave. However, I can work out a weekend or something. I'll write Martha some helpful hints when I get settled down. Right now, tell her not to bring any furniture. Everything, including glassware and china is furnished and quite adequate stuff. She will need to bring her kitchen utensils—pots, pans, table linens, and probably bed linens and blankets. I am not sure about dependents, but we are only furnished Army blankets. Some bed linen is furnished. She had better ask some of her friends who kept house over here. They will know more about it than I do. <u>By all means, bring their car.</u> It is an absolute necessity. I only mention these things now as I know she will be starting to pack soon. What are her plans for the interim until she gets her port call? She shouldn't dread the trip alone too much. The kids are big enough not to be too much trouble and everything is taken care of at the ports.

There is some anti-aircraft now in Karlsruhe which is not far from Heidelberg. I wonder if that is where they will be. I hope Martha and the boys can get over in time for John to not miss too much school. The schools are quite OK, I think.

As for [her brother] John's recall, I too am heartsick about that. Thank heaven it didn't come before the wedding. It would have upset everyone too much. I believe he will be given some time to settle his affairs before he actually goes. I am glad that he has had nine months on his new job as that will help when he comes back. Also a recent raise. It just isn't fair that men his age have to give two blocks out of their lives. . . .

* * *

The last letter from Munich is missing several pages but seems to be written on or around June 5, the day before Mary was to leave for Berlin. Much of the surviving part of the letter wrapped up her journey with Mary Liz. The letter ends with "I'll send you a cable when I get to the hospital. I want to take my car to the garage before I go to work. I'll write when I can, but maybe not for several days."

There is a three-month gap in letters. During this time, Mary moved to Berlin, but the next letter was written when she was back visiting in Munich, indicating that she was able to do some travel from behind the iron curtain.

Munich
Mon, Sept 3, 1951

I'll start a letter now, while I have a little time, but won't finish it and mail it until I get back. At the moment, Bess, Tom and I are sitting relaxed in Bess's apartment with a terrific downpour going on outside.

I've had such a wonderful weekend and have been so happy being here. I feel so completely [at] home here and as if I had never been away. I am so glad I came. It has done me a world of good.

Although I didn't tell you so I imagine you guessed that I flew down and am flying back. My plane (Air France) was supposed to leave Berlin at 4:35 on Friday, but for some reason we were two hours late in leaving there. They made a couple of announcements about it over the public address system but since they were in German, I only got a few essential facts. While we were waiting, they gave us a ticket entitling us to a free pastry and coffee in the airport restaurant. I was afraid to eat much of the sweet stuff because I didn't know whether or not I might be air sick. The plane was a big four engine job—full, but I was the only American on board. The flight was direct to Munich 2½ hours and very smooth. It was more like riding on a bus than anything else. I felt fine, except I was pretty hungry by the time we got in at 9:15.

. . . I have to be at the airport at 5:20. I can't fly back directly. I'm going by Pan American first to Frankfurt and then change planes for Berlin. I am due to reach Berlin at 10:15. My plane fare cost me $54, but it was certainly money well spent.

. . . Well, honey, this seems to about cover my weekend. I'll not finish this until I can add a line that I am safely back in Berlin.

12:00 PM Well, I'm back safely. The plane was only 45 minutes late tonight. It was a nice plane, the one from Frankfurt to Berlin at least. However, we went through much rain and lightning and a lot of people got sick. I didn't feel a bit queasy and even ate the cold plate they serve.

* * *

Only one letter from Berlin has survived. Although Mary discussed some travel plans in it, we know that travel in and out of Berlin was complicated, so there's no way of knowing if the plans were realized. Mary's sister, Martha, and her husband, Jack, arrived in Germany, and Mary did visit them several times.

Berlin
Wed, Sep 5, 1951

. . . I talked to Jack last night and we made tentative plans for the 22nd. He will meet me in Frankfurt and we will drive out to see Nene [a family friend]. I am sort of planning on spending that night with the Wermuth's and hope Jack will drive me to Stuttgart Sunday. I haven't mentioned the latter to him yet. He said he is now in the BOQ [bachelor officers' quarters] and shares an apartment with two other officers. He mentioned that he will be in Frankfurt for three weeks starting the end of September.

After I talked to Jack, I called Nene to see if our proposed visit would meet with her approval. She sounded delighted. She said the baby is wonderful, weighs 13 pounds at 7 weeks, and looks so silly in dresses that she has already put him in pants.

* * *

There is a four-month gap in letters and Mary had moved from Berlin to Wiesbaden when the letters resumed. It is unclear why or when she moved. However, it is clear she does not enjoy her situation as she did in Munich. She continued to travel, which would have been easier to accomplish based out of Wiesbaden than from behind the iron curtain in Berlin. The first trip we have record of is an extended stay in a ski resort in Davos, Switzerland.

Davos, Switzerland
Thurs, Jan 24, 1952

This has been a most peculiar birthday, but it certainly started out right when your cable was delivered to me first thing this morning. I must admit that I was expecting to hear from you today and it was wonderful not to be disappointed. Thank you all for the cable and for the loving thoughts which sent it on its way.

I hadn't told Kelly that it was my birthday, but of course when the cable came, I had to explain what it was. Tonight when I came in, she had a calendar with pictures of Switzerland on it as a present for me.

I spent quite a day today. I started off at 9:30 with a lunch packed by the hotel. One of the instructors from the ski school took ten of us down what is known as the Parsenn. We rode a sort of funicular up, the trip taking about ½ hour. We were really on the top of the world up there 2693 meters, approximately 8600 feet. Of course we took the trip down in easy stages, weaving back and forth. We stopped for lunch about halfway at a ski-hut. The place we ended up, Kublis, was an hour's train ride from Davos. The instructor said we skied about 14 miles altogether. I must admit I got pretty tired, but it was a wonderful experience. We were way above the tree line, of course, and the peaks of the Alps stretched off in all directions. The big snowfields extended seemingly endlessly. The day before in the afternoon, we went up the Strela—2300 meters—by means of a funicular and two T bar ski lifts. We skied part the way down, then went back up, then skied all the way down to the village. Tomorrow I am going up the Parsenn again and we are coming down a different way. The past two days haven't been as instructive as far as formal improvement of skiing technique goes. However, they have been fun and good experience in skiing on all sorts of terrain under all sorts of snow conditions. We have certainly been blessed in the weather so far.

I really wish I could stay here for another week. I feel I am getting such a lot of good out of this week. I am sunburned, rested and I think being out in the air all day is wonderful for me. I imagine I have gained weight too as I have been eating like a horse. This is the first real vacation I have had since coming overseas. All of my other leaves have been spent traveling and were not restful. In other words, I am glad I came. The only drawback has been that Kelly and I didn't quite see eye to eye on most things. Not that we argue, but she gripes all the time about how much everything costs. And to me, money spent on my own pleasure couldn't be better spent. Oh well, it is a little thing. She is a nice girl, but I realize now that we didn't have much in common. I would have been better off to have come here alone. I go off on my own every day anyway. I am quite chummy now with the people in my ski class and we all share a common interest.

Well, as I said before, I could stay for another week. I can't just now as Evelyn has to go to a three day conference right after I get back. Also, I'm saving one week for a short trip to Holland and Denmark in May and two weeks at home in July. And that is all the leave I'll have this year.

Thank you again for your cable. The only bad part about being away on leave is that I miss my mail from home. I imagine I'll find some when I get back.

* * *

Back in Wiesbaden, Mary planned one final extended trip with some ARC nurses. This time they would drive to Holland.

Wiesbaden

Fri, Apr 18, 1952

After frequent changes, I have at last gotten my plan for my leave at least partially settled. On Friday 2 May I am going to drive with three of the nurses to Amsterdam. We will be there two days and drive back Monday 5 May. They have only a three-day pass so that is all the time we can

spend. On Tuesday, I think I'll go to Heidelberg for overnight. Then I'll go to Munich and from there pay a farewell visit to my beloved Bavaria. Garmisch, Oberammergau, Berchtesgaden and Salzburg. Mary Liz is going to try and arrange to be off so that we can do something together over the weekend of the 10th and then I'll be back to work on the 12th. I have decided to abandon the trip to Copenhagen, as you can see. I have so wanted another trip to Bavaria and I think this will make a lovely and relaxed leave.

We had a great problem getting reservations in Amsterdam. When I was talking to Mary Liz, she gave me the address of a nice pension and so I telephoned them and got reservations. The address, incidentally, is:

Dr. Van Olterlo
Nassau Kave 106
Amsterdam West

Well, honey, all my love for now.

* * *

Wiesbaden

Tues May 6, 1952

Now I must backtrack and "do" the trip to Holland. We got started a few minutes after eight and made good time. We took a picnic lunch and ate by the side of the road. We got to Amsterdam at 4:00 PM. The roads in Amsterdam were very good but heavens, the bicycles!!! I have never seen anything like it and this was my European country to drive in.

The place we stayed was really something. The house was old and sort of crumbly with the steepest stairs I have ever seen. They had beds crammed into every nook and cranny. My room was about 5 feet by 6 feet with a bed which let down out of the wall. The other girls were in a double room with two beds and a third bed was in a porch off of it. There was a toilet on each floor, but only one bath in the house, and there were 11 guests there while we were there.

But the people who owned the place were just lovely. As soon as we arrived, they served us tea and cookies. We had arranged to have dinner there that night and the husband cooked it. All the guests ate at a long table in the kitchen, which was in the basement. The food was magnificent. They made you feel so at home that you felt like guests and not like paying guests.

Mrs. Van Olterlo (our Hostess) booked us a tour for Saturday through American Express. In the morning we took a sightseeing tour of Amsterdam, which included a trip through the Rijksmuseum with many famous Rembrandts, Hals, etc. I enjoyed that because as you may remember, I took a course in Northern art in college.

Our tour included a trip to the fishing village of Volendam where we had lunch. Volendam is one of the villages where they wear the typical Dutch costumes, complete with wind shoes. All very picturesque. After lunch we had about a 20 minute boat ride to the island of Marken in the Zuiderzee. That island is completely unchanged for centuries. The natives have intermarried so much that they are pretty moronic looking. They seldom leave the island. Their costumes are quaint. Boys and girls are dressed alike until the age of seven. They all wear skirts, aprons, bonnets and have long hair. It is impossible to tell the boys from the girls.

Sunday morning at 9:30 we took an hour and a half boat trip through the canals of the city. They have sightseeing boats almost like buses. When we got back we had a second breakfast. Then we picked up Mrs Van Olterlo and she gave us a personally conducted tour through the bulb

fields. Unfortunately [it] rained most of the afternoon, but we went anyway. The fields were just beautiful. Squares of massed tulips of different colors stretching for miles. They make lays [*sic*] of the Tulip blossoms and we bought one and draped it over the car. On the way to the bulb fields we drove through the town of Haarlem. Then we went to the resort of Noordwijk on the North Sea. We had tea at a lovely hotel there and came back through other resorts. Mrs Van Olterlo gave us the whole afternoon and refused to let us pay for her time.

In the evening we had dinner at the world-famous restaurant, The Five Flies. It is all little rooms with old furnishings. Very quaint and very good. Mary Louise took the 10:00 PM train back to Nurnberg.

Monday morning, we left about 8:30 and drove to The Hague. We didn't spend too much time there, just enough to get some idea of the city. Then we drove on to Delft and had a second breakfast. Then we started back to Germany. We had lunch about two at a place near Arnhem. We got back to Wiesbaden about 8:00. Our whole trip was 700 miles. We took four, five gallon cans of gas and that lasted almost—we had to buy 5 gallons about 50 miles from Wiesbaden.

I really just loved Holland and felt we saw an awful lot in a short time. When I paid my bill, which covered three nights, three breakfasts, one dinner and all day tour on Saturday, it was only $13. Isn't that amazing?

* * *

After the Holland trip, Mary made several "fond farewell" visits to some of her favorite cities and multiple trips to Heidelberg to visit Martha and her family. We know that she returned to Berlin for the christening of her godson, Alexander Hempel, the firstborn of Mary's secretary in Berlin. The only new destination she visited was a quick trip to Hattersheim, Germany, where the Hempels had moved to after deciding to leave Berlin. In total Mary visited seventy-eight European cities in two years' time.

— Cities Visited by Mary —

Austria	Salisbury	Bremerhaven	Capri
Innsbruck	Stratford-up on-	Esslingen	Florence
Kufstein	Avon	Frankfurt	Genoa
Salzburg	Warminster	Fussen	Milan
Vienna	Winchester	Garmisch	Naples
Belgium	Worcester	Hattersheim	Pompeii
Brussels	York	Heidelberg	Rome
England	**France**	Landsberg	Venice
Bath	Antibes	Mittenwald	**Luxembourg**
Bowness	Avignon	Munich	Luxembourg
Cambridge	Calais	Oberammergau	**Monte Carlo**
Canterbury	Limoges	Rothenburg	Monte Carlo
Carlisle	Marseilles	Schongau	**Scotland**
Cheltenham	Montpellier	Starnberg	Ayr
Chester	Nancy	Stuttgart	Edinburgh
Derwentwater	Nice	Weilheim	**Switzerland**
Dover	Paris	**Holland**	Berne
Keswick	Reims	Amsterdam	Davos
Lincoln	Toulouse	The Hague	Lucerne
London	**Germany**	Volendam	Montreux
Oxford	Bad Reichenhall	**Italy**	**Vatican City**
Peterborough	Berchtesgaden	Bolzano	Vatican City
Ripon	Berlin	Brenner	

The Car

A major, but often overlooked, character to Mary's grand tour was her car. The fact that she even owned a car in 1950 was remarkable. Women were not able to get a loan without it being co-signed by a man until 1979, so it is unclear how she financed her purchase. The family thinks Mary's father, Hal Ingles, purchased the car and Mary paid him back. In the letters there are several references to Mary making payments of one hundred dollars to her father for the car.

We know that the car was a 1950, two-door Chevrolet Styleline Special, standard shift with seat covers, radio, heater, and directional signals. It did not come overseas on the same ship as Mary, and she had to travel back to Bremerhaven when it arrived. It is clear from her letters that she intended to use the car extensively and then sell it shortly before her two-year tour was complete. With Germany still recovering from WWII, she was sure to get a good price by selling it overseas.

The car must have run very well because with the exception of an incident in London when a parking valet left the ignition turned on for two days and drained the battery in August 1950 and a problem with the generator in May 1952, there are no references to breakdowns or problems. On September 16, 1950, after having the car for a few months and already taking it on several long trips, including one to England and Scotland, she wrote:

> I have put 5600 miles on my car already. I had less than 1000 when I picked it up in Bremerhaven. I'm going to try to make arrangements to have the 5000-mile service done next week. It has been completely satisfactory so far, and I have never regretted bringing it over for one minute. I'm really quite sold on Chevrolets, judging from the performance of this one thus far.

* * *

She took the car into service the following week at the PX garage but complained about the cost ($10.55, of which $6.75 was labor).

Gas rationing was still being implemented during Mary's time in Germany. This fact presented logistic problems for her longer trips. Before undertaking her long trip in the spring of 1951, she wrote:

> I've also coped with my problem of gas until I get to Paris. Tom is going to lend me one five-gallon gas can. Colonel Parker gave me some French EES gas coupons, good for 40 liters. So I'll have enough to get me to Paris where I can get my own coupons. I'll pay him back with coupons (French) when I get back.

* * *

When returning from her ski trip in January of 1952, she wrote the following about the car:

> Our trip back yesterday was long, 12 hours, but uneventful. We had to change trains twice which broke up the trip a bit. We got to Mainz at 9:00 PM and Dorn, my ARC driver, was there to meet me in my car. I never used a carton of cigarettes to better advantage than I did to pay him for taking us to the train and meeting us. He probably would have done it for free because he loves to get a chance to drive my car.

* * *

In the last months of her tour, Mary began plans to sell the car. On May 6, 1952, she reported the following:

> My big news is that I sold my car today for $1400. The executive officer of the hospital called me this morning and said that an officer from France was interested in buying a good used car. And he told him about mine. The officer [Lieutenant Farmer] came to see me later and paid me $500 down. I'm going to keep the car until June 1 when he pays me the rest. Wasn't it a break that I decided to come back to work for this one day? It is such a relief to have it settled and with absolutely no trouble at all. He seems delighted with the car and I was delighted with the deal. He can't possibly welch on the deal because I have $500 of his money. Also I feel the fact that he was willing to pay that big a deposit is a sure sign he really wants the car.

* * *

There was also a flurry of correspondences about the purchase of a new car for her. In fact, in the following letter, cars, old and new, were the main story.

> Wiesbaden
> Mon, May 12, 1952
> . . . Now, for the big news in Daddy's letter about the [Chevy] Bel Air he has ordered for me. I am simply overwhelmed and thrilled to death. You know how much I would love it. I have wanted one ever since the first came out but could never talk myself into feeling I could afford one. You are much too good to me always.
>
> Well, you can see I am in seventh heaven over the prospect. I just couldn't be happier about any material possession. You know how cars are a passion with me and to finally be able to own such a classy one seems unbelievable. You shouldn't do so much for me, but I love you for it.
>
> I guess I just didn't sell my present car quite soon enough. Yesterday on the way up to Munich, it started making the most awful noise. I stopped at the MP station in Karlsruhe, and they called the ordinance emergency truck. Something had gone wrong with the pulley in the generator. The man worked on it for an hour, and it was better. He said it would get me to Wiesbaden. Before I had gone 10 miles it was worse than before. I limped into Heidelberg about four, having had nothing to eat since breakfast. After a conference with Jack and Charlie L. I decided to stay overnight and take it to the garage the first thing in the morning. I called Ev and told her I would be late getting back and then just relaxed with the Schraders. Of course, it was wonderful to have them to fall back on.

This morning, I had the car at the garage at 7:45. I told them a real pitiful tale about being stranded in Heidelberg, being AWOL [absent without leave], etc, and they took it right in. I went back and had breakfast and picked the car up at 9:30. That particular problem seems to be corrected, but tomorrow I will have a new muffler put on it. Mine has a hole in it and I had agreed with the man who was buying it to replace it. Both Jack and Charlie (he is an ordinance) think I did well to get $1400 for it. I have over 19,000 miles on it now and won't be driving it much before June 1, when Lt Farmer comes for it. Up until now it has been really a wonderful car, so I have no complaints.

* * *

The final reference to her Chevy Styleline is on June 3, 1952. She wrote about having to say goodbye to her beloved car:

> . . . I went to Heidelberg Sunday and came back Monday as I was off Monday because I worked Memorial Day. It was my last weekend with the car, so I decided I had better take advantage of it. Yesterday Lt Farmer came for the car. I have the money and have bought a cashier's check and have it ready to mail tomorrow. I tell you I had a hard time to keep from crying when he drove off with the car. I have loved that car and we have been through such a lot together, good and bad. It was really a 100% satisfactory. I am completely sold on Chevys. One of the nurses who is in Lt Farmers outfit told me that he has been bragging to everyone about what a wonderful car he was getting, what good care I have taken of it, etc. It has really had continuous TLC and he _is_ getting a good car.

* * *

The Work and the Life

While traveling was clearly the main focus of Mary's letters, she did give some insight into the duties and lives of ARC workers in the 1950s. With an organizational structure that mimicked the military, the ARC was stationed at US military and naval hospitals across the globe. According to the American Red Cross website, its mission is to "furnish volunteer aid to the sick and wounded of armies in time of war" and to "act in matters of voluntary relief and in accord with the military and naval authorities as a medium of communication between the people of the United States of America and their Army and Navy."

Mary always made it very clear that she was a social worker employed by the ARC—not a nurse. She worked with hospital staff, but in the early years of her career, she was more involved with overseeing the many different volunteer programs facilitated by the ARC.

Her references to work were few and far between. When she first arrived in 1950, she provided some short accounts of training and receiving her assignments. In her first letter after docking, she wrote one of her longest passages about work:

> . . . When I arrived in Stuttgart there was Miss Henry at the station to meet me! She had had to come over to Hqrs for a meeting so came to meet me. And I am going to Munich as I cabled you. Technically I am not supposed to know yet, but she told me right away. She stayed and had lunch with us, and then had to leave. She is going to meet me in Munich where I will go on Friday.
>
> RC Hqrs are at Esslingen which is about 20 minutes from here by car. This is the nearest point on the railroad, so we are housed here in the Gray Zeppelin Hotel. It is a hotel just for military personnel. They turned us loose this afternoon, but tomorrow and Thurs we will be "processing" at Esslingen. None of the rest of our group know his or her assignment yet.

I sure am lucky in all of this. You remember Miss Henry wrote me how Miss Jaboolian (FD [field director] at Frankfurt) bawled her out so because she had more adequate staff. Well, it seems that they got into a terrible fight over who should get me. Miss Henry says Hqrs got mad at Miss Jaboolian over the way she acted about it—therefore, I am going to Munich. The more I hear about the Frankfurt set up, the gladder I am that Miss Henry fought the good fight and got me for her hospital.

The sad part is that they have sent Mary Liz to Frankfurt temporarily where she is filling in as a social worker. She is to go to Nuremburg in Aug or Sept when the social service executive at that hospital goes home. She called me tonight and she is miserable. She didn't want to say much on the phone, but I gathered that Miss Jaboolian is being mean as heck to her because she got her instead of a social worker. Shirley is also at Frankfurt on temporary duty.

I only tell you all this so you will see how lucky I am. I also knew you would want to know about Mary Liz and Shirley. I am going to try and see them real soon.

* * *

The following day she added:

. . . Today we spent the day at Hqrs in Esslingen. It is a darling little town about 25 miles from here. It was completely untouched by the way. I am going to take my camera tomorrow and try and get some pictures to send you. Hqrs is in a lovely old home with a beautiful garden full of red roses in bloom.

We spent the whole day being talked at—getting accounts settled etc. I will be paid only once a month from now on and will actually draw $215.08 each month. Since our room and maintenance (we are allowed about $2.25 a day for food) are paid, I should be able to make payments to Daddy real soon. I want to get settled first.

The orientation was well organized—much better than Washington. We put in another day tomorrow. The others still don't know their assignments. I sure am lucky. Everybody is very nice and friendly, and the tempo here seems much slower. I may revise that statement later, but it is my first impression.

* * *

In her last letter before going to Stuttgart, Mary provided a little more information about life in the ARC.

Stuttgart
Thurs, Jun 29, 1950

This will be the last epistle from Stuttgart as I leave for Munich tomorrow at 11:55. I have to make a brief trip to Esslingen in the morning to get my voucher settled. Then I'll be off. My trunks will go with me, and Miss Henry will meet me at 4:00.

Trudy got her assignment today. In Augsburg. That is quite near Munich, so we will get together once in a while. She is quite pleased. She doesn't go until Monday.

I had one piece of information today that I didn't like and that was that my assignment in Munich is only temporary. Miss Corey (she is the director of hospital services for the theater) said that there would be a general reshuffling of personnel in September. I asked her if temporary status meant that I would be moved or that I may be moved. She said it meant that I may be moved, so I'm not going to worry about it. I'm counting on Miss Henry to hang on to me.

I had two interviews with Miss Corey today and spent the rest of the day reading reports and directives—the usual introductory procedure.

. . . Everything possible is done to make things easy for you. All the Red Cross people are so friendly and seem genuinely interested in you as a person. They seem to want you to be comfortable and happy. I hope I won't have to revise my feeling, but that is my first impression. The way I feel now is that I am already hating the thought that I will have to leave when I go back to the States. That is silly after four days, I know. Maybe I'll be fed up at the end of another four.

Well, I must stop and get ready for bed. I hope that I'll have some mail from you about Monday. It seems a long time—two weeks tomorrow.

* * *

When she arrived in Munich, where she was to be assigned for a year, she included information about the living arrangements.

Munich
Sat, Jul 1, 1950

Well, I have finally reached my destination, but I'm still unsettled in my living arrangements. Last night I had to go to sleep on a cot in the hall because everyone was here. For the next few days I will use the room of one of the girls who is going on leave. Later in the week I am going to move to one of the apartments. For a couple of weeks I will have to share a room. The girl I will room with is going back to the States about July 20 and then I will have a room to myself. In the fall, some other people will be going home and Rae has it planned that I will share an apartment with the ones she likes the best. Actually, on first meeting,

I certainly agree with her on her choice. I have not seen the apartments but understand they have three bedrooms, living room, kitchen and bath and free maid service for cleaning and laundry. They're in an apartment house where the Red Cross staff working with the able-bodied troops in this area also live.

It was extremely hot yesterday and the trip down on the train was most uncomfortable. Anyway, I arrived at 3:30 and one of the girls met me. We came right out to the hospital, which is quite impressive. It is very large and the grounds are beautiful. It was formerly a Catholic hospital. Part of it is still used as a children's hospital run by the sisters. ARC has nice offices on the ground floor of one of the buildings. Our quarters are on the 4th floor of the same building. There are about 7 rooms and a bath up here. The rooms are enormous and furnished adequately, but nothing matches. Each girl decorates her own. They also have rigged up a kitchen of sorts, 2 hot pots, a toaster, ice box (literally) and stock basic supplies. They have a kitty and one girl assigned to do the shopping. We eat breakfast up here. It is all really very comfortable. They have only recently succeeded in getting some inner spring mattresses which they rave over after German mattresses.

There is a nice friendly family feeling here and no tensions, at least on the surface. Rae is called Rae by everyone and she is being wonderful to me. She couldn't make me feel more at home or wanted.

They have two maids, one for cleaning and one for laundry. I think the Army provides one and the girls pay the other. They do everything, even wash underwear and clean your white shoes. I'm certainly going to have to learn some German so I can talk to them. ARC also has a man who works in the craft shop, washes the cars and is a general handyman.

Anyway, after I arrived and met a few people, I came up and took a bath. When the others came up after work we had a high ball, dressed and went to a reception by the new CO [commanding officer] of the hospital. It was informal and I wore my blue plaid cotton. We went through the line and only stayed a little while. Then we went to the Officers Club in town for a very good dinner. One of the girls has a Fiat station wagon. The club is very elegant—was Hitler's favorite art museum.

Well, I guess that is all for now. I think I had better get dressed and go down to see Rae. She is taking the duty this weekend. One nuisance is that I have to wear gray dresses as the others don't have their Blues. Since I didn't have any several girls have donated and I have to get them altered. I can't see why I can't go ahead and wear the blue, but Rae says some of the girls would object. Why? I don't know.

* * *

In the only surviving letter written to her brother, John, on July 7, Mary summarized her experiences thus far:

> . . . I never appreciated the telephone companies at home enough. The telephone system here is beyond belief. When you want to make a long-distance call, you have to book it and it may take hours. When you finally get through the connection is so bad that you can't hear a thing. Twice today I had to give up after I got my party because we couldn't hear. Then I had to book the call all over again and wait another two hours. In one day I learned the Army alphabet—Able, Baker, Charlie, etc. It is a necessity. You have to spell everything.
>
> I have seen a lot of destruction, especially in Munich, although they are doing a lot of repair work here all the time. Already I have gotten so I don't see it anymore. When I get my car, I'll be able to see more of the town. My car will reach Bremerhaven on the 19th.
>
> I have really only been on the job three days, but I'm finding it quite hectic. My first impression is that everything Army and Red Cross is not very well organized. Little things like not having enough pencils, having extremely inferior electrical equipment, impossible telephone service, etc., makes everything you do so hard. On the other hand, some things, especially in regards to your living are made very easy. We have a maid who keeps our room spotless, makes the bed, cleans our shoes, take shoes to the shoemaker, washes dishes, makes coffee for breakfast, etc. Also, one of the Catholic sisters brings us coffee in the morning and the afternoon. This was formerly a Catholic hospital, and the sisters are still here.
>
> All in all, I'm still very much in a state of confusion and numbness. I guess it will take time to work it all out.

* * *

From July until December, there were only scant references to work, typically no more than "I had to work today" or "It is slow at the office so I will start a letter now and finish it later." However, Mary wrote the following on Thanksgiving:

> Munich
>
> Thurs, Nov 23, 1950
>
> It's Thanksgiving and I am on duty at the office. Since things are very quiet, I think I'll take some time off to write you a few lines. I can imagine the dashing around you are doing today. As nice as it is to have the family together (at least part of it) on holidays, it sure means a day of hard labor for you. I sure wish I could be there.

MARY AT HER DESK IN MUNICH

I'll eat my Turkey dinner here today. The food is really quite good considering the fact that it is "institution" food. I think the Army serves much better food than the Navy, comparing the two hospitals I have worked in.

I think I'll stay home the rest of today—I only work until noon—and sort of catch my breath. I have been on the run for days. I like being busy, but you have to stop sometimes.

I just learned yesterday that I will get a raise in pay effective 1 Dec. They have changed the system of regular increases, and it turned out that I was actually due one on 1 Nov. To get it only one month late is a record for Red Cross. That will boost my salary from $308 to $324. Actually, I really should be saving money instead of just living from hand to mouth. In addition to my salary, I get a $2.25 maintenance except when I am on leave. As you know, I skipped my car payment this month. I felt I had to because of Christmas, plus wanting to get a little money ahead for future leaves. Starting next month, I'm going to try to save $50 for leaves in addition to sending $100 for the car. Income tax deductions have gone up, so I don't know how much of this new raise I'll get. Eventually after the car is off my mind, I would like to try allotting $100 a month to the bank. If I can do that and stay over here two years, I should be able to save a little money.

I'll have to stop now as the patients are beginning to pour in.

PS I just figured out that with the maintenance, my gross salary is in the neighborhood of $4600 a year. By golly, I have just got to save some of that.

* * *

World news did have an impact on Mary's life, particularly the looming US involvement in the Korean War. On the 6th of December 1950, she wrote:

> The war news is just heartbreaking. I know it is ostrich like, but I just try not to think about it. Of course, I do follow the news, but I just can't torture myself all the time with it. You feel the tension enough as it is.

On December 7, 1950, Mary shared the following:

> . . . We got a little more information today about the future of the Red Cross case work program, but actually it leaves us about as much in the dark as before. The dope is that the program is definitely going out and the Army will take over the civil service social workers. Of course, we will have the opportunity to take appropriate civil service exams and will be offered jobs if we want them. In the States, the ARC psychiatric social workers will start being retrenched in April. The medical social workers will stay on a little longer to help orient their successors. Red Cross will make no changes at all in the Far Eastern Theatre and at the moment, the dope seems to be that they will make no changes over here either. If that is the case, we will stay out our contracts and be retrenched when we go home. However, there still seems to be a lot of doubt about whether we will be left unchanged or not. So you see, we really don't know any more than we did. I just pass it on to you to keep you posted.

* * *

During her first Christmas in Germany, Mary provided insight into how the ARC staff create a "home away from home" for themselves.

Munich

Sat, Dec 9, 1950

. . . None of us can get away at Christmas. Too many activities with which we must all help. On Christmas morning we all have to go to the hospital and hostess at a coffee hour for the Medical Detachment. We are planning to get together—those of us that live in the apartments—Christmas Eve to open our presents and have a little party. The whole staff is having a party Tuesday before Christmas. We have each drawn names to give presents. There are many other things in that I can't even think of.

We're going to have a Christmas tree in our apartment and have inherited quite a few decorations from previous occupants. We already have an Advent Kranz. [*sic*] It is a wreath with four candles in it, one to be burned each Sunday during Advent. We have it suspended from the chandelier in the living room. Aileen has an Oberammergau nativity set, which we will have on the table so we will be quite festive.

Aileen went to the commissary today and bought home a 2 rib roast of beef. So the four of us are cooking a real meal tonight. We have fresh cauliflower too, also tomatoes and Bess is making cornbread. We don't get fresh meat and vegetables very often.

I got Aileen 6 sherbet dishes for Christmas. We are going to give each other presents for the house. These are glass with green glass base.

Bess and I went shopping this morning. I didn't buy much. I drew Bess's name for the party and got her a brass candle holder and a decorative red Christmas candle for it. The Christmas candles they have over here are different from anything I have ever seen in the States. They are fat and have lovely decorations on them. The holders have a spike in the middle to fit the candle over and a wide base

to catch the wax. The Germans put candles on the table all the time in the living room to serve as a cigarette lighter.

. . . Eleanor, our third social worker, has moved in with Bess, which is too bad as neither of us can stand her. Tomorrow a civilian is moving in with them. A psychologist who works at the hospital. Seems like a nice girl. We all miss Ruth and Louise. However, Billie is in Paris this weekend with her German boyfriend.

I must go see what there is to be done about fixing dinner. We are waiting for the meat to thaw.

. . .

PS Had a nice letter from Cornelia today telling me of their weekend in White Plains. Also a Christmas card from Mrs Doepel—my first except for one the maid gave me. I have about finished my cards except for the ones that I forgot about. For example, Miss Henry's sister sent me two little presents in Rae's Christmas box, so I quick sent her a card. We're going to hang our cards around the living room as soon as we get a few more.

Munich

Sun, Dec 17, 1950

I'm having a quiet Sunday for which I am always grateful. I like to go away when I can, but it is kind of nice to stay home too.

The stores were all open yesterday afternoon, so we took off for town right after lunch. It snowed all day yesterday, so we plowed around in a blizzard. It was sort of fun, even though there were mobs everywhere. Our prize achievement was a punch bowl and ladle—4.25 DM ($1.00) at Woolworths of all places. We needed a bowl for the party Tuesday night. In <u>Women's Home Companion</u> there was a picture of a punch bowl made from a dish pan, so we bought a round white enamel dishpan. We are going to pile greens around it and think it will be fine. The ladle is also white enamel. Woolworths was really the worst mob I have ever seen, but it looked just like the ones back home.

We also bought a gingerbread house for a centerpiece. It is about 12" wide and 8" high and is totally edible. It is all decorated and has Hansel and Gretel and the witch in front. It is really adorable. Only 7 DM, about $1.50.

We bought a tremendous Christmas tree—it touches the ceiling—and spent the last evening decorating it. We have only one string of 16 lights, but many balls. Billie had bought four boxes of them for herself, which we are using. The Christmas balls are made in Czechoslovakia and are lovely. We have rigged up a spray of greens with a red bow for the front door. Aileen took another idea from <u>Women's Home Companion</u> and fixed up a coat hanger with ribbons suspended from it to hang our cards on. So you see we have been busy and think our apartment looks quite nice. Billie baked a mince pie last night which we are going to eat ourselves today.

. . . We have heard re-broadcasts of the President's speech yesterday. I feel that he is doing the only thing in proclaiming a national emergency. It certainly is. As far as I am concerned, while I did not come over here on a war time assignment, I feel I must stay until ARC sends me home. While I can, I am going to enjoy peacetime pursuits. I feel that if there is trouble, I'll be as safe with the hospital as I would be anywhere. Our instructions are that we remain with the hospital as the nurses do. We all have been issued field service equipment. I have not wanted to go into all this before in writing to you, but I want you to know how I see my situation.

* * *

Munich

Mon, Dec 18, 1950

We have finally finished decorating our tree. We had to wait until today to buy some tinsel. It really looks very nice. We have been doing last minute preparations for the staff party here tomorrow night. One of the girls is going to bring down and play a small field organ so we can sing Christmas carols. They all drew names, so each of us only had to buy one present. I drew Bess's name and got her a silver after-dinner coffee spoon with the Crest of Bavaria on it. She is collecting spoons. They are really quite a nice thing to collect as each city has its own crest, etc.

I have a small box to send to Nene, but I'm so late getting it off, she may not get it. I got her a spoon with the Bad Lolz crest and a little octagonal painted wooden box for bobby pins that I got in Oberammergau. Actually I originally got it to send to you but forgot to put it in your Christmas box.

I had your letter mailed on 12 December today, sending me clippings and Christmas cards.

I'm glad you liked the etching I sent Martha. I really fell for them. I may get one for you someday when I see one I think you would like. I also want one for myself. I think they are quite special.

One of my letters to you must have gone astray. I know I wrote you that I received the Christmas box. I even remember saying that the packages looked so lovely and made me quite homesick as I could picture you sitting at the dining table wrapping them. I am also sure I told you that I couldn't go anywhere for Christmas. Working for the ARC is almost as bad as working for the telephone company as far as holidays are concerned. I shall be at the hospital serving coffee and donuts to the detachment Christmas morning.

The curtains are hung and I think they look very nice, although Aileen doesn't think they are very bedroom-y. I guess I am just used to them and have memories associated with them.

* * *

In April 1951, Mary gave a glimpse of some of the tragedy that must have been a regular part of an ARC worker's day:

Time to go home. Work has picked up. I have another tragic case 18 year old boy with sarcoma—leg to be amputated tomorrow. Prognosis of a couple of years at best. These things really get you. The other boy whose case was similar died in the Azores before they could get him home. Sorry to end on such a sad note.

* * *

Also that month, Mary shared that she was being relocated to Berlin. Even though her assignment in Berlin was supposed to last a year, she was only there six months at the most. By January 1952, she was stationed in Wiesbaden. She continued to travel while stationed in Wiesbaden, but her letters contain more bitter comments about the assignment and the people she was working with. While she didn't share much about her living situation in Wiesbaden, she did give more information about her work responsibilities.

One of the largest volunteer organizations of the ARC at the time was the Gray Ladies, so called because of the gray and white uniforms they traditionally wore. Mary appeared to be in charge of the Wiesbaden chapter, having to give talks to women's groups and oversee training. On January 3, 1952, she wrote:

. . . This has been a very disjointed week. On New Year's Eve, my dietician neighbor made Crepe Suzette's for the two of us and we killed a bottle of white wine with them. She didn't have any Brandy to use on them, so she used Chartreuse—quite satisfactorily too. New Year's Day we kept Red Cross closed. In the afternoon we donned Class A uniforms and went to a big New Year's reception given by the Generals. Since one of the generals' wives is one of our Gray Ladies, we felt particularly that we should go. It was a big mob scene, of course, but it was handled quite well.

Yesterday was a working day—in fact, I worked until 9:00 PM writing my bi-monthly narrative report, which usually runs to 12 to 16 typewritten pages. Since I also spent 2½ hours New Year's night at the hospital trying to calm down a patient whose wife telephoned him from the States that she was leaving him, I felt quite justified in taking today off. I haven't accomplished much except to stand in line for hours in the Post Office and American Express. I sure loathe and despise the latter organization. I could write a book on it. I haven't much use for the post office either, for that matter.

* * *

In February 1952, Mary made another reference to the Gray Ladies:

This was a long day, 8:00 AM to 7:00 PM. Evelyn wanted to take her day off for having worked on the holiday. I stayed until one of our Gray Ladies came to run the Bingo and then left her in charge.

* * *

In April of the same year, Mary made one of her few references to the emotional toll of the work done by the ARC. She wrote:

> This has been a miserable week for in our hospital history. We had the fourth death since last Sunday today. We go along for months, sometimes without any deaths or people on the seriously ill list and then we run into a spell like this. It depresses everyone.
>
> I had a meeting of my prospective Gray Ladies today and they seemed like a pretty good bunch. Only thirteen out of the 20 showed up. I am just as glad as I would like to keep the class at 15 and I have a couple of other good prospects in the offing. Martha Hill called me from Heidelberg yesterday to ask if I felt Judy would make a good Gray Lady as she had applied to them and given them my name as a reference. I was a little at a loss as to what to say. I told them about her losing Phil and wondered if working in a hospital might not revive all that emotion, etc. However, she does seem to be steadied down now and she has such a nice manner and approach to people. So I "said good" for her in general.

* * *

Also in April, she wrote of a presentation she must give to a women's club. Since Mary did not speak German, we assume that the women's club was made up of wives who are with their military husbands stationed in Germany.

> I gave my talk to the women's club today and I felt that it went alright. I had a few butterflies beforehand, but I was very calm and relaxed when I got there. My Gray Lady class is next week and I shall be very relieved when it is over. Evelyn is on leave this week but having Jan here is a big help. She is fitting right in.

* * *

As the class approached, she wrote:

> This next week will be a nightmare as I'll be all tied up with Gray Lady class Tuesday, Wednesday and Thursday. Ev will be back from her leave Monday, which will be a big help. Today, of course, I worked in the morning and then had to stay at home on call this afternoon. Tomorrow will be the same. I'm going to work a little early so that I can line up the coffee hour and then sneak off to church around 8:30. We don't start serving until 9:30, but there are many preliminaries to be attended to.

* * *

And then the night before the class started, she wrote:

> My Gray Lady classes start tomorrow and so I'm all wrapped up in that. I have to do some more preparation tonight for my first lecture tomorrow. I'll sure be glad when it is all over.

* * *

As Mary's tour was drawing to an end, she included details of how things were wrapping up and what she could expect when she was stateside. On May 12, 1952, she shared the following:

> I have so much to write about tonight, but we'll start with the biggest and best. I got back to learn that I have my port call for 21 June!! Now I really begin to feel like I am coming home. The dope seems to be that we report to

Bremerhaven on 21 June and sail about 24th. Of course, I'll have to go to headquarters first, so I suppose I'll leave here about the 19th. Now don't count too heavily on those dates, because many things could change them, but it should mean that I would be home soon after the 1st of July. I just pray that we land in New York on a Friday so that I can have the weekend at home before going to Washington. If we land in the middle of the week, I'll have to go right from the boat to Washington.

As for the leave situation, I have saved a couple of weeks, which is all I can count on. I am going to ask for some leave without pay, but I don't think I'll get it. ARC takes a very dim view of LWOP [leave without pay]. It fouls up things like retirement deductions, Social Security, income tax, etc. Furthermore, they are desperate for staff and probably have a job waiting for me right now. They usually approve LWOP only in very emergency circumstances. However, I shall try, but don't count on it.

* * *

Two days later she had the following information:

I talked to headquarters yesterday and got some more dope. As things now stand, we will arrive in Esslingen the evening of the 18th, clear headquarters on the 19th and 20th and go to Bremerhaven on the night of the 20th, arriving the morning of the 21st. The only stupid part about that is that we reach Bremerhaven on Saturday morning. They won't need us surely before Monday, so we'll have to sit out a weekend in that dump.

Headquarters also told me yesterday that they have decided to make the staff here permanently three people. Accordingly, they are sending us another recreation worker on Tuesday. I don't yet know who she is, as they are expecting several this week from the States and won't decide who goes where until they arrive. Maud C is supposed to arrive to replace me on 9 June, so except for the inevitable confusion of new people, transferring property, responsibility, etc, we should have plenty of help during the next month.

* * *

Mary mentioned that she was glad to be "getting out" when she was, as there were many changes that were being implemented that she didn't care for. On May 19, she reported:

Friday was a hard-working day as I was all alone. Also, they lowered the boom by announcing that we would lose all of our German help after 30 June. Our German help—secretary, Jeep, driver and a cleaning woman—have been paid out of what is called occupational funds for a form of German reparations. Now these funds will no longer be used to pay help of private organizations such as Red Cross, Exchange Service, etc. Also no more free domestic help for families. Of course, our headquarters has known this was going to happen for months, but they haven't yet told us whether funds will be available for ARC to pay the salaries of these people. Well, thank heaven I am going home. However, I still have to be the one to tell these people their jobs are finished, which is not very pleasant.

* * *

Shortly before leaving, Mary wrote of another tragedy in the ARC community:

Mary in fatigues in Berlin

This has been a rather hectic week. I wonder how often I have written that sentence. They're all hectic, I guess. One very sad event was on Monday night when one of our nurses was killed in an automobile accident. I didn't know her very well, but the real tragedy is that she has no family at all—a friend is listed as next of kin. They are having a memorial service here for her tomorrow. I was actually instrumental in arranging that. I was discussing the matter with the chaplain and he said that the CO didn't think it was necessary. I pointed out to the chaplain that the girl had no family and that if her outfit didn't have some sort of service for her, possibly there would be no service. So egged on by me, he went back to see the CO and there will be a service. After having so much to do with it, I feel I have to go, even though I didn't know her very well.

My new recreation worker arrived Tuesday. She was very young, has been in ARC only a year and is quite inexperienced. I'm glad to have two old hands like Ev and Jan to break her in. She seems a little overwhelmed so far, but she is a sweet little thing and will work out all right I think.

By the end of May, Mary seemed to be counting the days until she would leave. On the twenty-eighth, she wrote:

Three weeks from today I shall leave Wiesbaden. I am really living for that day. Although I'll still have all of the harassment of the trip ahead of me, I think it will be a wonderful relief to not have any job on my mind for a while. I haven't actually received my orders yet and sure wish they would hurry up. I have absolutely no confidence in our post field director here who is supposed to be taking care of getting the orders for us. If he fouls us up I shall be ready to kill him. Mary Liz is going a week before we are, so there is one foul up already.

As I told you, unless I arrive in New York on Friday (or July 3rd), I will have to go right to Washington. If I do have a weekend at home, I'll have to go to Washington on Sunday so as to report to headquarters Monday morning. It would be very nice if you could drive me down, but consider July 4th weekend traffic. Well, we'll just have to see about that.

You asked about my future assignment and of course I just don't know anything. I belong to Eastern area, so will be assigned somewhere between Virginia and Maine and out to Indiana. I did ask for Washington area, but I am not dead set on that. I'll just wait and see what they have in mind. As soon as I clear National, which shouldn't take more than a day or two, I'll go to Alexandria. What I hope is that they'll tell me my assignment right away. Then I can come home on leave and report to my new station. However, knowing ARC as I do, I imagine I'll be left hanging until after my leave.

* * *

On June 12, Mary made one of her final references to work:

What letters I do write these days are pretty sketchy, I know, but as you say, a lot of things can be saved now to tell you. I sure feel I am leaving just in time. We have lost our secretary, and the hospital has a new CO who obviously doesn't like Red Cross. God is good to me.

* * *

And for all of her complaining about the Gray Ladies class, Mary's last reference to them was one of fondness:

Friday, I had the Gray Lady graduation, which went very well. The Gray Ladies almost ruined me however. Just at the end of the ceremony—with all the hospital staff, husbands, visitors, etc.—one of them got up and presented Evelyn and me with beautiful silver cigarette boxes with our names engraved on them. I tried to say thank you, but I just couldn't get the words out. I was so completely taken off balance.

* * *

Berlin and the Hempels

About a year into her tour, Mary was sent to Berlin. She first learned of her new assignment on April 5, 1951, and wrote the following:

Well, I have some real news for you. I just learned yesterday that I will be transferred to Berlin reporting June 11th. My first reaction was "Oh no!" However, I have gotten my emotions under control by now and I'm beginning to get used to this idea.

The hospital there, 279th Station Headquarters, has 150 beds and runs about 100 patients. As with all station hospitals the patients are all short term, more or less minor things. All serious or long term patients are sent on to General Hospitals. Of course Station Hospitals have many dependents as patients. I will be Assistant Field Director and will be head of the unit. The staff will be one recreation worker and some Gray Ladies. At present they have

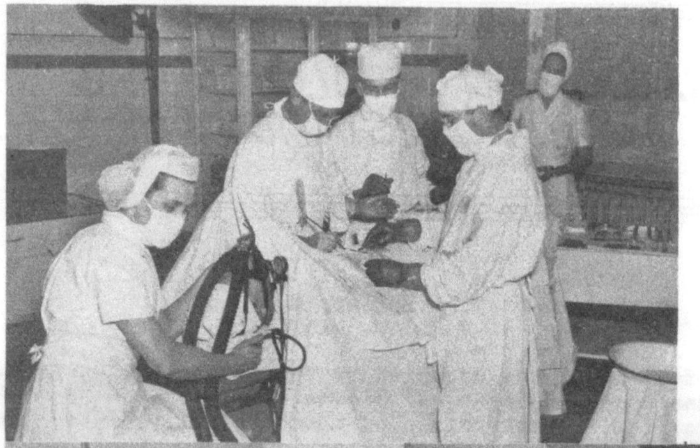

Around

the

Clock

at the

279th

Station

Hospital

Aerial View of the 279th Station Hospital, Berlin

Entrance

Main Building

ARTICLE FROM EUCOM MEDICAL BULLETIN ENCLOSED IN LETTER

two recreation workers there, one of whom will be transferred. The other one who will probably remain is named Martha Hill. She's from South Carolina and has only been over here a few months. I don't know her. I will share an apartment with her—reported to be very nice and near the hospital.

Part of my initial dismay was caused by dislike of being in a cage. My car will do me no good and you can't leave the city or even go in all of the city. You know how much I have loved my little weekend jaunts. I don't like the thought of driving up there either. However, you can go over a specified route which is constantly patrolled by MP's. I have been told that if I am traveling alone, an MP will probably escort me through the Russian zone. Several of the girls have expressed interest in driving up with me, so I don't think I will have to go alone. Once I get there I'll have to fly out or go on the train. Also I am told you can get passes to drive out if you want. It isn't far to Hamburg (British zone) and only overnight on the train to Bremerhaven—I can go to see Mary Liz.

One bad part is that by the time I get there, I'll not have a single day of leave left until 1952 and no three day weekends as I wrote you.

On the good side is that everyone who has ever been stationed in Berlin has liked it. Because people can't go scooting off on weekends there is a very close knit American community there. Everyone knows everybody else and do things to amuse themselves. Berlin is a big city—Opera concerts, lovely stores. All the girls have said they will come to visit me. You have to have a sponsor to visit there, but I can sponsor them.

Well, that seems to cover about all I know on that subject. I have an article from the EUCOM Medical Bulletin about the hospital which I am sending you.

* * *

Mary made arrangements to relocate and was ready to report to work on June 11, 1952:

Aileen and I have been planning our trip to Berlin. We think we'll start out early Wednesday 6th of June and go to Heidelberg, which neither one of us has ever seen. Then we'll go to Kossel Thursday night and finish up the trip on Friday. That will give me a weekend to get oriented and settled before I start to work. Aileen has a good friend who is a nurse up there, which is her main reason for going. I think I wrote you all this before.

* * *

Because only two letters survived from when Mary was stationed in Berlin, we know little from this time of her life. One of these letters was written in Munich when she had arranged to return to visit her previous posting and friends. She made several references to how therapeutic the visit was, which suggests that things were not going well in Berlin.

Munich
Mon, Sep 3, 1951

I'll start a letter now, while I have a little time, but won't finish it and mail it until I get back. At the moment, Bess, Tom and I are sitting relaxed in Bess's apartment with a terrific downpour going on outside.

I've had such a wonderful weekend and have been so happy being here. I feel so completely [at] home here and as if I had never been away. I am so glad I came. It has done me a world of good.

. . . Bess and Tom met me [at the airport] and took me to the Haus der Kunst for dinner. After we got home, Bess and I talked to the wee small hours. I am staying with Beth. I haven't seen much of Aileen as she has a guest, a girl who has been in Japan and is en route home via Europe.

Saturday morning I took Bess to work and then went to Frau Kroners for a permanent. She gave me such a welcome. I guess it was the first time she had ever had a customer come from Berlin to Munich to have a permanent.

I picked Bess up at noon (I drove her car) and we went to a nice club for lunch. Then we went to the PX and I bought myself a nice nylon slip. At the PX I ran into Betty, my OT [officer trainee] friend with whom I skied last winter, and we had a nice visit over a cup of coffee. Bess and I got home about 3:30 and both took naps for two hours. In the evening Bess and Tom and I went to a lovely German restaurant for dinner.

Sunday, Tom came for breakfast and then the three of us went to church at the hospital. Then we drove out to Starnberg for lunch. That is about 15 minutes from Munich and is a lovely lake with the mountains in the distance. It was a beautiful sunny day. After lunch we drove around back roads. I loved this country so.

About five, Bess's cousin and his wife, who were stationed in Salzburg, arrived to spend the evening. We had a few drinks and then went to Haus der Kunst for supper.

This morning Bess had to work again. Tom and I went out to Pat and Warner's for breakfast. We had a nice visit and then picked Bess up at noon. Now we have had some sandwiches and are all just relaxing. . . . I've been so happy and relaxed with people I like and who like me. It was almost like coming home. Miss Henry is away so I didn't get to see her.

Beth has been so worried about Tom. He has been in the hospital with a terrific blood pressure. He is out now, but has been put on a very strict regime. I don't know if

I ever told you, but Bess is very much in love with Tom. Unfortunately, her feelings are not fully reciprocated. He is obviously very fond of her and quite dependent on her, but that seems to be about as far as it goes. Tom is 50, you know, and has never been married and I think is a pretty wary bachelor. I'm the only one Bess has ever talked to about how she feels and I think it has done her good to have me here this weekend. She has really talked my ear off about it. It is an unfortunate situation because I don't think it can work out anyway without her getting hurt.

Well, honey, this seems to about cover my weekend. I'll not finish this until I can add a line that I am safely back in Berlin.

12:00 PM Well, I'm back safely.

. . . Found your letter of 26 August here. Will answer it and write more tomorrow. Now for bed.

PS I'm enclosing a copy of my orders. Thought Daddy might be interested in the Russian translation.

* * *

The only other surviving letter revealed an amusing snafu as well as a reference to Margot and Hans Hempel, a German couple who Mary befriended.

Berlin

Wed, Sep 5, 1951

Your letter, which came today, was written August 28th and 29th and mailed the 31st, so I guess I am only one week behind you at present.

I'm sorry that you had to take a bromide after reading my letter about the infiltration course. I debated about

ШТАБ-КВАРТИРА
БЕРЛИН ВОЕННАЯ ПОЧТА
ПП 742   АРМИЯ США

HEADQUARTERS
BERLIN MILITARY POST
APO 742   US ARMY

                              27 августа 1951 г.

                    /Дата//Date/

КАСАЕТСЯ: Приказ на поездку из Берлина/Германия/ и обратно.

SUBJECT: Orders for travel from Berlin Germany and return.

АДРЕСАТ: Г-жа: Мери О Ейнглес, Уд.личности № э 498 583

           /Фамилия,,в/звание, личный номер, род войск/
           /Name, rank, service number and service/

Вышеуказанное лицо,   Американка

The pers named above   /Nationality/

национальности, уполномочено отправиться из Берлина/Германия/
is authorized to proceed from Berlin Germany and return.

и обратно,   31 августа 1951 г. - 4 сентября 1951 г.

           /Срок командировки// Inclusive dates/

Поездка соб. автомаш. марка   № 1С   разрешена.

ПО ПРИКАЗУ БРИГАДИР-ГЕНЕРАЛА ДАНИЭЛЯ:
BY COMMAND OF BRIGADIER GENERAL DANIEL:

                                        Чарльз Г Тьюлл
Служебное.   СSO   США
Official.   Пом.-Адютант

ORIGINAL

HEADQUARTERS
BERLIN MILITARY POST
APO 742   US ARMY

ADJ 510-8-189   27 August 1951

SUBJECT: Travel Authorization

TO: Mary O Ingles (ARC-17) AGO Card No E 498 583
          American Red Cross

     1. Indiv named above is auth to utilize available rail, commercial air, surface trans, and/or to travel by privately owned conveyance from Berlin, Germany to Munich, Germany

effective o/a 31 August   1951 and return o/a 3 September   1951.
     2. This authorization must be accompanied by a Russian translation furnished herewith.
     3. This authorization permits passage through the Russian Occupied Zone of Germany via Berlin-Helmstedt and return. US Army messing, billeting, and other facilities will be provided only after prior indiv arrangements have been made, and then, only upon discretion of the commander providing the facilities.
     4. Travel beyond the Occupied zone of Germany will be by passport properly visaed for the countries to be visited. Personnel traveling on basis of passport and visa will travel in civilian clothing. Return to Germany will be governed by Military Entry Permit.
     5. No means exist outside the US Occupied Zone of Germany and Austria for the conversion of mil payment certificates into dollar instruments or local currency.
     6. Military payment certificate currency will be disposed of in accordance with standing instructions, when absence from this military payment certificate area will be for a period in excess of five (5) days.
     7. Indiv named above will possess sufficient negotiable dollar backed instruments or appropriate foreign currencies with which to defray all expenses incident to such travel.
     8. Cost of all trans will be borne by the individual concerned. No reimbursements are auth.
     9. TBMAA on a space available non-revenue basis.

BY COMMAND OF BRIGADIER GENERAL DANIEL:

                              CHARLES H. TUELL
                              CWO, U S Army
                              Asst Adjutant

even mentioning it to you. I wasn't in any danger, but it was an exhausting experience. The payoff came several days after. One of the WACs [Women's Army Corps] who was supposed to have gone through it with us didn't show up. The CO called the Post CO to see if he should take any disciplinary action against her. The report is that the Post CO nearly fell off his chair when he heard that the women had gone through the course. It seems that although the order read that all officers and men would go through the course, he hadn't realized that that would cover female officers too. He had not intended for the women to go through. Isn't that typical of the Army though? Well, I did it, and I'm glad. I am sure I wrote you that my eyes were fine after a couple of days.

I've just been reading an article in the August 11th <u>Colliers</u> on the subject of keeping dependents in Europe. I really can't help but agree with the man on many of his points. As desirable as I think it is for families to be together whenever possible, the dependents are certainly a problem, no matter how you look at it. I talked to Nene last night and she told me about the article. Of course, she and her friends are seething over it.

Speaking of magazine articles, I suppose you read the one on West Point in the July <u>Mademoiselle</u>. If not, I have it and can send it to you.

. . . Your enclosure about Celeste Holm was the first I knew that she would be in <u>Oklahoma</u> here. That's wonderful! She was the best thing in the show, I thought. I have gotten my tickets and I'm taking Margot and Hans to see it. This Friday, I'm going to hear the Berlin Philharmonic with Furtwangler conducting Beethoven's Ninth Symphony. I have two tickets and have invited Dr Rohde, one of the German doctors to go with me. He is very nice and attractive, and in my opinion, the best doctor—German

or American—at the hospital. He is going to the States in December to stay.

* * *

Margot Hempel was a secretary working at the hospital where Mary was stationed while in Berlin. Although Mary and Margot spent only a few months together, the bond between the women was a tight one. They continued to correspond when Mary left Berlin until Margot's death in 1983. Margot and Hans asked Mary to be the godmother of their first-born, an honor that required her to return to Berlin after she was posted in Wiesbaden. We are still in touch with the Hempel family. It is a friendship that has lasted several generations.

Wiesbaden
Sat, Jan 19, 1952

Just a line while I have 5 minutes. I am waiting now for Kelly to call me from Rhein/Main and then I'll drive over to get her. Dottie, ARC secretary in the Field Director's office, is going with me. She was also in Panama and is a good friend of K's.

I'm enclosing the letter I received from Margot, my secretary, in Berlin. It shows you what a grand person she is and isn't her English marvelous? The people she refers to are:

Arnba—their French poodle.
Angelika—2 year old niece.
Trudchen—Sister-in-law.
Hans—her husband.

The children are her brother's. Her husband worked in Turkey before the war and is trying to go back. He is an engineer.

When Kelly goes back, I am going to have her take Margot 100 marks as my present to the baby. I think she would rather have money to buy things she needs or apply on her hospital bill. [The letter from Margot has not survived.]

* * *

From the letters when she was posted in Wiesbaden after Berlin, it seemed as though Mary's enthusiasm for her employment and travel opportunities had waned. Maybe she was just tired of being away from home, but there were a few references that suggested something went badly with her assignment in Berlin. As for Wiesbaden, she was there just to count the months before she could leave. Following her January 1952 trip to go skiing in Davos, Switzerland, she complained:

This should be a long letter, but I am sort of tired tonight, so I don't know how long I'll hold out. I haven't even unpacked yet. Getting back to work today was an awful come down. It was wonderful the way I didn't even think about the job the whole time I was in Switzerland, however, that made facing reality today that much harder. I don't remember for sure when I last wrote you. I believe it was after I spent the first day on the mountain and skied 14 miles. Anyway, the weather continued to be beautiful all week. On Friday we went up to the mountain again and skied down a different way. Saturday, was spent back at the school slope really working on my technique. The sun shone all week except for a couple of hours Saturday morning. It snowed Friday night, but the sun was out by 11:30 on Saturday. I really wished I could have stayed another week. By that time, I could have been a quite a good skier. Also, I could have benefited from another week of rest and good food. Well, I only have five more months to do, and I guess I can stand this madhouse that long.

* * *

In February, Mary wrote twice about Margot. On the seventh, she sent another letter from Margot to Grace and wrote:

I'm going to enclose another letter which I received from Margot. When Kelly went back, she took Margo some cigarettes and message from me. I also sent her 100 marks as my present to the baby. I told her I was sending it early as I knew she needed some things and also it might help out on some little comforts when she goes to the hospital. I am sure you can see from her letters what a lovely girl she is.

* * *

Then on the twenty-fifth, Mary shared:

I will have to make the trip to Berlin before I come home. As I wrote you, Margot has asked me to be Godmother to the baby, so I'll go for the christening. I probably won't go before the end of May.

* * *

On April 12, Mary announced the arrival of her godchild:

My perspective [*sic*] godchild has arrived—Alexander Hempel—I received a cable Thursday. I cabled back and will write tonight.

* * *

HANS, MARGOT, AND ALEXANDER (ANDI) HEMPEL

MARY HOLDING HER GODSON, ANDI

And on May 1, Mary she added the following details:

> I had a letter from Margot today. The baby was delivered by Caesarean section. The christening is set for June 1, so I'll be up there over that weekend. She asked me to send a letter to the chaplain verifying that I am Protestant. Chaplain Wood said he would write it for me. The baby's full name is Alexander Mario Hans Hempel—Mario for me.

* * *

Curiously there are no letters about the christening, although we know she did return to Berlin for it. On Wednesday, June 3, 1952, she wrote:

> I don't think you are missing any letters from me. I have never mentioned Daddy's letter or cable about my trip to Berlin. The whole business upset me so terribly I decided we had better talk about it after I get home.

* * *

What "business" she was referring to is unclear. Based on the continued strength of her friendship with the Hempels, I don't believe she was upset by the christening. It is also unclear what her father wrote in a letter and cable about her trip to Berlin. Perhaps he was cautioning against making the trip. There was one remaining reference to the family. Less than two weeks after the christening, the Hempels relocated and reached out to visit with Mary. She wrote on June 12:

> In the midst of everything else, Margot called me on Monday to say she, Hans and the baby were leaving Berlin for good, and are coming to a little town near Frankfurt

called Hattensheim, where Hans's mother lives. As I have written you before, Hans is on the Soviet blacklist, and he has just gotten too afraid to stay in Berlin.

Anyway, they wanted me to come to Hattensheim on Wednesday as Hans had to go elsewhere job hunting, and that was the only day I could see all of them. So yesterday I took a 5:55 local train to Hattensheim. Margot, Hans and the baby met me and gave me such a warm welcome. I had such a nice evening with them and then they put me on a 10:05 train back to Wiesbaden. Hans expects to be back Sunday and they'll plan to come to Wiesbaden to see me Sunday evening.

The baby is cute, but at two months looks pretty much like a baby. He is fat and healthy, and they are so happy with him. We took lots of pictures, although it was a bit late-ish.

* * *

Could Mary's friendship with a family that was on the Soviet blacklist be the reason that no letters have survived from her time in Berlin? Is this the "business" in her father's letter and cable that upset her so? We will never know, but it seems a likely possibility.

The Siblings

A final story line in the letters from Germany displayed the relationships between the three Ingles siblings: Martha, Mary, and John. I think the closeness of their ages and the fact that as children they moved frequently between army bases encouraged them to be very close. Despite the distances between them and the complications of overseas communications, they seemed to stay in touch with each other, especially the sisters. And they all communicated with their mother, Grace, who was a

Margot, Mary, and Andi

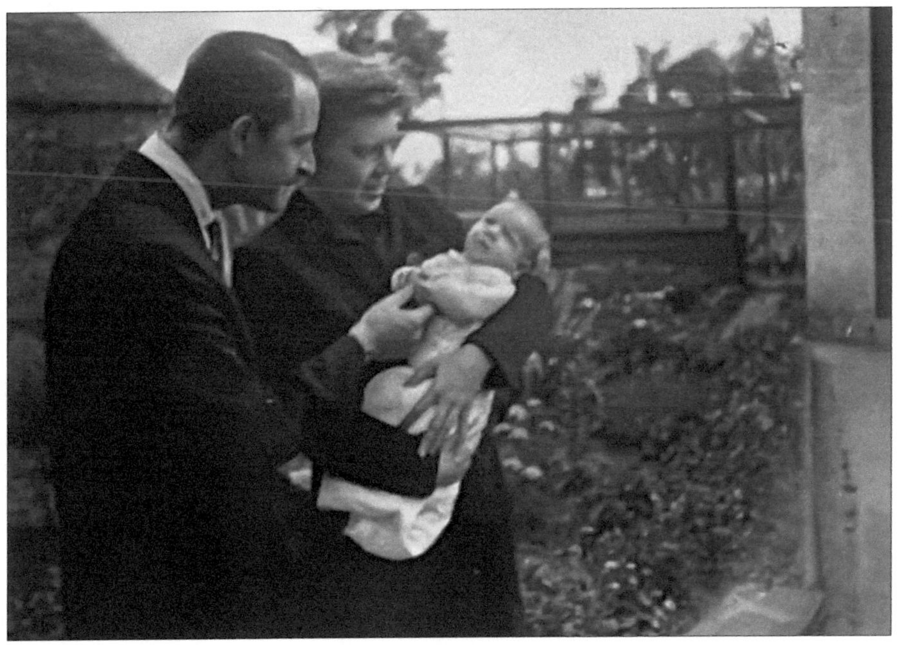

Hans, Mary, and Andi

HAL AND GRACE IN WHITE PLAINS, NY

conduit of information. In the one surviving letter to her brother (who she affectionately called "Johnny"), Mary gave us an example of their closeness:

> Munich
> Fri, Jul 7, 1950
>
> Dear Johnny,
>
> I'm sure that mother has been sending my letters on to you, but I thought I would write you a little line myself. You might return the favor when you get a chance.
>
> I do want to tell you how much I appreciated the wonderful time you showed me in Washington. It was wonderful that we could have such a nice time together before I took off.

* * *

Martha was plagued by physical and mental health challenges her whole life. Mary's letters had multiple references or questions about Martha's wellness. However, in keeping with the norms of the day, the actual conditions, especially if they were mental illness related, were always vague. The following two letters demonstrate the careful tracking of how things are at home, as well as a reference to what will become an important family event: the introduction of my mother to the family.

> Munich
> Tues, Sep 19, 1950
>
> I received letters from both you and Martha today telling me that the operation is to be tomorrow. I almost wish I hadn't gotten them until it was all over, but on the other hand, I am glad that I can know when and at least send a few thoughts in your direction at the right moment. Don't feel that you can't cable me because I have no code address. I can't see why the few extra cents the address costs should

matter. I sent Martha a cable today to the hospital and I hope she gets it OK. I know everyone will be relieved when it is all behind us.

Martha referred in her letter I got yesterday to something you had not mentioned, that is, that John has a girl in whom he seems quite interested. Please write me about it. You know he won't.

* * *

Munich

Mon, Oct 2, 1950

Just a brief note to send along with the money order. This brings the balance down to $700.

I am also enclosing the program from a concert I went to tonight. It was the first concert Bruno Walter had conducted in Germany since before the war. He got a terrific standing ovation. It was really sort of thrilling. Thought Martha might like to see the program.

I had your letter of Tuesday and Martha's letter today. Your letter sounded completely exhausted and frantic. It just made me sick. We all impose on you too much. I hope you won't get into a fret if the house isn't perfect when the Reagans come. They will know what you have been through. When Martha goes home, please don't wear yourself out running back and forth to West Point. If necessary, give her $50 to keep the Sergeant's wife another month.

Martha's letter sounded wonderful. She was feeling better. Jack had never been sweeter to her. Everyone had been so nice, etc. It is nice that she is getting something good out of the whole experience.

During Mary's time in Germany, her younger brother, John, met, courted, and married the love of his life, Audrey Primrose. Mary did not meet Audrey until she had been officially a part of the family for over a year. Audrey and Mary could not have been more different. Audrey was high school educated, had worked as a secretary, and had traveled only a few hours' distance from her birthplace. Mary was highly educated and well-traveled. Initially Mary seemed enthusiastic about Audrey entering the family.

Munich

Fri, Oct 20, 1950

. . . Your letter and Daddy's too, about the weekend with John and Audrey made me so happy. You both sounded so sincerely pleased with her. I guess that we should have known we could rely on John's judgment and good sense. Even if nothing ever comes of it, you will know that he knows what he is doing. I'm waiting to hear from you that John knows that I know about her so that I can write to him. I wish he would have someone take some snapshots of her and send them to me. It is hard when you have no mental picture of a person. The thing that seems best of all is that John is so relaxed with her and they seem to have so much fun together. I loved Florence's reaction, especially since she hardly knows John. However, I guess she knows you pretty well and knows how much he means to you.

You haven't said in a long time about whether John has heard anything further from the Army. I assume he hasn't had anything definite at least or you would have mentioned it. I can't help wondering how he is managing to escape, especially when they are calling people like Jerry Gross. Of course you know that I don't mean that he is "managing" things, just a figure of speech.

* * *

John and Audrey on their visit to White Plains, NY

Munich

Thurs, Nov 16, 1950

Does John have a picture of Audrey? Do you think he would like a leather picture frame? You see, I am getting desperate [for Christmas gift ideas]. I sent him three toy cars for his birthday. Silly, I know, but they are mechanically wonderful, and I thought he would have fun showing them to his friends.

* * *

Munich

Wed, Dec 6, 1950

I am glad that you had such a nice weekend with John. I know you all felt grateful for it. You will be interested to know that he hardly mentioned Audrey in his letter to me. All he said was that he was sorry I hadn't been able to meet her. He wrote me a very nice letter, which I shall answer the first moment I get.

* * *

Munich

Mon, Dec 11,1950

I think it is wonderful that John has gotten an apartment at long last. I sure hope he can have some enjoyment of it for a while. I wrote him a long letter tonight, so this one may end up a little short.

* * *

The letters from late 1950 through April 1951 are either full of travel news or are missing. There are not many mentions of the siblings other than occasional references to receiving letters from Martha. Early April was when Mary took her organized tour of Italy. She was not receiving mail during this trip, but she was mentally tracking the preparations for a major family event. John had proposed to Audrey on New Year's Eve, and they were married on April 21, 1951. Mary was back in Munich shortly before the event and wrote on April 19:

> I guess you leave for Washington today. You can be sure my thoughts will be there every minute for the next few days. I think it is wonderful that the kids both got raises just now. I didn't realize until one of your letters I read last night that Jack isn't going to Washington for the wedding. Who is John having for an usher in his place? I am very sorry he couldn't go. However, I know Martha will be more relaxed about the children with him at West Point.

* * *

HAL, AUDREY, JOHN, AND GRACE AT THE WEDDING

On the day of the event, Mary did all she could to be with the family in spirit. She wrote:

> Munich
> Sun, Apr 22, 1951

> It is a beautiful, sunny Sunday morning. I got up and went to communion at 8:00. I wanted to go, particularly since my wonderful trip, and also to say a little prayer for John and Audrey.

> I thought so much about all of you yesterday. Last night at 9:00, I put my thoughts on you hard as I knew it was 3:00 in Washington. I was at a movie, but I remembered to do it anyway. I just know that everything went beautifully and will really live it when I get your letters. I'm afraid it all still seems a little unreal to me. I guess it will until I get home and actually see John and Audrey together. I had a darling letter from John on Friday, which I shall always keep. I love him so.

> . . . I liked Audrey's wedding invitations very much. I couldn't have done better myself.

> I know you looked stunning at the wedding (J & A's). I am so anxious to see the pictures. I hope they will send me a complete set. I'll return them after Nene sees them. They will certainly help to make it seem real to me, I think.

* * *

Shortly after, Mary followed up with more thoughts about the wedding.

> Munich
> Tues, May 1, 1951

> . . . I do want you to know that I got your two wonderful

letters about the wedding. It just sounded about perfect. I have read and reread them. I am so happy so many people who mean a lot to you and to John could be there. As much as I wish I could have been there, I really can't feel anything but happy about everything. It sounded so right and dignified, if you know what I mean.

There are so many little questions I would like to ask. Like who did Martha walk back down the aisle with? What did they serve at the reception? What did the wedding cake look like? Oh, I just wish I could talk and talk about it. I am so glad Chappie ushered you in. That was just as it should have been.

I'm sorry, the newspaper write ups were unsatisfactory, although I thought the Herald one was OK. I don't think the picture of Audrey is a bit good, even when I don't know her.

The wedding presents sounds so lovely. It was wonderful how people came through. I know John will be particularly touched by the presents from the McDonalds and the Brinkers.

* * *

Although they had never met, Mary and Audrey began exchanging letters.

Wiesbaden
Sat, Jan 19, 1952
. . . I'll write Audrey this too, but be sure and tell her not to buy Hummels in the US with me over here and Martha coming. We can get her all she wants for very little money. I haven't priced them recently, but they only run around $2 or $3 each and I'm sure they are more in the US.

* * *

Wiesbaden

Mon, Jan 28, 1952

. . . I have ordered a locket for Audrey for John. I want to write her about it tonight, right away. I'm having it made in Switzerland. I hope it is what she wants.

* * *

Wiesbaden

Mon, Feb 25, 1952

I had two letters from you today and also a note from Audrey. She had received the locket and was sending it on to her mother to have the pictures made for it. That locket has really travelled Davos to Wiesbaden to White Plains to Tomah to Washington. She said she hadn't told John about it so is planning to surprise him. She also said they expected to start east on March 10th, so you'll be seeing them soon. I guess Martha will still be there, so you'll have a terrific house full. As always, I just pray it won't wear you out. Seeing John off to Europe this time is surely different from the last time n'est-ce pas?

* * *

By spring of 1952, Mary was anxiously awaiting the arrival of Martha and her two sons, John Robert and Stephen, to join their father, Jack, in Germany. The big day finally came.

Wiesbaden

Sat, Apr 5, 1952

Well, they are here and I have just talked with Martha. I told her I would write you this afternoon and she will write in a day or so when her feet are on the ground. She said she had cabled you from Bremerhaven.

Well, as you know, they were 24 hours late getting to B. The crossing was apparently completely awful. A virus bug was rampant and all three had it. Apparently, an intestinal flu with diarrhea and vomiting. Stephen was very sick on aureomycin for days and only checked up the day they docked. However, Martha said he is eating again and seems OK now. She had the bug too, now has a cold. But she seemed in wonderful spirits and completely uncomplaining. She said Mr. Southgate was wonderful to her and just took over completely. Because of Stephen she decided to go straight through to Heidelberg on the train and Mr. Southgate notified Jack who in turn called me.

Martha wants me to come down tomorrow and I shall start right after church, where I shall say a prayer of thanks for their safe arrival. I talked to both of the boys, and they sounded adorable, their voices so alike I had to ask which was which. Martha said the apartment is wonderful and the maid good. She speaks no English, but the maid next door is helping as interpreter.

I've accomplished nothing all day. I didn't dare budge until I got Martha's call, which didn't come until 1:30. Now my car is being washed so I haven't transportation. It is a nice day today and I sure hope it will be tomorrow too for my trip to Heidelberg.

Jack told me on the phone yesterday that John is due to reach Bremerhaven on 8 April. So I now have seeing him soon to look forward to too.

Honey, I'm too excited to think about anything but seeing Martha and the boys tomorrow. I'll write you fully tomorrow night.

PS Martha said Martha H. had already called her. My Red Cross friends are surely coming to the Fair.

* * *

Shortly before his first wedding anniversary, John was sent to Germany and stationed in Baumholder. Martha and her family were in Heidelberg, and Mary had managed to visit them a few times. Mary was planning for her departure from the country. Communicating was not easy, and John and Mary had little control over their leave schedules, but the three siblings worked hard to have a family reunion, an event they anticipated even before John arrived.

> Wiesbaden
> Mon, Apr 7, 1952

I should be hearing from John in a day or so. One of my Gray Ladies today said she thought the reunion of the Ingles family should be written up in <u>Stars and Stripes</u>. Ha!

* * *

> Wiesbaden
> Mon, Apr 21, 1952
> [John and Audrey's first wedding anniversary]

Tonight you will be having dinner with Audrey and I don't imagine any of you will be too gay. I just wrote John a letter and I am sure he is lower than a snake's belly tonight.

I pulled an awful dirty trick on John Saturday for which I am profoundly sorry, but which was far from intentional. As you know, I was tentatively expecting him up for the weekend and he said he would call. Well, Saturday dawned bright and beautiful and I still hadn't heard from him. I hated to waste the weekend, so I decided to try and call him at his outfit. I booked a call at 10:00 but it didn't get through until noon. I had made it a person to person call and when I finally got the unit the Sergeant said John was out on inspection tour of the area with the Colonel and

that he had sent a runner for him. I said "Oh don't do that," but he said, "I've already sent for him, ma'am." John finally came to the phone and was sweet about it, but I felt just terrible. He said he couldn't come and had written me, but I didn't get his letter until this morning. It was mailed and arrived at the same time as your letter from Thunderbolt.

He hadn't been able to find any place from which he can make personal calls. Also, his situation there seems completely snaffu-ed, and he is apparently mowed under. His letter sounded so disgusted and discouraged. I hope maybe we can work out something for next weekend since I'll be away the two weekends after that. I just wrote him and sent him dope on trains and suggested that [if] he can't get away overnight, I could drive down for the day on Sunday. I also suggested possible places where he could make phone calls—public phone places. I sure hope he'll be able to call sometime this week.

Well, after learning that John couldn't come, I called Martha to see if I could go there for the weekend. She was delighted. They had asked two couples and three officers whose wives have not yet arrived, to come in for drinks, and then they were all going to the club for dinner and dancing. So of course she was glad to have me in the party. They were all very nice people and it was a pleasant evening. Jack played golf both Saturday PM and Sunday AM, so Martha and I had a real good visit. Sunday she and I went to church while the boys went to Sunday school and then the Sunday play school.

* * *

While still working to get the whole family together, John and Mary had one visit. Mary's reaction to Audrey took a turn at this time. It is clear she took a distaste to Audrey's "intrusion" into the family right from the start. Unfortunately, the tensions never really resolved, even after Audrey and John had been married for sixty years.

Wiesbaden
Mon, May 19, 1952

Saturday AM I worked and John arrived at about 12:30. It was just wonderful to see him. I thought he looked just the same and very well, not too thin or fat or too tired. He weighed himself while he was here—160 pounds, which he says is just what he likes to weigh. I had made arrangements for him to stay in the doctor's BOQ so we went over there with one of the doctors and he left his things. Then we came to my place and I changed my clothes. After that we went downtown and he had some lunch. I shopped a little at the PX, walked around, drove around a little for a while. I had to return to the office to cope with a problem that came up. After bathing and changing, we had a bottle of sparkling burgundy in my room. Then we went to the nicest officers' club and had a good dinner. They had an excellent band which John enjoyed particularly. We danced a little, saw a fair floor show, had a few drinks and then were home about around midnight. Sunday, I was at work before 8. John met me there about 8:15, and then we went to church together at 8:30. I had to work the rest of the morning. John had to prepare some material for a lecture, so he worked on that while I was serving the coffee and Donuts. I closed the place at noon and after I changed my clothes, we went to one of the hotels for lunch, then John picked up his things, dropped me and started back about 2:30.

So it was really quite a nice weekend and we had a good visit. John of course hates his setup, but he is so levelheaded that he is able to weather it without any abiding scars. John has always seemed very mature to me, but this time he

seemed more so than ever. The only thing I noticed was that he seemed so serious, and I missed his old twinkle. We didn't laugh very much. Another thing that I have to learn to accustom myself to is his complete absorption in Audrey and detachment from his own family.

In other words, I thought he had changed quite a lot in the past two years. Martha had seemed so completely the same that I guess I wasn't prepared to find John as changed.

Now, I hope my reaction isn't going to upset you. I don't mean a single syllable of criticism of John. He was so sweet as always, and I love him dearly. One thing we did laugh over heartily was John's description of his visit with the aunts.

I talked to Martha Saturday morning, and she seems to have thoroughly enjoyed her trip to Vienna. I'm sure she has written you about it. I am so glad she got to go. I called her while John was here, so she got to speak with him. John is not sure he can get off over the weekend of the 6th when Martha wants us to reunion in Heidelberg. His CO is apparently mean as H--- about giving passes. Well, I guess this is all for now.

* * *

On June 9, 1952, the three siblings were finally able to have a short family reunion. This was a source of tremendous joy for them and their parents. It was a story told many, many times by all involved for the rest of their lives.

Wiesbaden
Wed, Jun 3, 1952

Martha just called and John has this weekend off. He is going to drive to Heidelberg Saturday AM. In the PM he and Jack are going to Baden Baden to play golf. Saturday they will play golf at Mannheim. I told Martha I would try to come down on the train Saturday morning. It seems like an awful effort, but it will be my last chance to see all of them, so I guess I'll make it. I'm so spoiled from having the car that having to go anyplace on the train seems terribly difficult.

* * *

Wiesbaden
Sun, Jun 9, 1952

Well, things just pile up too much for me to try to go to Heidelberg this weekend. I talked to Martha Friday and suggested they all come over Sunday and have dinner. I was really very glad I didn't go because I accomplished quite a lot and feel much less panicked than I did.

The Schraders and John arrived about 12:30 today and it was a beautiful sunny day. We took a lot of pictures of all of us together which I shall send on in due course. We all went over to Kronberg Castle for a nice lunch. The boys were good, ate well, and we all enjoyed being together. Right after lunch, John felt he had to start back to Baumholder, so we left the Schraders at Kronberg and John dropped me off at Wiesbaden.

I won't see any of them again before I leave, as the Schraders are going to Bavaria next Saturday. It wasn't so hard to say goodbye to John as I'll see him again in six months, but it hurt to say good bye to Martha and the boys for another two years.

* * *

Wiesbaden
Mon, Jun 16, 1952

Here are some pictures which should gladden the heart of a certain mother and grandmother I know. I am so pleased at how well they turned out. I have the negatives and can have enlargements made when I get home if you want. I had sets made for Martha and John. I offered to send some directly to Audrey, but John wanted me to send them to him first. He said Audrey is always asking him for pictures, so he wants to send them himself.

* * *

Mary returned to the States in July of 1952. Regardless of any dissatisfaction she may have had with the last part of her posting in Germany, she had developed a deep love for the country. She would be posted there at least two more times during her tenure with the ARC. The Hempel family remained an important part of her life. They were frequent visitors whenever Mary was in Germany and even travelled to the US to see her. They would remain in touch until Hans and Margot passed in 1972 and 1983, respectively. Alexander, Mary's godson, and Mary would stay in touch the rest of her life. Alexander's family and the Ingles-Christensen family are still in regular contact in 2025.

Back: Martha Schrader, John, and Mary Ingles. Front: John Robert and Stephen Schrader taken June 1952 in Wiesbaden

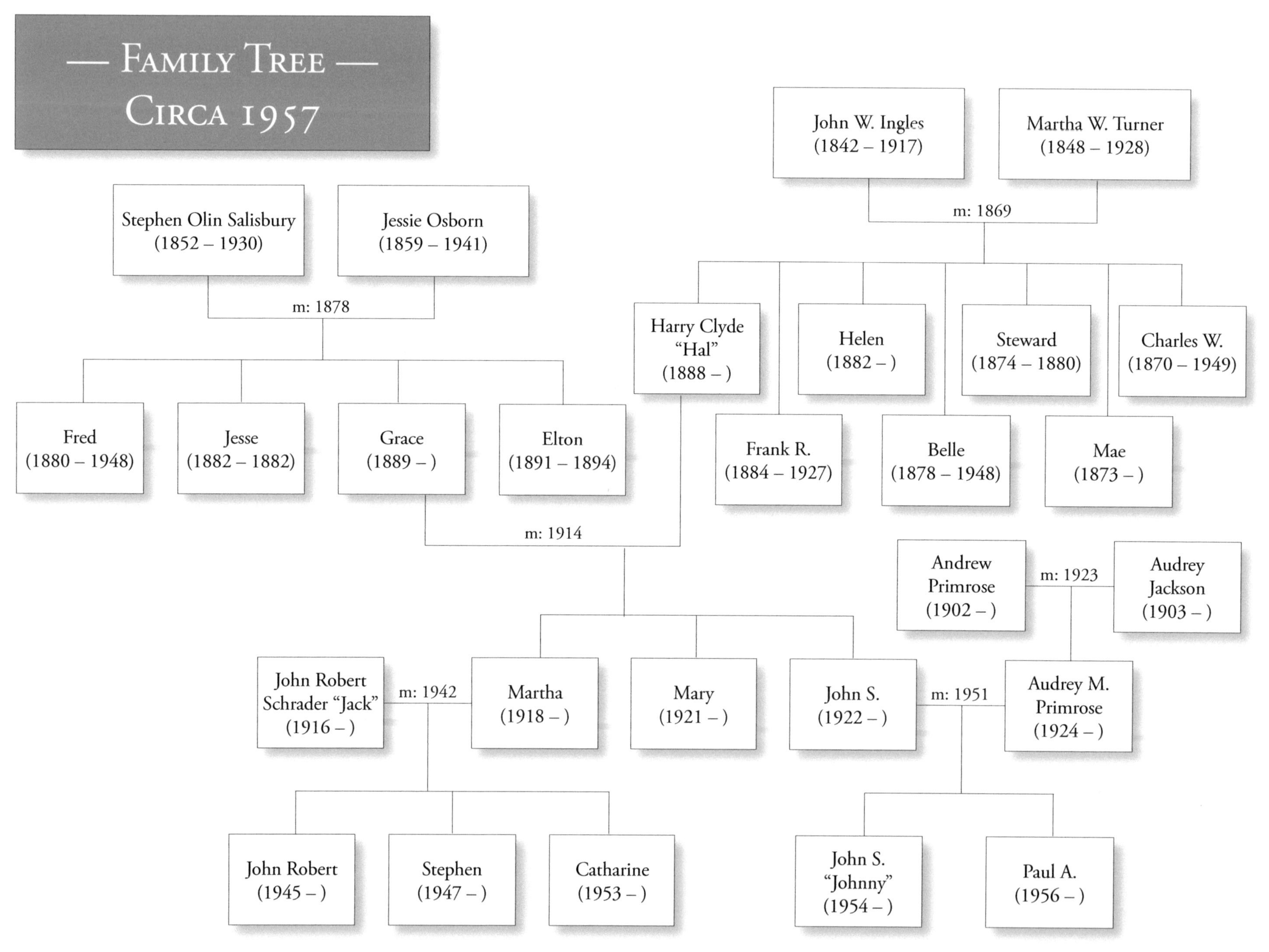

— Family Tree —
Circa 1957

John W. Ingles
(1842 – 1917)

Martha W. Turner
(1848 – 1928)

m: 1869

Stephen Olin Salisbury
(1852 – 1930)

Jessie Osborn
(1859 – 1941)

m: 1878

Harry Clyde "Hal"
(1888 –)

Helen
(1882 –)

Steward
(1874 – 1880)

Charles W.
(1870 – 1949)

Fred
(1880 – 1948)

Jesse
(1882 – 1882)

Grace
(1889 –)

Elton
(1891 – 1894)

Frank R.
(1884 – 1927)

Belle
(1878 – 1948)

Mae
(1873 –)

m: 1914

Andrew Primrose
(1902 –)

m: 1923

Audrey Jackson
(1903 –)

John Robert Schrader "Jack"
(1916 –)

m: 1942

Martha
(1918 –)

Mary
(1921 –)

John S.
(1922 –)

m: 1951

Audrey M. Primrose
(1924 –)

John Robert
(1945 –)

Stephen
(1947 –)

Catharine
(1953 –)

John S. "Johnny"
(1954 –)

Paul A.
(1956 –)

JAPAN

Historical and Cultural Context for the Japan Letters (1956–57)

Post–WWII US occupation of Japan ended in 1952, but the country was still digging out of the devastation caused by the war when Mary arrived. Tokyo was a major world city and growing at an astounding rate. Japanese culture was embracing Western styles and was beginning to export its own influences. Japan joined the UN in 1956. There were, and still are, several US military bases in the country. And where there are military bases, there are ARC workers. It was to one of these bases that Mary was assigned when she traveled to Japan in 1956.

Personal Reflections on the Japan Letters

Mary arrived in Japan on June 11, 1956, after a two-week ocean journey. The trip seemed more pleasant than her voyage to Germany six years earlier. The ship went by way of Hawaii, which she experienced for one day, and many of the passengers disembarked there. The rest of the passage was uneventful.

Mary's assignment in Japan, which she didn't learn until she arrived in the country, was to a small, remote hospital at the very southern tip of the country, in Sasebo. It was, and still is, a naval base. Travel from such a remote location was complicated and impractical. So, while the

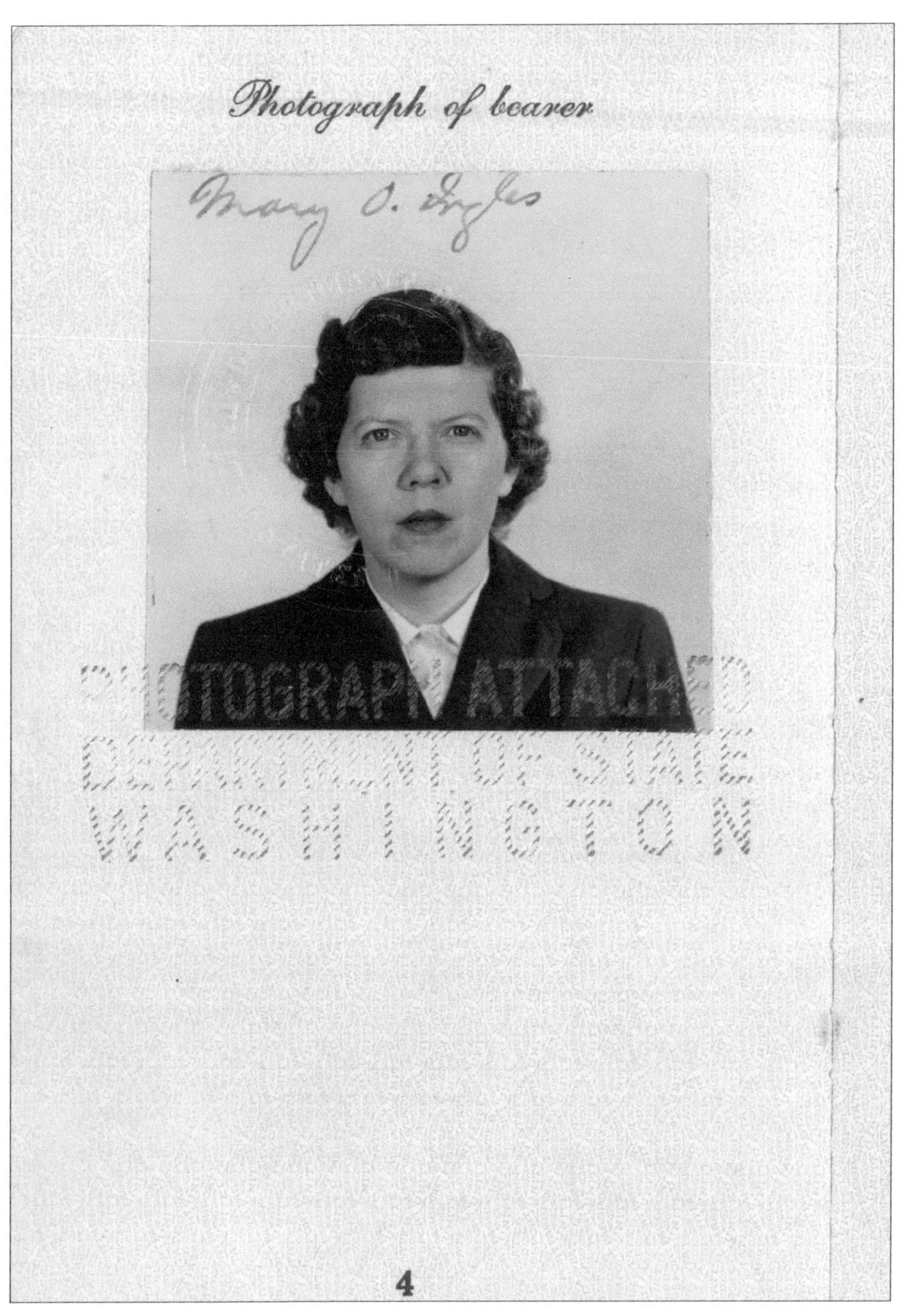

Mary's passport (1956 – 1960)

ARC community seemed to flit in and out of barracks in Germany, in Sasebo they all banded together to make what little social life they could together. The community in which Mary found herself included the men who were stationcd in Sasebo and those who came in and went out when ships were in port. The men were allowed in the women's quarters—a change from the protocols in Germany—and she seemed to socialize more freely with the officers. Mary's letters were full of recounts of ruggedly, yet creatively, put-together social events, including many KT (the army code for cocktail) parties.

Since Western style clothing was not readily available and clothes had to be custom made, Mary now took a new interest in fashion. Much to her surprise, she was asking her mother to send dress pattern books and fashion magazines to her. This newfound interest in style seemed to extend to her living space, as well. She wrote of attempts to make her room appealing and comfortable for social events.

Mary's stay in Sasebo was short—just six months. Few letters survived, and there are large gaps in those that were saved. Unlike the Germany letters, where she rarely talked about the job, we get more insight into the life as an ARC worker in these letters. At the end of her tour, she shared many details about her new assignment in Korea.

FASHION

MARY BEGAN HER JOURNEY to Japan by sailing from San Francisco. She spent several days there before embarking and noted the elegant style of the women in the city by the bay.

***

San Francisco
Hotel Broadmoor
Fri, May 25, 1956

. . . I went to the City of Paris [a famous San Francisco department store] and opened a charge account and recorded my personal business with their personal shopper. I also bought a hat. I felt so underdressed in San Francisco without one. It is a blue straw, coolie type, not overly large and I think surprisingly becoming. I made an appointment at Helena Rubenstein's in the C of P to have my hair done at 10:00 in the morning.

. . . [I] wandered through C of P, I. Magnin and Macy's. The weather is unbelievably beautiful. The gorgeously dressed women are still wearing their mink stoles.

I'm enclosing the fortune that was in my Chinese cookie last night. It is certainly apt and perfect for me, n'est-ce pas?

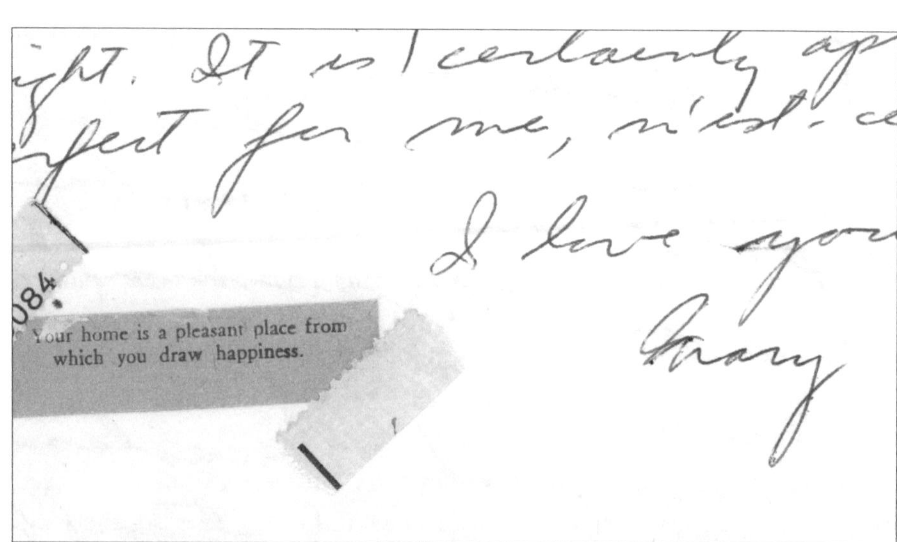

FORTUNE COOKIE MESSAGE FROM SAN FRANCISCO: YOUR HOME IS A PLEASANT PLACE FROM WHICH YOU DRAW HAPPINESS.

* * *

While in San Francisco, Mary arranged to spend a weekend with family friends living in Palo Alto. She wrote of the activities and her wardrobe.

San Francisco
Hotel Broadmoor
Sun night, May 27, 1956

. . . The weather has been perfect ever since I've been here. Sunny and clear, but cool enough for suits. It was a little warmer in Palo Alto, but still cool. I wore my blue shantung with white collar and cuffs to church and thought I looked real nice with my new hat.

* * *

Upon arrival in Japan, Mary received the bad news that her footlockers did not make the journey. This inconvenience forced her to delve into the world of dressmaking.

Tokyo
Tues, Jun 12, 1956

Well, I just had a blow. My foot lockers did not come on the ship with me. Now I probably won't get them for at least two months. The whole thing makes me very mad, because it was all the fault of National Headquarters. When I got to San Francisco, they told me I should have mailed them my luggage checks as soon as I checked the foot lockers. No one told me to do so, so of course I hand carried them across country. The main problem will be shortage of civilian clothes—particularly party clothes and only three blue uniforms. Well, I can't do anything about it, but it is maddening.

* * *

Tokyo
Sat, Jun 16, 1956

I wrote you last on Thursday afternoon. I went with two of the secretaries from the office to the club at the Washington headquarters for a drink. We then went to—of all things—a German restaurant—Alt Heidelberg. We had a good dinner featuring Wiener schnitzel and beer. They then took me to a street lined with little Japanese shops and poked around until about 9:00. I made my first purchase. It is a length of Yakata cotton from which the summer kimonos are made. Very cool. It is Navy blue with a very small design of Japanese characters spotted here and there. It only costs $3 and is enough to make a dress. As much as I dislike the idea, I'm going to have to try having some clothes made. It is hot and will be hotter in Sasebo. I have so few clothes with me and will be without foot lockers for weeks. I am told that I will have to have summer party clothes as life is very social there. I can't do anything about a dressmaker until I get there.

* * *

Mary arrived in Sasebo by late June. Shopping, often with a companion, seemed to be a regular activity for her. Besides shopping for fabric, Mary regularly shopped for items to send to family members back home.

Sasebo
Sun, Jun 24, 1956

. . . I spent the rest of the afternoon and evening writing letters, reading, looking at fashion magazines to get ideas for clothes to be made.

Today has been a beautiful day weather wise, clear and cool and low humidity. I went to church with Ginny and one of the teachers, Bea Hill. After lunch, Bea and I went downtown and spent the afternoon poking in and out of the shops. It was lovely weather and fun. I bought a beautiful piece of raw silk with a colorful print on it to have made into a party dress. It has a white background, and the print is birds and things in greens, reds, blues and golds. Sounds awful but it is effective. I also bought some thin cotton, almost a voile, white background with a flower print. I got a small porcelain electric teapot 2 cup size so that I can heat water for instant coffee in my room. It is white with almost a moss rose design on it. I got two cups and saucers of Noritake china which almost match the teapot. The teapot costs ¥700 ($1.94) and the cups ¥180 each ($0.50). I paid ¥3600 ($10) for the silk material—5 yards—and $4.50 for the cotton (¥1620)—6 yards. I plan to have it made into two pieces with two different sleeveless blouses. I may regret my dressmaking ventures, but I have to try it.

. . . I packed my strapless bra in my footlockers and will need one with the new clothes I plan to have made so I have ordered one from Sears Roebuck to be sent to me airmail.

. . . Incidentally, everyone says to wait until I go to Hong Kong to get linens. I haven't forgotten your interest in place mats. I'm also looking at pearl earrings. I have seen a couple of pairs for you that I liked, but will just look for a while. I am quite taken with the so-called black pearls which are actually a pale blue. Do you think you might like some of those? If you think of anything else you want, let me know. I also haven't forgotten the little ashtrays. The name of that type of china escapes me at the moment.

Tell Audrey that the figurine of the musician that Jane sent her is a Hakata doll. They are made near here, about 3 hours away, and are quite famous and special. I hope to take a trip to see where they make them one weekend soon. There are a myriad of different ones and are especially noted for their wonderful facial expressions.

* * *

An interest in dress patterns developed along with the interest in fabric.

Sasebo
Mon, Jun 25, 1956
. . . See if you can find me some McCall's, Simplicity or Vogue pattern books. They are put out like magazines for summer clothes. I even poured over Sears Roebuck catalog for dress ideas. On second thought, I guess it is silly to have you send them. By the time I get them summer would be over. Still, I might as well have them and even the fall ones as they come out. Even if I didn't get much made, the other girls like to look at them, so see what you can find.

I know you are getting a big kick out of my sudden interest in clothes. I am myself. It is the chief topic of conversation here and I am surprised to find myself being as interested as I am.

* * *

The errant footlockers were found and delivered by the end of June. But even with access to the items in them, Mary was beginning to have items custom made for her. Papasan, the dressmaker, became a regularly mentioned character in Mary's letters.

Sasebo

Wed, Jun 27, 1956

. . . Tomorrow night I'm going to take my first venture with Papasan the dressmaker. I am going to start him on the cotton print which I bought for about $0.70 a yard. I had the maid wash the material today and it didn't seem to fade, so here goes. He only charges about $2.50 to make a dress.

. . . My trial balloon is a skirt and two blouses from the cotton print. Well, we'll see.

* * *

Sasebo

Thurs, Jul 5, 1956

. . . We are going to Papasan's for fittings on the dresses we are having made. Yesterday I brought another lovely piece of cotton print, yellow background with blue and brown figures. I am going to have a skirt made from it, I think. I had seen the piece when I was looking for curtain material but it was too expensive for curtains. It is actually only about $0.90 a yard, but I didn't want to spend $15 for curtains.

* * *

Sasebo

Sat, Jul 7, 1956

Yesterday I went to Papasan's in the evening and had a fitting for my dress. I'm not too encouraged, but I'll be able to tell better when I go back next Wednesday.

* * *

Sasebo

Mon, Jul 9, 1956

. . . The piece of material enclosed is the print of my curtains and bedspread. They brought them out this evening and they're going to look really nice. The flounce on the bedspread is a light blue, as near the blue in the print as I could get. In typical Japanese fashion, they always manage something peculiar. Since the material was cheap, I asked them to wash it before they cut it. They did all right, and then made it up and brought it back without ironing it. I'll have the maid iron them tomorrow, but that sure seemed a stupid way to do something. I paid ¥1700 to have them made, just under $5, so the whole job costs about $13. I'm thinking about getting enough of the blue for a valance across the top of the windows. I'll see how the curtains look after I get them up. There is enough print left for a dresser scarf. I think I can get the maid to hem that up for me. When I get my bedroom all fixed up, I'll find someone with a flash attachment on a camera to take some pictures of the room for you.

* * *

Sasebo

Thurs, Jul 12, 1956

. . . I'm also including a piece of material from the dress Papasan made for me. He made a skirt and two blouses, one with sleeves and one without. I got them yesterday and I'm fairly pleased with the results. The sleeveless blouse fits quite well and the skirt is fine. The other blouse looks pretty, but he made it too tight under the arms. He tried to rectify it, but he didn't help much. He just cut it too short from the top of the shoulder to the underarm. I can wear it, of course, but I don't like clothes that fit up too tight under my arms. The workmanship on the clothes is beautiful, with much attention to detail. The one blouse has covered buttons and he covered them so that each one has the same little design from the material on it. He only charged me ¥1200 ($3.34) for the whole job.

* * *

Sasebo

Sun, Jul 15, 1956

. . . After that, I took material for three dresses to Papasan. I go back Wednesday for the fittings. I decided that I had better get the summer material made-up if I was going to get any wear out of it this summer.

* * *

Sasebo

Wed, Jul 18, 1956

. . . I've just returned from Papasan's where I had three dresses fitted. I am to go back again Saturday. When I get them all, I'll have Ginny take pictures of me in them and send them to you. I think you'll be pleased to see that I am getting somewhat away from the strictly tailored things.

* * *

Sasebo

Fri, Jul 20, 1956

. . . Yesterday, I received the third fashion magazine. It has a picture in it of one of the dresses I am having made. I'll cut it out and send it to you when I get the material scraps back from Papasan. I go to him again tomorrow.

* * *

Sasebo

Mon, Jul 24, 1956

I'm enclosing a sample of material and a picture of the dress I had made from it. I like it very much. The other two I picked up today were not quite so successful. I'll also enclose samples, but I don't have a picture of the blue one. It is something like this [drawing] with a little bolero jacket like so [drawing]. I am going to have to take it back for some this-ing and that-ing. Please send back the sample of the yellow print. It is the only scrap I have and I'm going to have them cover a new belt buckle as the one they did is broken. It will hold out a couple of weeks, I think.

* * *

THE WORK AND THE LIFE

MARY WAS NOT FOCUSED on travel in Japan like she was in Germany. She spent more time in Sasebo and socialized with the men and women posted there, not just other ARC workers. Her career with Red Cross was progressing, and her duties began to shift. She started her assignment in Tokyo, where she received news of her new posting.

Tokyo

Mon, Jun 11, 1956

I will start this now and probably finish it later this evening. I found six letters from you and Daddy and the crossword puzzles when I arrived which was more than wonderful. I got another one today written 5 June, which gave the reports on the tests. It is so wonderful to be in touch. I'll go back over the letters when I have time and really answer them. Right now I'll bring you up to date on me.

First of all, I am being assigned to Sasebo which is on the island of Kyushu just about as far away from Tokyo as you can get and still be in Japan—something like a 30 hour train ride. I'll be in Tokyo the rest of this week and maybe over the weekend as I have to wait for travel orders.

The Sasebo assignment is everything I didn't want— Navy and one worker station (not even a secretary), very small hospital, about 70 patients. People tell me that it has its compensations, such as good living accommodations, etc. Well, I am disappointed, but I am trying to keep an optimistic outlook. I will find out more about it in the next couple of days. The address will be:

American Red Cross
Station Hospital
U.S. Fleet Activities
Box 20, Navy 3912
c/o FPO San Francisco, Calif.

You'd better start using this address right away. They did say I might not be there more than three to six months.

* * *

Tokyo
Tues, Jun 12, 1956

. . . I have found out a little more about Sasebo. The hospital is in a permanent building, and we are billeted in BOQ with schoolteachers. Apparently, the Officers Club is also in the same building. Due to isolation, you apparently find your social life and recreation within your own local group. Sasebo is a couple of hours from Nagasaki. The

hospital is only running about 40 patients. I will, of course, be doing recreation as well as everything else. The worker there has just trained a new group of 17 Gray Ladies. There is a man field director at Sasebo and his secretary, who lives where I will and the three of us will be the entire ARC staff. Everyone speaks highly of the field director—Bob Berg.

* * *

Tokyo
Wed, Jun 13, 1956

. . . I spent all day talking to various people at headquarters, reading reports, etcetera. I'm actually all through there now. My orders are in the mill, and I'll get them Friday and leave Monday morning for Sasebo, arriving Tuesday evening. The girl I am replacing will be with me until the following Monday.

Tomorrow I'm going to the Tokyo Army Hospital to see the place and have lunch with Helen Husted. Last night, incidentally, I saw Anne Duga who was one of the Belvoir nurses, at the Dai Iki. She is at Tokyo Army Hospital, and she invited me to come to a party out there Friday night. I believe there are some other army people out there that I'll know, so I'll have to check into that.

Friday I'm going down to Yokosuka for the day. That is the big Navy hospital over here and the one to which we will be sending our patients. I want to get a feel of the place and meet the ARC staff as I'll be working with them. It is an hour from here by train. I thought it would be a good idea to take my first train ride as a short haul before starting the long jaunt to Sasebo. The FDA [field director, Asia] at Yokosuka is Cecily O'Connor whom I knew slightly over in Europe.

* * *

After approximately a week in Tokyo, Mary traveled to Sasebo. Glendy Chapin occupied the position Mary would assume, and they had a week together so Mary could learn her new responsibilities.

Sasebo

Sun, Jun 24, 1956

. . . I don't believe I have written you since Thursday. Glendy, Ginny (FO [Field Office] Secy) and I had dinner with the nurses. They live in three Quonset huts near the hospital. They have a kitchen and do most of their own cooking. They fixed a real nice dinner and served it in the yard. There are 7 nurses altogether, the chief nurse and the surgical nurse are in their 40s and the others are in their 20s. One of them is married, and since her husband's ship is based here, they live in town somewhere. I like the chief nurse Mary Jane Brown a lot. The others seemed nice enough, but they are so much younger mostly.

Friday I was in the office alone most of the day as Glendy was coping with her packers. The Gray Ladies gave a farewell luncheon for her at the club to which I was invited, of course. I worked Friday night as a hillbilly band from one of the ships was scheduled to entertain the patients.

. . . While we were downtown today, we took a lot of pictures of the really vulgar signs they have in front of the various dives. This is very much a port town at its worst. The local populace lies in wait for the American sailors, and the place has the highest VD rate of any place in Japan. Don't let all of that alarm you. I just mention it as a prologue to the pictures when I get them developed and send them home.

* * *

Sasebo

Mon, Jun 25, 1956

. . . One thing I haven't told you about this assignment is the real reason I think they sent me here. The girl who was here last fall was apparently a very unstable person. Being on her own was just too much and she went hog wild in many directions. She ended up with a complete mental breakdown and had to be sent home. Consequently, it is very important that ARC have a very stable person here to counteract the bad impression left from that. Glendy Chapin has done a marvelous job in pulling the place together and in reestablishing a place of respect for Red Cross here. I feel that one reason I was sent here is that they know I can manage on my own, will maintain a high level of personal and professional performance, and will do credit to the organization. I'm not patting myself on the back too hard, but I know I can do all those things, so in that sense it is a real compliment that they sent me here.

There was a sizable American community here, almost 100% Navy. Everyone has been extremely candid and have gone out of their way to be nice. At this point I really feel that the job will not be too demanding. The Gray Ladies are a wonderful group, well trained and capable. They want and can take a lot of responsibility and I'm going to let them. My living is comfortable, and I really think I'll enjoy it here for a few months, so rest easy in your mind about me.

. . . Glendy is still here. She finally got her orders today but can't get a reservation on a train until Wednesday. I am glad to have another day or so with her as I can use some help in learning some recreation. I have to learn a little about crafts too—me of all people!

* * *

Sasebo

Wed, Jun 27, 1956

. . . Today I worked all day. I spent most of my time on recreation planning. I am having to dig around in the files, teach myself games, and really work at it. Well, at least it's a change of pace and form. Glendy left on the 4:30 train and six of us went down to see her off. Two of the Gray Ladies, two of the teachers, Ginny and I. Seeing people off at the train station seems to be an old Sasebo custom. They have a phonograph playing "Auld Lang Syne" even. There are only two trains a day, so they are an event I guess.

* * *

Sasebo

Thurs, Jun 28, 1956

. . . As I have written you so, Sasebo is certainly not the end of the world. There used to be a lot of Army here, but they have all pulled out. The only Army function left is a petroleum depot and there are about 8 Army officers there. The Navy has taken over everything. The hospital used to be an Army one, but is now Navy. This is all to amplify the information Edith O'Connell gave you, which was a bit out of date.

I've heard people talk of Beppu. It is quite a distance, about 8 hours by train I think, so it isn't any place I can go on a weekend—would need at least three or four days to make it worthwhile. One weekend soon I will go to Fukuoka—about 3 hours away and another to Nagasaki, also about 3 hours in the other direction. At this point I have travelled enough for a while. I'll save the short trip until I begin to feel the need to get away from Sasebo.

Mary doing field work in Japan

I got my first paycheck today. They stopped the income tax deduction 1 June, so my check was $201.86. That plus my $90 maintenance will give me more than enough money. Saturday I am going to open a checking account at the Bank of America, which is the military banking facility here. What I can save here will go toward a trip to Hong Kong next spring.

* * *

Mary rarely wrote about individual cases. However, she did mention one case that made her feel like she was making a real contribution.

Sasebo

Fri, Jul 20, 1956

. . . I have finally gotten a patient in the hospital that I can do a little casework with. He is a Chief Boatswain's Mate who got a sliver of metal in his eye. The future of his eyesight is in doubt. I have been visiting him for a while every day and I really feel that I am doing him some good. I provide someone for him to talk to about his apprehensions etc. Since in this job so much of my time and energy goes into recreation, it helps me to once in a while feel that I can help someone and use the training I have.

* * *

SOCIALIZING

IN GERMANY, MARY'S SOCIAL life was primarily driven by who was available to travel with her. She did some entertaining in her lodgings, particularly around the holidays, but those events were primarily limited to other ARC women. In Japan, socializing was much more focused on dinners and drinks and seeing local sites, either in Tokyo or around Sasebo, and often times men were included.

Although Mary commented that she didn't really care for Tokyo, while there, she took advantage of several unique experiences.

* * *

Tokyo

Tues, Jun 12, 1956

My evening with Florence was very nice. We had a couple of drinks and a nice dinner at Dai Iti Hotel, where she lives. I have always been very fond of Florence. She is a warm, sweet person in her late 40s, smart as a whip. I am sorry that Sasebo is not one of the hospitals which she supervises. We were joined at dinner by Helen Husted, who has just come from Valley Forge and is the field director at Tokyo Army Hospital. I had known her slightly in the States. During the evening I discovered she is a native of White Plains and a Smith graduate—class of 27.

* * *

Tokyo

Thurs, Jun 14, 1956

I'm out at the headquarters office with a little time to kill, so will put a few lines on paper.

Julie and John really showed me a wonderful evening last night. They picked me up about 6:45 and we went to the Dai Iki for drinks. We were joined by a Col Olmquist, a friend of theirs, over here on a trip. Then we went to a Japanese restaurant. We parked our shoes out at the door and sat on cushions on the floor. We had sukiyaki, which

I thought was very good. We ate with chopsticks and had sake—rice wine which is served hot. The sukiyaki is cooked at the table and the girl kneels right there and keeps serving it. It is beef, onions, mushroom, bamboo shoots, bean sprouts, bean curd, chrysanthemum leaves, etc. They had a floor show of typical Japanese dancing and singing. They also got some of the Americans up on the stage to dance with them. Special sort of folk dances that everyone seems to know.

When we left there, we went to a tea house for coffee. That place really defies description. It was circular, five stories high. In the basement at the bottom of the central well was a fishpond with carp swimming in it. Around was an aviary with tropical birds. The ceiling at the top was stained glass. Each floor has tables on sort of balconies around the center well, with a band on the second balcony which plays continuously. The walls throughout are upholstered in purple satin. As you go up the stairs there are cabinets in the walls with collections of European glass, china, snuff boxes, etc. Well, I just can't give you a picture in words.

When we left there, we went back to Dai Iki for a liqueur, and I got home at after 11:00.

Wasn't that a wonderful thing for them to do for me? I liked John so much. Julie was darling and such fun as always. I thought she looked very well. She said she had gained 20 pounds and seemed happy about it. They are moving to Camp Zama in two weeks, so I'm so glad I got here while they were still in Tokyo.

* * *

Tokyo
Sat, Jun 16, 1956
Friday morning I took off for Yokosuka on the 8:45 train. It is quite an experience to try to get around when you can't read a sign or understand a word. However, I had no trouble on the train. I befriended, or was befriended by, two American kids, about 10 and 12. They were going to Yokosuka to swim. They told me when to get off the train and where to catch the bus to the base. They were cute as bugs. When I got off the bus at the gate, the ARC field director happened by in his Jeep and drove me up to the hospital. The girls at the hospital were most candid and very helpful and I had a nice day. I picked up my orders and got back to Tokyo about 5:00. Barbara Hart—ARC Secretary—and I went to the Imperial Hotel for dinner and then did a little window shopping on the Ginza. The Imperial has been turned back to the Japanese, but it is still very much frequented by American tourists. We had a nice steak dinner, wonderful service.

Sun, Jun 18, 1956
Continued—Saturday 8:00 AM, Elise called and said she would be in for the afternoon. It was a hot day, but sunny and clear. In the morning I took my orders out to get my transportation set up. I leave at 10:30 Monday morning. I have a reserved seat in the coach for the daytime and a lower berth for night. I have to be at the station ½ hour ahead to check my luggage there. I arrive in Sasebo at 1:00 PM Tuesday. It is going to be quite a trip.

I met Elise at noon and we went to the Imperial and bought tickets for an afternoon city sightseeing tour. Since it left from the Imperial, we decided to have lunch there. The tour was pretty good. It is run by a Japanese Travel Bureau for foreigners and had an English speaking guide.

It took nearly four hours so we came back pretty exhausted.

We showered and had a drink sent up and then went to a Japanese garden restaurant featuring hundreds of fireflies. Being Saturday night, the place was mobbed with Japanese and we felt pretty out of place. The dinner was poor. We didn't know what to order, so had broiled chicken, small and tough.

* * *

Once Mary arrived in Sasebo, she began decorating her room so she could entertain people there.

Sasebo

Wed, Jun 27, 1956

After Glendy left, I took some of the furniture she had in her room. A chair, two end tables and the tatami mat for the floor (rice straw mat). So my room begins to look a little less bare. My next project will be to get some curtains and a bedspread.

* * *

Sasebo

Thurs, Jun 28, 1956

Today at the ship's store, I bought 4 zabutons. They're large, square, flat cushions [upon] which the Japanese sit on the floor. We do a lot of floor sitting in our rooms here, as none of us have much furniture. So now I am prepared to extend my hospitality. They were only $0.95 apiece.

* * *

Having been in Sasebo for just over a week, Mary wrote of a group outing that was planned.

Sasebo

Sat, Jun 30, 1956

Weather permitting, tomorrow a whole bunch of us are planning to take the special services boat out to what is called the 99 Islands for the day. I'm told the islands are just outside the harbor and there is good swimming. The boat leaves at 11:00 and we are taking a picnic lunch. If it rains, we will have our picnic in the game room here at the club. I don't know for sure who all is going, but the crowd includes five of the nurses, one of the doctors, four officers from one of the ships, Ginny Conrad and me. I hope the weather is good as it should be fun. We are going to the commissary this afternoon to buy the food.

* * *

Sasebo

Sun, Jul 1, 1956

It looks like our excursion plans for today are out the window. It isn't raining, but it is an overcast, muggy day. We were all set to go anyway, but they cancelled the boat because not enough people had signed up. The plan now is to cart our food over to the nurses' quarters and picnic in their yard.

. . . Yesterday afternoon Jenny and I went downtown and I got a little coffee pot fixed for ¥30, less than $0.10. I shopped and finally found some material for drapes and bedspreads. It is a beige background with blue, red and yellow print and I got plain blue for the flounce on the bedspread. It was ¥140 a yard, about $0.35. On Monday, a man from one of the ships is coming to measure for them. Ginny helped me figure out how much to buy. My windows are three together. I'm just having side drapes made and have gotten three bamboo screens which roll up and down to put across the middle. So you see I'm working on getting my room a bit livable. I have two bare bulbs hanging from the ceiling and we'll pick up some Japanese shades to cover them. I'm not going hog wild on Japanese decor, but the rooms are Japanese in style so you have to get things in keeping. I'll send you samples of the material when I get the leftovers back.

* * *

Sasebo

Mon, Jul 2, 1956

. . . Our picnic got rained out, but we had it anyway in my room. We ended up with nine people. It was really fun. We sat on the floor and ate sandwiches and had drinks. We played cards, dice, and various parlor games, and the party lasted from 1:00 PM until midnight. It is permissible for us to have men come to this floor, which might have its drawbacks, but it was just good, clean fun.

The people came out this evening to measure for my bedspread and curtains. The girl from the desk downstairs came up to interpret and Ginny drew a sketch. I'm not at all sure that they understood, but it will be interesting to see what comes out of it.

* * *

In a long letter written on the Fourth of July, Mary referenced several different types of social events. The first was bingo, which was a regular weekly event probably for patients and staff. In the second paragraph, she mentioned a ward party, which she would be running. One of the main duties for the ARC was to provide recreational events and activities for the patients in the hospital. Planning and executing these events were fundamental parts of Mary's job. The Welcome Coffee at the Base CO's home would be an event designed for anyone working at the naval base in Sasebo. And finally, the event planned by Mary's new acquaintance, Gay, was a private event. Mary commented on how different it was for her to have so many social engagements and alluded to the fact that she was socializing with men more than in the past.

* * *

Sasebo

Wed, Jul 4, 1956

Happy 4th of July.

Guess what? I won at Bingo last night again, not once, but twice. On the second win, however, three other people also won, and on the drawing, I lost out. On my real win, I got a pair of binoculars. I had hoped to get a radio, but the only one had been won earlier. In a way it is too bad that I won because now I'll have to go on playing each week. Since you have to buy your cards ($1.00), if you play regularly, you actually end up paying for whatever you win. The binoculars are small ones, 8 by 30, but are in a nice pig skin case. I wouldn't want a big heavy pair anyway. I really didn't know what I'll do with them, but they will come in handy if we ever take a boat trip, for sightseeing, etc.

Yesterday was another miserable day, pouring rain all through it. This morning it was not raining, and the sun was even trying to get through. It was good to see a spot or two of blue sky when I woke up. I am taking the morning off today but will go to work this afternoon and tonight. I've planned my first real ward party for tonight, so I guess I'll see what a good recreation worker I am.

I went to the Welcome Coffee yesterday AM. It was held at the Base CO's house. You would have liked to see those quarters. They have just been completely renovated and rumor hath it that the job cost $10,000. There is a tremendous living room and the whole downstairs is painted a lovely shade of blue with white woodwork. At the window she has printed pongee draw curtain—the print of leaves (small) of blue and red and gold. That stuff costs $1.50 a yard, and I can't imagine how many yards there are in that house. I imagine that is actually not too expensive for silk pongee, is it? Anyway, the house was beautiful.

I've been seeing a lot of a real cute girl named Gay Murphy. She was formerly an airline hostess. She came out to Tokyo just a month ago and married her Navy husband. In typical Navy fashion, they had a week together and then his ship went out for a month. She's been living temporarily at the BOQ, but moved into a private rental yesterday. She is a lot of fun and is going to come up to the hospital to help me with my party tonight. Through her, Ginny and I have met a group of officers from one of the minesweepers. They are the ones we had to our picnic on Sunday, played bingo with last night, etc. Friday Gay is having them and us to her house for a housewarming. Their ship goes out next week. That seems to be the pattern here. You make friends with groups from various ships operating in and out of here and play with whichever group is in the port. Most of the men are married and quite young. But it is all good clean fun. It is certainly quite [a] different life from any I have known. But I am game to give it a try.

Saturday Gay, Jenny, Joyce Blue (a Navy wife who came over on the ship with me and who has a car) and I may drive to Arita. It is about an hour's drive away and this is where Noritake china is made. The girls are interested in china, and I will go just for the ride.

Well, I guess you can see that I'm having a pretty good time thus far. The atmosphere here is relaxed and informal, people friendly. Living at the club has its advantages as you don't have to go out for meals in the bad weather. Can even have room service if you want it.

* * *

A few days later, Mary wrote of more social events.

Sasebo
Sat, Jul 7, 1956

. . . Nine of us converged on Gay Murphy for her housewarming dinner. She had done a wonderful job considering she had no ice box and only two primitive gas burners for a stove. She had filled the bathtub with ice and had beer and cokes in there with the salad, deviled eggs and watermelon resting on the ice. She had made spaghetti for the main course. She didn't have enough dishes, so she served the spaghetti on everything from solid plates to a large platter. I drank my coffee from a cream pitcher. It was all fun and I could only admire how well she did with nothing to work with.

A couple of the men brought Ginny and me home and came up for a drink. After I finally got to bed, I spent several hours battling mosquitoes and getting well chewed on in the process. I finally managed to kill two and that seemed to be the end of the foray. It was nearly 5:00 AM before I got to sleep. Fortunately, I didn't have to get up early, so I slept until 10:30. I had brunch around 11:30 and then had my hair done.

Today is a clear sunny day, but hot. This afternoon, Ginny and I decided to take a taxi up to the top of the mountains to see the views from there of the town and the harbour, etc. The road up is terrible, narrow, winding, full of potholes. About halfway up, the taxi broke down. We paid them off and started to walk up. We had only gone a little way when the same taxi caught up with us. We went on a little further and the taxi broke down again. Just then the two men who managed the local branch of the Bank of America (Americans) came along. They took us on up to the top, and we spent about an hour taking pictures and exercising my new binoculars. We had a sandwich and a drink when we got back, so now I am writing you. I have no plans for the evening other than to shower, have dinner and go to bed early. I don't have any plans for tomorrow either, although I think I'll try to find the little church again. If it is a nice day, we might try to take the boat trip to the islands. Which we couldn't take last week.

Yesterday I picked up a couple of Japanese paper lanterns to hide the bare bulbs hanging out of my ceiling. They look real nice. I also bought the other day, some cotton square scarves that the Japanese use to wrap around their bundles. These are very colorful with birds and flowers etcetera, and I've put them on the wall for color and interest.

I won't start another page now since I can't mail this, but since I can't mail this till Monday, I'll leave it open.

Sunday

Well, I have had another lovely day to report. Last evening we had dinner about eight and stayed for the floor show, which was pretty good for out here. They announced during the evening that the boat trip would take place today. For $1.50 we would be served lunch and any drinks we wanted, so we got organized right away to go. Gay, Ginny, one of the teachers, me and our three friends off the *Firm*, which is the Minesweeper.

We left at 11:00 and there were 35 people altogether.

We went out on an LCU [landing craft utility], which is a small landing craft. We traveled for about an hour and then they ran the boat up on a sandy beach. On the way out, the club served a wonderful buffet. Hot dogs, hamburgers, fried chicken and baked beans, potato salad and ice cream. They had all kinds of drinks. Four of the waiters from the club were along to serve. We stayed at the beach for about 3 hours. Most people went swimming, but you know, I'm never very interested in that. We explored the island, played baseball and just lolled around. It was a gorgeous, sunny day. The harbor is really beautiful. The scenery here is almost tropical. I put my new binoculars to good use and also took a roll of film.

This evening after showers and changes of clothes we all had dinner on the patio at the club. Now some of them have gone off to the movies and I am here to write to you and get to bed. Since the weather turned nice the club serves dinner and the band plays every night on the patio, which is directly under my window. That is not a distinct advantage, as it complicates sleeping. Last night, being Saturday, the band played until 2:00 AM, which is why I just couldn't get up for church this morning. Tonight, they'll stop at 11, thank goodness.

Well, as you can see, I'm leading a most unusual life for me. I'm really enjoying it for a change. I gather that these spells of gaiety come and go depending on whether you know anyone on the ships which are in the port. I could wish for a little more stimulating female companionship as Ginny, with whom I am thrown constantly, is a bit of a bore. She's hard of hearing—wears hearing aids. Looks like I'm having a run of being associated with people with that handicap. At least she is always ready to do things, and it is good for me to have someone pushing me to get out a bit. The three teachers are awfully nice, but they are extremely close to one another and rather a closed corporation. Well, I'm definitely going to stop now and climb into bed with my book.

* * *

On some occasions, Mary combined business with pleasure, as seemed to be the case with her field trip to the Pearl Farm.

Sasebo

Thurs, Jul 12, 1956

. . . Tuesday, I arranged a trip to the Pearl Farm for some of the patients. It was planned that one of the Gray Ladies would go as official chaperone. At the last minute, one of the patients dropped out, so I went along in his place. The Pearl Farm is only about 20 minutes' drive from Sasebo. The Gray Lady had called ahead that we were coming, so they had a demonstration set up for us. They showed us all the kinds of pearls, and they gave a demonstration on how they culture pearls. I found it very interesting. The old man there spoke quite good English. He said that his company is the second largest in Japan, next to Mikimoto. I am also enclosing a brochure he gave me. The patients seemed very interested too. We were planning to take small groups of patients—the vehicle at our disposal can only carry seven, including the driver—on short trips to points of interest around here each week.

Tuesday was a long day as I had to go to work in the morning to get the trip cleared and organized and go back in the evening because I had some entertainment scheduled. Incidentally, the entertainment was a little combo of sailors from one of the ships, and they were wonderful. The boy who played the piano was as good as Eddie Duchin. Really terrific. I got home from the hospital about 8:30

and took a fast shower and changed. One of the men who works in the bank was having a birthday party for himself and had invited Ginny and me. It was quite a party and only six people and I left while we were on the 6th bottle of champagne. A few diehards ended up in a nightclub downtown, but I couldn't take all that on all workday night.

Last night I went to bingo but had no luck. One man at our table won $25 and another a free round of drinks for the table, but that was the extent of it.

* * *

On several occasions, Mary wrote about going to floorshows. I assume these are held at and coordinated by the officers' club. Floorshows were a common form of entertainment in the 1950s. They were typically a collection of musical, dance, and comedy acts performed in restaurants or nightclubs.

Sasebo

Sun, Jul 15, 1956

. . . Last evening, Ginny and I had a late dinner on the patio and stayed for the floor show at 10:00. It is now a little after 9:00 AM. I have had some coffee and in a little while I will get dressed and go to church at the Navy Chapel at 11.

We haven't seen our friends from the *Firm* since Wednesday. I guess they are finding their amusement elsewhere. The club has just come out with a ruling that men must wear coats and ties after 6:00 PM. Formerly, they could wear sports shirts. In this heat the result has been to drive the men away from the club. The order is reputed to be the Admiral's idea, but then the higher ups always get the blame. However, I think it is a stupid move in a tropical country.

The boat trip which we enjoyed so much last Sunday was

scheduled for Saturday this week and was for officers and their families. I'm sure it was mobbed with kids. Next week it will be on Sunday for adults only, so we may go then.

Gay Murphy's husband is in port, so we haven't seen much of her this week. Her husband Tom is such a nice person.

Every Sunday night at the club they have an early show floor show for the children. Then they all get up with their mothers and daddies and dance the Bunny Hop and the Mexican Hat dance. It's really cute.

* * *

A wide range of social activities filled Mary's days and letters through the month of July.

Sasebo

Mon, Jul 16, 1956

. . . Yesterday I went to church with Clint Hanks. He is an Army Capt in the Transportation Corps, one of the very few Army people here. His family have gone back to the States and he is going in September. In the meantime, he lives here at the BOQ and sort of squires all the girls. He takes me to work almost every morning, which is wonderful in this heat. After church, he, Ginny and I went to the club on the base for lunch. It is air conditioned and is commonly referred to as the Waterfront Saloon. It is really a very nice club. It used to be a Navy club when this one was the Army Club. But now they are both under the same management.

Mr. and Mrs. Johnston invited the three of us and one of the teachers to their house for sukiyaki dinner. He is an Army Warrant Officer and they are older—have five grandchildren. They had a Japanese girl to cook the dinner and

we had a nice evening.

Next Saturday they are having a shipwreck party at the club and we are all up to our ears and planning costumes. I have a dilly if only I have the nerve to wear it. I bought a huge red and white cotton beach hat downtown. Ginny has loaned me a red nylon taffeta half-slip—many ruffles. I will wear a strapless bra and pull the half slip up under my arms. It has elastic at the top. Then I'll wear the red nylon panties that Lois gave me for a going away present. The slip comes almost halfway to my knees. Gay and Tom Murphy are having a gang up for cocktails first. I think we'll all need a little liquid courage to put on our costumes.

Did you ever know me to have such a social life? One nice thing is that living right here, we feel free to go down to the parties without a date. There are enough of the men here at the BOQ whom we know so that we never end up just a bunch of girls.

* * *

Sasebo

Fri, Jul 20, 1956

. . . Wednesday night I went to Bingo but had no luck. Last night, Ginny and I went down to the base club for the monthly Hail and Farewell. Each departee is given a wooden honey bucket with an engraved label on it and a bottle of champagne. They pour the champagne in the bucket and then take it around for each person to have a sip out of preceded by a kiss. It makes for a gay party. A honey bucket is shaped like this [drawing] and the kissing is done under the handle, if you get the idea. We came back up here for a buffet supper.

. . . In the evening is the Shipwreck Party. Gay told me today that she has invited 30 people to her place for KTs first, so it should be quite a party. I hope they will have a photographer at the party so I can send you pictures of the costumes.

Sasebo

Tues, Jul 24, 1956

. . . At six, we went to Gay's for KT's. Then back and into costume and down to the party. The party really went kind of flat. Gay was furious because she had invited a lot of men from various ships. They all came to her house for the free drinks but then took off and didn't come to the party at the club. So we ended up with barely enough men to go around. Men have the most impossible manners when they don't have their wives around to keep them in line.

* * *

Sasebo

Wed, Jul 25, 1956

. . . [Social] Life has slacked off a bit the last couple days, which is just as well. Monday night I was getting ready for bed when some of the "boys" showed up and started a party across the hall. We drank screwdrivers (vodka and orange juice) and I really learned a lesson. I was quite sick all night. No vomiting, but head spinning and stomach churning. I should have known better, but you have to try everything once. From here on out, I'll stick to Bourbon.

* * *

Sasebo

Sun, Jul 29, 1956

. . . Friday, Ginny and I went on a moonlight boat trip sponsored by the club. About 100 people went. We left the club by buses at 6:00 and were driven to camp Ainora, about 20 minutes. It is now a Japanese army camp, but during the Korean conflict, it was the staging area for troops going to and from Korea. You know, it gave me a kind of creepy feeling to see all those Japanese soldiers. It was too close to all the movies I have seen of World War II.

At Camp Ainora we boarded the LCU. They had brought a band from the club, had a bar set up, etc. We travelled about an hour to an island where there was sort of a little park and hotel, very picturesque. A crew had gone out ahead and had tables, buffet and bar set up. The band played and some people went swimming. They served a wonderful buffet, barbecued steaks, fried chicken, corn on the cob, salad and watermelon. At about 10:30 we started back, coming around and up the harbor. The trip back took three hours. There was nearly a full moon and a cool breeze and it was lovely. The only problem was that it was really too long, and everybody was so sleepy. We finally got back home about 2:00. I had another one of my mosquito battling sieges. I finally ended up sleeping on cushions on the floor, directly under the ceiling fan so that I could stand to have a sheet over me and keep the mosquitoes off.

I didn't get up until nearly noon on Saturday. After brunch, I went to the Ship Store and did some shopping for things I need at work. . . . When I came back, I stopped in the bar for a sandwich and lemonade. A woman I know introduced me to two officers off the cruiser Los Angeles, which is in port for a few days. After chatting with them for about an hour, they invited me to have dinner with them. I got Ginny to make a fourth and we had a really pleasant evening on the patio.

So now it is Sunday morning. In a little while, Ginny and I are going down to the Waterfront Saloon to meet Gay and Tom for brunch after they get out of church. Beyond that, I have no plans for the day.

* * *

In early August, Mary took a weekend trip to Unzen, an area known for its active volcano and multiple hot springs. It is renowned for great natural beauty, although Mary made little reference to the scenery.

Sasebo

Mon, Aug 6, 1956

I'm afraid that there will have been a little gap between letters by the time you get this one. As you know, I was away over the weekend, so this is the first chance I've had to write.

The weekend was OK, but was far from an unqualified success. We started out at 7:55 by train Saturday morning. We got off at a place called Isahaya and got on a bus for a two hour ride. The trip up wasn't too bad. The bus was not overcrowded and the scenery was very pretty at spots. The roads, of course, are unpaved and terribly rough. The drivers deserve medals for maneuvering those big buses around. We drove along the sea part of the way and later up a real mountain road. We finally arrived at Unzen at 11:30. The buses have girl conductors who apparently point out points of interest (in Japanese, of course, so lost on us) and sing to you.

The hotel was sort of old fashioned, but our room was lovely. Japanese style with Japanese bathroom like the one in the picture in the folder I'll enclose. As soon as we got to our room they brought us glasses of iced tea. We had

brought sandwiches with us, so we ate lunch in our room. I think, I wrote that Clint Hank went with us. He is an Army Captain in the Transportation Corps. He had a western style room in another part of the hotel.

After lunch, we all stretched out on the floor for a nap. Then we took hot baths. The place is noted for its hot Sulphur Springs. The hotel had a community hot sulphur bath house, but Ginny and I used our private one which was hot, but no sulfur. The tub is 2 levels, stone lined, sunk into the floor. You wash before you get in and then get in a big tank and soak. The water is not changed between customers. The toilet is in a separate cubbyhole and was queer, but usable.

Ginny had a headache and didn't feel so hot, so we left her, and Clint and I walked around the town. The Sulphur Springs spout up all over the place and the whole place smells like rotten eggs. The town is strictly a resort and not much.

When we got back, we ordered ice and had a couple of nips out of Clint's wisely brought bottle of bourbon. We had dinner at the hotel and God knows what it was we ate. They told us they would prepare us a Western style meal, but it was awful. It wasn't even hot.

After the sun went down, it was lovely and cool. We went out again after dinner and walked around the town some more. It looked better at night. At all the hotels they furnished kimonos and in the evening all the guests wander around the town in their kimonos, with the name of their hotel woven into the pattern. We were sorry we hadn't worn the ones furnished us, but Clint is over 6 feet tall, so his only came to his knees. We bought a couple of souvenirs and played pachinko machines—Japanese slot machines.

When we got back to the hotel, our "beds" were made up—three futons (sort of quilts) piled on top of each other

Mary modeling a kimono

on the floor. It was lovely and cool and I slept with a quilt over me. I really slept very well, much to my amazement.

Sunday morning we had breakfast—tomato juice, ham and eggs, toast and coffee at the hotel. It wasn't too bad. We took a bus at 10:30 and rode up the most fantastic road to the top of the mountain. The view was lovely, but it was hot. When we came back, we all bathed again and then went to another hotel for lunch. All they could serve us was ham and cheese sandwiches and Japanese beer. We then walked to a pond and went rowing. We came back to the hotel and slept for an hour. Then we started the homeward track which was unbelievably awful. The bus was jammed with sweaty, smelly humanity and the dust!! It just poured in and over you. I'm still tasting it and my hair is just a matted mess. I can hardly wait to get it washed tomorrow. When we changed to the train, there was no 2nd class so we rode for two hours on wooden benches in 3rd class. Windows wide open, soot pouring in. We finally got home at 10, not having had any dinner and indescribably dirty. We had a steak dinner right away and then showered and showered and collapsed into bed.

Well, it was an experience, but I tell you I'm not sold on this traveling over here. It is really too bad that I have been to Europe because I can't help but compare and these places can't stand comparison. Food is a big problem. You don't know what you dare eat and what you get is inedible. I shall have to be content to stay in Sasebo for another good while before tackling any more weekend trips.

* * *

News from Home

Letters from Grace to Mary contained many tidbits, anecdotes, and health reports about the family in the States. By 1956, Martha and Jack Schrader had added a daughter, Catharine, to the family. John and Audrey Ingles had a son, John (called Johnny), and in August a new family member, Paul Andrew Ingles, joined the clan. Mary enjoyed hearing of family news and encouraged her mother to send more details. Letter writing seemed to be an important activity for both.

All the following excerpts were written while Mary was in Sasebo.

Sun, Jun 24, 1956

. . . I hope Daddy's good progress continues. I'm always interested in every detail you know.

* * *

Mon, Jun 25, 1956

. . . Talking to you by letter is wonderful recreation and my greatest pleasure. You see, I didn't find it hard to get back into letter writing swing again, did I?

* * *

Thurs, Jul 12, 1956

. . . I am real glad that Martha had Dr. Daisley give Catharine a thorough checkup. Actually, that child has never eaten well, that I can remember. I hope the tonsillitis business is cleared up quickly. I suppose that we'll be in for periodic tonsillitis until she is old enough to have them out. I am glad that she is being good when she stays with you. Maybe if you two can be together alone sometimes you'll get better acquainted.

* * *

Mon, Jul 16, 1956

. . . I'm always grateful to Daddy for taking such good care of my affairs. I appreciated both of his letters about Loomis Sayles and Perpetual. His description of J and A's house sounds good. Two hours a day commuting seems like an awful lot, but I guess we were spoiled by the fast service in White Plains.

I'm anxious to see the new pictures of little Johnny. I hope Audrey won't wait until Christmas to send me one. I would rather have my Christmas present early. I don't have a picture of him here at all.

. . . Please never apologize for writing me what you call "family trivia." You know, I am interested in every little thing that goes on at home. It makes me feel so close to you.

* * *

Wed, Jul 18, 1956

. . . I had Daddy's letter today telling me of his success as a squirrel trapper. I think it is wonderful that he actually did the deed with the trap he designed and built. Maybe he should apply for a patent and go into the squirrel trap making business. However, I really hope you can find where it got in the house, so you can prevent future recurrences.

* * *

Sun, Jul 29, 1956

. . . I have had a couple of letters from you, which as always, means so much. I am sorry the Schrader family had their bout of summer flu, but I'm glad it wasn't worse. Your

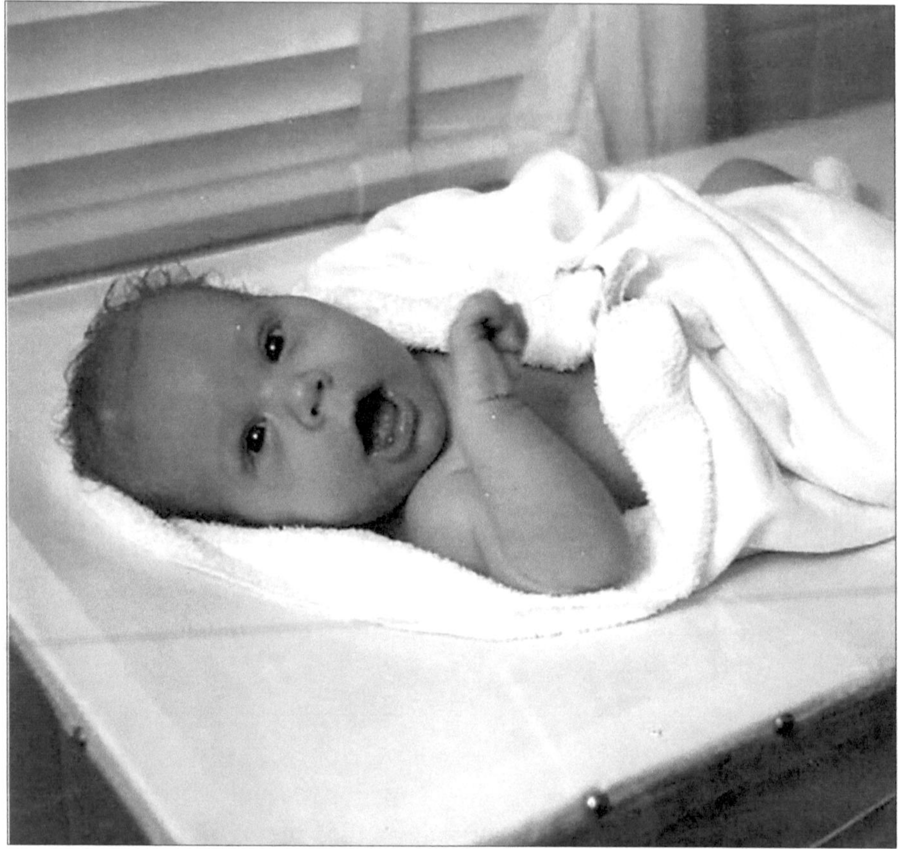

PAUL ANDREW INGLES JOINS THE FAMILY

little jaunt to West Virginia sounded nice. I think it would be nice if you could take the boys up for a couple days in August.

* * *

Tues, Aug 7, 1956

. . . I'm always pleased when you write about the children's speaking of me. I don't think it is too surprising that Catharine associates me with you in your house. She saw me there so much. I am glad that she remembers me.

Your evening with Eugene sounded so nice. I'm glad

you and Daddy both had it. I'm so glad that you have the air conditioners. I sure could use one. Our summer heat goes on and on.

* * *

Wed, Aug 15, 1956

. . . Since you called the baby Paul in your letter, I assumed that Paul Andrew was the final decision. Don't say so to J&A, but I feel partly responsible for the Paul. Once last spring when I was over there, we were discussing names. I mentioned that I liked the name Paul because I had liked everyone I had ever known who had the name. Audrey had not seemed to be considering it before but seemed pleased with the idea. Anyway, I do like it, so will let myself think I had a hand in choosing it. I love our Johns and Stevens, but I think it is sort of nice to have a new name in the family.

Monday when I was downtown I saw an ashtray with a picture of a little boy chasing butterflies with a net in it. It made me think of John Robert and I couldn't resist buying it, so right now it is on the table beside me.

. . . It is a relief to know that Stephen's eyes are OK and I am very anxious to know how the tutoring is working.

* * *

Tues, Aug 21, 1956

. . . I have had so much good mail from home in the last couple of days. Two letters from you, one from Daddy, one from Martha, one each from John Robert and Stephen. [John Robert] wants me to catch, preserve and send him butterflies. His letter is really a classic. That is a very tall order and I don't see how I'm going to meet it. I know I can't catch them. Maybe I can find someplace that sells them mounted. I also rather doubt if they can get through customs.

* * *

GOING TO KOREA

IN OCTOBER ARC HEADQUARTERS representatives visited Mary in Sasebo. They delivered some unexpected news.

Sasebo
Sun, Oct 14, 1956

The headquarters visitors brought me news of their plans for me, which I shall have to tell you. By not writing it, I am being inhibited from writing at all.

I will remain in Sasebo until around the middle of January and then I am to go to Korea. I will be promoted to field director and will be in charge of the one large hospital over there. In addition, I will be supervisor for the staff in the four small hospitals scattered about Korea. It is, of course, a job of considerable responsibility and a real promotion in every sense of the word. The large hospital (400 beds) is at Ascom City, about 18 miles from Seoul. I am told that the hospital is new, built by US—but of temporary Quonset Hut type construction. The ARC staff lives in the nurse's quarters—also Quonsets—and I will have a room and bath to myself. The hospital and quarters have steam heat, inside plumbing and are quite comfortable. The staff at the large hospital consists of a field director (me), one caseworker, a head recreation worker, two recreation workers and a secretary. The smaller hospitals have one recreation worker, each. Living at Ascom City is civilized to the extent that

STEPHEN AND JOHN ROBERT SCHRADER CIRCA 1955

the staff wear their regular uniforms—hospital dresses—on duty and civilian clothes off. The smaller hospitals are still pretty rugged—fatigues, combat boots, outside plumbing, etc. But I won't be involved except for periodic field visits to them. The promotion to field director will be permanent, both as far as the theatre and Stateside assignments are concerned. It will, of course, mean a salary increase—I don't know exactly how much—and will place me in a new salary range so that I can go higher. I have been at the top step of my present classification for nearly three years.

Well, to sum it up, I am not charmed at the idea of spending a year in Korea. However, I am gratified to receive the promotion and to feel that ARC has enough confidence to entrust me with such a responsible position. I will be the senior hospital staff member in Korea. Of course, headquarters personnel will visit occasionally, but for the general run I'll be on my own. The challenge and experience of this job will be greater than almost any place else in the Red Cross.

Now this is important. This is not to be mentioned to anyone outside the immediate family until I give you the word—especially not to anyone who is in any way connected to the Red Cross. There is always the possibility that the plans may be changed for one reason or another. Furthermore, no one but headquarters and me knows about it. The people in Korea do not know and of course no one here. Red Cross is a pretty small world, and it would be pretty damaging to me if word sifted back to headquarters from the States before they were ready to announce their plans. They told me that probably by the end of November, they would be able to announce it officially.

My first reaction to the news was how much I hated to write you about it. I know it is going to upset you as I am sure you have been praying for months that I wouldn't

have to go to Korea. I had held the same hope, but if I have to go, I am glad that it will be in a position of professional advancement for me. Surprisingly enough, the girls I have known who have been over there all liked it. Even when living was a lot more rugged than it is now, they felt the job was terrifically satisfying. You really feel needed. Needless to say, with no dependents there and very few American women, the social life is reputed to be pretty terrific. I guess you can have as much or as little as you want. I am far from jumping up and down with glee, but so far I haven't been too charmed with Japan so I do not feel I am leaving too much. Since I have to put in two years over here, I may as well get as much as I can professionally out of it. This job here has been pretty piddling and certainly hasn't added to my professional stature. In view of the future, however, it has given me an easy setting in which to get acclimated and I won't be going into a new job in in exhausted condition.

. . . One thing about Korea is that you can really save money. There is nothing to spend it on. I am told that the girls live comfortably on $90 a month maintenance. Also, you get R&R (rest and recreation) once every four months. That is 10 days in Japan, which is not charged against annual leave. The tour there is not more than one year. They told me that I might even get transferred back to Japan in the fall of '57 so as to give me a decent length of time in my last assignment.

Well, I have filled a whole letter on the subject, but I wanted to tell you as much as I could about it. Please try not to get too upset over it. I am not. There are a lot of "pluses" in the plans and I am not dwelling on the "minuses", so please don't you?

Well, back to present day activities. The area people stayed until yesterday afternoon as they couldn't get a train reservation out sooner. They were very complimentary about the job I have been doing, found no fault and gave me a few helpful suggestions. They said they seldom make a field visit which was so uncomplicated. Yesterday I took them and three other girls to Arita. We toured the Fukazawa Porcelain factory and poked around in the shops. The weather was lovely, and we all enjoyed the day.

* * *

There are no more letters from Japan, although Mary stayed there for several more months. In January of 1957, she moved to Korea.

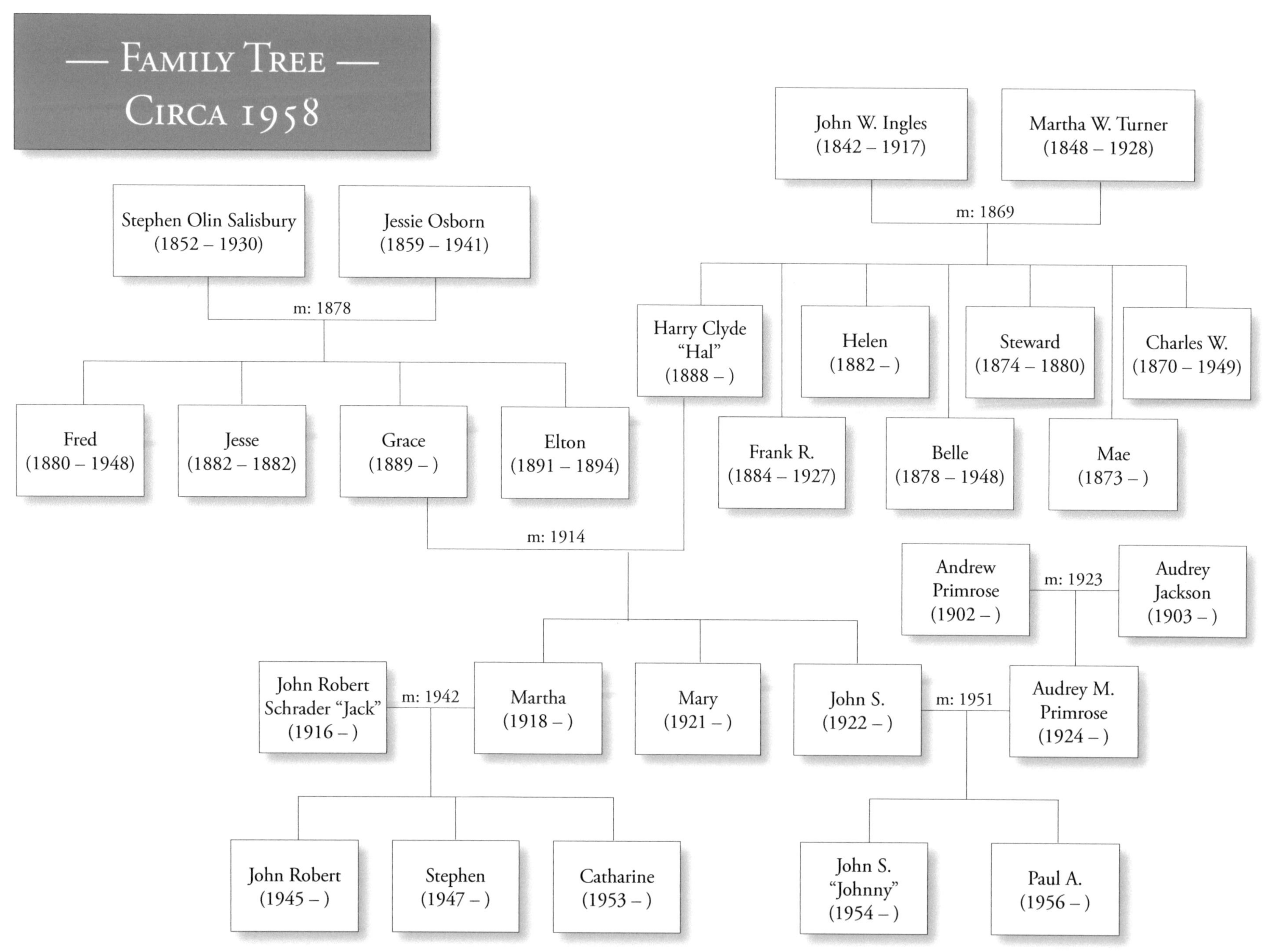

— Family Tree —
Circa 1958

John W. Ingles (1842 – 1917)
Martha W. Turner (1848 – 1928)
m: 1869

Stephen Olin Salisbury (1852 – 1930)
Jessie Osborn (1859 – 1941)
m: 1878

Harry Clyde "Hal" (1888 –)
Helen (1882 –)
Steward (1874 – 1880)
Charles W. (1870 – 1949)

Fred (1880 – 1948)
Jesse (1882 – 1882)
Grace (1889 –)
Elton (1891 – 1894)

Frank R. (1884 – 1927)
Belle (1878 – 1948)
Mae (1873 –)

m: 1914

Andrew Primrose (1902 –)
m: 1923
Audrey Jackson (1903 –)

John Robert Schrader "Jack" (1916 –)
m: 1942
Martha (1918 –)
Mary (1921 –)
John S. (1922 –)
m: 1951
Audrey M. Primrose (1924 –)

John Robert (1945 –)
Stephen (1947 –)
Catharine (1953 –)

John S. "Johnny" (1954 –)
Paul A. (1956 –)

KOREA

HISTORICAL AND CULTURAL CONTEXT
FOR THE KOREA LETTERS (1957–58)

MARY WAS SENT TO Korea after the official end of the Korean War, but the United States still had a military and hospital presence there. The country was trying to rebuild, but the infrastructure was in need of significant repair. Things like getting water, making a phone call, or driving on a decent road were all challenges. Technically it was not war time, but it was closer to the action than any of Mary's other postings. Although America was not yet involved, Vietnam was in the midst of a civil war that would erupt into the conflict that shaped much of the next decades.

PERSONAL REFLECTIONS ON THE KOREA LETTERS

MARY USED TO SAY that her time in Korea was very much like the TV show *M*A*S*H*. She was staying in Quonset huts in Army Service Command (ASCOM) XXIV Corps (also known as Ascom City) in Incheon's Bupyeong district. The conditions were primitive. The weather was uncomfortable. The group was isolated. Travel was restricted. The few medical cases Mary references were severe and tragic. But there was a sense of community and socializing that seemed to get everyone through the tough times. Early in her letters, she wrote that the key to success for a woman in this environment was to establish an arrangement with an officer or doctor where they

MARY'S DOG TAGS

MARY CIRCA 1957

relied on each other for companionship but not get too involved.

As to the professional side of this assignment, things were very good for Mary. To be sent to Korea, she received a significant promotion. When she wrote of the work, generally, she seemed to have things well under control. She also wrote a considerable amount about her finances, including her income, her investments, and her upcoming purchase of a car when she returned stateside.

The harsh living conditions created a longing for simple comforts. Mary made her life more livable by acquiring a record player, a slide projector, and a hair dryer. These seemingly mundane items brought her a little bit of joy in an otherwise unpleasant place.

All excerpts from letters in Korea were written in Ascom City unless otherwise noted.

THE WORK AND THE LIFE

WHILE IN GERMANY, MARY wrote very little about her job and responsibilities. In Japan, she shared a bit more on these topics. When she went to Korea, she wrote quite a bit about her job, colleagues, and responsibilities. Perhaps this change was due to the fact that she had received a promotion and many of her responsibilities were new to her, so she believed they would be of greater interest and importance. Or perhaps she was trying to relieve Grace's apprehensions about her daughter being in Korea. Mary provided information about the living situations, her co-workers, and the internal politics of the ARC and the army.

Thurs, Jan 17, 1957

Well, here I am in Korea. It is 8:00 AM and I am keeping out of the way for a little while, so will get off a few lines. If I can find out how to send a cable to you, I'll do so, but don't know yet how convenient that will be.

Yesterday was a very long day, but everything went very smoothly. I got up at 4:00, finished my packing and got the bus at 5:00. I dozed mostly on the bus and finally got to Tachikawa at 6:30. It was on a small scale, much like any busy airport. I had been well briefed in advance on procedures, so I knew what to do. I checked my bags temporarily, picked up customs forms which I filled out while I ate breakfast in the snack bar and with three Marine officers. At 8:00 AM, I checked in with the Marines, and they took excellent care of me. The Sgt took my customs forms and processed them so I didn't have to stand in line, got my bags, tagged them and put them in the outgoing baggage room. About that time, Lois Beck who is head of ARC Clubmobile program arrived, so I had a second breakfast with her. She was on the same flight with me, which was a help. A little after 9:00 our flight was called and after some standing around we were loaded on a bus and driven to the aircraft. Our plane was a tremendous C-124—a double decker job which can carry over 200 passengers. The enlisted men were "upstairs" and the officers and women—there were three women—in the lower part. These planes open up in front and they can carry trucks, tanks, etc. The seats were modified bucket seats, but not uncomfortable. The cabins are not pressurized, so once the engine started, the noise made any conversation impossible.

The flight took just under five hours. It was a beautiful, clear day and absolutely smooth. Once we were airborne, we could move around a little on the plane. It was pretty crowded, so there wasn't much place to move. For almost an hour we had a stupendous view of snowcapped Mount Fuji sticking out from above the clouds.

Before boarding the plane, we had signed up for box lunches, which were distributed at 12:00. They were very good. Two sandwiches, two pieces of fried chicken, hard boiled eggs, olives, pickles, Coke, apple and a container of milk. I dozed a little, read a little, and mostly just sat.

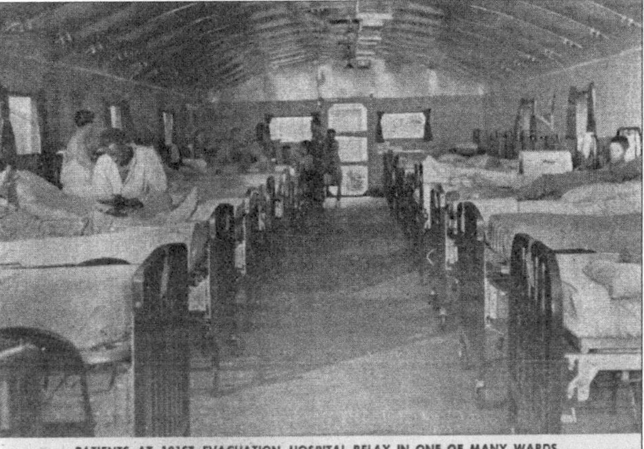

ASCOM, Korea (S&S)—A colorful 13-year record of service in Europe, the U.S. and Korea is proudly being maintained by personnel of the 121st Evacuation Hospital here.

Commanded by Maj. Thomas G. Nelson, the hospital admits nearly 700 patients a month through its doors for resident treatment. More serious cases, approximately 170 per month, are evacuated to Japan. Some 3,500 men a month in Korea are also treated by hospital teams in their own unit areas for minor ills.

With a primary mission of supporting all United Nations Forces in Korea, the 121st Evac. Hospital specializes in neurosurgery and the treatment of infantile paralysis, hemorrhagic fever, and hepatitis.

The hospital was originally activated in March, 1944, at Camp Swift, Tex. Not long afterward it moved to England, then to France and Germany. It came to Korea in August, 1950.

PATIENTS AT 121ST EVACUATION HOSPITAL RELAX IN ONE OF MANY WARDS

BETSY DENMAN, OF RED CROSS, JOINS CARD GAME IN HOSPITAL'S RED CROSS SECTION

ARTICLE FROM STARS AND STRIPES

We landed at three and Elaine was at the front of the ramp to meet me. There is snow everywhere here, but it wasn't too cold yesterday. After retrieving my luggage we got on a bus which brought us to Ascom City—about a 30 minute ride.

Temporarily, I am in a Quonset hut with Mary Ann Siegfried, a rec worker, and Margie Riggs, the secretary. There are two bedrooms and sitting room and bath, and I am sharing Mary Ann's room. Eventually I will move into Elaine's quarters. She's going on leave to Hong Kong 23 January and will come back for her things about 1 February before going to Japan, so I'll be in these quarters for at least a couple weeks. The girls have the hut fixed up nicely and it is fairly comfortable. The heat is provided by a kerosene stove in the living room. The rooms are partitioned off but the partitions don't run to the ceiling, so the heat can get around, more or less.

. . . At this point, I can't give you much in the way of impressions, except that everyone is extremely friendly and the girls seem like a real nice bunch. I'll be filling in more details as time goes by.

* * *

Thurs, Jan 17, 1957

I wrote you once today, but this evening I have the time and the inclination, so will write again. I've had a busy but quite pleasant day. It was really quite a mild day and sunny. Much of it was devoted to getting myself provided with the clothing I'll be needing. We wear army issue wool shirts and slacks on duty for warmth. So today I obtained 2 each of those and took the shirts to the tailor to be altered. The pants were OK. I also get a field jacket and liner, a parka, 3 pairs of wool socks and a pair of field shoes and a visor cap. So by tomorrow I'll be dressed like everyone else here. I'll send you some pictures when I can get all decked out. I want to be prepared before it turns real cold, as it undoubtedly will soon. There is not much snow now.

I went to the hospital this morning about 9:30. They were having coffee hour, which gave me a chance to meet quite a few of the hospital staff, including the CO. The latter is Lt Col Regan, and from what I can gather he is a bit of a character. He had duty in London at some time and is more British than the British. Swagger stick, twirling mustache, clipped speech, etc. One little foible is that he insists that the chiefs of service, (including the Red Cross, and therefore me), sit at his table in the mess hall for all meals except breakfast. You have to ask his permission to be excused if you want to dine elsewhere. For dinner he likes to dine at 6:30 or 7:00 and you can't get there ahead of him. Therefore, you go to the club which is next to the mess and wait until he is ready to dine. He has his own wine closet and has wine with his dinner which he does not offer to anyone else. At this point I find it all quite amusing and ridiculous. But I can see where it may become a bit of a nuisance. He is very hard to talk to—makes no small talk. Tonight I discovered that he knew Pat Wehr when she was married to Frank Given, so that kept the conversation going for quite a while. His sympathies, incidentally, were all with Pat.

What with my running around on the clothing business today, I didn't have much time to get into the job. I did go around a few wards with Elaine. The hospital is not fancy but seems adequate. It is all sort of large Quonset huts off a large central corridor. The ARC has one of these huts to which a sort of ½ hut attachment has recently been added. It is freshly painted and is really quite nice. There are five small offices for six people, so the two rec workers share an office. It's really OK.

I was in the PX today and it is surprisingly well equipped. Everything is within the area of three or four blocks—equivalent that is. I am still not completely oriented but it seems to be compact and accessible. My initial impression is all good and they seem to try to do everything possible to make you comfortable. All in all, is quite civilized.

* * *

Sat, Jan 19, 1957

It is Saturday PM and all goes well. My foot lockers arrived today as have all but one of the packages I mailed to myself from Sasebo. I will not be able to get into the foot lockers until I get settled in my own quarters as there just isn't room where I am now. A new caseworker is arriving Tuesday and will have to move into these quarters, so we will really be jammed up for a couple of weeks.

Last night I made my first visit to the library and was really thrilled to death with it. It is very well organized, many new books, and will be a real joy. I drew out Nora Loft's new book, "Afternoon of an Autocrat" and an old Neville Shute book which I had somehow missed. At the moment I am reading a book Mary Ann received for Christmas, Margaret Case Harriman's "Blessed Are the Debonair."

I got the rest of my clothing yesterday, so I'm now decked out like everyone else in wool slacks and shirt field shoes and parka. I'll have someone take my picture one of these days to send you.

I think I had better give you a rundown of my staff here as I'll be mentioning them from time to time and you'll want to know who they are. At present, the head recreation worker is Judy Hunter, but she is leaving on

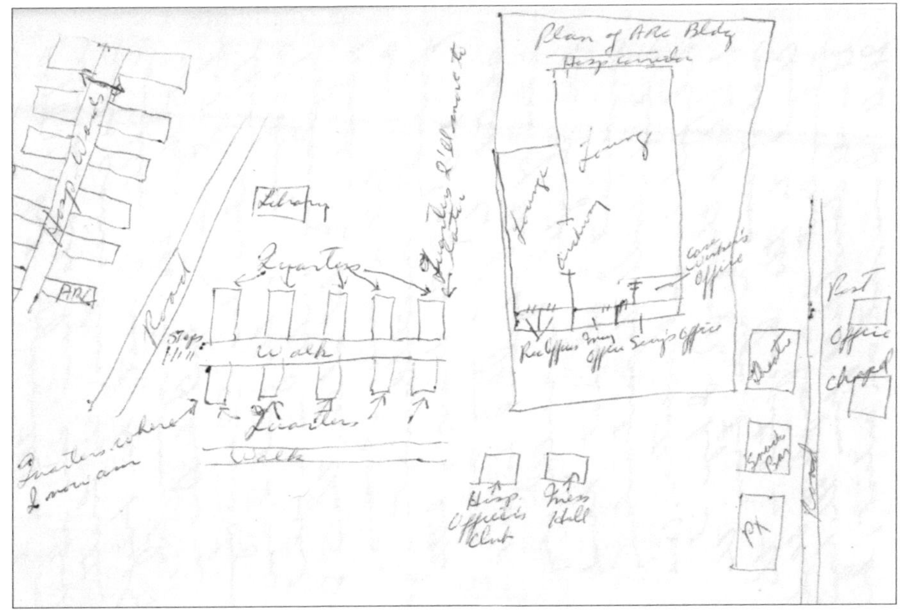
Layout of Ascom City

4 February. She will be replaced 18 February by Betsy Denmark, who I do not know. The recreation workers are Marianne Siegfried, whom I knew slightly in the States and whose room I am sharing, and Louise Powell. Lou lives in different quarters and I have hardly seen her so far. The secretary is Margie Riggs, who lives in this hut. She is young and peppy, but apparently a good worker. The new caseworker who comes Tuesday is Loretta Coughlin. I met her briefly at headquarters. She is young too but I really don't know a thing about her. Elaine Lynch, of course, is the girl I am replacing, and she's a real peach—bit older than I am, but a nice, warm, friendly middle western girl.

I'll try to draw a little sketch to give you some idea of the physical layout here. Everything is really very convenient and close at hand, which will be particularly helpful in bad weather. See back of this page. I hope it makes sense to you. From the Chapel to the hospital is the equivalent of a couple of blocks. It is all downhill from the hospital. Well, I'm not an artist, but maybe that will give you a vague idea. I superimposed a diagram of the ARC building.

* * *

Mon, Jan 21, 1957

. . . Today Elaine and I have been doing inventory, transferring funds, etc. We are getting things pretty well cleared up. Tomorrow a new caseworker arrives and I'm going to Seoul to meet her plane. I'll go and return on the bus. Sort of a case of the blind leading the blind, but I have to get my feet wet sometime.

* * *

Wed, Jan 23, 1957

. . . Yesterday the new caseworker arrived and I had to go to the airport to meet her. They ran a bus in to meet the planes which was due to leave here at 12:00. When I got to the place for the bus, I found that it was going first to Seoul. I was afraid the plane might come in early and I wanted to be sure to be there. So I was offered, and accepted, a ride in a 2½ ton truck that was going in for the luggage. So there I was, bounding over the Korean countryside in the cab of a truck between a Korean driver and a negro Lieutenant. I had the thought "If my mother could see me now!" I got to the airport about an hour early. I had brought a book along for just that reason, so I was quite content. The plane was on time and we came back on the bus without incident. The airfield is Gimpo of which I am sure you heard during the war.

The new girl—Loretta Coughlin—is an attractive young girl aged 24, and she seems to be settling in nicely. She's been in the ARC a couple of years so should be pretty well grounded in the work.

Last night I was able to move into a room in the quarters I will occupy permanently. I will still move into Elaine's room later, but I'm glad to have a room to myself and to be able to unpack a bit. Just moving my things down took up most of the evening. Tonight, I got into a couple of foot lockers and got some of the things I really needed, but will not really settle in until I'm in my final room.

Today was Elaine's last day and she left tonight for Hong Kong. Although I know there will be many times in the next few weeks that I will wish she were here, in a way it will be better to be able to really settle into the job with only one head, etc. I think I have a very fine staff here, all of whom seem to know their jobs and we can sort out the problems together. I am very sorry that Judy Hunter, the head rec worker is leaving. I'm very impressed with her and would enjoy working with her and knowing her better.

* * *

Less than a week after Mary arrived, the hospital was called upon to help with a major aviation disaster in Seoul. It was a trial by fire for Mary, but she was pleased by how her staff responded to the crisis.

On ARC stationary
Sun, Feb 24, 1957

Well, what a weekend this has been!! I'm sure you have heard about the crash of the C-124 Globemaster near Seoul on 22 February with 159 people on board. The plane crashed around 7:45 PM. I was at the 8057th Club having dinner with William and George Dewey when the hospital adjutant who was also there got the call. He notified me immediately and William brought me back. By 8:30, our entire ARC staff was on duty. The casualties started arriving about 9:00 and by 2:00 AM the hospital had admitted 127 survivors. A ward was set up in our ARC Lounge and we admitted 33 patients to it—all in for observation because of exposure. No nurse or corpsmen were given to us, so Betsy and I ran the ward.

I went home to bed between 3:00 and 7:00 AM and left Betsy in charge. I knew that Saturday would be my big day when requests for reports would start flooding in and did they ever! I never left the telephone all day and had the staff scurrying all over the hospital.

Actually, the whole operation was handled magnificently by the hospital. By noon on Saturday, all but 26 of the survivors had been discharged from the hospital, including our "ward" full.

I worked all Saturday until 8:00 PM and am in the office this morning as the phone keeps ringing. It seems like everyone in the States who has someone in Korea is trying to find out if they were in the crash. There are still a number from the plane who are missing, and some bodies have been recovered. Of those we admitted only one was placed on the SI [seriously injured] list.

The plane had just taken off from K14 [military airport in Seoul] for Japan and crashed in the Han River.

I have just finished writing a very lengthy report of our activities in connection with the emergency and I'll send you a copy if I can get an extra one when it is typed up. I haven't the strength to rewrite it all here.

It has been hectic but also a wonderful experience for me and the staff, and I am very proud of the job we have done. You never mind working long hours and hard if you feel like you are doing a job.

* * *

Mon, Feb 25, 1957

Well, the first of the shouting and the tumult seems to be dying away. We have continued to be very busy mopping up loose ends of the disaster operation of the weekend. I called headquarters today and gave them a verbal report and they seemed quite pleased with us. In looking back over it, I'm pretty satisfied. Of course, there are little things which could have been handled better, but we didn't goof on anything.

* * *

Wed, Feb 27, 1957

. . . I am enclosing a copy of the report on our disaster activities which I sent to headquarters. I thought you would be interested. Please save it for me. Every time the "field director" is referred to that's "little old me."

* * *

Seoul was a hub for ARC workers, and this arrangement put Mary in contact with many people she had worked with over the years. She frequently commented on what a small world the Army and the ARC was.

Sat, Jan 19, 1957

Did I write you that one of the nurses here was stationed with me at Belvior and another one at Munich? Also, the dietitian was with me in both Munich and Aberdeen. None of them are particularly friends, but it is always nice to see a familiar face. I also ran into a patient yesterday who had been a patient at Belvoir. I didn't remember him, but

AMERICAN RED CROSS

Report on ARC Activities at 121 Evacuation Hospital
22 - 25 Feb. in Connection With Plane Crash

On 22 February 1957, a C-124 Globemaster with 159 people aboard crashed in the Han River, approximately 20 miles from this hospital, a few minutes after taking off from K-14 at 1939 hours bound for Tachikawa AFB in Japan. At 1955 hours, the hospital was notified to prepare to receive casualties.

The Field Director was notified at 2000 hours by the Hospital Adjutant at the 8057th Officers Club where she was having dinner. Notification was also made to Miss Coughlin, SCA, Miss Siegfried, RW II, Miss Riggs, CS II, and Mrs. Dodge, RW II, from 618th Medical Co. who happened to be visiting our hospital. The FD notified Miss Denman, RW III, and Mrs. Powell, RW I. The entire staff, including Mrs. Dodge, was assembled in the office by 2030 hours. Upon reporting to Hospital Headquarters, the FD was informed that casualties were just beginning to come in and our staff was requested to stand by.

Supplies of comfort articles and paper cups were assembled in the office in readiness. At about 2100 hours, we were sent 13 patients from a ward that was being cleared to receive casualties. We obtained coffee from the Mess Hall to serve to these patients and other personnel as desired. The recreation staff started card and table games to occupy the patients. A request was received from the laboratory for a supply of cold cups which we provided.

At about 2230 hours, we were informed that 50 beds would be set up in the Recreation Lounge to take care of the patients we already had and for others to be admitted. A crew of men arrived and set up the cots which completely filled both sections of the Lounge. Staff assisted in making up the beds. Between 2300 hours and 0200 hours 23 February, we admitted 20 additional patients to our "ward", all of whom were survivors admitted for observation for exposure. About 0200 a doctor came down and checked these new admissions. As each came in, our staff served him hot coffee and helped him get bedded down. We set up a roster of patients so that we would know who we had.

During the evening, the FD reported periodically to Hospital Headquarters to inform the Commanding Officer of our activities and receive instructions. A number of calls were received for supplies of comfort articles and cigarettes to be taken to the wards receiving the crash patients. During the night a total of 127 survivors of the crash were admitted to the hospital. Only two were placed on the S.I. list.

At about 2330 hours, the Chief of Medicine requested the FD to see the pilot of the plane and another officer member of the crew who wished their wives, who were waiting at Tachikawa for their return, to be informed that they were safe in the hospital. At the same time a similar request was received from an enlisted member of the crew. The FD interviewed the patients and then cleared the requests with the Hospital Commanding Officer. He gave permission for us to give the service requested. A call was made to Mr. Horne, AFD at Tachikawa AFB who arranged for contact with the wives concerned.

Cont'd on Page 2

PAGE ONE OF FOUR-PAGE REPORT

he remembered me. It is nice to be back with the army.

* * *

Tues, Jan 29, 1957

. . . Incidentally, did I tell you that Lou Chatham who was at Belvoir with me is over here in the Clubmobile program? I've tried to call her, but have not yet succeeded in making connections. She is some distance away from here.

* * *

Wed, Feb 27, 1957

Mary Katherine Cuppy arrived today and I have just left her after having dinner together. All nurses arriving in Korea come first to our hospital to get their clothing etc., so she will be here for a day or so at least. She arrived just before dinner and I met her and Col. Fuller, our Chief nurse, at the club for a drink and then we all had dinner together. Col. Fuller had us up to her quarters for liqueur afterwards. Mary Kay looks fine. She is so sweet and it is almost like homefolks having her arrive.

She has walked into a mess because although her orders read that she used to be the Chief Nurse for Korea, the chief surgeon for Korea says he won't have a nurse in his office, so no one knows what she is going to do. She outranks our present Chief Nurse, so she can't very well come to this hospital. I think she may end up here eventually as our Chief Nurse goes home in May. It is an awful mess, but she is taking it all very philosophically and says she'll go wherever they want her to. As long as she has patients to take care of, she'll be happy. She is a very adaptable person and not one to complain about things being beneath her rank, etc. She was going in to do battle with the surgeon tomorrow.

* * *

Sat, Mar 2, 1957

. . . Mary Katherine Cuppy's problem has worked out for the time being. She is going to be at this hospital for a month as Assistant Chief Nurse to familiarize herself with our setup. Then she will go to the 43rd MASH [Mobile Army Surgical Hospital] for a month. Then, in all probability, she will come back here as Chief Nurse and also have an additional duty of being chief nurse of Korea. Of course, I'm delighted that she will be here. The chief nurse is awfully important to the ARC in the hospital and with M.K., I will have no problems.

* * *

Thurs, Aug 8, 1957

. . . A Sergeant I knew at Belvoir came in to see me today and we had a nice old home week. It is always such fun to run into people you have known. Two of the new nurses were at Munich when I was.

* * *

Sat, Aug 17, 1957

Here's a "small world" item: yesterday afternoon Captain Melner, who works in the personnel center here, called Betsy and asked if she and I could go out last night with a couple of friends of his who were down from the 24th Division. When Betsy explained about Florence being

here, he also got a date for her. Well, when they arrived, one of the friends turned out to be Charles Wahle, you know, Cecil's husband and the good friends of the Harveys. The other man with him was named Dan Brewer, who also knows the Harveys and it turned out that Mel Melner, whom I have known for months, also knows the Harveys. They were all stationed in Germany and/or Benning together. In fact, the occasion for the men being here was an 18th Infantry Reunion in Seoul Friday night. You sure never know who you are going to run into, do you?

* * *

Tokyo
Sun, May 11, 1958

. . . I've been running into people I know all day. This morning, as I was leaving for church, I saw an ARC man I knew in Korea. In church, another ARC man I know sat next to me. I went to the Osaka for lunch and ran into two nurses and a doctor from the 121 and another doctor from the Tokyo Army whom I had met when he was on a trip to Korea.

* * *

In many cases, the line between work and socializing was blurry. When Red Cross or Hospital brass arrived, Mary was to meet with them and entertain them.

Fri, Mar 15, 1957

. . . Sunday, I had to go to the hospital in the morning to take care of a case problem that came up. At 11:30, Mr. Salverud and his party arrived. Mr. Beam, the field director here, and I had invited the various brass to luncheon for him at the 8057th Club. We then went to the hospital and the executive office and I gave Mr. Salverud a briefing and a tour. Sunday evening, Florence, Betsy and I had dinner at the buffet supper at the hospital club and saw the movie "The Revolt of Mammie Stover." (Lousy.)

Monday, I conferenced with Florence most of the morning, and in the afternoon went to K-14 to meet Jeanette Ross. Colonel Reagan let me have his car and driver, so I had a comfortable trip. In the evening, Mary Katherine Cuppy and Col. Fuller (Chief Nurse), had us all over to the club for a drink before dinner and then we had dinner together at the mess. Afterwards we went back to the club for the movie "The Swan."

Tuesday and Wednesday all day, we're taken up with various conferences. Tuesday evening seems to be the sort of a blank, except that we continued our conferences into the evening.

Florence and Jeanette had early appointments in Seoul on Thursday, so Wednesday evening William drove us all up to Seoul. We joined up with Lois Beck, director of the Clubmobile Program, and Col Don Miller and all had dinner at the club there.

Thursday and today have been days of picking up the pieces on the job. Last night I went to Bingo but came home immediately thereafter. Tonight, I have washed my hair and here I am.

The visit in general was quite satisfactory. I think that the visitors were satisfied with the way things were going in general. They had many nice things to say about the way I had handled the emergency of the airplane crash. My report has been sent to National Hqs and a condensed version is being published in the "Rice Bowl," which is a monthly newsletter published in the theatre for the ARC staff.

Nothing too startling grew out of the visit. Our secretary, Margie Riggs, has submitted her resignation to go home and get married, and they seem very doubtful about filling her vacancy. That will make life quite difficult for us. Of course, they will fill it in time, but it may take several months if a replacement from the States has to be waited for.

A new staff member is going into one of the small hospitals over here the end of the month, so I'll have to pick up supervision of her.

There is not going to be a general conference this Spring, so the trip to Tokyo for that, which I was kind of hoping for, is out. When we are in Korea, we get what is known as R&R (rest and recreation) every 4½ months which is a week in Japan not charged to leave. I'll be due one about 1 June, so depending on how things are going I may get a trip in then.

. . . In one letter you made the comment that you had thought there was a hospital in Seoul. Perhaps I never really explained the hospital setup over here. The 121st is the only real hospital in Korea. Despite the name of "Evacuation Hospital," we serve as the general hospital for Korea. There are four other very small hospitals which run 30 to 50 patients. One of these is strictly a convalescent hospital where we send patients for a week or two before they are ready to return to duty. The other three are what are called MASH Units—Mobile Army Surgical Hospitals. They are very small—can't keep patients more than 15 days. So you see that when anything serious comes up, we get the patients. After the crash, most of the patients were flown to us by helicopter. At our hospital we can't keep patients more than 60 days, so anyone who can't be reasonably expected to go back to duty in that time is evacuated by air to Japan. I hope that will sort of clear up the picture for you.

* * *

Tues, Sep 17, 1957

Next Monday I have to go to Seoul for a KT party and dinner. Some ARC brass from Washington are coming for the Grand Tour. You would think Korea was like going to New York. I haven't yet figured out how I'm going to get in and back. Transportation is always a problem. They have just announced that gasoline consumption is to be reduced 25% and they are doing it by putting 1/3 of the vehicles into storage. So that is going to make it even tighter. Ah me!

* * *

When Mary had been at Ascom City for about six months, an unexpected change of command rocked the community. Mary wrote about the leadership and the influx of staff on several occasions thereafter.

Wed, May 29, 1957

. . . The trouble which broke wide open yesterday has been brewing for some time. I, and everyone else too, am convinced that the root of it all is a violent personality clash between our CO and officer who is the 8th Army surgeon. While there has understandably been fault on both sides, it has been obvious that the 8th Army Surgeon has been out to break Colonel Regan. I couldn't begin to recount all the mean, harassing things—big and little—which he has done. The hospital has been given absolutely no support command-wise, logistic-wise or personnel-wise. Well, the 8th Army Surgeon sits closer to the throne so he finally won. Down he came yesterday to deliver orders to Colonel Regan and Colonel Albrecht, our Executive. Colonel Regan is ordered to command the 44th MASH—a tiny 30 bed hospital and Colonel Albrecht is ordered to the 8th Army Surgeon's office on three days' notice with no advance warning. Both officers were so crushed at first that they were immobile. But today they have rallied and have gone to higher headquarters demanding that their orders be rescinded until a full scale investigation is made. Colonel Regan saw the 8th Army Chief of Staff today and is going to Japan Friday to take the matters up there.

Everyone in the hospital has been in a state of shock but have rallied 100% behind Colonel Regan and Colonel Albrecht. We are all hoping that there will be an investigation and we will all be given a chance to get in our licks in their favor.

Actually, I have found that Colonel Regan has his foibles, but basically he has tried to do a good job. As far as I'm concerned, we have had continuous interest and support from him. I feel even worse about Colonel Albrecht. I consider him one of the finest, most capable officers I have ever worked with. I have never had a more interested and helpful executive. I could go to him with anything—big or small—and know that I would get his thoughtful, undivided attention and all the help that was within his power to give. I feel that he is just caught in the whiplash of this situation and is being crucified unjustifiably.

Well, I have gone on and on, but I am sure you can see why I did not feel that I could go away at this time. If the officers leave and new ones come in, I should be here to establish our unit relationship with them. If there is an investigation I have to be here to speak for our unit. I called headquarters today and told them briefly what was happening, and they agreed that I should stay here. I have switched Loretta's leave up so she will go next week when I would have gone. If things have stabilized by the time she gets back, I'll go then—about 21 June.

I've been in some funny situations before, but not like

this. Things have come to a sorry state in the army when things like this can happen.

* * *

Tues, Jul 23, 1957

We have gotten in four new doctors this week and such an unpromising lot I have never seen. It seems to me that we hardly have an honest to God American in the Medical Corps anymore. Among our doctors now we have one Canadian, two Lebanese, two Puerto Ricans, one Hungarian, two Germans, one Japanese and one American. They have all received all or part of their medical training in the US and of course are U.S. Army officers, but it is a regular United Nations.

* * *

Wed, Jul 24, 1957

I reread your letter last night and noted you asked about Colonel Regan. He was in the hospital in Japan a couple of weeks. They decided that they had removed all of the malignancy on the first operation and could not do anything more at present. He is to go back in three months for a check-up. He was returned to Korea and took over command of the small hospital to which he was originally ordered. I have neither seen nor heard from him since I got back from leave. I haven't particularly wanted to, of course. At any rate, I don't think it would be politic for me to identify myself too closely with the previous regime.

Major Nelson is still in command here, although there are all sorts of rumors floating around about his leaving. Lieutenant Colonel Albrecht, our former executive, is in Seoul. I saw him when I was in Japan as he was on R&R

at the same time. I'm very fond of him and hope he will be down from time to time.

* * *

Mon, Jul 29, 1957

. . . We are suddenly getting a lot of new people in and I really feel like an old timer. With a 16-month tour for the military, there is constant turnover. You tend to feel that the new ones are not as nice as the ones who are leaving, but I'm sure they will be when you get to know them.

Actually, I'm not too happy about the hospital at this point. Our CO and executive are pretty worthless and aren't giving us much direction or leadership. There is a feeling that the place is sort of drifting. The only encouraging thing is that the 8th Army Surgeon, who has caused so much trouble, is leaving in September. He is Gen White's fair haired boy and is going to Hawaii to join Gen White. So regardless of who his replacement is, it will be a cause for rejoicing. The medical setup over here stinks and I sure hope someone can straighten it out.

* * *

Thurs, Aug 8, 1957

. . . In regard to our United Nations medical staff, many have had all or part of their training in the US and are well qualified. So set your mind to rest about that.

* * *

Sat, Apr 19, 1958

. . . Wednesday night I went to the square dancing and most of my new gals turned out for it. Thursday evening, all the new gals came down and I showed them my slides of Korea. It was a sort of combined hair washing venture. They are having water troubles in their hooch so all of them wanted to use my shower for a shampoo. They are [a] real nice bunch of girls.

I know you were probably confused about which is which, so I'll list them again for you.

Lynn Schmidt. Lynn came first and was secretary in Japan. She is to be a rec worker here, but has had no previous experience in that line. She is 24 and comes from California.

Jackie Darnell. Jackie is a social worker. She is from Virginia, aged 28 and came here from Walter Reed.

Ruth Vaughn. Ruth is secretary. She is only 21, pretty as a picture and darling from Tennessee. She is very efficient and is already proving a big help to me.

Pat Harris. Pat is a rec worker who is to be with us for six weeks and then go to a small hospital. She's 26, tall, good looking, brunette from Alabama. She's very musical, plays the piano and sings.

Well, that's my crew of as of now. Jody is still here but leaves the 24th. Frankly, it will be a relief to have her go.

* * *

As in other locations, Mary rarely wrote about the cases at the hospital. And when she did write of them, she included very few details.

Tues, Jan 29, 1957

. . . One of my problems here is coping with hospitalized ARC personnel. The Clubmobile program has about 50 girls over here and there has been one in the hospital ever since I came. Different girls, but always at least one. In addition to giving them interest and TLC, I am responsible for getting many medical forms filled out on each one. I also have to arrange for them to get outpatient care as needed. I just mentioned it as it is a new aspect of the job for me.

* * *

Wed, Jun 19, 1957

. . . Yesterday afternoon they had a special air evacuation of our three broken neck patients. They flew in the largest sized chopper to take them to K14. Almost everyone on the staff was out with their cameras to get pictures. I took quite a few and hope some of them come out.

* * *

Thurs, Jun 20, 1957

. . . The picture Jody took of me and the chopper came out real good. I have ordered some prints for you. I may not get them until I get back from Japan, however.

We have two more cases of polio in the hospital. I sure hope we aren't in for an epidemic. I am sure I wrote you that I had the first two shots of the series in February. The third shot isn't due until after seven months.

* * *

Wed, Jun 26, 1957

. . . You asked if the broken neck patients all were injured in the same accident. They were not. One broke his neck from driving into shallow water. Another was a psychiatric patient who fell on the ward while "running away from the devil." A third was a Jeep accident and the Korean had been shot in the back. I don't know the details on that one. They have all been sent to the other hospital

FROM LEFT TO RIGHT: LYNNE SCHMIDT, RUTH VAUGHN, MARY, PAT HARRIS, AND JACKIE DARNELL. PICTURE TAKEN IN REC HALL DURING COFFEE HOUR.

now. I think I wrote you about them sending a big chopper to take thc three GI's out.

* * *

Thurs, Jul 18, 1957

We are still quite busy at the hospital. Much flu. It is not too bad a variety. Patients only sick a few days, but they do run a high fever for a couple of days. While I was away we had over 100 cases admitted in a couple of days. It's slacked off a bit and is now picking up again. Korea had been quite free of it until we got in three boatloads of troops transferred from Japan, who brought it with them.

* * *

Thurs, Jul 25, 1957

The flu is on the up-sweep again. They have 400 men sick at the replacement depot and admitted 40 of the sickest to the hospital this evening. We get a new batch every time a ship comes in. I am taking a fatalistic attitude about it. It is all around and I am likely to get it, as likely to get it as the next person. So there's just no use in worrying about it. I'm in general good physical condition and that is about all I can do about it, so don't you worry about me. If I get it, I'll get over it. And if I don't, that's fine. Fortunately this is not too bad a bug.

* * *

Sat, Aug 31, 1957

Loretta had to have a BMR [Baseline Monitoring Report] today, so was in the hospital overnight. She's supposed to be on duty today but will be late so I have opened up the building and will dash off a few lines while I am waiting for her to have her breakfast and come in. She has scemed so run down and pepless since she was sick earlier this month that I insisted she go and see the doctor yesterday. He's prescribed some vitamins and said he thought it was just post-infection fatigue. However, he ordered a BMR just to be sure. Major Keeton, who takes care of all the women patients, is a wonderful doctor—very thoughtful and so sweet. He has an interesting background. He is a 7th Day Adventist. He is strictly vegetarian, neither smokes nor drinks. He observes his Sabbath religiously from sundown Friday to sundown Saturday. He takes his work very seriously and I have a great deal of confidence in him as a doctor.

* * *

Fri, Sep 27, 1957

The Clubmobile Girls and their ailments are causing me many problems. The one with the injured coccyx is being medically evacuated to Japan on Tuesday. She is taking it very badly, which is not much help. Another girl had gotten herself tied into knots and hadn't had a BM in weeks so I've had to arrange a medical consultation for her. The doctor feels it is all psychological, but if she can't get herself unkinked, she may have to be sent home. I sympathize with all their problems, of course, but it all serves to keep me pretty busy.

* * *

Sat, Sep 28, 1957

. . . Such a tragic thing happened yesterday. One of our chaplains who was stationed here a short time and whom

I liked very much, was in a Jeep accident and is paralyzed below the waist from severance of the spinal cord. That is permanent, even if he survives. A horrible thing to happen to anyone, but in this case it has been particularly upsetting. His name is Chaplin Quick—a Baptist or Methodist, I think—Luther might know him.

* * *

Fri, Apr 4, 1958

This place is getting more Stateside every day. Since last night, I have been involved in looking after the wife of a seriously ill patient. The patient is a civilian American employed by the Air Force in Japan. He was on a business trip to Korea when he was taken ill and brought to the hospital last Friday. He is married to a Japanese girl. He is not expected to live, so the Air Force flew his wife over from Japan last night. Arrangements were made for her to have a bed on one of the wards and all day I have been looking after her, getting her meals to her, etcetera. She is a sweet little thing, speaks quite good English, very self-effacing and really no trouble. It sure reminds me of being in a stateside hospital.

* * *

Tues, Apr 15, 1958

This has been a day and a half. I believe I wrote you about our having the Japanese wife of the seriously ill patient over here. Well, it was decided yesterday that he was fairly much under control and that she should go back to Japan. She didn't want to go, but the Army and the Air Force were anxious for her to get out of Korea. She came over without a passport or a visa and they were afraid the Korean Government would get wind of it and cause trouble. The Koreans and the Japanese hate each other. So anyway, she left the hospital about 7:00 this morning and took off for Japan about 10:00. Almost simultaneously the patient died and the Air Force turned the plane back and brought her back to Korea. An Air Force chaplain met her and brought her back to the hospital. I, of course, had been alerted to be with her. It was rough. She was completely hysterical. Blamed the doctors for sending her away, for killing her husband, etc. She was beyond all reason. I brought her down to my room and stayed with her until arrangements could be made to get her started for Japan again. There was not much I could do for her, except listen and try to be a friend to her. The chaplain finally took her off to K14 and to start her back to Japan. I, of course, was emotionally exhausted when it was all over. Well, it is over now as far as I'm concerned.

* * *

Sat, Apr 19, 1958

. . . One nice thing that came out of the troubles I had with the Japanese girl whose husband died this week is that two of the doctors have gone out of their way to tell me how grateful they were to me for the help I gave them in handling her. One of them said that this experience had converted him to a staunch rooter for the American Red Cross. So that made me feel good.

* * *

While there were probably many chances to attend training lectures, Mary referenced only one that she found particularly interesting.

Tues, Jul 16, 1957

. . . I went to a very good lecture this afternoon by Colonel Glass, who is the chief of psychiatry from SGO [Surgeon General's Office] in Washington. He talked [about] stress in isolated areas, of course, relating it specifically to our situation in Korea. It was extremely well presented and enlightening and gave us all a lot of insight into our own and others' reactions to our environment.

* * *

Sat, Jul 20, 1957

. . . When the psychiatrist gave his talk the other day, he was describing normal reactions to living in an area of deprivation, such as we do. One group of people will fight it and others will run away from it. The latter group escape into things such as hobbies, readings, writing, long letters home, etc. I think I really fit into that latter group. At any rate, I count as one of my greatest blessings, the fact that I have you to write to and to know that regardless of what I write, you are interested. I'm so lucky to have a loving family on whose interest in and love for me I can always count.

* * *

During a trip to Tokyo in July for R&R, Mary went to the ARC Headquarters to see if she could learn anything about her next assignment. When and who will be relocated were topics that took up much ink.

Sun, Jul 14, 1957

. . . When I was at headquarters, I tried to find out what their plans were for me. I really believe they don't know at all at this point. With all the changes in military command and shifts of troops over here, they are having a hard time predicting their staff needs. I definitely got the impression that they were quite satisfied with the job I am doing and were particularly complimentary regards to the way I and my staff had conducted ourselves through the recent commands upheaval here at the hospital. Their dilemma, if they have one, in regard to me is that if I stay a full year in Korea, I would hardly have time to get going on another assignment before I go home. So as I see it, they have the choice of either transferring me in the fall or leaving me in Korea until I go home. There are seven jobs for FOs [field officers] in the Far East—four in Japan and one each in Korea, Okinawa, and the Philippines. We can't discount the last three. Only one FO in Japan, Elaine Lynch, is going home before March '58. However, changes are coming shortly in both the Philippines and Okinawa, which may mean shifts of people from Japan. So all in all it is hard to figure out, although it is an indoor sport in which we indulge. However those of us in the field never have the full dope, so whatever way we figure it, it is bound to be wrong.

* * *

Tues, Jul 30, 1957

I'm sure you must realize that there is little chance that I'll get an assignment near Washington this time. The only two field director jobs are at Walter Reed and Bethesda, and I am too "junior" for either of them. I wouldn't want Walter Reed even if it was offered—that's too much of a job. The other FD jobs in Eastern Area are: Portsmouth, Va., Bainbridge, Md., Philadelphia Naval, Valley Forge, Pa., Fort Dix, St. Albans, Newport, R.I., and Chelsea Naval (Boston). So you see, there just isn't a great deal of choice. My preference, job wise at least, would be Valley Forge or

Fort Dix, mainly because they are Army. Well, we shall see what we shall see. I just thought I had better prepare you.

* * *

Mon, Aug 12, 1957

As you asked about the possibility of an assignment in area office in Alexandria. That is not really a possibility at this stage of my career. It would mean a promotion and as you know, I only just made field director. The people who go into those jobs have generally had a number of years as field director first. It isn't a job I aspire to very much—it means constant travelling and always trying to help on problems the hospital and staff haven't been able to work out for themselves. I may have to take the job someday, but I would say it was at least 10 years in the offing.

. . . I have my days of hoping I get another assignment before I go home and other days of feeling I would just as soon finish out my tour here. I hate the thought of another move, working into a new job and hospital etc. Actually I have so little control over the matter that there isn't much point in my trying to decide what I want anyway. Well, we'll see.

* * *

Mon, Aug 19, 1957

. . . Florence [Tupper] is still here. She goes to Seoul in the morning. I am going to ride in with her as I want to bring back some supplies from the warehouse.

We have talked over and around the subject of my assignment. Florence—as recreation consultant—of course is not the one who has too much to do with the field director assignments. However, she obviously was instructed to

sound me out on what my thinking was on the situation. I reiterated to her my complete lack of interest in extending my tour beyond June. I also told her that I did not want to go to a new assignment for the last three to four months of my tour. In other words, if I'm going to be moved, I wanted it to be this fall. If I can't be moved, then I would rather finish out my tour here. She was extremely frank with me in discussing the status of the various field director jobs and the people they have available to fill them. I think she understands that I am not volunteering to remain in Korea until next June, but that if that is what they feel is best for the overall theater, I will accept it.

I'm really very ambivalent about it. In many ways I am quite satisfied with my assignment here. When I look at what else might be available, I really think I have the best job in the Far East. Korea hasn't gotten me down thus far, and I've really seen no reason why it should in the future. The summer will soon be over, and I didn't really mind the cold weather at all. I prefer it to the heat. Also, I hate the thought of packing, moving, having to make new contacts, friends, etcetera. So if it breaks that I stay here, I think I'll mostly be glad.

So please, don't you get upset if it works out that way. I've said, and I mean it, that as long as I have to spend two years over here it doesn't really matter where I spend it. One place is about the same as another. At least here I like my job and I am with army and I have lots of friends. So what more could anyone ask? Well, we'll just have to see what happens.

* * *

Thurs, Aug 29, 1957

We are getting scads of new people in every day. We

have been through a famine in personnel and now we are entering a feast period. I haven't been able to keep up with all the newcomers, but the ones I have met seem like nice folks. There are now only about 20 people at the hospital (in the officer group, that is), who have been here longer than I have. If I stay until next June, I'll outlive them all. The tour for the army is now 16 months, but the current rumor is that it is going to be cut to 14 months.

* * *

Wed, Sep 4, 1957

What are referred to as "Dear John Letters from Uncle Sam" are being received right and left by various reserve officers over here. Many have had 17 or 18 years active duty and now are being released in 60 days' notice. It is a nerve shaking experience all around—for those that have gotten them and for those who are afraid they are going to. My friend Johnny Brooks has gotten one. It is part of the general cut back in the Armed Forces, I guess.

* * *

Thurs, Oct 31, 1957

Our new CO—Lt Col Brown—has arrived and assumes command tomorrow. He seems real nice on very brief contact. I have to go to a staff meeting on Saturday morning "prepared to brief him on my section."

. . . Just to put your mind at ease, I really feel fine. Last week my sinuses were kicking up and I thought I might be coming down with something, but I have no symptoms this week at all. The reason I hate to take all the shots is that they will make me feel lousy and I just have to hold together. I sometimes feel like I am dragging the whole

stuff around on my own strength. With the exception of Betsy, they just don't have the right feeling of responsibility. They're good kids, but so often they are just that—kids. Well, of course carrying the responsibility is what I am paid for, so I have no cause for complaint. I guess it is a sign of old age when you begin to feel that there is a younger generation behind you and that they don't measure up or something.

* * *

Tues, Nov 5, 1957

. . . Headquarters called today to see if Betsy would consider extending her tour for two months. She has been due to go home on 30 January. She said she would, as she didn't want to get home in the middle of winter anyway. My answer to a similar question would have been quite different. Betsy has already had one six-month extension on her overseas tour at her own request. This additional extension has still to be approved at National, so may not come about.

* * *

Tues, Mar 18, 1958

. . . I have had another busy day. I guess they are all that way and will be, so I may as well stop saying it. I had a good long conference this AM with Col Buchmann and Col Elliott (Executive) on a number of things. They were so helpful and interested and I came away feeling real good. I can cope with all the staff turnover as long as I am getting good support from the hospital.

June Williams started another new innovation today in the mess. A salad bar where you can help yourself to several choices of salad and choice of dressing. These little things are so important and when they happen, you wonder why no one ever did them before.

* * *

Fri, Mar 28, 1958

Well, one more week down. I got a little more dope from headquarters today. Some good and some not so good. The good part is that they are going to let Jody stay an extra week until 26 April. Of course, Jody isn't much help, but she is a body and gives us some recreation coverage. The rest of the good is that the case worker had an airport call for 24 March and should be in Tokyo this weekend. She may get over here by the end of next week or the first part of the following week. They are sending me a recreational worker on TDY [temporary duty] on 15 April. She is to go to one of the small hospitals over here about 1 June. My main job with her is to get her oriented to administration, casework and Korea, but I am to use her as a rec worker too.

The bad part is the other three—head recreational worker, recreational worker and secretary—are coming by ship and won't leave the States until 3 April or after. So it will be the end of April before they get here. So that is the story as of this minute.

* * *

Tues, Apr 1, 1958

I hasten to write to tell you that I am feeling better about life in general today. I finally got caught up with myself this afternoon and feel like I can face tomorrow. Yesterday was a humdinger and I know that the letter I wrote last night showed it. The new caseworker is in Japan

and should be over here by the end of the week. Just getting bodies in here will help, even though they are new and have to learn. I don't mind taking time to teach new people who are willing to learn and show some intelligence. It is more frustrating having to waste time with a droop like Jody, who hasn't learned anything after nearly a year and never will. In just two days I can appreciate what Betsy had been struggling with all these months. I realize I didn't give her enough sympathy and understanding.

* * *

Fri, Apr 4, 1958

. . . Our new caseworker Jackie Darnell arrived last night and I went out to K14 to meet her. She has just come from Walter Reed, so the 121 is quite a shock to her I fear. She was so tired from her trip over that I didn't have her come to the office until this afternoon. She seems like a nice girl—28 and very nice looking. I hope that she won't find the adjustment too difficult and can get organized and start carrying part of the load in a hurry.

* * *

Thurs, Apr 10, 1958

. . . I felt badly about the letters I have written lately as they have been completely full of my troubles here. I have them all right, but I always feel guilty when I dump them on to you. Today was a bit better as Lynn was back on the job. Jackie came to work for a while but is still full of cold, so I sent her home this afternoon at least. She was there to cover the office while I made ward rounds this morning.

I had a call from headquarters today that our new secretary is arriving tonight. Lynn is going out to meet her at the plane. She volunteered, and I was glad to have her do it. I know very little about this new girl—Ruth Vaughan is her name—except that she is only 21 years old. That is awfully young. Florence told me on the phone that she is a sweet young thing, very eager, has had good references. She has been working with Red Cross in the States. Well, we'll see. But it still seems awfully young to me. I think I was a fairly mature 21, but I sure wasn't ready for Korea at that age.

On Tuesday, the rec worker who is eventually to go to one of the small hospitals is arriving for six weeks TDY at the 121. Her name is Pat Harris.

The hard part is having so many new people all at once. No matter how capable they are potentially, I have to find time to orient them and get them started and answer every new question that comes up. I really feel like I have the whole thing on my shoulders, and actually I do.

* * *

Postcard written
Sat, April 12, 1958

Dear Mother, Will dash off a card in case I don't get a letter written tonight. I'm fine, but busy, busy, busy. The new secretary came in Thursday night is a doll, pretty as a picture and smart. Has been in the hospital in the US for seven months and I am very impressed with her. Think she will be a wonderful help. I'm on duty this weekend—working Saturday and Sunday. Am playing some bridge tonight. Starts in a few minutes. Will surely get a letter written tomorrow. All my love, Mary

* * *

Sun, Apr 13, 1958

I'll backtrack and tell you a little of my doings. Thursday night, the new secretary, Ruth Vaughan arrived. Lynn met her, and I didn't even see her until Friday AM. As I said in my postcard, she was a darling little girl, very pretty, sweet and southern from Tennessee. She had worked at the hospital at Fort Campbell, KY, for seven months before she came overseas. This of course means she is familiar with the work, which is a godsend. She is very eager and intelligent and I'm sure is going to prove to be efficient and a big help when she gets oriented. She made her first public appearance at the Hail and Farewell party Friday night and really took the place by storm. I don't think she will want for social life over here.

* * *

Thurs, May 1, 1958

. . . I've been busy, busy, busy and have had so many things on my mind. My last two staff members finally arrived today. They were supposed to come in last night, but their plane had to turn back due to bad weather, so they finally arrived about 2:00 this afternoon. It's too soon to make an opinion, but I really wonder about the assignment of the head recreation worker to Korea. She is 52 and not in very good health and I just wonder how she will take it. She seems like a good old gal, but I still wonder. She will have to take over when I go to Japan next week, but I guess the place won't fall apart. Her name is Rusty Warmdahl.

The other girl, Alice White, is also older, 45, but seems like a good solid gal. A recreation worker.

* * *

Sat, May 3, 1958

. . . Ruth Vaughan, my darling little secretary, is having her first weekend on duty and she is having a busy one. She has had to call me several times for guidance and help but is doing very well. I really wish you could meet her. She is a doll. She has the loveliest speaking voice, almost like a girl on TV with the weather reports only not as suggestive. Ruthie is really a terrific combination—beauty, brains and a sweet, darling personality. She likes me too, which is very flattering.

* * *

Another common topic was commenting on army duties and the complications that disrupted what should have been routine activities.

Sun, Mar 17, 1957

. . . Yesterday we had a surprise alert called at noon. Since I have never drawn my field equipment, I would have been in a bad way if we had actually had to move out. As it was, we only had to pack up our supplies and be ready to go. I have my field equipment now and tomorrow Doug Hunt is going to send a man down to pack and roll it properly for me. So another time, I'll be ready. I am sure that later on we will have an exercise when we actually move out and may eventually spend a night out in the field. I haven't been through all of this since I was in Berlin, so I feel kind of rusty. It was all part of duty with the Army, of course.

* * *

Mon, Jul 15, 1957

This was another day of pouring rain. Everything leaks and these Quonsets offer no real protection—everything is just waterlogged. I really worry more about my things this year than I did last as there seems so little I can do to protect them. There is no way at all I can rig a dry closet. I have so little closet space anyway that I have to keep a lot of things in my foot lockers. I just pray that everything won't be ruined. The De-moist things in the closet get completely saturated in a few days. Lucy is going to bake them out again tomorrow for me. She has done it once already.

I really think that of all the seasons in the Orient, the rainy season is the worst. I can take the cold in the winter and even stand the heat, but this is the bottom. Just to make it ducky, rats the size of cats are rampant and mosquitoes chew you to death. A lovely place!

I shouldn't mention these things as they will probably upset you. I'm sorry.

* * *

Thurs, Jul 18, 1957

I finally succeeded in getting my passport pictures made tonight. I believe I wrote you before I went on leave about our having to get special visas now to go back and forth to Japan. Among other things, we had to have three more passport size pictures. I had gone down two evenings already and the man was never there. Now our passports have to be sent to Taijoch [Taihoku, now Taipei] in Formosa for the visas to be extended. It is all part of the enmity between Japan and Korea. They do not have diplomatic relations with one another and the nearest Japanese consulate is Taijoch. You would think they would do it in Japan, but they won't. Ah, me!!!!

* * *

Sat, Jul 20, 1957

We are in a most ridiculous situation. Tons of water pouring out of the heavens and no water inside at all. I don't know the course of the latter or how long it's going to last. They announced yesterday that there was a water shortage, but they didn't turn the water off until in the night. This morning there is none. The pumps have probably broken down again. We always keep a couple of whiskey bottles full of water for emergencies, so I was able to brush my teeth and have enough to heat up for a cup of coffee. I had to flush the toilet this morning and so used the water in the tank from before they turned the water off, so now I can't do that again. Ah me, the joys of primitive living.

In every letter I seem to be complaining bitterly about the rainy season. But gosh, it is awful. Everyone is so uncomfortable and depressed and we feel so sort of help-less to cope with it. I have put a lamp with 100 Watt bulb in one of my closets. I'm afraid to leave it on when I'm out when I'm not in the room because of fire hazard, but maybe it will help a little.

* * *

Sun, Jul 21, 1957

. . . Incidentally, all the water finally came back on late yesterday morning. It seems they were putting in a new filter plant, so have to turn off the water periodically.

* * *

Mon, Jul 22, 1957

. . . Tell Daddy that MATS [Military Air Transport Service] does not fly in and out of Korea. There is no such thing as real passenger service. All the planes we fly are primarily cargo planes with bucket seats. On every trip I have made the whole center section has been boarded with cargo. The C-124s are big enough to carry trucks and tanks if necessary. They really are mammoth—look too big to fly. When they carry personnel, they have two floors on them and can carry 200. But he is sure right about their utter disregard for schedule. Well, it all comes under the heading of experience, I guess.

* * *

Thurs, Aug 8, 1957

. . . I had a number of projects at work that I wanted to get accomplished before Betsy got back. I have finally succeeded on most of them. It does you good to set a time limit on yourself sometimes as it is easy to let things ride. Now, the pool table is installed and in use, the furniture repaired, the leak in the storeroom finally fixed and the bars put on the office windows. The latter became import-ant after the building was broken into twice in one week. Getting things done over here is hard because you just have to keep hounding people. Well, anyway I have a feeling of achievement and having gotten these things done, at least.

* * *

Mon, Aug 12, 1957

. . . The medical supply officer told me that every effort is being made to get a form of central heating installed in the nurses' quarters before winter. That would certainly be a boon this winter. The kerosene stoves are fairly effective, but so dirty.

* * *

Wed, Aug 21, 1957

. . . I had a rather frustrating day. I had arranged to ride to Seoul with Florence to bring back more supplies, thereby avoiding duplication of transportation. When the car picked me up, two new doctors were in the car. Instead of being able to come right back, I had to wait around all day while they conducted their business and didn't get back until 4:00. In addition, with them in the car plus their belongings, I couldn't bring back all my supplies, so now I'll have to make another trip. So I felt the whole day was wasted. I couldn't make any complaint as the hospital was merely trying to make the best use of transportation but it was frustrating. With Florence being here, I didn't feel like I have been on my job since last Thursday. Tomorrow I am really going to have to get in and dig and pick up the loose ends.

. . . We had a typhoon alert last night. It has poured buckets all day, but the storm has changed course. As so often happens, the water pumps have broken down and we are short of water inside—no hot water—while being washed away outside. That's the way it goes and means I can't have a much needed shampoo tonight. I have to do my hair about every five days over here.

* * *

Thurs, Aug 22, 1957

Boy, we are really having a time with water, or lack thereof. We haven't had a drop inside for 48 hours now. Yesterday it rained, so we put out every container we could find and by catching drops off buildings etc., managed to gather a couple of buckets full that we are using for toilet flushing purposes when it becomes absolutely necessary.

They are trucking water to the hospital for drinking and cooking and Lucy got us one 5 gallon can for our quarters that we are using for drinking, toothbrushing and what little spit bathing we are doing. They sent trucks loaded with GI cans out today to collect water from various streams so that they could flush the hospital toilets. The last time there was a real water shortage, the water was never turned off completely, so the toilets could be used and we had some water for washing, etc. The report is that there is a break in the main pipeline somewhere. Anyway, no one seems to know how long it will last. I particularly need a shampoo but there is nothing I can do about it. Well, all this isn't related to upset you, it is just our major news item at present.

* * *

Sat, Aug 24, 1957

I have finally managed to have a sort of shampoo and bath. I got about two gallons of water and heated enough of it to make the whole lukewarm. I put it in a metal waste basket and sat in the shower. Using an empty coffee can for a dipper, I washed my hair and then poured the rest over me. I only got one soaping for my hair, and most of that still feels like it is in there, but the net result should be some improvement over the filthy, greasy mess I had.

Such action becomes necessary after our outing this AM. We were alerted at 8:00 and loaded into trucks about 9:00. We drove about 30 minutes—very dusty—to a training area where the EMs went through a tent pitching exercise. We just sat around in the broiling sun and watched. They called a mock air raid, and we all had to scramble into ditches. We finally got back about 12:30. We had to wear fatigues, helmets and packs, so with the sweat and the dust, we were pretty sad sacks when we got back.

As you probably gathered, we are still without water. Thanks to Lucy we have had water from that trucked to the mess hall for all essential purposes. We have carted in buckets full from various ditches and puddles to flush the toilets. Actually we are not suffering acutely, but it is a bit inconvenient and unpleasant. Well, it all goes to make the experiences to laugh over in the years to come. We haven't been able to have any laundry done all week, of course, but so far I have had enough changes to make it. We have every hope that we'll have the water back in a day or so.

* * *

Sun, Aug 25, 1957

Well, the big news is that the water finally came back on again about 4:00 this afternoon. I was taking a nap and was awakened by a peculiar sound. I finally identified it as water coming out of the tap in the utility room, which the maids had apparently left turned on. We have no hot water, but having the cold is wonderful. I am sure they'll get the boilers going tomorrow so we'll have hot.

* * *

Fri, Sep 27, 1957

My room is such a mess that I can't find anything. This is some paper Betsy brought me from Japan and is all I can put my hands on at the moment. [The paper is very decorative with birds, trees, flowers, and bamboo on the edges.]

The reason for the mess is that the painters moved in at 7:30 yesterday morning. We got the word they were coming on Wednesday so could use Wednesday night to get

things cleared away for them. The job of the entire building took two days. Last night all I did was make my bed and get in.

This has really been a hellish week. They painted the ARC Monday and Tuesday and our quarters Thursday and Friday. Wednesday we had the recreation workshop and today, the ARC Brass I had dinner with Monday night in Seoul descended for a visit and I had to go to lunch with them. And to top it all off, we had an alert today. None of us went to the field but we had to go dressed for battle and go through various of the motions.

. . . Now it is Saturday morning and I am still in bed, mainly to keep warm. It has gotten quite cold—40° yesterday morning—and we have no heat in quarters yet. They are supposed to start working on a new heating units for the quarters on Monday. They always do things backwards over here. The quarters have just been painted and now they're going to have to knock holes in the walls to put the heating ducts in. I don't think I mentioned that the painters didn't have any white paint so all they have done is paint the walls and will come back later to do the ceiling. I think the reason that I have resented the painting the most is that I had to give up my lovely soft gray walls for bilious green. In all fairness, I must say that having the living room and hallway painted—they never had been before—is a big improvement.

* * *

Sat, Oct 26, 1957

This is a nice relaxed day, at least so far. I slept in this morning and didn't get up until 9:30. Have had a couple cups of coffee, checked in with the office and here I am, still in my PJ's, sitting by the stove in the living room. There are signs that we will eventually get some heat, as it is now working in the quarters at the top of the hill. Unfortunately, I live in the quarters at the bottom, so I guess ours will be the last to get the heat. I have always been happy to be at the bottom of the hill before because we are next to the boiler house, which has meant we had hot water if there was any at all. However, being at the tail end of the heating system may make it not so desirable. Anyway, those who have the new heating system working think it is going to be a great improvement, so there's hoping.

. . . We are getting ready for our three-day field exercise on Monday. It is not going to be too bad I don't think. I will go out Monday afternoon and on Tuesday. The rest will take turns going out for a couple of hours at a time.

* * *

Mon, Oct 28, 1957

. . . Today was the start of our three-day field exercise. I went out to the bivouac area at noon with a group of the nurses just to look around and get oriented. We were only out there about ½ hour. Tomorrow we are going out again on sort of an orientation tour in the morning. In the evening, they are going to serve dinner out there for everybody. I hope the weather is better as today was foggy and overcast with intermittent rain. The men are sleeping out tonight and tomorrow night.

Today they got to the point of knocking holes into our rooms and installing the ducts for the heating system. Tomorrow or the next day they are supposed to come in and paint the ceilings so you can see life is just one ducky mess right now.

* * *

Fri, Nov 1, 1957

Lots to report tonight, the most wonderful being that we have heat at long last. When I came home from work tonight, it was turned on and you can't imagine how wonderful it felt. So far it seems to be working very well. It will probably need adjusting. Also I wonder if it will really do the job when the weather gets cold. Like all the heating over here it seems to me to defy all the laws of thermodynamics. They are all installed with the heating ducts at ceiling level. Since hot air rises, the floors are always cold. This system consists of an oil burning furnace outside between each two rooms. A T shape duct enters the bathrooms and the hot air flows out into the bathroom and into each room. The arms of the T enter each room through a hole cut in the wall. In the bathroom below the sink, is an outlet duct, which is supposed to recirculate the air from the room through the blower. As I say, it would seem to me the system should be in reverse, but that's the way it is. There is a large oil tank for all the quarters and the oil is piped in to the separate furnaces. It certainly should be cleaner than the potbelly stoves in each room, and certainly less of a fire hazard.

Another news item is that the box with my clothes—knit dress, etc.—arrived today. They looked lovely and I do appreciate you taking care of them for me. The package apparently came in on the same boat with the book and the record but was delayed at the PO one day.

. . . The painters came and went today and I have just spent a good part of the evening getting settled again. I have stored things away in my cubbyhole that Johnny had fixed for me and rearranged my room a little, so I think it looks better.

. . . Like everything in Korea, the heating system for example, the painting job was done backwards. They did the walls, then the ceiling. Consequently, there are drips of white paint down the walls. They wiped it off and left white smears. At least now that is done, and the heat is in. Maybe they will be able to leave us alone. It seems like the quarters have been full of little men for weeks.

* * *

Tues, Nov 5, 1957

. . . Tomorrow I go on my [undecipherable] to Seoul. It is a terrible ordeal, as you have to wait [at] each place and battle with them to stamp your passport today and not make you come back two days hence. I have to go to the 8th Army to pick up my orders, to the bank to pay for my ticket, to Hong Kong Airways to give them the receipt from the bank, to the American embassy, to the British Legation, and the Korean Ministry of Foreign Affairs. I expect it will take me all day. I imagine, before I am through, I will wonder why I ever thought going to Hong Kong was a good idea.

* * *

Thurs, Nov 7, 1957

Well, I had a long day yesterday in Seoul but managed to get all my business accomplished. This was my itinerary:

1. ARC office to pick up my orders.
2. American embassy for amendment to my passport—1½ hours.
3. British Legation—30 minutes. This only after I all but wept when they said to come back at 4:00 PM.
4. Korean Ministry of Foreign Affairs. I worked them down from return in two days to come back at 4:00.
5. Lunch at the Officers Club.
6. Bank.
7. Back to where I had lunch as I left my camera by mistake. Recovered it OK.
8. PX.
9. Red Cross Office to kill a little time.
10. PX. I called my office and got a couple of additional shopping requests.
11. Hong Kong Airways Office.
12. Korean Ministry of Foreign Affairs.

When I got home, I thought I was all set, passport all ready, ticket in my hand and travelers' checks bought. Crowning blow was that I had a chance to examine my passport closely, I found that my exit permit from Korea was good for only 15 days from the date issued. (6 November). Since I don't exit until 22 November, I now have to go back to the Korean ministry and have that fixed. Isn't that a nuisance? I paid $175 for my airplane ticket and bought $700 in travelers checks. I think that should see me through. I am told that every place in Hong Kong will accept personal checks drawn on a stateside bank, so I could do that if I need to.

Now this is good news. One of the special service girls whom I have known quite well, Ginny Weisel, will be in Hong Kong when I get there and will be there until the 24th. Florence comes on the 25th so I will not be completely alone, hardly at all. Ginny has finished her tour and is going home around the world. She is also going to be staying at the Peninsula Hotel, so you can put your mind at rest on that score.

* * *

Tues, Apr 22, 1958

Yesterday I was talking to Col Ahufeldt, our new CO, and happened to mention my 15 month long exasperation at not having a phone in my own office. He immediately started buzzing buzzers and told the adjunct to get me one, so I think I may really get one. He made a trip down to our building today to look over the office set up and agreed that I really needed one. He seems really interested in us and our program and is going to be real nice to work under.

* * *

Mary also complained about the behavior of some of the men she had to deal with.

Wed, Jul 24, 1957

. . . I have a new, but unwelcomed admirer. There's a little Puerto Rican doctor who has just arrived in Korea and is a patient. He is going up to one of the divisions. However, for two days he has dogged my steps and has been quite a nuisance. Says he is coming back down to see me, etc. It is the kind of thing that comes from being friendly sometimes. Ah me!

* * *

Sat, Dec 7, 1957

. . . I have gotten myself involved in a party tonight, rather against my will, but there was no way out of it. Betsy goes with the executive officer of the Personnel Department here. He called her and said they were laying on a party for

the 8th Army AG who is their big boss and asked her to get a couple of the girls. Since the officers at the personnel center came to our rescue so nobly when Mrs. Hahn was here, I felt I had to reciprocate. My chief hesitancy is that I have met the 8th Army AG, and as the saying goes, he shows me zilch. One of those guys who drinks too much and then has his hands all over any girl within his reach. My date, however, is Captain Eichenberger, who is the adjunct at the personnel center and a real nice guy. He has promised to protect me at all costs. The things you have to put up with in the line of duty, as it were!!! Men!!!

* * *

Mon, Apr 28, 1958

. . . I had a fairly busy weekend. The three men from the 7th Division came down Saturday and we went up to the 8057th Club for dinner and the dance. It wasn't too successful a venture as they arrived in a fairly inebriated condition which didn't improve as the evening went along. On Sunday I went to church and then to brunch at the 8057th in the afternoon. George Guy, the only one of the three who put in an appearance on Sunday, took Lynn and me to Inchon and back and then left about 4:00.

* * *

In spite of all of her complaints, Mary repeatedly encouraged Grace not to worry about the situation. All excerpts following are taken from letters written in Ascom City.

On ARC stationary
Sun, Feb 24, 1957

. . . Please don't go on feeling so unhappy about my

being in Korea. I'm not being a Pollyanna when I say I am not in the least unhappy. I am not even uncomfortable particularly. Sure, it's been cold and will soon be wet and then hot. Sure it's dirty, etc. But those things aren't important. Everyone is in the same boat, so we just laugh it off and make the best of it. I have the best job in the Far East as far as the ARC is concerned. If I do it well, it is going to look wonderful on my record. I think it is an opportunity of a lifetime and I am lucky to get it. As far as much personal life is concerned, I'm having a good time. You know as well as I do that where you are doesn't matter. It's who you are and who you are with.

So, if sometimes I comment on some aspects of the situation that sound unpleasant, don't get upset about it. I don't try in my letters to just point to the bright side and I don't think you want me to. I try to be honest with you always.

Well, I have work to do now so will stop.

* * *

Mon, Jun 17, 1957

. . . Don't feel desperate about me being in Korea. It isn't so bad. I know it's strange and different, but after all I live in the bosom of the Army, and that is my real home. I always feel like I belong in such a setting. I try to describe the place as I write, but I guess I can never really make it real for you.

* * *

Sat, Jul 20, 1957

I hate to be filling all my letters with complaints, but there doesn't seem much else to write about. It is so all consuming, all pervading. On the whole, despite what I write, I am in quite good spirits and have not lost my balance or cheerful outlook. I am so glad that I have learned long since to amuse myself and to keep myself occupied—primarily with reading. I have just finished a new book by Howard Swiggett, "The Durable Fire." Not world shaking, but OK. Now I am reading "The Lancet" by Garrett Rogers. I will make another trip to the library today and get some more ahead.

* * *

Sat, Jul 27, 1957

I am sorry that in recent letters I have complained so much about the rainy season. I don't want you lying awake nights worrying about me. It is unpleasant, but no harder on me than anyone else. Sure, I would prefer to be living more comfortably but I can take this. It could be a lot worse. For example, the girls in the Clubmobile units in the divisions have only 8 holes outside and water for showers only an hour a day some days. So I have luxury by comparison even if the water does go off now and then, I'm not unhappy, so don't you be.

I'm in fine spirits today, and your two letters just added to the extra fillip to my day. You are always so good about writing me, and you have no idea how much I count on your letters.

* * *

Mon, Aug 12, 1957

. . . I sometimes think I must sound like a nauseating Pollyanna when I write you so often that I am not unhappy over here. I wish you could achieve more acceptance of it and not worry so much about me. I think I will always consider it one of the most valuable experiences of my life. I admit there are lots of frustrations and inconveniences, but it is not all bad by any means.

* * *

Mon, Mar 31, 1958

I am busy though. Today Loretta was still here and yet I ran with my tongue out all day—didn't leave the office until 6:30. I have to make every decision for Lynn because she is new, and for Jody, because she's stupid. For example—the latter—I was interviewing a patient about a problem and Jody came in and asked if she could interrupt for a minute. She was supposed to take five boxes to the post office to mail ARC property. I had ordered the truck and given her minute instructions. Well, the big problem was that the truck driver couldn't lift the boxes himself. So what should she do? My answer was to get a couple of the ambulatory patients sitting in the lounge to help. Well, that gives you an idea of her brain power. I was glad to have Betsy get away without killing her, but I may end up doing it myself before the next three weeks are over. Fortunately, Lynn seems to be [a] real reliable, calm girl with a good head on her shoulders. When she gets a little more experience, I know I can rely on her.

What kept me so late today was that I was having to check in the money collected from the medical detachment. For the ARC Fund campaign. It is always very disillusioning. They contacted 220 of the men (all but about 10 of the detachment) and only got $137. Eighty-three of the sods turned in empty envelopes, and one envelope had one penny in it. 110 gave $1.00 or more and 27 gave less than $1.00. A number of those whom I have done the most for gave nothing. Well, I guess there is nothing one can do about it. I always hate the fund drive time and it is just unfortunate that this year it has to coincide with a time when I'm having to beat my brains out because of no staff.

I am sorry to pour my troubles out to you, but I have no one else, particularly now that Betsy is gone. I would be a lot better off if I weren't so conscientious, but I do feel my responsibilities and I can't be satisfied if I don't do the very best I know how. Really, though, with ARC having such a time getting money, I wonder how the organization is going to be able to go on. I may find myself out of a job one of these years. Also, unless they cut back programs, they are going to kill off the staff they have. My present situation is only temporary and we are much better off overseas then we are stateside. They keep us pretty well staffed over here. I am sure when I get on the job back in the States, I'll look back on these two years as a real vacation. I have to admit that there have been a lot of times over here when I really haven't had enough to keep me busy, so if I am snowed under for a few weeks now, I shouldn't complain.

Well, I really did blow off, didn't I? Well, I feel better, so don't let it worry you. I guess I'll putzi [*sic*] around a little and go to bed. I got up at 6:00 to tell Betsy goodbye and then went back to bed and overslept, which didn't start my day off very well. I had to deliver a death message first thing this morning, which also didn't help my day very much.

* * *

Sun, Apr 13, 1958

. . . One thing that has been somewhat encouraging is that our fund drive dollar wise has been going better than it did last year. We have already taken in about $125.00 more than we did last year and I think some more will come in. The nurses have been surprisingly generous. It is always surprising to see which ones really give and which ones give a token $1.00. The $5.00 and $10.00 seem to come from the most surprising people, those who didn't seem particularly friendly or cooperative toward ARC.

* * *

As Mary's time in Korea draws to an end, it was clear her work had been exemplary and the powers that be in the ARC had noticed. She went to the regional headquarters in Tokyo to determine what her assignment would be when she left Ascom City.

Ascom City
Mon, Apr 28, 1958

. . . I just found today that I will be going to Japan for a few days the week of 12 May on ARC business. I haven't had a chance to figure out the transportation yet, so I don't know exactly when I'll be going and coming back. It all came up in a telephone conversation with headquarters today. My last two new staff members are due to come Wednesday and with those already here getting broken in, I guess the place won't fall apart if I go away for a few days. I would like to work out transportation to go over on Friday so I'd have the weekend in Tokyo before I get down to business on Monday. I think maybe I can arrange to go over on the medical evacuation plane on Friday, which would mean a fairly comfortable trip. It will be a nice break as I really had my nose to the grindstone these past months.

* * *

MARY AT HER DESK IN ASCOM CITY

Ascom City
Thurs, May 1, 1958

One of the reasons that I'm glad this trip to Tokyo is breaking right now is that I have had quite an offer from ARC on a new job. National wrote FEA [Field Office Eastern Area] headquarters saying that Eastern Area is interested in me for a job of Home Service Field Representative. This idea originates with my old and good friend Mildred Jenkins, who you know. You remember that I worked with her in New York and she lived in White Plains. It is a big promotion. I am now a grade 18 and this would jump to grade 21. I would work in Eastern area office at Alexandria primarily, but would have to travel quite a bit, visiting chapters etc. It would mean giving up hospital services which as you know I am pretty partial to. It is an awfully hard decision to make and I do want to talk it over with headquarters people. The pros, of course, would be that I would be working for Mildred Jenkins again and I have the greatest admiration and respect for her. I would be more or less stabilized in Alexandria even though some traveling would be involved. It would be a very good promotion and could in time lead to bigger and better things. I have very good background for the job because of my experience in Home Services at National and in North Atlantic area. The cons are that I am not too sure I would enjoy the work. I hate to give up my hospital work, which basically I like so much.

I really didn't want to have to make the decision on this until I was back home and could talk to Mildred and find out more about it. My present plan is to ask headquarters to write back to and tell National that I will consider the job, but that I would like to wait until I get home to make a positive decision if they can wait that long. Secretly, I feel that they will wait because they can't have too many candidates in mind. Without patting myself too much on the back, I can say to you at least that there aren't many people in ARC with my experience and background. Also, before leaving Hospital Service, I would like to know what they have to offer me in the way of an assignment and promotion possibilities. Also, I would like to know if the door would be open for me to come back to Hospital Services if I didn't like the job and in what capacity. Of course, if I am to get ahead in ARC, I am going to have to eventually leave the field and move to the area level. This offer has come much sooner than I anticipated and might prove a real steppingstone to something big. Another thing, of course, is the hospital work stateside is becoming a real headache with staff shortages, night and weekend duty, etc. This would be pretty much a nine to five office job with lots of the pressures off. I could either live at home or get myself an apartment in Alexandria and live like a human

being for a change. Also, no more overseas tours.

Well, you can see that there are a lot of angles to consider. I really feel self-confident enough in my position to hold off on making the decision. They may not like it too much. But I refuse to be stampeded into making a decision.

My plans for going to Japan have pretty much jelled. I am going over on the medical evacuation plane on Friday 9 May, and thus will have the weekend in Tokyo the following week. I'll be both at the hospital at Camp Zama and in Tokyo at various meetings and conferences. I haven't firmed up when I will come back, but it'll be almost the end of the week. I'll be glad to have a chance to talk to headquarters people about a myriad of things that seem to have cropped up recently. In a way, it seems like too much to have to dash to Japan just now, but I am getting real frustrated with trying to work things out through letters and telephone calls over which you shriek and then they cut off at the end of 10 minutes. For my free weekend, I am going to have headquarters get me a nice hotel room at the Dai Ichi and I shall relax and take hot tub baths, get my hair done and I am sure will feel completely rejuvenated.

This is an awfully self-centered letter, but I know you like to know what is on my mind and I think you will see there is plenty. What a relief it will be to get on a boat and have nothing to think about except coming home to my loving family.

* * *

Ascom City
Sat, May 3, 1958
. . . In regards to the question of my job when I get home, I called Miss Penhale Friday and told her that it was

a decision I didn't want to make until I got home and could go into it thoroughly with Mildred Jenkins and Rae Henry. She was very understanding and agreed with my point of view. She is going to write back to National and tell them that. So now we will see what happens. I am relieved to have gotten that much of a decision made and like Scarlet, "I'll think about that later."

* * *

Ascom City

Mon, May 5, 1958

. . . Miss Penhale called me from Tokyo today to tell me that they had had a wire from National that SMH (hospital service) [Service Medical Hospital] in Eastern Area were counting on me for "a big hospital" in Eastern area. Apparently they didn't want to lose me to home services so are getting their licks in. Penny thought I would like to know in case it might make a difference in my decision to request for postponement of any decision at all until I get home. I told her that I appreciated the testimonial from SMH, but actually I had assumed they would want me if I decided to stay on in SMH. Well, it's flattering to have people fighting over you, and it just proves that I am in a position to bargain a little. I am toying with the idea of using this as a point of bargaining in the event SMH should be planning to assign me someplace I didn't want to go. Just between us I am really not too interested in the Home Services job. I think I am happier in the SMH and may well in time advance to Area level in that service. So right now, I am just biding my time and we'll see what happens. I think I'll ask Penny when I am in Tokyo what she would think of my writing personal letters to both Mildred Jenkins and Rae Henry, to the effect that I appreciate their

interest, want to talk it over thoroughly with both of them, but not commit myself in any way. Since they work in the same building, I could even make it a joint letter. In fact, I am really looking forward with relish to my first visit to the Eastern Area office. Penny, at least, agrees that I am within my rights to postpone the decision. In fact, I think my stock has gone up a few points in her eyes to know that there is all this interest in me in the home area.

* * *

Ascom City

Wed, May 14, 1958

. . . First of all, I want to report to you on one matter I more or less got settled at headquarters yesterday. They wrote me several weeks ago and wanted me to extend my tour until the middle of July because they would not have a replacement for me until then. As you can well imagine, I took a very dim view of this. Yet on the other hand, I hated to be selfish and insisted on going home on schedule when I had no real emergent reason to do so. So we have been sort of kicking it back and forth for several weeks. As usually happens, we finally reached on a compromise. They are going to send as my replacement a field director who reports to the West Coast on 18 June and are going to put in for transportation for me about 28–30 June. They had planned to send this particular girl to another station and replace me with a girl who reports to the West Coast on July 1st. By talking to them in person, I was able to convince them that I should have the first replacement. I've worked hard to maintain standards at the 121 and I don't want to see it without leadership for over a month. On the other hand, I feel I have more or less personally shot my wad and the place will profit by a newer, fresher point of view. As it is, even if my replacement flies over, she may not actually get here before I leave, but there should be a gap of only a few days at the most.

What this means personally is that I won't be home until about the middle of July instead of the 1st of July. But that is better than August as it would have been if I hadn't fought my battle.

I deliberately did not write you about this until I had more or less settled it. I know you will be unhappy about the delay, just as I am, but one can't always have things just the way one wants them. A couple of weeks isn't very important in the long run. I could probably have put my foot down and flatly refused an extension. But after all, I do work for these people and plan to continue doing so, so I had to give a little as long as they were willing to give a little too. I was real glad of the opportunity to discuss it with them face to face as I think they really understood and accepted my position and good relationships are intact.

So please you, too, try to understand and don't get upset about it. Of course, I don't know yet what transportation and probably won't until up to the last minute. They told me they requested their transportation spaces for each month on the 1st of each month and then are dependent on what the military allots them. So, I'll just have to ride along with that and keep you informed as I learn myself.

I wrote you pretty much in detail about the Home Service versus the Hospital Service jobs. All that is postponed until I get home and that is the way I want it, so I probably won't be mentioning it again.

* * *

Socializing and Traveling

As in Japan, travel within Korea was not easy, so most socializing was done on base, although Mary was able to do so traveling to Japan and Hong Kong for R&R. The socializing seemed to be part of the job. It also had to have been a way to deal with the hardships of the posting. Mary wrote of different social activities from the first letter from Ascom City.

Ascom City
Thurs, Jan 17, 1957
Last evening, I went to a farewell party for one of the Clubmobile girls who is leaving. It was at the Officers Club nearby. The girls had arranged transportation, in fact the base commander, Col Webb, sent his sedan for us. The club was quite nice and we had a good steak dinner. Of course I met many, many people and my mind is sort of confused at about it all. I was pretty tired anyway and the champagne didn't clear my mind much. We came back about 9 and I fell into the bed and slept very well.

* * *

Ascom City
Sat, Jan 19, 1957
Today there is a dance at our hospital Officers Club to which it is expected that everyone will go. After the dance the girls have invited various people to this hut for a party for Elaine. I am told that the social activities are unusually quiet just now—a sort of reaction to the holiday hilarity. That really suits me fine.

* * *

Ascom City

Mon, Jan 21, 1957

Saturday evening I went to the dance and the hospital club. It was OK. I met some nice British officers there. The dance broke up at 11:30 (Curfew here is 12:00—one must be in quarters, or at least the compound by then) and the girls had invited a tremendous number of people to a post dance party in our hut. It was really crowded and confused and didn't break up until 2:30 AM.

. . . In the evening, Elaine called and asked me to go with her to a club at the 68th AAA Bn [Antiaircraft Artillery Battalion] for dinner. It is about five or six miles from here and on Sundays, they feature a cook your own steak night. We went with Elaine's beau Col Courser who is CO of Ascom (Army Service Command) and Col Dougherty, who is replacing Colonel Courser. Being out with the brass meant traveling in style, a 1956 Chevrolet staff car. We had a very nice evening and a grand dinner. Elaine and I were the only American women at the club. But there were quite a few Korean girls. Such get ups you never did see.

The solution to your social life over here seems to be to latch on to a nice steady escort, married or not being of no matter. It ensures that you get out and around and if you can find someone who has his own transportation, so much to the better. Both the colonels last night are married of course, but they are real nice dates. The secret, of course, is to find someone who will be just a good companion without any emotional involvement. Well, we'll see what we will see.

* * *

Ascom City

Fri, Jan 25, 1957

I finally broke down and told the girls that it was my birthday, so after work we all got together for a drink. They even came up with a birthday cake, a brownie with a candle in it. At 10:00 last night, I had a call from the girls in Sasebo. They were all around the phone and sang "Happy Birthday" and then I talked briefly to each one. Wasn't that sweet of them?

Tonight four of us went over to another club where they feature a Friday night to seafood dinner. It was delicious and I ate the best meal I have eaten since the steak last Sunday. I'm sorry to say that our mess is very poor, so it is a real treat to get out once in a while.

* * *

Ascom City

Tues, Jan 29, 1957

. . . I wrote Daddy last night and closed by commenting that the evening stretched ahead. About 10 minutes later, Doug Hunt, who is CO of the medical detachment, called and asked me to go to the club at the 44th Engineers. We went with another officer, a nurse, and the Catholic chaplain. It was only a short distance from here. We had a pleasant evening, just visiting in front of an open fire. Tonight the gang is gathering to play Clue, which is a new game, sort of a Monopoly type I guess. I've never played. In fact, I'm going to have to stop here and change my clothes.

Later: Well, it was a nice evening. We played Clue—six of us and then had coffee and fruitcake. Just a nice homie evening with no drinking or carousing.

MARY AT THE CLUB

* * *

Ascom City

Thurs, Jan 31, 1957

. . . Tomorrow night I am going to the 8057th Club with Lou Powell, one of the recreation workers, and her steady date to a seafood dinner and dance. Saturday is the Army Nurse Corps Anniversary, with KT party and dinner. I'm going to the KT party and have a dinner date with Colonel Dougherty. I wrote you that I had been out to dinner with him the first Sunday I was here.

The post theatre is about 50 yards from my quarters and at the moment the most terrific screams are emitting, therefore I am assuming that the movie must be a blood curdling one.

* * *

Within weeks of arriving in Korea, Mary was spending much of her time with a married colonel, William. It is unclear the exact nature of their relationship, but she did confess that he was "the only man [she] ever wanted." There seemed to be an idea that "what happened in Korea stayed in Korea," but eventually Mary realized that there would be consequences for their relationship—whatever it was. Throughout their relationship, she regularly wrote to her mother, telling Grace of their socializing. There was a lot of drinking, dining, and dancing, and one has to imagine that the frivolity was an escape from the difficult conditions of daily life.

Ascom City

On ARC stationary

Sun, Feb 24, 1957

. . . Last night, William came over at 8:30 to return my photograph and we had a drink and I sort of unwound. I went to bed about 10:30 so have had a good night's sleep. I'm feeling fine and I'm going strong today.

* * *

Ascom City

Wed, Feb 27, 1957

. . . Tomorrow night, Betsy and I are going to the KT Party in Seoul for the assistant director of the ARC Clubmobile service who is leaving. The girl, Ruth Stoltz, was at the 98th in Munich with me. Fortunately, William was invited too, so he is taking us in.

* * *

Ascom City

Thurs, Feb 28, 1957

. . . Have run into complications on our trip to Seoul tonight, as several generals are descending on Ascom this afternoon and William doesn't know how long they will stay and whether he'll be free soon enough for us to make the trip. We'll have to see.

* * *

Ascom City
Fri, Mar 15, 1957

. . . Last Saturday I got a call at 8:00 AM that Mr. Salverud, the ARC Director of Operations for the Far East, was going to visit Ascom on Sunday. So I had to scurry around and arrange for his visit. Florence Tupper arrived about 1:00 on Saturday. As soon as I had her settled, I washed my hair and she came over and visited with me while I put it up and dried it. I had arranged a party for the evening of Florence, Betsy, William, Colonel Webb and Colonel Preiss and me. We went first to Colonel Preiss's quarters for cocktails and then had dinner at the 8057th Club. We came back to the hospital club for the dance and afterwards went to Colonel Webb's quarters for scrambled eggs and coffee.

* * *

Ascom City
Sat, May 25, 1957

. . . The girls who live in our hootch are having a KT party tonight before the dance. Last night we decided that we had to paint the bar, so we really went to town. The top has silver enamel paint, the sides gold enamel with red and green polka dots. A bit gay, n'est ce pas?

. . . Next weekend I'm going to a party at what is known as UNCMAC—United Nations Command Military Armistice Commission. Several of us are going. They are sending sedans for us. There will be a buffet supper and

dance and plans include a tour of the DMZ (Demilitarized Zone). It is something I have been wanting to see and this seems like a good opportunity. We are constantly bombarded with invitations to parties all over Korea. We could go someplace every weekend if we wanted. I don't much care to go usually, but this seems sort of special, so I think I will give it a whirl. Hope the weather stays nice.

* * *

Ascom City
Mon, Jun 17, 1957

. . . I had a real nice weekend. I went into Seoul on the bus and William met me for lunch. I made connections with Lois Beck, who let me use the room of one of her Clubmobile workers, who was on leave. At 1:30, I went and struggled through a permanent. I had them give me another Toni, as I wasn't familiar with the other brands they had and was afraid to experiment. I think it turned out OK. At least I hope so.

William picked me up at 6:00 and we went to the 8th Army Club for a KT party and dinner given by G4 section to which William is now assigned. After the dinner most of the party left, so William and I joined Colonel Regan and Kathleen for the rest of the evening. I ran into a number of the officers I had met up at UNCMAC as they have now moved to Seoul.

Sunday morning, W and I had breakfast at 9:30. Then Johnny Brooks, who happened to be up there, joined us. We went to the PX and wandered around. Had lunch then Johnny brought us back to Ascom. At 6:00 we went to a KT party and BBQ at the 55th QM Club—182nd anniversary of the QM. We came back to the 121st club and saw the "King and I." It was lovely, I thought, and stuck very closely to the Broadway show.

Tonight at 5:00, we had wiener roast for the patients on our new terrace. The mess hall provided all the food. In fact, they just turned over the evening meal to us. We had a charcoal broiler and roasted the hot dogs and served potato salad, carrot sticks, olives, cookies and punch. It was very successful and the patients seemed to enjoy it. I stayed up and helped Betsy with it.

. . . William told me that there is a very good possibility that he will get the job of G1 with 7th division. For his sake, I hope he does. The division is to be reorganized on the new Pentomic plan and it would be wonderful for him to be in on that at the beginning. It means that he would be even further away than he is now, which is bad for me. He hates his present job, so I'm sure hope he gets this. He expects to know by the end of the week.

Well, I guess that winds me up for now. Tomorrow night Father Bernie, the Catholic chaplain, is taking William and me out to dinner in Seoul. Father B. leaves for the States this week.

* * *

Ascom City
Wed, Jun 19, 1957

. . . At present I plan to leave here the night of the 29th (Saturday) [for R&R in Japan]. The plane goes at 12:50 AM, so it keeps you up all night. I plan to stay at the Dai Ichi Hotel in Tokyo. I'm going to have to call headquarters tomorrow and will ask them to get me a reservation there. I will stay until Saturday 13 July. Now, as to mail— you might send me a couple of letters mailed between 27 June and three July, addressed c/o Florence Tupper, ARC Headquarters, APO 500. The rest can wait for me here at the 121.

I still don't know just what I'll do. The 4th comes in there, so I figure some of my working friends might be available for a little tripping over the weekend. I want to go to Yokosuka and have also written to Jane van Alta who is at Yokohama. I guess the best thing is just not make any firm plans until I get there and can see when people will be available. I am not overly enthusiastic about the whole project, but it will probably do me good to have a change of scenery.

. . . Last night, Father Bernie drove me to Seoul in a jeep and we had dinner with William and Colonel Regan. It was a pleasant evening and it was real nice of Father Bernie to arrange it. He even bought us champagne. He leaves for the states tomorrow, so he had cause for celebration. In case you have wondered, William is not Catholic—is Baptist in fact. However, we have both been good friends with Father Bernie who is a real nice guy.

* * *

Ascom City
Sun, Jun 20, 1957

. . . I had to call headquarters today, so asked them to make a hotel reservation for me. They will confirm it by letter. I begin to feel like I am actually going, which I never did before. I'm getting things done ahead, like reports etc., so I can feel free to go.

. . . My plans for this weekend haven't jelled at all. I hope William will come down as I won't have another chance to see him for a long time. He's pretty sure his transfer to the 7th Division will go through. The job is not G-1, but as commander of the armed battle team which is part of the new divisional organization. That is his branch, you know, and like all officers he is most pleased to have troop duty. I sure hope he gets it.

* * *

Ascom City
Sat, Jun 22, 1957

. . . It is a rainy day so I am quite content to stay in. William is coming later, so I have that look to look forward to.

He called last night and he is getting the 7th Division job as expected, effective 1 July. He was on the crest of the wave, and I am so happy for him.

* * *

Ascom City
Sun, Jun 23, 1957

. . . I have had a nice weekend. William came down yesterday at 5:00. We went to a small KT party for several of the nurses who are leaving, had dinner at the mess and later went to the dance. He came down again today for about 3 hours as he was able to get an unexpected ride. He is leaving tonight for Japan on TDY. There is a possibility that he will still be there for part of the time I'm there. I hope so as it would make it so much more fun for me.

* * *

Ascom City
Wed, Jun 26, 1957

This may be the last letter for several days. I am starting out tomorrow night, so we'll probably be in a rush with packing and getting off. As things stand at the moment, I will take the bus from here at 9:30 to go to K14. The plane isn't scheduled to leave until 0050, but we have to check in at 11:00. The plane arrives in Japan about 5:30 AM Friday morning. I will be staying mostly at the Dai Ichi Hotel.

In fact, I think I'll just keep my room there even if I go off on some short jaunts. It would save having to cart all of my things along and give me a base. The room is only $4 a day. My day by day plans are still not jelled. The first few days will depend pretty much on whether William is over there or not. But you know, you can always locate me through ARC headquarters and I will keep them advised of my coming and going.

* * *

Ascom City
Thurs, Jun 27, 1957

Well, I'm finding a little time to get off another letter before I go. I have everything all packed and I'm waiting for William. He got back from his TDY to Japan last night. He's coming to take me to dinner at K14 then see me onto the plane. He is always so thoughtful and does so much to make things easy for me. The best thing of all is that he thinks he is getting R and R next week and will come to Japan on Monday or Tuesday. That means he will be over there most of the time I am, which should make all the difference from the fun angle.

* * *

Tokyo
Sat, Jun 29, 1957

Well, here I am, but I have quite a tale to tell about getting here. Everything is fine, so don't start worrying before you read on. I mailed the letter I wrote you just before leaving last night and scribbled a note as to my arrival on the envelope, which I hope you saw.

Anyway, William arrived to pick me up at 7:00. We went first to the passenger terminal, checked in my baggage, verified I was booked and learned that roll call would be at 11:00. We then went to the club and had a couple of drinks and leisurely dinner. When we got back to the terminal, we learned that the flight the night before had been cancelled due to bad weather, so there were to be two flights. I was booked on the second one. William stayed until nearly midnight and then left me more or less in the TLC of the of Red Cross man who was booked on the same flight as I. Shortly before 1:00 the first flight was called and everyone loaded. Ten minutes later they were back on the ground. One of the engines had conked out on takeoff and the plane came back in. The passengers unloaded and there was much milling around. During all this time I was lucky enough to have a seat as there aren't too many in the terminal. After a while, they announced that the first plane couldn't take off again, so they started transferring some of the people to the second flight manifest. In a little while they called me and said that I had been bumped from the second flight to make room for someone from the first flight who was on emergency leave orders and thus had a higher priority. There was more waiting, and finally they announced that those leftover from the first flight plus the bumped from the second were released until noon. Since my baggage had already been loaded on the second flight it would stay on the plane and I could claim it at Tachikawa. They got a truck to take me and about 15 officers (I was the only woman) to the BOQ. There were only six beds available, four in one room and two in another. The officers saw to it that I got the double room, even though that meant one bed wasted and most of them had to bed down on sofas in the club. I finally got to bed at 4:00 AM. Of course, I

had nothing with me but my purse, so I couldn't wash or bathe and had to sleep in my underwear. I had to use the ladies room at the club as there was only a general latrine in the BOQ.

I slept more or less, mostly less, until about 9:00 and then had breakfast at the club. While I was there, Harriet Burns, who is ARC worker at Pusan called me. She was on her way back to Pusan after attending a meeting we held last week, after which she had been up to visit Bonnie at the 43rd. She joined me at the club for a while and then we went back to the terminal and she had to check in at 11:30 for her flight at 1:30. So I had company for a while. At 12:00 they announced that they still had no information when I would get out (and the others) so we were released until 2:00.

I went to the Snack Bar for some lunch after Harriet left and then had a stroke of luck. I got into conversation with a Navy captain who told me that two Navy C-54s were coming in to bring Admiral Jerrold and his belongings. He said if I checked at Base Operations, I might be able to get a ride on one of the planes which were going back as soon as they unloaded. So I beat my feet over there and sure enough got booked onto the Navy plane. They rounded up about 50 people to go back on the two planes. I didn't get on the Admiral's plush seat job, but did get on the cargo plane. The planes were going to the Naval Air Station at Atsugi. I told the Army liaison officer about my baggage being at Tachikawa. He promised to phone ahead to arrange for transportation to take me from Atsugi to Tachikawa, about an hour's drive, and then into Tokyo.

We finally got off at 3:30. On the plane there were two regular seats and the rest bucket seats. I, being the only lady, was given one of the seats and my seatmate was a very nice Signal Corps Captain. The flight was fine—smooth and fast—just four hours. I forgot to say that before we left K-14, I learned that there would be no more flights to Japan until Monday, so I sure was lucky to get rescued by the Navy.

It was raining when we landed, but the transportation was all arranged for us. Three Air Force men and I had a sedan to take us to Tachikawa. When we got there, I found my baggage OK, but ran into a snag. It seems that the car had not been dispatched properly and couldn't take me to Tokyo. There was a bus into town at 11:00 (it was now 9:00), but I was too exhausted to wait. Fortunately, I had some yen with me, so I got a taxi to take me into Tokyo. It cost 2400 yen ($8.00) but at that stage it was worth it to me.

When I got to the hotel—about 10:30—they had my reservation and all was well. I had them send me up a sandwich. I did a little unpacking, took a beautiful hot bath and fell into bed at 11:30. I slept until a little after 9:00. I had my breakfast now and when I finish this will get myself organized and start out. My room is very small, but it has a private bath and is quite adequate—only $4.00 a day.

My plan for today is to go over to Osaka and get some yen, buy a couple of things at the PX (soap powder, etc.), get my hair done, look up some phone numbers so I can contact a few people. Will try to contact someone for dinner tonight and tomorrow. I also want to go to the Japan Travel Bureau and get some information on possible trips for next week. Monday I'll have to go out to headquarters for a while.

William expects to come over Monday night, arrive Tuesday AM. Of course, with the foul up on the flights, he may have trouble. However, colonels usually get taken care of.

Well, I guess that brings me up to date. I'll keep writing, of course, and give you my plans as they develop.

I just reread this and wonder if you will be able to read it at all. I am writing it sitting in bed and this ballpoint pen is a mess. At best, I guess I'll just have to hope you can decipher it.

At this point I feel quite relaxed. After all the trouble I had to get here, it is wonderful to have nothing I have to do, no pressures, deadlines, etc. The hotel is air conditioned. The weather outside is overcast, but it isn't raining—at least not at the moment. I don't imagine it is too warm outside.

Well, I'll mail this when I go out. The biggest advantage to this hotel is it is only a block from the Osaka—Army Hotel—so I have the advantages of that such as branch PX, yen sales, Post Office, APO, Beauty parlor, etc.

* * *

Tokyo
Sun, Jun 30, 1957

Time for the next installment. Things are going along quite well, quietly and without much excitement, but generally smooth.

Yesterday after I finished my letter to you, I went over to the Osaka Hotel and got some yen, made a couple of purchases in the branch PX and tried to get an appointment to get my hair done. No soap on the ladder, so I made an appointment for 10:00 this morning. I had lunch at the Osaka, a lovely big salad bowl with blue cheese dressing. After lunch I went to the Japan Travel Bureau in the Imperial Hotel to make inquiries about some trips. While I was in there Elaine Lynch came along. She is stationed in Yokosuka, but was in town for the day. She had only about 30 minutes before she had to catch her train, but we went back to the Osaka bar and had a beer and a brief visit. There we ran into an officer whom we both know on R&R from Korea, so he joined us briefly.

I guess I forgot to say that earlier in the day I had done some phoning to friends. I called Elsie Hanson—my wave [WAVE, Women Accepted for Volunteer Emergency Service] friend—and she asked me to come out to Camp Drake for dinner. She was expecting Helen Husted—ARC FD at the Tokyo Army Hospital, who is also a friend of mine. She contacted Helen and I met her at the garage where she was having her car repaired. She drove me out to Drake. We had a couple of drinks at Elsie's and then went to the club for dinner. Helen brought me part of the way and I took a taxi the rest of the way.

This morning I got up in time to have breakfast and go for the hair at 10:00. When I finished that, I had lunch at the Osaka and then walked over to the Ginza. I wandered about for a while, brought a summer pocketbook, but it started to rain so I grabbed a cab back to the hotel. It is now 2:00 PM. Yesterday I also called Helen Penhale, who is the director of the hospital services. She has invited me to come out to Washington headquarters about 4:30 for drinks and dinner. So I'll get ready to go shortly. Tomorrow I am going out to headquarters and to PX and bank. Beyond that I haven't any definite plans. I rather imagine I may pick up a dinner invitation at headquarters.

The weather hasn't been too good so far. It has rained every day and both days have been overcast with intermittent showers. However, I am told it has been pouring steadily for a week, so I guess I should be glad it isn't worse. It is quite cool. I have worn my short red coat every time I have been out. Right now it looks almost as if it might clear.

I'll be glad when William gets here Tuesday because then I won't be on my own. I haven't heard from Mr. Jennings yet, but in my letter I told him I wouldn't be here until the first. If he doesn't contact me, I'll call him after William leaves. He goes back on the 9th.

* * *

Tokyo
Mon, Jul 1, 1957

. . . Yesterday evening I went out to Washington headquarters and had KTs and dinner with Helen Penhale, Jeanette Ross and Margaret Halson—all of the hospital service brass. They were most cordial and I had a pleasant time.

This morning I went to the office at 11:00 and talked to them about for about an hour. They were very interested in hearing about all the change and command troubles at the hospital. I had lunch with the hospital people and then spent about two hours in the PX doing various shopping commissions. I bought myself an electric fan, which I mailed to Korea. In fact, I mailed two big boxes. I haven't finished up out there yet, but will have time later. Mostly today I wanted to get other people's shopping out of the way. Next time I can poke around for myself. I had to go back to the office at 3:00 for a conference with Jeanette Ross. This evening I am having dinner with Florence Tupper. In fact, I'm going to have to stop this and get dressed as I have to catch the bus in about 30 minutes. I'm about through anyway, and I can mail this as I go. I find that mail at the Osaka is only picked up at 10:00 AM each day, but I guess you get your letters OK anyway, I hope.

* * *

Hakone
Wed, Jul 3, 1957

How I wish you could see this place. It is gorgeous and so completely away from it all. But first I'll backtrack to yesterday and bring you up to date.

Around 4:00 yesterday we went out and I took William to the Shirobooka. That is the fantastic coffee house where John and Julie took me. I am sure I wrote you about it. All purple satin walls, Rococo design, with balcony on balcony and an orchestra playing. He was fascinated with it, as I was sure he would be. We then went back to the hotel and bathed and dressed and went for dinner at Suehiro's—also where John and Julie took me—for sukiyaki dinner. It was William's first experience at eating on the floor with chopsticks. He had a time with the chopsticks but seemed to enjoy it. After dinner we went to the Queen Bee, one of the big cabarets. It was an experience. They had a huge dance floor with two orchestras alternating. It is a place where they have hostesses to hire and were they ever dolled up in backless, strapless, practically fretless evening dresses. Just watching them was worth going there. There were two floor shows and in each there was a strip dance. So you can see the whole evening was an experience. I certainly could never have gotten to the latter place without an escort.

This morning we had breakfast at 8:00 and then I packed and we caught the 10:21 train. We arrived at the town of Odawara at 12:03 and took a trolley for 30 more minutes right up into the mountains to Miyanoshita where this hotel is on the trolley. We met up with a very nice older couple from New Zealand with whom we ended up having lunch after we arrived.

This hotel almost defies description. It is made-up

Travel brochures from Japan

of a lot of buildings and is sort of scattered all over the hillside. I have a tremendous double room and bath. A little on the old fashioned side, but mostly comfortable Western style furnishings.

By the time we checked in and got cleaned up, it was almost 2:00. We had an excellent lunch and then decided to explore the hotel grounds. The gardens are beautiful and we wandered up the hill and down dale and all around. We also poked around in the shops. I bought myself a necklace of carved ivory and earrings to go with it. I have been wanting some white summer jewelry and this set only costs $5.00. I also bought you a couple of Imari ashtrays. They aren't what you wanted, but I have never yet found just what I know you want.

When we came back, we sat in the lounge for a while and listened to a string orchestra play tea time music. Then we came up to my room and had a couple of drinks. We bought a little bottle of bourbon with us as drinks are very expensive on the Japanese market. Now I've had my bath and will finish dressing for dinner in a minute.

We will be here until Friday. Plans for tomorrow haven't jelled. Today was not too nice weather wise. Intermittent showers. If it is at all good tomorrow we might get a car and guide and tour around this very scenic countryside a bit. We are near Mount Fuji and there are several lakes in the vicinity.

* * *

Hakone
Thurs, Jul 4, 1957

Happy 4th of July! It seems a very strange place to be on July 4th, but then I'm spending all of my holidays these years in queer places. Today is not a bit attractive. There is low hanging mist or clouds and although it doesn't appear to be actually raining at the moment it sure could at any moment. I had wanted to take a sightseeing tour today, but if we do it's a cinch we won't see Mount Fuji. At the moment I am waiting to go to breakfast, so it is hard to tell what the day will bring forth.

Last night we had a good dinner at the hotel and then went to the Gohra Hotel to dance. The latter is about a mile from here and is a special services hotel. I had considered staying there, but everyone told me they had only dormitory type rooms with the bath down the hall. I've had enough of that type of community living and when I am on vacation, I like to luxuriate in a private room with a private bath.

The weather is still unpromising. We have decided to see how it is this afternoon and if at all possible we will hire a car for a tour. The bigger attractions here are of the scenic variety, and it hardly seems worth it unless it clears somewhat. In the meantime, I'm going down to have my hair done. It needs it badly and they used some sort of cream rinse last time which left it sort of oily.

I'll leave this open for now and add more to it later. I mailed the letter I wrote yesterday at the Gohra, but heaven knows when it will go out of there.

Later . . . Well, the hair bending adventure wasn't too bad—at least I feel a bit cleaner and more attractive. We have now had lunch and are about to start out by car, despite the weather, which hasn't improved. At least we'll see more than if we sat in the hotel. The poor weather is just unfortunate, but it is to be expected this time of year.

I've just counted the steps on my way up from the dining room. There are 71 up to my room. We have decided that they only assign rooms in this building to the young and healthy. William has 89 steps to his room, so he is worse off than I am. The fact that we have separate rooms is obviously a source of consternation to the Japanese, and we have had a good laugh over the fact that this building is called the "Hermitage." All the buildings are named—"Restful Lodge," "Comfy Cottage," etc. There is really no plan or sense to the layout—corridors wandering in every which direction. We keep coming on parts of the hotel that we haven't seen before.

Later. Well, the ride was a farce. We got up into the clouds and it was like pea soup fog. As you have said so often, "I felt like Helen Keller out for a ride." But we weren't out for a couple of hours and made a stop at the Hotel Hakone for a beer. At least we tried.

Now I'm in the process of getting ready for dinner. We are going up to the Gohra for dinner and dancing. We figured that since it is a holiday, it may be a little more festive up there. We planned to go back to Tokyo tomorrow in the morning, I guess, although we haven't discussed it specifically.

* * *

Tokyo
Sat, Jul 6, 1957

I'll get a start on this while I have a couple of minutes. I believe I last wrote Thursday, just before we went to dinner. Anyway, that evening we went to the Gohra Hotel and had a good dinner. Afterward we danced and had a nice evening. Despite the holiday, there weren't too many people there, which rather surprised us as it is an Army resort hotel.

Yesterday, of course, the sun came out and would have been the perfect day for a sightseeing we had done the day before in the fog. It was hot, though. We took a bus down to the station at Odawara—30 minutes—and got the 11:00 train back to Tokyo. It was a hot and dirty ride. By the time we got to the hotel, checked in and cleaned up, it was 2:00 before we had lunch. The lunch here at the hotel was delicious. This hotel is air conditioned, which is a real blessing.

In the afternoon we went out to Hardy Barracks and I stopped by the office and found two letters from you June 29th and July 1. We went to the PX and I did a little shopping. Got a present for you and one for Daddy, bought a light meter for my camera—Japanese made and only $15—and knocked off a couple of more things on my shopping list for other people.

When we got back to the hotel, we had a couple of drinks and called Elaine Lynch and Judy Hunter. We made plans to see Elaine this afternoon when we are going down to Yokosuka.

After much study of a little book called "This Week in Tokyo," we decided to have dinner at a place called "Papagayo." It is a Mexican restaurant of all things. The food was not good, but the place fairly attractive. They had a nice little combo. At 10:00 the floor show started. It consisted of no less than six different girls who did individual dances, all of which were strips. I'm beginning to think that you can't go anywhere in Tokyo without seeing a striptease. Actually, all the girls had beautiful figure and skin, and it wasn't too offensive.

Now it is Saturday AM and we have had breakfast. We are going to Yokosuka after lunch on the train. Will look around Ship's Store and have a drink with Elaine. She wanted us to stay for dinner but I don't think we will. It is a hot day and by the time we ride the train and plow around, we'll be a mess. We both feel that we couldn't go to the Navy Officers' Club on a Saturday night without

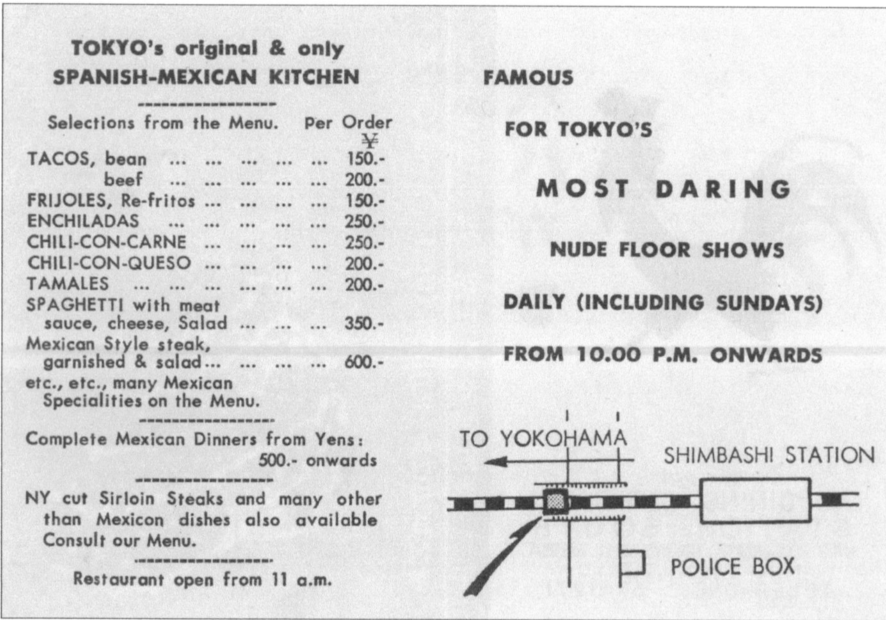

PROMO PIECE FROM MEXICAN RESTAURANT

a bath and getting dressed up and it is too much to carry along a change of clothes. Anyway, we have to catch an 8:00 train to Nikko in the morning, so we'll want to be in early tonight.

* * *

Nikko
Mon, Jul 7, 1957

This is another beautiful spot. We have just arrived, so I haven't gotten out to explore and give a full report. The hotel is old—built in 1873 according to the above—but has large comfortable rooms and a nice old-fashioned bathroom. The day is cloudy but cool and not rainy. We had a lovely train ride up, all electric train with reserved seats and snack service. The trip took just two hours. We left at 8:40 this AM.

We had a nice day yesterday, although it was a rather hot one. William had some errands to attend to in the morning and I stayed in my room to write some letters. We had lunch at the hotel and caught a 1:45 train to Yokosuka—about 1¼ hour trip. The train was crowded and we had to stand most of the way. We went to the Ship's Store Ashore and Ship's Store Afloat. I didn't buy anything except some records and a sapphire needle for my phonograph. We went up to Elaine's room about 4:30 and she gave us drinks. We hadn't planned to stay for dinner and weren't dressed for it. However, she insisted, and she borrowed a coat and tie for William from the club.

The club is beautiful, as you would expect the Navy club to be. As we went in, we ran into Elsie Hanson. She had had her dinner, but she joined us anyway. We had an excellent roast beef dinner and William took turns dancing with all the girls. They had a very good floor show and we left as soon as it was over at 10:00. We got a 10:52 train back.

Will stop now and add some more later.

We are just back from a 3½-hour tour which included most of the important sites. The tour was made up of three cars of people and a guide. We saw the big shrine here, which is really gorgeous, the best one I have seen. Then we drove up the mountains over switchback road such as I have never seen. We saw a lovely lake and at nearly 5000 feet and then rode back down the mountain on a cable car. This is a truly gorgeous setting, quite high mountains (highest 8500 feet) rushing mountain streams, waterfalls, etc.

It started to rain just at the end of the tour and is raining steadily now. Fortunately it didn't interfere with our tour. We have had a couple of drinks now and I am bathed and dressed and will go down for dinner in a few minutes. Our train back to Tokyo doesn't go until 5:00 PM tomorrow. I am hoping for a nice day as I would like to get some pictures. I took a few today but I have doubts as to how they will come out.

. . . Monday AM, Jul 8, 1957

Will add a few lines and then will close this. The day is overcast but not rainy as yet. Check out time is at 12:00. I am getting ready now to check out (10:00) and we will check our bags here. Then we will go get a bus to the Nikko-Kanko Hotel for lunch. It is an Army hotel, about an hour's bus ride from here.

I'll mail this when I get back to Tokyo and will write again in the next day or so.

* * *

Tokyo
Tue, Jul 9, 1957

Well, I'm back in Tokyo again and am through tripping until I make the big trek back to Korea.

I believe I left off around Sunday afternoon. The hotel was quite dull. After dinner we had a couple of drinks in the bar. The bartender showed us how to use an abacus (Japanese call it soroban) and we had fun playing with that.

Yesterday it was quite pretty in the morning. The sky was cloudy, but the sun came out every once in a while. We planned to take a bus ride up to the Army Hotel—about 18 miles away to have lunch. We inquired at the hotel and were told where and when to catch the bus and that it would have "Yumoto" on it in English. Well, we sat at the bus stop for 1½ hours and dozens of buses went by, but none marked "Yumoto." We finally gave it up and when we went back to the hotel, they allowed as how sometimes the buses were only marked in Japanese—a big help. Anyway, it was kind of fun to sit on the sidelines of a Japanese village and watch the people go by.

We had lunch at the hotel and afterward took a long walk all over the little town. It started to rain, so we took refuge in a beautiful antique shop. The little man brought out all his treasures to show us, and we saw some lovely things. I ended up buying a beautiful ivory figurine, about four inches high, a young Japanese girl in kimono and obi. I like it very much and it will be something to remind me of this trip. It costs ¥6000, which is about $17.00.

Our train left at 5:15 and we got back to Tokyo at 7:20. By the time we got back to the hotel had a drink, bathed and dressed and had dinner, it was time to go to bed.

Today William has to leave. He has to check out of the hotel at 11:00. He has ordered a car for 1:30 and we are going out to Tachikawa. We have made arrangements to see Judy Hunter this afternoon. She was at the 121st—Betsy's predecessor—and is now stationed at Tachikawa. William's plane leaves at 6:00 and I think I'll have dinner out there with Judy and come back into town by train. So that is the plan for the day.

Tomorrow I shall have my hair done and will go out to headquarters for a while. Jeanette Ross has to do my evaluation as she is leaving soon, so I have to go over that with her. I have some more shopping to finish up too. I'm definitely planning to go back Friday night. If I can get booked on a flight that will give me the weekend to get unpacked and settled down before I have to go back to work on Monday. Also, if I should not get on a flight Friday, I can go Saturday without cutting my time too short.

I am sure you have gathered from my letters that this has been a good trip. I had qualms about coming, but I guess things usually work out better than you think they will. Of course, Williams being here has made all the difference.

I guess you gather that I decided against trying to call you. I just didn't think I could take it. I hope you weren't disappointed, or at least didn't count on it. The distance is too great and the time until I come home too long. I get homesick enough without aggravating the situation.

Well, I'll close this now and mail it when I go out. We are going by the bank and post office en route to Tachikawa

* * *

Tokyo

Wed, Jul 10, 1957

Well, it's time for another installment of my doings. Yesterday was mostly devoted to getting William off to Korea. We had lunch at the hotel and at 1:30 a staff car came

for him. We stopped at a Hardy Barracks en route as I had to go to the bank and get a check cashed. I stopped by the office and picked up a letter from Daddy written 3 July. We then went on out to Tachikawa, where we met Judy Hunter. We all went to the club and had a couple of drinks and a visit and then went back to the terminal and saw William off at 6:15. Judy and I went back to the club for dinner. We were just finishing when Lee Galender, who is an ARC secretary who used to be in Korea, came in. So we sat on to visit with her. About 8:00 Judy was paged and went out to the lobby and came back with William. The plane had never gotten off the ground due to engine trouble. He had some dinner and at about 9:30 they sent a car to take him back to the plane. We didn't hear from him again so assume he got off.

Judy and I went over to her quarters for a little while and then I taxied to the station and took the train back to Tokyo—an hour's ride.

This morning I had breakfast in my room and at 11:00 I had my hair done at Osaka. I had lunch there and I'm now back in my room. It is a miserable day—pouring rain. However, in a little while I think I'll go out again and try to finish up some of my shopping errands.

Yesterday I got a message through headquarters that Jan van Alta had been trying to contact me. I called her and am going down to Yokohama tomorrow to have dinner with her. She wants me to stay the night, but I won't. I have booked on a flight for Friday at 6:00 and have to check out of the hotel by 11:00. I have to get a bus to Tachikawa at 1:30 and I think it would rush me too much to start the day in Yokohama.

Tomorrow morning I have a 10:00 appointment at headquarters with Jeanette Ross to go over my evaluation. I'll finish up some PX shopping while I'm out there.

I was glad to know from Daddy's letter that you had

received some of my mail from Japan. I have written quite often, I think, so I hope it has all been coming through promptly. I haven't made plans for this evening and I don't think I will. The weather is so miserable and I think I could use a quiet evening by myself. I've been in a tear ever since I have been here. I bought a $0.25 book at the PX so can amuse myself nicely. I'll have dinner here at the hotel.

I don't think I'll have a chance to mail this at the APO tomorrow, so I'll leave it open and maybe add more later.

Later. Well, it kept up pouring all afternoon, so I decided against going out. You know how I feel about shopping anyway, and I certainly didn't feel like getting wet to do it, so I've had a restful, if bit lonely afternoon. I even took a nap. Now I have had my dinner and I'm in PJ's and settled in for the evening.

The dinner was exceptionally good. Every Wednesday, this hotel features a roast beef dinner, which is served from the cart. It takes four people to serve it, the waitress, the chef who carves the beef, a waiter who puts watercress on the plate and hands it to the chef, and another waiter who puts gravy on the meal. The beef was rare and tender, in fact, delicious.

I've talked to Jane again. I'm going to take the train to arrive at Yokohama at 3:00 and she will meet me. I will come back after dinner. It is only 25 minutes by train and the station is less than two blocks from the hotel.

I've discovered a new drink on this trip. William always has martinis before dinner, which I don't like, so I have been having a dry Manhattan. I've never liked Manhattans much as they are too sweet, but this is quite good. I think they use dry vermouth instead of sweet. Have you ever tried one? I had one tonight, even though I was by myself.

I called Elise this afternoon and will call one or two others tonight. This is sort of my last chance as I will be late getting in tomorrow.

One of the mysteries of this trip is that I never heard from Mr. Jennings, although I wrote him about two weeks before I came. He must be away.

Well, I have nothing more to add tonight. I don't know if I'll have time for another letter before I leave, but we'll try to work one in. I usually manage to find a few minutes to dash off a few lines.

PS So far I have received 3 letters from you and one from Daddy since I have been in Japan. I wonder if that is all you have sent. I may find another when I go to headquarters tomorrow.

* * *

Ascom City
Sat, Jul 13, 1957

I am back, safe and sound. I wanted to send you an EFM. However, you send them through the PO, which closes at 12:00 on Saturday. There is a positive deluge going on outside—started in the night—and I just didn't get organized early enough to get the cable off. I'll send one Monday and hope that you will get it before you have begun to worry.

. . . I had a very busy day Thursday. Fortunately, it didn't rain much, so I was able to dash around without getting soaked. Wednesday night, Lucy Haag called me from Korea and asked me to pick up and bring back 16 uniforms for the waitresses in the mess hall. Thursday AM I called the firm and arranged for them to deliver them to me at 2:00 as I had to sign for them. I had a 10:00 appointment at headquarters so went out there and then had lunch at the PX [and] did a couple of errands which included getting the stuff wrapped and mailed to Korea. Then I dashed back to the hotel and received the uniforms. Then I dashed down to Ginza and in and out of two department stores trying to find [a] porcelain electric teapot for Lou Powell. I found it at the second place, tore back to the hotel, changed clothes and caught the 3:15 train to Yokohama.

Jane van Alta met me at the station and took me on a brief tour of their main shopping street. We then picked up Van, who was playing in a tennis tournament. We went to their quarters, which are quite nice but small, only two bedrooms. We had a couple of drinks and a wonderful steak dinner, and they took me back to the station about 10:00.

We had a real good visit. They are such great people. Their boys are enormous. Pete is 15 and nearly six feet tall, and Freddie, at 10 is nearly as tall as I am. Freddie made me think so much of Stephen—only not so beautiful.

Friday was a "hurry up and wait" sort of day. The box of uniforms completely threw me as it was so big and heavy and I already had more luggage than I could handle. Fortunately, Larry Albrecht, our former executive, was in Tokyo on R&R. So I called him and asked if he would bring them back. He agreed, so after I checked out of the hotel about 10:30, I got a cab and took them to him at his hotel.

From then on I had nothing to do until I caught the bus to Tachikawa at 1:30. I was in my wool uniform and slacks and didn't want to run around. So mostly I sat at the Osaka and had my lunch there. Eventually I got the bus and out to Tachikawa at 3:15. I immediately bumped into three officers I know from here who were going back on the same plane. Judy Hunter and Lee Gallander came over and joined us at the terminal. After we had completed the checking in about 4:30, the men

insisted we dash over to the club for a drink as we had until 5:15. I was against it but went anyway and had a coke. The plane loaded at 6:00, but it was 6:50 before we took off. The flight was completely uneventful—just 4½ hours. During the flight, the copilot invited me up to the flight deck for a little while. We flew in a C124—bucket seats and much cargo. I had ordered an in flight lunch which was quite good.

As I came down the ramp from the plane an Air Force officer told me that there was a sedan waiting for me. Lucy and Betsy had gotten the hospital sedan and driver to come and meet me. Wasn't that sweet of them?

. . . The pictures I am enclosing are ones Judy took of me when I rode the chopper up to see Bonnie. I thought the boys might get a kick out of them. In the one where I have my hands out, I have started toward the plane and then remembered my raincoat, which Betsy had been holding for me.

* * *

Ascom City
Sun, Jul 14, 1957

Well, I guess I'm experiencing a letdown over being back. I spent a most dull day yesterday and have the same prospect for today. It will almost be a relief to go back to work tomorrow.

Yesterday it poured rain all day, so I stayed in except to go to meals. I did get unpacked and settled in again. I went to the library and got a couple of books. I'll get used to the quiet routine again soon, but after two weeks of being on the go constantly, it will take a little readjustment. What I really should do is find me a new boyfriend in the local area. I have had it too good and been too spoiled by William. It is even almost impossible to talk to him by phone where he is now.

* * *

Ascom City
Mon, Jul 15, 1957

. . . I am really not as depressed as this letter probably sounds. I am pretty cheerful on the whole. But I do miss the distraction of a social life which added so much to my first six months in Korea. Well, maybe things will pick up in that area too. My real problem now is post-vacation let down.

* * *

Ascom City
Tues, Jul 16, 1957

. . . I'm enclosing a small picture of William, Johnny Brooks and me that Betsy took on one of our picture taking jaunts this spring. William is on the right (my left in the picture). Not too good a picture of him. It makes him look older and heavier than he is. He's really very slender. He is just not photogenic.

. . . I think William may come down this weekend. He has some business in Seoul Friday and is going to try to stay over the weekend. Telephone communications to his present location are terrible. The telephone exchanges here have weird names. To call him, for example, I call Bayonet and then ask for Boxcar.

* * *

Ascom City
Sat, Jul 20, 1957

. . . I don't believe William will come down today. I talked to him Thursday night and he was doubtful. I don't blame him for not making an unnecessary trip in this weather, although I could use with a little social distraction.

* * *

Ascom City
Sun, Jul 21, 1957

. . . I had a rather slothful day yesterday, but in the evening, I decided there was nothing to be gained by staying in. Lou had some people in for drinks before the dance in honor of May Nelson's birthday, so I went along with the crowd to the club. I hate going stag, but I had a fair time and danced with several people. I have been here long enough so that I know nearly everyone which helps.

Today I didn't get up until around 11:00. There is a party this afternoon for one of the doctors who is leaving. Then there will be the regular Sunday night buffet at the club and the movie, which I'll see if it is anything bearable.

* * *

Ascom City
Mon, Jul 22, 1957

Yesterday afternoon I went to a KT party, had supper at the club and saw a poor movie. That was my big excitement for the day.

* * *

Ascom City

Sat, Jul 27, 1957

I think this weekend is going to be a big improvement over the last two as William is coming this afternoon and I think he will stay until tomorrow. There's a big party at the club tonight which should be fun. It isn't raining at the moment but is overcast so might start at any time.

* * *

Ascom City

Mon, Jul 29, 1957

. . . My weekend was a nice one for a change although William wasn't here very long. He got here about 4:30 on Saturday. I had some beer on ice waiting for him. Later we went to the 55th club for dinner and then to the dance at our club. There was a nice crowd there, more people than usual, and I enjoyed being back in circulation again. Sunday we had breakfast at 9 and William had to leave right afterwards.

* * *

Mary was not unique in her situation. Having a relationship with a married man was certainly something that happened before and since the late 1950s and seemed to be the norm in Ascom City. But I have to think that Mary's openness about it with her mother was rather unusual. After Mary and William's trip to Japan, Grace wrote a letter of recrimination (which we don't have but can imagine the contents) to which Mary responded with one of the most poignant letters in the whole catalog.

Ascom City

Thurs, Aug 8, 1957

First of all, you don't ever have to be hesitant about writing or telling me anything you want to at any time. The most important thing in my life is the truly wonderful love and understanding we have for each other. Nothing could ever change that.

There is not going to be an "argument across the miles," honey. I am fully aware that the Japan trip was a mistake. I regretted from the start that I allowed it to come about. I didn't want you to think that I deliberately did not write you about it in advance. Although we had discussed the possibility, I honestly did not think that it would come about and that William would be able to get leave at the same time. When it broke that way, I let myself get carried away by the complete acceptance of that sort of thing that there is in this Never Neverland of Korea. I kept telling myself as long as I knew I wasn't doing anything wrong, it didn't matter what interpretation others might put on it. But, of course, that isn't so. I didn't feel right or comfortable about it at any time.

Ever since William left Ascom, I've been trying to make up my mind to break off completely. We have discussed this a number of times and he will go along with whatever I decide. It is a hard decision to make because it means depriving myself of my one source of pleasure in this God forsaken place. I think I have finally made that decision, although I haven't told him so yet. I am committed to going and taking some girls to a party he is giving on the 24th, the first big party for his new unit. But I think that will be the end.

I'm sure that you do not think much of William. I sincerely wish you could know him as I do. He is a fine person and one whom I truly trust and respect. He had many misgivings about the Japan trip and repeatedly pointed out to me that I was the one who was risking my reputation. So you see, I can't project any blame onto him. I was the one who allowed both of us to act ill advisedly. If I am to be completely honest with you and with myself, I'll have to admit that he is the first man I have ever met that I really wanted. If he were available, I would do everything in my power to get him. But since he isn't, I know now that I'll have to stop seeing him.

I don't want you to think that I have been hurt by this experience. Actually, I think I have benefited in many ways. You might say that this has made a woman out of me. It has shown me that I am not strange and peculiar, and that I can respond normally to a man's attentions. Without fully realizing it, I think I have always been afraid to relax and be myself with men. William has repeatedly told me that I always underestimate myself. So this has been a most flattering and ego-boosting experience and I think I have gotten a great deal from it.

But—the time has come, in fact is overdue, for the two of us to discontinue a relationship which can only become more complicated for us both if it continues. It isn't easy, and my life here henceforth bids fair to being pretty bleak, but it is the only course of action that is right and possible.

I have written and rewritten this letter four times in the last three days. I was dissatisfied with the former ones because I realized I was still hedging and rationalizing. I feel that I have finally gotten it down honestly and I count on you to understand.

I think you know that I never consciously tried to withhold anything from you. If it seems sometimes that I do, it is because my own thinking is not clear. You'll never know how much it means to me to be able to share my life with you. I know absolutely that regardless of what I may do, it won't make any difference in our love for one another. I always try not to do anything which I know will upset or hurt you. You have never failed me, but in this case, I failed you. That hurts more than anything else. I can't undo that I'm afraid.

I love you more than you'll ever know.

* * *

Mary spent almost a full year in Korea after this letter and continued to socialize with William, as well as several other people.

Ascom City
Sat, Aug 10, 1957

. . . There was a real nice party last night given by one of the doctors for a couple of others who are leaving. It was too hot to stay inside, so we moved the chairs out on the sidewalk between the quarters. Practically everyone in the hospital was there and it was just pleasant and relaxed.

There's another party tonight before the dance. This is really quite a partying crowd, but whenever anyone gives a party, they post a notice in the mess hall saying "everybody come." I think that is good form because it keeps the group from becoming clique-y.

* * *

Ascom City
Mon, Aug 12, 1957

. . . Even my experience with William, which was always fraught with potential disillusionment and heartbreak, has left me only with a feeling of gratitude. I know I didn't always handle it too well, but I haven't been hurt by it. In fact, I have gained a lot from it. I think I explained it all in my other letter. At least I hope I did.

* * *

Ascom City

Mon, Aug 19, 1957

. . . William came down to see me yesterday, the first time I have seen him in two weeks. We had a good talk and I think have gotten things fairly well worked out. We will continue to see one another from time to time, particularly for special events. For example, on 7 September the senior officers in his division (the 7th) are having a farewell party for General Jark, their CG [commanding general] who is leaving and he wants me to come. I have told him that I will.

Incidentally, he came down with the news item that one of my Smith classmates was working with Special Services up there. When I asked him her name, he told me Mrs Lee, but he had completely forgotten to find out her maiden name. Isn't that just like a man? Anyway, whoever it is told him she knew me. He went back with the mission of learning more particulars.

* * *

Ascom City

Tues, Aug 21, 1957

. . . I had your letter today written after you received mine of 8 August. As you said, it is probably best to consider the matter talked over and not fill letters with it. I hope you will not be disappointed in me if I continue to report on seeing him from time to time. I think that I will, and I am not going to feel I can't mention it to you when I do. Incidentally, his party on the 24th had to be cancelled because of a conflict with other festivities relative to the upcoming change in commanding generals in

the 7th division. I mentioned it in yesterday's letter that I expect to go up for a high level party for General Jark on 7 September. No other plans have been made.

* * *

Ascom City

Wed, Aug 22, 1957

. . . Charles Wahle called me this evening. He expects to be down this way again sometime next month and wants me to go out with him. I told him I would. He is really up in the sticks. He said he had to drive an hour and a half to get to a phone on which [he] could call down here. We in the rear areas really don't have any understanding of the inconveniences the men up forward have to put up with.

* * *

Ascom City

Sun, Aug 25, 1957

. . . William came down yesterday afternoon. He had to go to a party in Seoul today, so decided to come here and go to the party on the way back. He has to go through Seoul to come down here. After he got here, he went up to the hospital to call on a couple of his friends who are patients. He and I had dinner with Johnny Brooks at the 55th Club and then came over to the dance at our club. This morning Betsy and Lucy made waffles and we all had breakfast together in our quarters.

* * *

Ascom City

Thurs, Aug 29, 1957

. . . Last night there was a KT party and buffet supper for a nurse wheel from the Pentagon who is making the grand tour. We get almost as many visiting firemen in Korea as we used to get at Belvoir. Anyway, it was a nice party and everyone turned out.

. . . Tomorrow night, Mr. Foy, the ARC FD, has asked me to have dinner with him at the 8057th. He has been there since June and this is the first time he has ever as much offered to buy me a drink and I think it is about time.

* * *

Ascom City

Sun, Sep 1, 1957

I went to Seoul on the bus yesterday morning, lugging a suitcase with a change of clothes. I had lunch and then braved the beauty parlor. I had my hair cut fairly short and so far the permanent seems OK. I still had quite a bit of permanent in my hair so they only gave me a very light one. I then went to Ethel Inglis's quarters and showered and changed. William picked me up there and took me to dinner at the OEC [Operational Evaluation Command] Club. We came back to Ascom in time to take in the floor show at the hospital club and he went back last night.

The biggest thrill at the OEC Club was the beautiful ladies room. It was completely stateside. Tile floors, metal booths, full length mirror, etc. I haven't seen anything like it since I left the States. It just shows what having dependents around can accomplish. The OEC is under the State Department and their personnel are allowed to have their dependents with them. Well, I never thought I would write a page raving about a ladies room, but it was

exciting. I told William he really ought to go see it, but he said that would make a fine headline: "Colonel caught in Ladies Room."

I think I mentioned yesterday that I'm going sailing this afternoon with Major and Mrs. Crane. It is a beautiful day and I think it will be fun. We are going about 2:00.

* * *

Ascom City

Mon, Sep 2, 1957

I had such a nice day yesterday. The weather was beautiful—cool and sunny. I wrote you that I was going sailing with Major and Mrs. Crane. The party also included Lou Powell, Tom Nelson (our CO) and Bob Richards (a dentist). We left about two and sailed out around Inchon Harbor for about 3½ hours. There wasn't much breeze, but enough to make it a nice smooth ride. Sailing is fun and relaxing, and getting out in the sun and air is always good for you. I wore blue jeans and a long sleeve shirt so I wouldn't burn and smeared Sea and Ski lotion on my face. My nose is a bit pink today, but no other damage.

When we got back, we had a picnic supper in Tom's quarters.

I always enjoy Paul Crane so much. I know I have told you that he is the son of a missionary, was born in Korea and was a medical missionary when he was called into service. He knows so much about Korea and it is always so interesting to talk to him. Last night at supper he told us a great deal about leprosy, which was most educational. It may not sound like good supper table conversation, but we were all extremely interested.

* * *

Ascom City

Wed, Sep 4, 1957

I didn't get a letter written last night and won't tonight so will dash off a few lincs on my lunch hour in order to keep your mailbox filled. I've been having a little local social life the past few days. Monday evening there was a small KT party for one of the doctors who was leaving. While I was there, a couple of the officers invited me to join them for supper as a group were cooking out. There were about 15 of us and we had delicious steaks and a pleasant evening sitting around.

Last night Betsy baked a cake in her electric frypan and we had about 10 people in for cake and coffee and to look at slides. Tonight is the monthly "Hail and Farewell" party. Tomorrow, Lucy has a Jeep for the afternoon. I'm going to take the afternoon off and ride to Seoul with her. I will get my hair done while she messes around on errands. I always like to have my hair done the first time after a permanent. Also this is the weekend I'm going up to the 7th Division to the big party for Gen. Jark and I want to look as nice as possible. So you see it is a nice week.

* * *

Ascom City

Thurs, Sep 5, 1957

. . . This is the weekend I'm going to the 7th Division for a farewell party for Gen Jark. William is sending his car down for me Saturday morning and I will leave here about noon. I am to stop at the 43rd MASH to pick up one of the nurses. He has arranged for me to stay with the ARC Clubmobile Girls at Division. The women's billets at the 7th are called "Seventh Heaven." William will bring me back Sunday and other than the party Saturday night, I

don't know what festivities have been planned. However, I have no qualms as I know William will take good care of me. I have never been up there and I think it will be interesting to see the division and that part of the country. It has been so dry recently that I fear the trip up and back will be pretty dusty. There are no paved roads beyond Seoul.

I had a nice time at the "Hail and Farewell" party last night. I joined forces with Maj Jorsen, who was our supply officer and a good friend of mine, and he took good care of me. He is leaving next month, as are many of my old buddies. With all the staff changes, I feel almost like I am starting on a new assignment.

* * *

Ascom City

Thurs, Sep 12, 1957

This Saturday, Johnny Jorsen is going to take Lucy and me walking in the village to take pictures. Women aren't allowed to walk alone over there without an escort, and I have never been. The exercise will do me good as I get very little outdoors exercise.

* * *

Ascom City

Sat, Sep 14, 1957

. . . Last night I went with Johnny Jorsen up to the 8075th for their steak dinner and dance. As you can see from my recent letters, Johnny has been beau-ing me around quite a bit recently. I have known him ever since I have been here. He used to date one of the nurses who has gone home. He's going home next month. He is not exciting, but a nice guy and it is convenient to have someone in the hospital to go around with. He is a major—MSC [Military Sealift Command]—Chief of Supply, married with three children. I just give you the details so you know who I mean when I refer to Johnny. I think I mentioned that he is going to take Lucy and me on a picture taking walk to the village this afternoon and tomorrow by Jeep to a place north of Seoul where the tombs of the ancient kings of Korea are.

Yesterday we worked out the staff leave schedule for the rest of the year. I can have leave about 25 November and I may go to Hong Kong then on a package tour. I think Florence Tupper will be in Hong Kong at that time, so I wouldn't be alone all the time. As you know, I'm not overly enthusiastic about the trip, but I have to use some leave and may as well go. I had hoped to go a bit sooner to do Christmas shopping, but I can't work it out so it looks like any presents I get will be late, I'm afraid. I'm going to have to send money to Martha and Audrey to get things for the kids. Incidentally, you never answered my questions about what, if any, linens you, Martha and Audrey might want, or anything else from Hong Kong.

The tour I'm considering is from Korea to Hong Kong via Hong Kong Airways. It is a British company which flies Viscount Turbojets, British pilots and maintenance. It is a 5 hour flight with a refueling stock stop in Okinawa. Their package, which includes plane fare and five nights in a hotel and breakfast, is about $258. There are less expensive package tours but I am not keen on such airlines as Korea National Airways, which has American pilots but Korean maintenance and crew. I'll keep you posted on what I decide to do, of course. It is hard to make up my mind to go at all. I feel I might regret it if I don't didn't go, but I do hate to have to go by myself.

I expect to carry over about 10 days unused leave into

1958. My hope is that I will be permitted to hold that and take it when I come home. That would give me a total of 6 weeks leave before I have to start a new job. There's nothing I would rather do than have a lovely long leave right at home.

* * *

Ascom City
Mon, Sep 16, 1957

. . . I had a real interesting weekend. Saturday afternoon Johnny took Lucy and me on a long walk through the two villages near us. I took a roll of film. Of course the villages are filthy and depressing, but interesting nevertheless. We must have walked about 5 miles in all. I took a nap and had dinner and Johnny took me to the dance.

Yesterday Johnny and Roy Ostermann—our adjutant—picked me up a little after 10:00. We took a can of ice with beer on it and a picnic lunch and started out. All and all we drove 94 miles, which is quite a jaunt in a Jeep over terrible roads. Our destination was the Tomb of the Kings north of Seoul. We had quite a time finding it, but finally did about 2:30. We'd stopped en route and had our lunch. On the way back we stopped at the Club at the 618th Medical Company. (Rest and refreshment stop.) I took another roll of pictures and really enjoyed it. It was terribly dusty, and we had an open Jeep, so we were quite filthy when we got back at 6:30. In the evening, I went to a very lousy movie.

. . . You asked about Betty's cake and the electric frying pan. It was one layer chocolate package mix job. It wasn't very good, but we were so pleased with her effort that we gobbled it up.

* * *

Ascom City
Fri, Sep 27, 1957

. . . Last night I couldn't stand to stay in my room, so I went to the movies and saw Walt Disney's "Cinderella," which I loved. Three of the new nurses had a house warming party before dinner.

Tonight Johnny Jorsen is taking me to dinner and the dance at the 8057th Club. I have managed to find enough clothes in this mess to get dressed decently.

. . . Now it is Saturday morning. . . . I had a fairly nice time last night. A good steak dinner and the dance afterward. Tonight we are having a KT party in our quarters before the dance for Ray Ostermann—our adjutant—who is leaving on Monday. Tomorrow a group of us have two jeeps lined up and have tentative plans to go to Suwon, an old walled town South of Seoul, on a picture taking jaunt.

* * *

Ascom City
Mon, Sep 30, 1957

. . . William came down Saturday afternoon and was here for dinner, our small KT party for Roy Ostermann and the dance. The KT party was in our hooch and was very successful. William left Sunday morning at 8:00 and at 9:00 Lucy, Ray Ostermann, Johnny Jorsen and I took off in the Jeep for Suwon, an old walled city about 45 miles from here. It was a rather overcast day and a bit chilly but not bad. The roads were terribly rough, but we enjoyed the trip. As always, the main purpose was picture taking. We had a picnic lunch beside a lake. On the way back, we

stopped at Anyang where they have dammed up a river and built a series of swimming pools, one above the other up a sort of Canyon.

We got back around 4:00 and after showers and a brief rest, we cooked steaks outside the BOQ. Later we came down to our quarters and showed each other our slides. I got back the roll I took from the Tomb of the Kings two weeks ago so Roy and Johnny wanted to see them.

Roy left for the States late this afternoon. Lucy and I rode over to the K-14 to see him off. He is going to be stationed at Fort Meade, so we have great plans of getting together when I get back to Washington.

* * *

Ascom City
Mon, Oct 28, 1957

. . . Saturday afternoon went by without event except that I was reading an international spy thriller which kept me engrossed. At 5:00 about 25 of us—nurses and Red Cross—loaded on a bus to go to the Dickers' KT party. It was a lovely party at Hartwell House—the General's mess. General and Mrs. D received us and then we went into another room for drinks and hors d'oeuvres. They had all the generals there and ranking 8th Army Staff officers. I saw Gen Kyster there and had a number of other people who I know, but you don't.

The bus took us all down to what is called Kimchi Kabana, which is actually one of the clubs. The girls all had dinner there and came back on the bus. William picked me up there and we went to the 8th Army Club for dinner and dancing and then came back to Ascom.

Yesterday, we had breakfast, drove around a bit and then had lunch at the 8057th club and William left at

1:00. I spent a good part of the afternoon taking a nap and in the evening saw "War and Peace" at our club.

* * *

Ascom City
Tues, Oct 29, 1957

. . . I guess I wrote that Thursday we are to have a Halloween costume party. I have about decided to wear the same get up that won me the prize in Sasebo last year. The only trouble is that I don't have the big hat anymore. However, Loretta brought back a coolie hat from Hong Kong, which she says I can wear. William may come down, so I guess I'll have to think up something for a costume for him too. He is thinking about taking a three day pass this weekend. If he does, I'll have him take me to Seoul (I have the day off Friday anyway) so I can see about my reservations for Hong Kong. I haven't been able to get my orders yet which is too bad as that will mean another day in Seoul getting visas, etc. It would certainly help to have transportation for that day, but I'll have to cope with that later.

* * *

Ascom City
Thurs, Oct 31, 1957

Happy Halloween. My plans for tonight and the weekend have gone all haywire, but I am going to the party anyway. William called yesterday that he couldn't come down at all this weekend. Although I wish I had a date for tonight, it is just as well he isn't going to be here tomorrow as I couldn't possibly take the day off.

. . . Next Wednesday is another Hail and Farewell party. This will be my 10th one and they are beginning to get in a bit of a rut as far as I'm concerned. However, I shall go of course, especially since Dolores and our new CEO will be being hailed.

* * *

Ascom City
Fri, Nov 1, 1957

. . . Last night I went to the Halloween party and again won a prize with my costume, a bottle of champagne. Tish and Dolores also won prizes so the ARC did all right. It was a good party and I enjoyed it even though I didn't have a date. I came home around 10:30 as I didn't want to be up late on a weeknight, especially when we are so short staffed.

* * *

Ascom City
Tues, Nov 5, 1957

. . . I have nice weekend plans and I wish my hair looked better. Saturday there is a KT party and steak fry at the BOQ for Tim Nelson, our former CO—who leaves Sunday. William is coming down for it. On Sunday I am going up to the 7th division with him to a party Sunday night. I will stay overnight and Monday AM (it is a holiday) we are going to the ceremonies dedicating the Memorial Chapel at the 7th Division. He will bring me back Monday night. It will be a nice change as I have scarcely been away from Ascom in weeks.

* * *

Ascom City

Thurs, Nov 7, 1957

. . . Mrs. Decker and Mrs. Mathewson (CG of KMAG [Korean Military Advisory Group]) are the only army wives over here. The OEC (State Department) have their dependents. Mrs D and Mrs M have to do so much official entertaining with the Koreans representing their husbands here and there. A hell of a life, I am sure. You're always seeing Mrs. Decker's picture in the paper visiting this orphanage, attending that luncheon meeting, etc. Almost like royalty.

Yesterday I ran into Mrs. Crane at the PX. She wanted to come down to the Hail and Farewell last evening, so I offered her a ride. She met me at 4:00 and rode down with me. I went to the party but came home about 10. The dinner was unusually good, but the party as a whole seemed to lack spark. You mentioned that I went to a lot of parties. I do, but there is such a sameness, the same people, same routine.

* * *

Ascom City

Tues, Nov 12, 1957

. . . William's exec, Bill McKean, came down with him Saturday. I had expected them about 3:30, but they had car trouble en route and eventually got here at 6:00. We went immediately to the farewell party for Major Nelson. It was KTs and buffet supper at BOQ 1. Afterwards we sang and danced to the phonograph. It was a fairly small group, a fair party, but not too much.

Sunday, we had breakfast and started out for the 7th Division about 11:00. It was a miserable day, poured continuously. We stopped at Seoul for lunch en route. We got up there about 2:30 and I got settled in my room at the females' billets. We visited at William's hooch until it was time to dress.

The party consisted of a KT party, dinner and dancing. William and I double dated with Bill McKean and one of the special service girls.

Monday was a lovely day, weather wise. I had breakfast at William's Mess. It developed that the Chapel dedication do was complicated. William's car was requisitioned to transport visiting dignitaries and he had to go to a command lunch afterwards, to which he could not take me, so I ended up not going to the ceremonies at all. I stayed at his club where I was properly looked after by his officers and had lunch there. He got back about 1:30 and as soon as I had collected my things, took off for Seoul. We stopped at the Korean Ministry of Foreign Affairs and I was able to get my exit permit corrected with no difficulty.

We had no sooner gotten in the headquarters when Ginny Weisell called and asked us to come up to the farewell party being given for her at the 8057th Club, so off we went. We had dinner there and William took off around 8:00 to go back.

As you can see, the whole weekend was rush, rush and party, party. It sounds gay and glamorous, but actually it isn't as much fun as it sounds. I shouldn't complain, but I do get sick of parties. They are all the same. I keep wishing there was something else to do in a way of social activities. It really gets tiring always being in a crowd, making useless conversation, drinking too much, (I don't, but an awful lot of people do) dancing to lousy bands and eating poor food. Well, that's enough steam blowing off. But this weekend was just too much of the madness. Guess I'm getting old.

Here's a piece of nice news. Elise Hansen called me last night and both she and Helen Husted (Field director at Tokyo Army Hospital) are going to be in Hong Kong when I am. Helen is going this Saturday for two weeks, so will be there all the time I am. Elise is going first to the Philippines, but will come to Hong Kong for part of the time. So it looks like I am not going to be lacking for company and I am glad Elise and Helen have found out through Florence Tupper that I was going to be there.

* * *

Ascom City

Thurs, Nov 14, 1957

. . . For the record, I leave on 22 November on Hong Kong Airways at 0800 hours. I believe I'll be at the Peninsula Hotel. I meant to call the airlines today to see if they had confirmed my hotel reservation, but I didn't have time. I will return on Thursday 28, November getting in around 4:30 PM. Don't try to write me in Hong Kong.

. . . Maj. Wells, the Chief Nurse, and I got drafted as official hospital hostesses again tonight. Gen. McNinch, the number one medical officer from Japan, and Col Sayler, 8th Army surgeon, were here for dinner and a medical meeting afterward. Maj Wells and I were required to sit at the head table at dinner. I'm always pleased at the recognition accorded Red Cross by these requests. Gen McNinch said to me tonight "You are getting to be the most familiar face I see when I come to Korea." I don't know whether it was a compliment or not, but at least he knows me and that I represent the ARC.

* * *

Ascom City

Mon, Nov 18, 1957

. . . We arranged a party for Margaret Saturday night and it went very well. She said she enjoyed it and I think she did. All of the men knocked themselves out to be nice to her. All danced with her and she was quite the belle of the ball. On Sunday she went to church with Betsy and William and I took her to brunch at the 8075th club before he had to go back. Last night she and I went to the movie, which was pretty poor, but something to do. She has really been no trouble. Has kept herself occupied nicely. I think the weekend provided her with a rest, which I'm sure she welcomed in the midst of her rather strenuous trip.

* * *

Ascom City

Wed, Nov 20, 1957

. . . I'll have my Thanksgiving dinner on the plane coming back. A queer place to have it. Since it is a holiday, William is planning to meet my plane. He is always so good and thoughtful. I have arranged for the hospital staff car to take me to the plane Friday. I have to be there at 7:45. Take off time is 8:30.

* * *

Ascom City

Wed, Dec 11, 1957

. . . William's division is on a week-long maneuver this week. He just called me from his tent in the field. I told him it was some war when you can make personal calls from the field. He called to tell me his exec. was coming to the hospital tomorrow and he wanted me to look in on him. If the war is over Friday, as expected, I may go up to the 7th Division this weekend.

* * *

Ascom City

Thurs, Dec 12, 1957

There has been much excitement in the quarters tonight because Lucy Hoog got her promotion to Major today. So we have been celebrating with her and have decided that the party we are giving tomorrow night will now have to be her promotion party. There are four of the nurses who have also gotten their Majors. Nice Christmas presents for all concerned. Wish we could hope that Jack would get his promotion as a Christmas gift.

. . . I thought I had written you that William is going to be stationed at the 1st Army headquarters at Governor's Island. He thinks he will get quarters on the post and is very happy about the assignment. His son is a senior in high school this year and they hope to get him into West Point this June. He has taken the exams for congressional appointments, but they haven't heard yet how he made out. He is their only child, so if he is at West Point, Governors Island is ideal. W has applied for paratroop training of all stupid things and hopes to get that in before reporting to Governors Island. Because of Bill's school, his wife wouldn't be able to move to New York before June anyway, so he feels that he may as well go to jump school this spring. Why an armored officer feels that he has to jump out of an airplane is beyond me, but he seems to feel that in the modern army, being a paratrooper is necessary if you're going to get anywhere. He admits that his wife reacted to the idea the same way I did. He doesn't seem to have any idea of transferring to

the Airborne—just wants to qualify and wear the wings. Men just never grow up, do they?

* * *

Ascom City

Sat, Dec 14, 1957

For all it was Friday the 13th our party last night was a huge success. We had our quarters decorated for Christmas and were all dressed in our Korean dresses. I think nearly 100 people came and that was some crush in our small quarters. A large number went on over to the dance and it was one of the best attended dances they have had in months. I didn't have a specific date but ended up going to the dance with one of the young doctors and had a real pleasant time. We changed out of our Korean dresses before going to the dance.

My weekend plans have altered slightly in that William is coming down here instead of my going up there. He called in the midst of the party last night and I could hardly hear him, so I don't know why he changed the plan. However, it makes no difference to me. I assume we'll go over to the 8057th for dinner and their dance.

* * *

Ascom City

Thurs, Apr 10, 1958

Last night was square dancing night. We had a pretty good turnout and it was fun. I am the star pupil because I know how to do "put your little foot" and the Jesse polka.

* * *

Ascom City

Sun, Apr 13, 1958

. . . As I said, the Hail and Farewell party was Friday, which of course knocked out any letter reading writing time I might have had. I left the party about 9:30 as I was tired and had to work Saturday and Sunday. I was having a good enough time, but I also am trying to keep myself in a state of health to withstand the pressure I am under.

Saturday, of course, I worked all day. I wasn't too busy work wise, but I didn't twiddle my thumbs either. The big event yesterday was the installation of a TV in our rec hall. There's a TV station in Korea which broadcasts films. Of states side programs yesterday we had "The Big Tops" and "Wide, Wide World." This afternoon we are having "Omnibus."

Last night I played bridge for a couple of hours, then went with Bill Howard, one of my doctor friends, to a birthday party of one of the dentists. It was a small, quiet affair. And I was home by 11:30.

. . . On Friday, I received a call from Col Berkowitz, who said he had dinner with Martha and Jack a couple of weeks ago. I appreciated his calling me very much. He is with KMAG in Seoul, but said he would come down this way sooner or later and would stop by to see me.

* * *

Ascom City

Thurs, Apr 17, 1958

. . . My life here continues hectic but is getting a little less so. I like all my new girls and I think we are going to have a real good staff here once they are broken in and learn their jobs. They are a very attractive bunch and should not want for lots of social life.

I'm not having much social life these days, but of course at this point I don't really care. I don't want any more "entangling alliances." I feel completely at home in the hospital crowd and feel free to go to the parties without any escort and know I'll be danced with. I am the senior member at the hospital. There is no one left who has been here as long as I have. Yesterday was my fifteen-month anniversary. The Army tour is going to be cut to 13 months after one July.

* * *

Ascom City

Sat, Apr 19, 1958

. . . Wednesday night I went to the square dancing and most of my new gals turned out for it. Thursday evening, all the new gals came down and I showed them my slides of Korea. It was a sort of combined hair washing venture. They are having water troubles in their hooch so all of them wanted to use my shower for a shampoo. They are a real nice bunch of girls.

. . . Last night the girls Jody lives with had a farewell KT party for her and then we all went over to the dance at our club. Bill Howard, who is a dermatologist and a good friend of mine, took me under his wing and I had a real nice time. All my girls were there and they all seemed to be having fun.

. . . I had a real nice letter from George Guy up at the 7th Division yesterday. He was William's Adjutant. He wrote to thank me for sending the girls up for their party last week and he is going to try to come down to see me next week and if he can promote transportation. Wants to take me to Seoul to dinner. He is a real sweet boy West Pointer class of 54.

* * *

Ascom City

Thurs, Apr 24, 1958

. . . Last night I went to the square dancing. I rather enjoyed it and would enjoy it more if I weren't sort of in charge of it.

Tomorrow night, Col. Buchanan has asked me to go to the dance at our club, the Hospital EM are having a unit party and we are going to put in our appearance there first. That is a good solution as I had been invited to the EM party but wouldn't have gone unescorted. This way I can do my duty and be in good company.

One of William's officers up at the 7th wrote me a note about 10 days ago asking me for a date for Saturday as he was coming down here. I answered his note accepting but haven't heard from him again, so don't know. Maybe he'll call tonight or tomorrow.

* * *

Ascom City

Sat, May 3, 1958

I may or may not have a date tonight. June Williams—dietitian—wants me to go out with a Lieutenant Colonel from Seoul whom she picked out for me. The question is that he is not sure he can get down today. I don't care much one way or the other, but there is no harm in meeting new people. I have plenty to do this weekend anyway, with my packing and sorting. I have washed my hair just in case and I'm writing this under the dryer.

* * *

Ascom City

Thurs, May 8, 1958

. . . Last night I went to square dancing, as I do every Wednesday. I have rather come to enjoy it, although I doubt I'll ever become a real enthusiast.

* * *

Tokyo

Sat, May 10, 1958

. . . I hope the postcard I mailed you from Tachikawa last night reached you promptly. As I said on the card, it was by far the nicest trip I have ever had between Korea and Japan. It was very comfortable—C 54. We had nine litter patients and the rest ambulatory and we had regular reclining airline type seats. The trip only took 4½ hours and the weather was lovely.

When I got into Tachikawa last night about 5:30 I had called Loretta Coughlin, who was stationed there. Now she had weekend duty so couldn't leave the base. She suggested I have dinner with her and stay the night. I decided I might as well so I taxied over to her apartment. I called the Dai Ichi and postponed my reservation until today.

Loretta and I had drinks and then went to the Officers Club for a real good dinner, then back to her apartment for a visit and thence to bed. Loretta was real homesick for Korea and lapped up all the news I had to tell her.

She had to go to work this am so was up and out early. I got up just as she was leaving and went over to a nearby club for breakfast. I then took a taxi to the station and came into Tokyo.

* * *

Tokyo

Sun, May 11, 1958

I haven't commented on the strange people staying at this hotel. On 24 May, Tokyo is playing host for the Asian Games, a sort of Olympics confined to the Asian countries. The hotel is filled up with their contestants from the Philippines, India, Pakistan, and many others. In addition, the Leningrad Symphony Orchestra is in town and in staying here. So that lobby also has a liberal sprinkling of long-haired Russian musicians.

* * *

Ascom City

Thurs, May 15, 1958

. . . Before I forget, I want to tell you about an amusing aspect of my trip back to Korea last Tuesday. First of all, one of the secretaries at ARC Hospital asked me if I would bring a pair of khakis over to her Lieutenant husband who was on TDY at K-14. So she gave me a parcel containing clothes and also $20 to give him. It seems he also sent an SOS for funds. When I got out to the terminal and went to check my bag in, the little Japanese man saw that my address was 121 Evac. He got very excited and showed me two larger packages addressed to ARC at the 121. I recognized them as packages of cookies, which we receive regularly from volunteers in Japan for the patients; each box must have weighed 50 lbs. The little man, of course, wanted me to take charge of them. Actually, after a little phoning, I found out that someone from the ARC office was supposed to pick them up and send them to us via air freight. However, I decided I might as well take them in tow and arranged to check them along with my baggage. So now I had Lieutenant Townsend's uniform, $20 and 100 lbs of cookies in addition to my own bag, coat and camera case.

While I was waiting for the plane, I saw a little colored nurse 2nd Lieutenant in the terminal and decided she, too, must be on her way to the 121. So I introduced myself and offered to help her along. She, of course, latched on to me like grim death. So that is how I made the trip—Lieutenant Townsend's uniform, 100 lbs of cookies and a colored nurse in my charge. I felt exactly like the Joads of Grapes of Wrath. Just to finish the tale, Lieutenant Townsend met me at the plane and was very grateful for the clothes and money. One of the nurses from the 121 was there with a car to meet both me and the new nurse so transportation was no problem. Oh yes, I almost forgot on the bus going out to Tachikawa there were two little petty officers going to Korea for the first time. They were full of questions and attached themselves to my entourage. They forgot or didn't know enough to sign up for box lunches, so Lieutenant Swain, the nurse, and I shared our lunches with them in flight. This business of traveling in American Red Cross uniform really puts you on the spot sometimes. But I am always glad to help people out anyways, and it was good public relations for the American Red Cross.

* * *

Ascom City

Sat, May 17, 1958

. . . Last night I asked Nancy Kinsley—the new nurse arrival whom I knew in Aberdeen—to have a drink at the club before dinner and then have dinner with me. After dinner we called Mary Katherine Cuppy and both talked to her. She had just gotten back from a trip to Persia. She is leaving for the US on 29 May and will be calling you when she gets to Washington. I'll see her Monday as we are having a big reception at our club for the Surgeon General of the Army, General Hayes, who is on a trip over here.

About 8:30 I went over to the club with another one of the nurses for the dance. There was a small crowd, but I danced with several people and had a pleasant enough evening. Tonight I am going to Seoul with June Williams to have a blind date with a Lieutenant Colonel she has been wanting me to meet. It will make for a nice change.

* * *

Ascom City

Sun, May 18, 1958

. . . I had a real nice day yesterday. I spent the morning at my desk in my room weeding out letters and accumulations of stuff. I haven't completely finished but made good headway. In the afternoon, Bill Howard and I walked over to the Armed Forces Day exhibit. We didn't even bother to look at the exhibits but took loads of pictures of the literally thousands of Koreans who were there. It was a lovely day weather wise. We came back and sat in the sun for a while over a beer. At 4:30, I took off with June Williams and a friend of hers for Seoul. She had arranged the date for me with another friend whom we met at the 8th Army Club. My date, Lieutenant Colonel Sifford, was very nice and we had a pleasant evening. He is stationed with KMAG way off in the boondocks, so I doubt if I'll see him again. The chief drawback to the trip is that we had to make it in an open-air Jeep which is not very comfortable riding to say the least.

* * *

Finances

Mary was always proud of her ability to provide for herself and thrive financially as a single woman. She lived frugally but would make a few luxury purchases. She also was a shrewd investor. When she was overseas, her father helped take care of her banking needs. He acted as banker and financial advisor. She consulted him extensively on business matters and often used the letters to her mother to convey messages to him. She also wrote to him directly, though not with the same frequency as she wrote to Grace. Her comments and questions about finances provide insight into the economy of the times.

In a time when women couldn't get loans without a male cosigning the papers, she relied on her father to enable her to own a car. Mary loved owning a car. It was truly her prized possession. Although she made very few references to a car when she was in Japan, apparently, she did have one shipped over when she was posted in Sasebo. The car did not come to Korea with her, but she did arrange for its sale and the purchase of a new vehicle when she returned stateside.

All excerpts sent from the following letters were written in Ascom City.

Wed, Jan 23, 1957

. . . I received Daddy's letter sending me the nice money order for $25 for my birthday. Thank you very much. He also said you were putting $100 in the bank for me. That is certainly wonderful of you. I have so little need of money at present that it is certainly better not to send me any more over here. I'm sure I'll find a good use for it sooner or later. I certainly hope that your giving it to me doesn't mean that you are passing up anything you want for yourself or to do for Martha and the children.

* * *

Fri, Jan 25, 1957

I'm glad to know that Daddy has received the $800 I sent. I appreciate his willingness to wait for the balance as I'll be able to manage it soon without disturbing my savings account. Speaking of the car, one of the officers here is very interested in it. He is being transferred to Japan next week and says he will go down and look at it. The big drawback, which I don't think he fully comprehends, is that the car is in Sasebo and he is going to Zama near Tokyo. Of course, that is his problem to cope with if he decides he wants the car.

* * *

Mon, Jan 28, 1957

Dear Daddy,

I received my W2 form from ARC for 1956 and I'm sending it to you right away so it will not go astray. I know you will need it eventually, even if my request for an extension of filing date is approved.

I believe this is the first year my salary has gone over $5000, which is quite a milestone. I am sure I'll never earn 10,000, but I might work up to $6–7000 one of these years. I also got a salary check today for $200. I think I'll send most of or all of it to you as additional payment on the $400 I still owe you. I have about $70 cash on hand plus the $25 money order you sent me and a $52 money order Jack sent to pay for Martha's pearls, so I'll have plenty of cash until I get my maintenance of $93 on 15 Feb. My salary check is dated 31 Jan, so I can't cash it until then. I'll have to send you money orders as this check can only be cashed in MPC's [Military Payment Certificates].

* * *

Thurs, Jan 31, 1957

. . . In Daddy's letter he told me about buying up the Anaconda stocks when they were offered. As I wrote him the other day, I am planning to send him $200 in money orders from this month's paycheck. I had planned that money go against the $400 I still owe him. However, since he advises buying the stocks, he can use it for that and you can write a check on the Chase account for anymore needed. I don't want to go into savings account, but there is sufficient in my checking account to cover $50–$100 more if needed.

. . . I finally clarified my living expenses. I pay $10 a month for the maids who clean our rooms and do our laundry. Soap powder, starch and shoe polish is also bought from this fund. I pay $3.00 a month club dues and $7.00 a month service charge in the mess. Meals at the mess cost $1.05 a day. Thus my basic living expenses are a little over $50 a month. This certainly shouldn't mean that I can pretty much live on my $90 a month maintenance. I bought a bottle of J.W. Harper Bourbon yesterday for $2.40. Bar drinks are $0.25 each.

. . . I would appreciate each month if Daddy would tell me the date he writes the check to Loomis Sayles so that I can enter it in my stub book. I try to keep track of that account even though I don't write many checks on it.

* * *

On ARC stationary
Sun, Feb 24, 1957

. . . I had a couple of personal disappointments yesterday. I had a letter from Mary telling me that the car sale had fallen through. That is very upsetting, especially since Mary has received word that she may be transferred soon. I haven't had the time to think it through yet as to just what I'm going to do.

* * *

Mon, Feb 25, 1957

. . . I had a letter from Mary yesterday. Still no sale for the car, but the transfer for her to the Philippines has fallen through for the moment, thank goodness.

. . . I had Daddy's letter advising me that he was buying the Anaconda stock, which is fine.

* * *

Sat, Mar 2, 1957

Seems like I have quite a few news items to report. First and foremost is that Mary called last night and has sold my car. In fact, you may already know this as she said she sent the money off to Daddy yesterday. The telephone connection was so poor that she didn't try to go into any details. In fact, I don't even know what she got for it, but she did sell it. I am so terribly relieved to have that off my mind at last. She said that after the other false alarm, she waited to tell me this time until the deal was all buttoned up. She is writing me the details.

When I got my check this month, my raise was included. My promotion became effective 16 January, the day I arrived in Korea, and my salary has been raised from $441 to $475 a month. That is the biggest single raise I have ever gotten from ARC. The new salary range goes up to $587 a month in annual increments of $13 to $25. The range starts at $400, so I am in on the 4th step. In January

1958, I'll go to $500. Now, after deductions for retirement, Social Security and insurance I'll be getting $432.04 a month. $200 of that, of course goes by allotment to the Chase Bank. When I can get to the post office, I'm going to get money orders for $200 from this month's check for you to deposit in my savings account.

I'm counting on Daddy to deduct the balance of what I owe him—$400—from the money Mary is sending him and to deposit the rest in my savings account. The money I am building up in that account is for a new car when I come home, and I want to build it up to at least $3000 for that purpose.

* * *

Sun, Jul 14, 1957

. . . Oh yes—I have over $900 in my Chase checking account, which is really too much. I would like Daddy to be looking around for a suitable investment for about $500 to $600 of that. If nothing better develops, I could transfer some to my savings account.

. . . I haven't figured it out exactly but believe my trip to Japan costs about $300. It is nice not to have to count pennies.

* * *

Sat, Jul 27, 1957

. . . In regard to Daddy's letter of investing some money, you know I'll do whatever he advises. If he doesn't do anything for a couple of months, I'll be able to spare some more money from my checking account. As you know, $200 a month from my salary goes into it after the $50 is taken out for Loomis Sayles; that still leaves $150, and that account is used very little, mostly for piddling little checks.

I know Daddy thinks my savings account is too large, however, my aim is to have about $5000 in it when I come home to spend for a car, new clothes and furnish an apartment if necessary. I have plenty of money over here for any trips I may want to take. I have over $700 in my Sasebo account and nearly $300 in uncashed checks here. As you know, I am not particularly enthusiastic about [a] Hong Kong trip, but I don't have to hesitate for financial reasons.

So anyway, I imagine I can safely invest up to $1000 if he can find me a good investment. I feel I would prefer AT&T stock if any rights are available to me. But whatever he advises, I will do.

* * *

Tues, Jul 30, 1957

. . . I was talking today to one of the nurses who was going home in August. She has ordered a new Olds Super 88 four door hardtop with all the trimmings which she is going to pick up in Detroit. She ordered it through a dealer in Japan and it was only going to cost her $3250. She figures that she is saving close to $500. I am going to look into that. One big disadvantage I shall have in buying a car when I first come home is that I'll have to register it in Maryland and pay that awful excise tax. It seems mean as I won't be in Maryland except for a few weeks leave before I go to my next assignment, but I guess there is no way around that.

* * *

Mon, Aug 12, 1957

. . . I am sure the prices at home will floor me. Money seems to mean so little over here. There is nothing to buy and what you do get is comparatively cheap. Well, I would rather be broke and in the US than rich and in the Far East.

* * *

Mon, Aug 19, 1957

I had a letter from Daddy yesterday which I can't seem to put my hand on just this minute. Anyway, the important thing in it was about converting my matured E bonds into coupon bonds. That transaction would be fine by me. I agree that it is a good time to do it tax wise. I'm sure Daddy knows that the only part of my 56-57-58 income which is tax exempt is the part I earn overseas, i.e. my ARC salary. I will have to pay taxes for 56 on my ARC salary up to 10 June 56 and income from investments. For 57, only on income from investments so that 57 is the best time to convert the bonds. In 58 I'll have to pay taxes on salary for the last half of the year.

As regards to the bonds, I don't really think I have too many which are matured. During 46 to 47, I was going to school and was largely unemployed. During 43 to 46. I bought them fairly regularly and again from 48 to about 52. Anyway, I'm perfectly agreeable to his converting any of the matured ones. I believe they are all co-ownership bonds with you.

* * *

Tues, Aug 21, 1957

I had Daddy's letter listing my matured bonds. He should get the letter I wrote yesterday telling him to go ahead and convert the matured ones. If there is an odd amount leftover, he can either put it in my savings account or you can write a check on my Chase account to bring the amount up to $100 to buy another coupon bond.

Speaking of the Chase account, will you please write them to send me another checkbook? I've used up all the stubs in my present one, although I have plenty of checks. That is a result of entering on the stubs the checks you write. I like the flat kind of book—size of one check with stub record on separate sheet in groups of three checks—I think it is the kind I left with you.

* * *

Mon, Sep 16, 1957

. . . Red Cross has started a new system of paying us overseas. Previously, whatever we received overseas was paid us once a month by a check good only for cashing in MPC. Now our checks are being sent to us direct from National, drawn on the Riggs Bank twice a month. We have been instructed that they must be cashed or deposited right away and not held. So I will be sending them home fairly often. So please have Daddy get me some deposit envelopes from the Chase Bank and also tell me how to endorse the checks for deposit in my savings account. I'm ashamed to say that I am not sure of the exact name of the place where my savings account is. I can send the deposits to the Chase Bank direct, but assume that after endorsing them, I'll have to send any checks to Daddy to put in the savings account.

* * *

Tues, Sep 17, 1957

. . . I'm enclosing a two weeks' paycheck made out for deposit in the Chase Bank. As I wrote before, we have to cash or deposit them right away. I can make deposits direct when Daddy sends me some deposit envelopes.

* * *

Sat, Sep 18, 1957

. . . I had Daddy's letter about my banking situation. I had no idea of having my deposit book shuttling back and forth across the ocean. I just wanted to be sure of how to endorse the checks I might want to send him to deposit for me.

* * *

Mon, Sep 30, 1957

I am enclosing another check for deposit in my checking account. Getting paid every two weeks seems to keep the checks pouring in. This is slightly more as my Social Security deductions are tapering off as they do at the end of each year.

* * *

Sat, Oct 26, 1957

. . . Did I ask Daddy to send me the booklets on the 58 Buicks or Oldsmobiles when they come out? I want to start dreaming about my new car a bit.

* * *

Thurs, Oct 31, 1957

. . . I didn't mean to imply that I am concerned over getting a little money ahead. I'm sure it will all vanish in short order when I get home, and I'll be feeling broke again. It's just a bit of a problem at the moment to get it all safely tucked away. Incidentally, I think Daddy could transfer another $500 from my checking account to my savings account. I've previously suggested that he invest some money, but in view of what you write me, I think I would prefer to have a nice fat savings account from which to buy my car, clothes and furniture.

* * *

Fri, Nov 1, 1957

. . . Tell Daddy I received the two deposit slips and the deposit envelope today. There was a spread on the 58 cars in the Stars and Stripes today, so I am more anxious than ever for the colored folders he will be sending me.

* * *

Tues, Nov 5, 1957

. . . Tell Daddy I received the folder of the 57 Olds today. I enjoyed looking at it but will be even more interested in the 58's. The price list he sent me on the 58 Buicks gives pause for thought. Maybe he'd better send me some pictures and prices on Fords. I don't want another Chevy and I really am beginning to wonder if I should throw my money away on as expensive a car as a Buick or an Olds.

* * *

Tues, Nov 19, 1957

. . . I received Daddy's letter about the Olds and also the brochure. It is a lovely car but so much money. He had better send me the dope on the Fords and the Chevys. I may change my mind but at the moment I am in an economical mood. My chief fear on a Ford or Chevy is the possibility of getting a lemon. I suppose you run the same risk with any make, but the percentages seem greater with those two. Well, I'll have plenty of time to mull it over. It seems that it is no longer necessary to place an order way in advance. You probably can get almost anything you want for immediate delivery. I also still want some dope on the Buicks. I remember that when I bought my Buick, it was $500 less than a comparable model Olds, which was why I bought it.

* * *

Thurs, Nov 21, 1957

I had your letter of 15 November in which you stated you thought I would receive it just before taking off for Hong Kong. Well, I did and was glad for late word. I also had Daddy's card telling me he has sent in my 56 income tax return. When and if I get the refund, he can deposit it in my savings account. I also received the article on car buying which he sent.

* * *

Sat, Dec 7, 1957

. . . I was interested in Daddy's dope on the Buicks and real impressed by the price. It looks like the situation is about the same as it was in 54 between Buicks and Olds—Buick can be had for about $500 less and I personally don't see that much difference in the Olds. Well, we'll see how it seems when I get home.

* * *

Fri, Apr 4, 1958

. . . One other piece of business while I think of it. I believe that Daddy told me once that I had to notify my Savings Bank 30 days ahead if I wanted to make a big withdrawal. If so, maybe you should notify them about June 1 that I am going to want to withdraw about $3000 about July 1 to buy a car.

* * *

Thurs, May 8, 1958

. . . I have entered the various checks Daddy wrote about in my stud book and my account checked out with my statement. I am glad the investment in the AT&T stock has been completed. Since I managed it out of "current income" the $500 daddy plans to give me from his retainer can go into my savings account until such time as another good investment turns up.

* * *

Thurs, May 15, 1958

. . . I appreciate Daddy's sending me the report on my "networth" [*sic*]. $22,000 is a nice tidy sum for a single gal, although I realize that the bulk of it came from gifts from you and Daddy and various other sources. As near as I can figure, I have accumulated approximately $8000 out of these two years overseas. So even if I haven't gotten anything else out of it, and I have gotten a great deal, I have gained that. If my living expenses come a little high for the next few years, I'll have to remember these two inexpensive years.

* * *

When Mary passed away in 2011, her net worth exceeded one million dollars. A nice tidy sum for a single gal, indeed.

THE RECORD PLAYER AND SLIDE PROJECTOR

TWO OF THE LUXURY items Mary invested in while in Korea were a record player and a slide projector. The record player seemed to be primarily for her own enjoyment. The slide projector played a role in entertaining as she and others would use it to share their slides at picture parties.

All excerpts are from letters written in Ascom City, unless noted otherwise.

Sun, Jan 27, 1957

I'm toying with the idea of spending the $100 you gave me for a Hi Fi. With no TV and very poor radio programs, everyone here is Hi Fi and record mad. They have in the PX an RCA 3 Speed 3 Speaker Portable Hi Fi for only $85. It is model #8, HIP-1. I would be interested to have Daddy find out what they cost in the States retail as I can imagine that it is quite a bargain. I may have to make up my mind pretty quick as I have found over here that if you don't get things when they have them, you may never get another chance. They get shipments of records in from time to time and they are also quite cheap. I imagine shipping when you move is quite a problem, but others have done it and tell me that the engineers will build a special box for them. I would like your reaction to the idea. Since I gave Johnny my little 45 RPM one, I don't have a record player at all and I think it would be a nice thing to own.

* * *

Mary must have made the decision to buy the hi-fi quickly because by February the family was sending her records to enjoy.

On ARC stationary
Sun, Feb 24, 1957
. . . The other disappointment was that the Belafonte record Martha sent me arrived broken. I just hate to tell her as I know it was expensive, plus $1.02 postage. Actually, she had packed it herself and the cardboard around it was a little smaller than the record. Thus, I think if you send me any records, they had best be packed by the store. I hadn't received the one you sent from Woodies, but will report on its condition when it comes.

* * *

Wed, Feb 27, 1957
Yesterday I bought a portable metal record case to keep my records in. I think it will give them better protection and also make the room looked less cluttered.

* * *

Sat, Mar 2, 1957
. . . I would like very much to have the Emery Deutsche Record. I haven't received the Vienna Record yet, so assume Woodies sent it regular mail instead of airmail. Actually, on records and things there is no urgency about my getting; we may as well use regular mail and save the postage. Any records you send me I will pay for. I don't want you to go on making me presents. You asked if we could order some records here. The answer is no. The PX gets shipments in from time to time and it is strictly first come, first serve.

* * *

Fri, Mar 15, 1957
. . . I bought a couple of records today. An Al Jolson one in which he sings all of his famous ones. Also, an organ one [with] popular tunes played by Mert Lindsey. The "Echoes of Vienna" must be coming boat mail.

* * *

Wed, Jun 19, 1957
. . . Loretta came back to work today, which relieves me of a lot of the pressure. She brought me the original cast record of "My Fair Lady" which I have been wanting. I played it tonight while drying my hair.

* * *

Sat, June 22, 1957

. . . I bought some more records today, a Mantovani, "The King and I" and "High Society." So I am having a nice concert this afternoon. It is a rainy day so I am quite content to stay in.

* * *

Tokyo
Mon, Jul 1, 1957

. . . I bought 8 records at the PX today and had them packaged and mailed them to myself in Korea. It was wonderful to have such a selection and I had difficulty restraining myself.

* * *

Sun, Jul 14, 1957

. . . You asked about what records I bought. One batch, which I mailed to myself hasn't arrived yet. The ones I brought back are "Sleeping Beauty Ballet," Horowitz playing Chopin, and Liszt's 1st and 2nd piano concertos. I really can't remember at the moment what the other ones I bought. I think I wrote you that previously I got "The King and I" and a record of "High Society." I am really getting far too many records. I must have close to 50 now. I bought a lot at first that I didn't care too much about just to have something to play. Now I will have to be much more selective. Packing is sure going to be a problem when the time comes.

* * *

Mon, Jul 15, 1957

My box of records arrived from Japan today and I am having a grand time playing them. Altogether I bought 10 this trip so it will take me quite a while to even play them through. I'll list them below and will check (*) a couple I think you would particularly like.

1. *I remember Paris—Songs and Piano Solos by Victor Autier. This is a capital record #T 10041. It has a gorgeous picture of Notre Dame on the cover. Songs are all in French but very nice.
2. *Holding hands at midnight—Dinah Shore—RCA Victor LPM-1154 Dinah at her very best.
3. Errol Garner—A Columbia #CL535. Piano with rhythm accompaniment. A little disappointing, too fast and noisy.
4. *Tribute to Dorsey, Vol 2—Tommy Dorsey and his Orchestra, RCA. Victor LPM 1433. I haven't played this one yet but know I'll like it. Has a lot of the good old TD numbers. "Shine on Harvest Moon," "East of the Sun," "The One I Love," "Blue Skies," "Embraceable You," etc.

The ones below I haven't played yet.

5. Music of Chopin—Andre Kostelanetz—Columbia, CL862.
6. Kreisler and Rumbaugh—Andre Kostelanetz—Columbia, CL771.
7. Rachmaninoff Symphony #2—Ormandy and Philadelphia Orchestra—Columbia, PRL 7020.

I wrote you about the other three the other day. I'll tell you about a couple of others I have that I particularly like:

9. Lord Adrian Foley at the piano. MGM Record PML 5017. Real nicc piano with orchestral accompaniment. Plays such things as "In the Still of the Night," "Long Ago and Far Away," "Wish You Were Here," etc.
10. Carmen Cavallaro—Selections from Rogers and Hammerstein—Decca AL12058. One side is all from "The King and I" and the other selections from "South Pacific," "Oklahoma," "Carousel" etc.
11. Bing Crosby "Drifting and Dreaming." One side is Hawaiian. The other straight old Bing.
12. "Cocktails, Anyone?"—Bob Creash Quintet. Unique. There are two numbers on this LP104 and LPM2. My recording was made in Japan, so one of the numbers may refer to that. This is lot of good numbers from the 20s.

Well, there are many others, but this should give you some ideas. All this is being written because you said you never know what to get.

For some reason I have gone quite wild on piano music. I don't know why particularly, but I always seem to pull out those records first these days.

* * *

Tues, Jul 16, 1957

I'm playing some more of my new records tonight and you would love both of them. They are the two Kostelanetz records I listed in my letter yesterday: Music of Chopin and Kreisler and Rumbaugh. The selections are all well-known popular ones by various composers, but wonderful listening.

* * *

Wed, Jul 24, 1957

Today I was able to get an LP record of "South Pacific" with the original cast. I will have fun playing it tonight and remembering when we saw it a few nights after it opened and before I went to Germany.

* * *

Tues, Jul 30, 1957

. . . Don't be upset about the record not coming airmail. I have lots of records and I'll enjoy the new one whenever it gets here.

* * *

Tues, Aug 21, 1957

. . . Today in Seoul I was able to get another metal box for my records. I've been trying for months. It is a relief to get most of them filed away properly. I have quite an investment in them now, about $100, and I want to take proper care of them.

* * *

Thurs, Aug 29, 1957

. . . I'm gradually working myself up to buying a slide projector. I can get a real bargain in one over here and I am sure I will want one sooner or later. The only thing that holds me back is that I have already accumulated so much stuff I don't see how I will ever get it all home. One of the main reasons I wouldn't mind staying in Korea is that I would only have to pack and move once.

* * *

Sat, Aug 31, 1957

. . . I have to tell you that the George Fryer record arrived yesterday but it was broken on arrival, cracked in half. Daddy had packed it well, but I guess not well enough. I guess you had just better not try to send me any more records. Of the three sent from home two have arrived broken. It is just a waste of money. I do appreciate you trying so hard, but it just isn't worth it. I was really disappointed and know you will be upset, but I have to tell you, so you won't try again. I'll just pick up records here as I see them. If you find something special for me, just put it away until I come home.

* * *

Wed, Sep 4, 1957

. . . Monday, I finally broke down and bought myself a slide projector and screen. I got a Bell & Howell projector for $39.50. The same one retails in the US for about $60. It took part of Monday afternoon to get my slides filled in the boxes that feed into the projector. It works real well.

* * *

Tue, Sep 17, 1957

. . . This has been another busy day at work, but not uncomfortably so. I didn't do anything for excitement last night. Tonight some people are coming in to show slides. One of our pleasures here is looking at each other's slides. The joke is that we have so many of the same thing, but we are all admiring each other's extravagantly. Now that I have a projector screen, I'm quite popular as a lot of people don't have the full equipment.

* * *

Mon, Sep 30, 1957

. . . Later we came down to our quarters and showed each other our slides. I got back the roll I took from the Tomb of the Kings two weeks ago, so Roy and Johnny wanted to see them.

* * *

Fri, Nov 2, 1957

. . . I played the "Around the World in 80 Days" record and liked it. I'm dying to see the movie and I'm sure the music will mean more to me when I have. I also bought a new record, "Miss Show Business," Judy Garland. It is her Palace performance.

* * *

Sat, Nov 2, 1957

. . . While I have been working on the [Christmas] cards this afternoon, I've been playing some of my records and enjoying them. I always sort of go in spells of playing records sometimes, don't play any at all for a week or so and then will start playing them every night. That is the nice thing about records. You can play what you want when you want. I must have nearly 60 records now.

. . . Did I ever write you about a record which I have enjoyed and [am] playing it now? It is MGM record PML-5017 "Lord Adrian Foley at the Piano." Real nice listening music. Another one I enjoy is Deca AL 12058 Carmen Cavallaro playing section selections from "The King and I" and other Rogers and Hammerstein shows.

* * *

Sat, Nov 16, 1957

. . . Last evening Margaret and I had dinner at the mess. After a drink at the club, I showed her my slides of Korea and we both turned in early. She was pretty tired from her junketing around and seemed glad not to have to do anything. She's not a young person—has six grandchildren—so I'm sure these trips take a lot out of her.

* * *

Sat, Apr 19, 1958

. . . Thursday evening, all the new gals came down and I showed them my slides of Korea. It was a sort of combined hair washing venture. They are having water troubles in their hooch so all of them wanted to use my shower for a shampoo. They are a real nice bunch of girls.

* * *

Sat May 3, 1958

. . . I have made a little more progress today toward packing. I took my hi-fi and records and slide projector to medical supplies and the GI there is going to pack them and build wooden boxes for them so they will be ready to ship. I took my projection screen and boxes of slides to the wrapping service and got them ready to mail. It may not sound like much, but it all has to be done sometime and the more I get done before I go to Japan the less I will have to do when I get back. I seem to have relatively little time to attend to personal things, so it is good to be able to get some things off my mind at least.

* * *

The Hair Dryer

In all the letters from Mary, an inordinate amount of ink was spent talking about getting her hair done. Mary was of a generation and social status where she did not wash her own hair if she could avoid it. Her preference was to go to a salon once a week for a wash, set, and occasional perm. Mary was not overly vain, but this routine signified how well she was doing in the world. It also indicated her professionalism. Maintaining a professional appearance always seemed more important to Mary than trying to be fashionable.

In some locations, like Korea, the ritual of going to the hairdresser was just not possible. So accommodations had to be made. Mary complained of having to wash her own hair and was generally dissatisfied with the outcome. Trying to make a bad situation a little bit better, Grace and Hal managed to have a hair dryer sent to Mary. The arrival of this luxury item was the topic of many letters. When it finally arrived, Mary shared her largess with the other girls. Washing and drying hair became a social event, probably accompanied with a few cocktails.

All the following excepts are from letters written in Ascom City.

Mon, Jan 21, 1957

. . . Sunday I went to church at 10:00, then had brunch in the mess hall. In the afternoon I washed my hair so it could get dry and I wouldn't have to sleep with a wet head. There is so much soot in the air here from all the oil stoves that your hair has to be washed every few days. My first effort was not an outstanding success, but it doesn't look too bad.

* * *

Thurs, Jan 31, 1957

. . . Tonight was "wash the hair" night. One of the nurses in my quarters has a hair dryer which she has offered me at any time. It is a big help as I can accomplish my project in the evening. With all the soot and frequent washings, I am afraid I'll emerge a brunette. You might inquire at the drugstore if they have any lemon rinse tablets. There is no rinse—cream or otherwise—available at the PX.

* * *

Sun, Mar 17, 1957

. . . Did I write that it looks like we may be going to get a beauty parlor in Ascom at last? Col Reagan is making space for one in the quarters area, and the PX seems willing to set it up. I've been working on both William and Col Regan about this ever since I have been here. What kind of an operator they can get and what it will be like remains to be seen. But we are all hopeful. Actually, I'll believe it when I see it.

* * *

Wed, Jun 19, 1957

. . . We were all delighted to get Daddy's letter that the hair dryer is en route. It is too bad it was too heavy for airmail, but we can wait.

* * *

Thurs, Jun 20, 1957

. . . Don't feel badly about not sending the dryer airmail. We will be happy to have it whenever it gets here. You are so good to get it so quickly. I hope it wasn't too expensive. I will gladly pay for it.

* * *

Mon, Jul 15, 1957

. . . I washed my hair tonight. Each time I do it now I hope that by the next time the hair dryer will be here. Some boat mail came in today and I don't imagine it has all been unloaded, so I may even get it this week.

* * *

Wed, Jul 24, 1957

. . . I heard today that a ship carrying mail caught fire about a week ago and a lot of mail was destroyed. I sure hope my hair dryer wasn't on that ship. I wonder if you insured the package. It is too soon to really start worrying about it, I guess. I also ordered a pair of play shoes and a box to file my slides in from Sears about six weeks ago and that package hasn't come yet either.

* * *

Thurs, Jul 25, 1957

The big news of the day is that the hair dryer came! It came through in fine shape. It looks like it is going to be just wonderful. We tested it out and I can hardly wait until I wash my hair. I would do it tonight except we have no hot water. I had planned to wash it tomorrow anyway, so I would be clean for the weekend. I'll report on my first venture with it. We all like the color. I can assure you that I will not be the only one to use it. So many, many thanks from us all.

I also got my package from Sears with the play shoes and the box of for my colored slides. So now I think that I have all the packages I have been expecting.

* * *

Sat, Jul 27, 1957

I used the new hair dryer last night and it worked wonderfully. Except for a few spots, my hair was dry in a little over ½ hour. I then removed the cap and placed the hose on the few damp spots, and I was soon all finished. I think I can do the whole job—wash, set and dry—in less than two hours. I'm really thrilled with it. Of course, when I come home, I shall go back to the beauty parlor routine as I still can't set my hair well. But the dryer will be worth its weight in gold to me over here. The other girls will be using it too.

* * *

Sat, Aug 10, 1957

I'm sitting in my hair dryer and what a joy it is. Besides being very efficient, it leaves my hands free to write and read. It is amazing how much convenience some of these modern appliances can add to your life. So again, merci mille fois.

* * *

Mon, Sep 30, 1957

. . . After all my Jeep riding in the dust, my hair was in sorry shape so I have just washed it and am under the dryer now. Speaking of hair, they finally started to work on our own beauty parlor today. I never thought I'd live to see it as it has been projected ever since I have been in Korea and actually long before I came. At this point, I would rather see them get started on getting some heat in our quarters. It has been really nippy today.

* * *

Thurs, Apr 24, 1958

I'm in a frequent writing position—under the dryer. This business of having to wash my hair every five days gets to be a real nuisance but thank goodness for my dryer. I can do the whole operation in 1½ to two hours.

* * *

News from Home

Just as before, Grace's letters to Mary must have been full of tidbits about family at home. Mary also got letters from her sister, Martha, her sister-in-law, Audrey, and occasionally from her brother, John. Her nephews John Robert and Stephen even wrote from time to time. Mary took great pleasure from the seemingly trivial details of home life. Everything from report cards to health reports were shared, and Mary responded with words of encouragement, care, and sometimes derision.

All the following excerpts are from letters written in Ascom City.

Wed, Jan 23, 1957

. . . From all reports the East is really having a terrible winter. I hope you weren't snowed in too long, but I know you can keep more than comfortable if you are. I sure hope that you are able to restrain Daddy from such foolishness as shoveling the driveway.

* * *

Tues, Jan 29, 1957

. . . Your letter was full of the [Eisenhower] inauguration and I'm glad you had such a good seat for it. . . . As
far as we were concerned over here, I didn't even remember
that it was Inauguration Day. We are so far removed, so
wrapped up in our day-to-day existence.

* * *

Mon, Feb 25, 1957

Our poor John Robert worrying about becoming a
teenager. He is such a worrier and takes life so hard. I am
glad he is beginning to do a little better in school. Surely he
will get over that hump sometime.

* * *

Wed, Feb 27, 1957

. . . I had a birthday card from Audrey yesterday with
pictures of the children. Although it was marked airmail, it
apparently came by ship. I wrote to her a nice letter last night.

* * *

Sun, Mar 3, 1957

. . . I had a nice letter from you yesterday written the
25th. I know you were always happy when you have one
or all of the children with you for a day or so, and it does
give Martha relief. I think it is wonderful for all of you that
you have had this year together. That is a rare blessing in
this Army life and one to be cherished. In all you have been
uncommonly lucky to have been able to see as much of
Martha and her children as you have over the years.

* * *

Fri, Mar 15, 1957

. . . Am re-reading all the letters I have around from
you and am not sure which I have answered and which not.
Anyway, I loved your recounting of your afternoon with
Catharine showing her your dolls. It was indeed a "blessed
moment" and one for you to cherish. Isn't it wonderful that
you two are being able to enjoy each other at last?

. . . I thought the report on Aunt Bobbie in Aunt
Helen's letter sounded pretty good. We know, of course,
that her illness is cyclical, and she may be just coming into
an "up" phase, but since she's getting real professional help
for the first time, maybe she can be helped to reach a good
level and hold it.

. . . I thought Audrey's letter sounded happy. She seems
to have more social contacts up there. I think that is good
for her not to have both families so close. She has to exert
herself more to meet people.

Daddy mentioned that he was toying with the idea of
getting a new Cadillac. I can't see that it is a necessity, but
if he wants one and has the money, why not?

* * *

Sun, Mar 17, 1957

. . . Each of Daddy's letters just bubble over about
Catharine. It is so wonderful that you both enjoy her so
much.

* * *

Tues, Jun 20, 1957

. . . Such a good letter from you today, all about John Robert's graduation and report cards. It is also encouraging about Stephen, particularly with school ending for him on such a happy note and camp ahead of him. He should be on top of the world. God bless him!!

By the time you get this, Jack may be home or just about. I can imagine the excitement which abounds.

* * *

Sat, Jun 22, 1957

. . . I've just been doing my monthly chore of going through letters before destroying them. It is fun and sort of gives me a general view of how things are at home. The time of this particular bunch was so good. The previous bunch had been so full of worry about Martha's illness, etc. This time it was all good—your New York trip, the Schraders' new home, the good end of the year for the boys, anticipation of Jack's homecoming. So I ended up by feeling real good about you.

* * *

Wed, Jun 26, 1957

. . . I'm sorry that Daddy had to lose another tooth, but I'm glad it wasn't any more of a problem. I guess this means a new denture for him.

* * *

Mon, Jul 1, 1957

. . . Your letter told of Jack's safe arrival home and I was so glad for the news. I had been wondering about it for several days.

Today at the PX, I picked up a couple of packages of Japanese stamps for the boys. I will enclose them in this letter. I couldn't remember if Stephen is really interested, but I got two identical packages anyway. If John Robert is the only one interested, maybe he can trade off the duplicate.

. . . I, of course, had heard of Col McKinley's death before I left Korea. I hadn't really connected him as being someone you knew. The rumor over here was that there was a real doubt as to whether or not it was suicide. One thing I heard was that there was no evidence of powder burns. Anyway, an investigation was being conducted. The other side of the coin is that there have been several suicides in Korea among the officers and also several mental crackups, so I don't know.

* * *

Mon, Jul 22, 1957

. . . I'm glad that the Schraders' new house is working out so well. It is so wonderful that Jack is there to pitch in on it. He is always at his best at times like this. You haven't mentioned how he and the boys are getting along. I hope he is showing Stephen the love and understanding he needs. You also haven't mentioned their camp experience since the first couple of days. I hope it is as happy for them as it was last summer.

Today is Martha and Jack's wedding anniversary. I didn't do anything about it, but I did think about it and them. I'm so glad that they are together for it.

* * *

Thurs, Aug 8, 1957

. . . Martha's letter was one of the happiest I can remember ever receiving from her. She just bubbled throughout with joy of having Jack home, pleasure in the new home, satisfaction with the children. Well, it was all good and made me so happy. I know also from your letters how at rest your mind is about her and her family and how much you are all enjoying one another.

Your party for the Camps and the McLeans sounded just perfect. How I would have loved to have been there!! I know full well that your parties just don't happen and that you put a lot of work into them. But when they go so well, I know it is all worth the effort.

I hope you will steam ahead with your redecorating project. You have had it hanging over you for two years. Make it your goal to have it completed before I come home. That is enough time so that you won't feel rushed, but will still give you a definite time limit.

* * *

Sat, Aug 10, 1957

. . . Martha also told me about John Robert's caterpillars roasting to death on the way to Tom's River. That was surely a disappointment after he had nursed them along for so long. Poor little guy. He flits from interest to interest but is always intense over each one.

* * *

Mon, Aug 12, 1957

. . . I was surprised that Catharine could pick me out of a picture. I know she is a very bright child, but I never felt I made much an impression on her.

* * *

Sat, Aug 17, 1957

. . . The little jaunt [Martha] and Jack took sounded perfect, and I am so glad they had it. Seeing old friends is a breath of life to Martha, and she has an astounding capacity for making and keeping wonderful friends. I envy her that aspect of her personality, as so many of my friendships are superficial and transitory. It is obvious that she has such a greater capacity to give of herself to others than I have, which invites abiding love and response from others. It is a wonderful quality.

I am glad too that Jack is initially satisfied with his assignment. It is going to be a long pull there and so many people seem to find the Pentagon assignments most wearing.

I know you enjoyed the Dunn's visit, and you know they wouldn't have arranged to see you if they didn't love you and want to see you. I might add that it is quite apparent that Martha's talent for friendship was inherited from her Mama.

I'm so glad the boys did so well for the Saint Albans' team. It is too bad Jack had to miss it. How I love those boys and how proud I am of them.

. . . I was amused by Catharine's "Yes Sir." Both the Japanese and the Koreans use, "Yes Sir," indiscriminately for men and women, so that we are quite used to it over here.

* * *

Sun, Aug 25, 1957

. . . I had your letter of 18 August today. By now I guess John, Audrey and the children are with you. I hope the visit is going well and that the weather is cooperating a bit. One thing I must say for the hot weather here—so far it has always cooled off pretty well at night.

As long as Martha is concerned about Catharine's health, I guess it is a good idea to have her checked thoroughly at Walter Reed. From all your accounts of her she doesn't seem to be acting like a sick child, but it is better to get everything checked than be wondering and worrying.

* * *

Wed, Sep 4, 1957

. . . Your letters have been full of the visit with J&A and the children. I imagine it will be over by the time you receive this, and I sure hope you aren't a complete wreck.

* * *

Mon, Sep 16, 1957

Today is Catharine's birthday and I have been thinking about her. In the last pictures Martha sent, she looked so much taller . . . more of a little girl and less of a baby.

* * *

Mon, Sept 30, 1957

. . . It is extravagance, I suppose, but I'm glad M and J are taking the boys to the Army Navy game. You took us when we were all at Monmouth and it was a real thrill for me. Navy won—Slade Cutter kicked a field goal in the last minute of play, remember?

INGLES BOYS, 1957

* * *

Tues, Oct 29, 1957

. . . I had your good letter written from the Homestead. I was particularly thrilled with your account of seeing the Queen. I'm so happy that you had that wonderful opportunity. God bless Luther.

I hope your whole stay at the Homestead was as nice as it started out.

. . . I do hope little Johnny is well over his flu and that none of the rest of them caught it. The vaccine has arrived over here and we'll be having our shots in a week or so. I almost hate to take them as the shots seem to be almost worse than the flu, but I guess I won't have any choice.

I am glad your Garden Club party went so nicely. Your parties always do and it is wonderful that you have your lovely home to entertain in.

* * *

Tues, Nov 12, 1957

. . . I'm amused by Daddy's letter saying he was making the dollhouse more for Martha than for Catharine. I think if the truth was known, he is making it more for himself, at least for the fun of doing it. It sounds like a most elaborate project.

* * *

Thurs, Nov 14, 1957

. . . I had good letters from you today, written 8 November. I am always glad to hear of your getting out and seeing people. As I read each letter, I always think how lucky you are to have Martha and the children so near at hand. They are certainly the brightest spots in your lives and how wonderful that you and the children can have these years to really know and love one another.

* * *

Tues, Mar 18, 1958

. . . The toy chest that Daddy is making for Catharine sounds like a real fine undertaking. I am sure she will enjoy it. I am glad her mumps ordeal wasn't severe. Now I guess we just have to hope that Jack doesn't get them.

. . . I am glad that Daddy feels so well. I do hope that if Doctor Murray is still not satisfied with the X-rays that he will go out to Walter Reed for another complete checkup. It has been nearly two years since he went there before.

* * *

Fri, Mar 28, 1958

. . . I'm glad Daddy was pleased with John's house, and I do hope Audrey was. Is Audrey P[rimrose] up staying with the children? I am sure it did Audrey good to have the little jaunt to Washington and hope she accomplished what she wanted to.

It is too bad you discovered still another tree with borers. It looks like all the trouble you went to get the builders to leave the trees in the lot wasn't worth it. At least you can use the clean tree the storm wrecked for your fireplace.

* * *

Sun, Mar 30, 1958

. . . I had Daddy's postcard written 24 March telling me that the X-rays showed his lungs almost entirely cleared up. That was very good news indeed. I am sure that his health wouldn't prevent your New York trip, so I hope you are there now and are having a good time. I agree that you both needed the trip.

* * *

Mon, Mar 31, 1958

. . . That was quite an experience you had with Catharine, getting caught in the chair. Kids do the darndest things, as you say, impossible things. You're always reading in the paper about one getting stuck in a pipe, locked in a bathroom or something. I am glad you were able to extract her without damage to her or the chair. It is things like that which make you leery of leaving kids with young babysitters or older brothers.

* * *

Wed, Apr 2, 1958

. . . I think you were real cute to go off by yourself and have a Chinese dinner. You ought to be devilish like that more often. I am sure Daddy and Catharine kept each other good company.

* * *

Thurs, Apr 10, 1958

Today is an important date—birthday for both of our Johnny's and now only two months until my tour is up. I had both little boys so much in my thoughts today and send them both so much love.

* * *

Sun, Apr 20, 1958

. . . Yes, you must have literally sent me pounds of paper in the past two years. And I to you. It is my lifeline. I mean that truly.

I agree that you should go out when you are invited. You and I are much too prone to be content to withdraw into ourselves. It is a big effort, but maybe when you get back you can pull yourself together and give a KT party or two. You have such a lovely place in which to entertain and you can always get in good help.

* * *

Mon, Apr 28, 1958

. . . I had a letter from John Ingles today, a real nice one. I also heard from Margot and she had received the money order. Again, my thanks for taking care of it for me.

I also had a letter from my friend Mary Wickman Campbell in Sasebo. Her big news is that she is going to have a baby in October. She's so happy as it was quite unexpected. She was 38 when she married last year and had been told by a doctor a number of years ago that she would never be able to have children. I guess all it took was a husband.

I had a letter from Martha today, too—a very nice mail call, actually—She said Stephen was fine again and looks well. Told of being amazed at the exhibition of John Robert's tumbling prowess.

* * *

Thurs, May 1, 1958

. . . This is an awfully self-centered letter, but I know you like to know what is on my mind and I think you will see there is plenty. What a relief it will be to get on a boat and have nothing to think about except coming home to my loving family.

* * *

Mary's eighteen months in Korea were clearly filled with hardship. But they were also formative for her personally and professionally. Toward the end of her tour, she went to Japan on business for a few days. When she returned, she penned the following.

Ascom City

Thurs, May 15, 1958

You know, one of the nicest things that has happened to me morale wise was the greeting I got when I got back here after my brief trip to Japan. It seems like everyone knew I had been away and it was almost like coming back to family. The close feeling you develop for people over here is one of the biggest pluses to duty in Korea. I think it brings out the very best in most people. After I leave, I know I'll forget the discomforts and inconveniences and will remember the warmth and friendships I have had here.

* * *

Mary returned to the United States the summer of 1958. She did several more tours to Europe, but the only letters that survived those postings were of R&R trips to various locations, including Egypt and Greece. In 1969-1970, she would have to return to Asia when she was posted to Saigon, Vietnam.

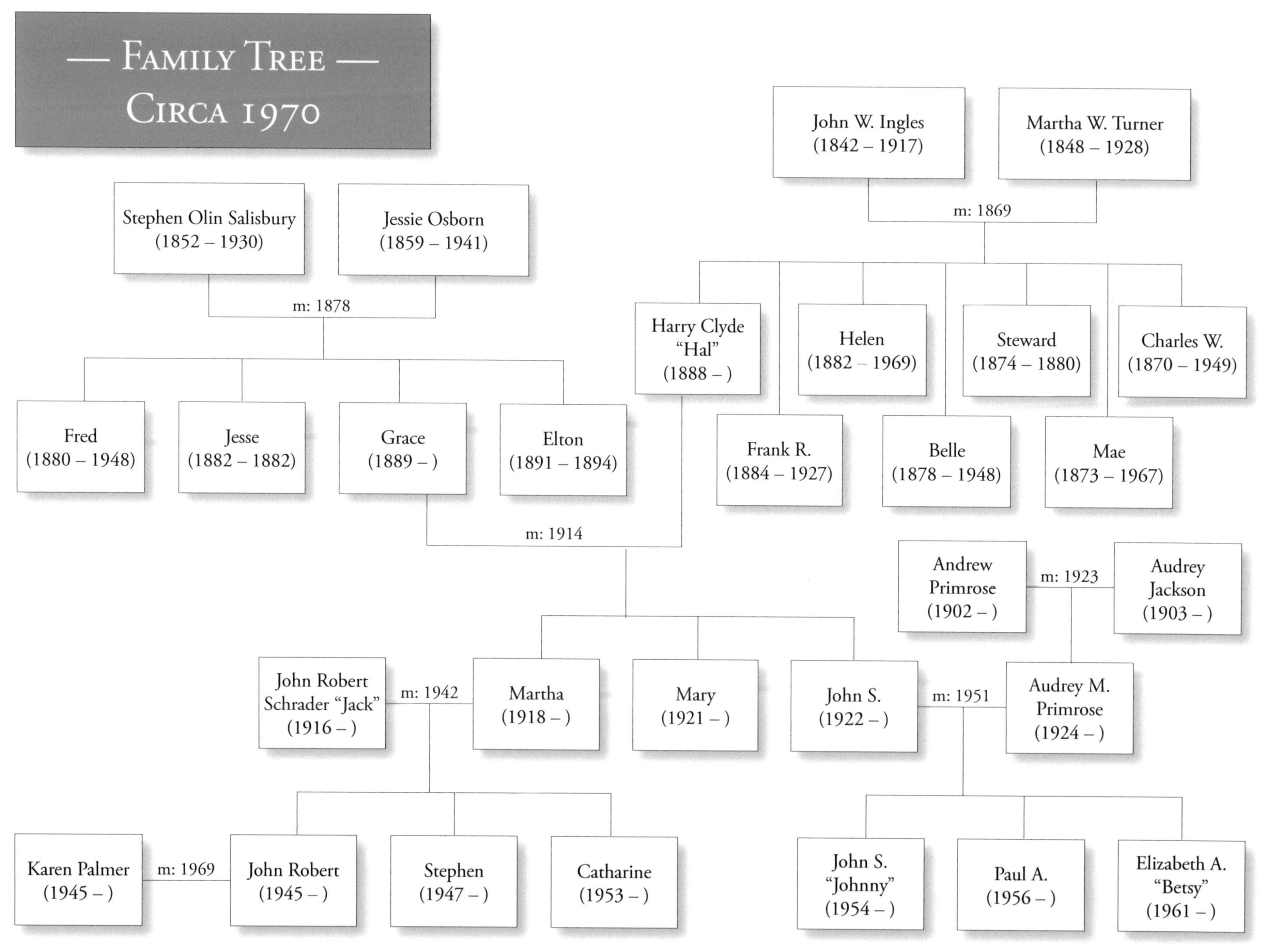

— FAMILY TREE —
CIRCA 1970

John W. Ingles (1842 – 1917)
Martha W. Turner (1848 – 1928)
m: 1869

Stephen Olin Salisbury (1852 – 1930)
Jessie Osborn (1859 – 1941)
m: 1878

Harry Clyde "Hal" (1888 –)
Helen (1882 – 1969)
Steward (1874 – 1880)
Charles W. (1870 – 1949)

Fred (1880 – 1948)
Jesse (1882 – 1882)
Grace (1889 –)
Elton (1891 – 1894)

Frank R. (1884 – 1927)
Belle (1878 – 1948)
Mae (1873 – 1967)

m: 1914

Andrew Primrose (1902 –)
m: 1923
Audrey Jackson (1903 –)

John Robert Schrader "Jack" (1916 –)
m: 1942
Martha (1918 –)
Mary (1921 –)
John S. (1922 –)
m: 1951
Audrey M. Primrose (1924 –)

Karen Palmer (1945 –)
m: 1969
John Robert (1945 –)
Stephen (1947 –)
Catharine (1953 –)

John S. "Johnny" (1954 –)
Paul A. (1956 –)
Elizabeth A. "Betsy" (1961 –)

VIETNAM

HISTORICAL AND CULTURAL CONTEXT FOR THE VIETNAM LETTERS (1969–70)

While the other postings, particularly Korea, had risks and hardships associated with them, Mary's Vietnam tour was the only time she lived in an active war zone. Roads were not safe. Guerilla warfare meant there was no clear front line, and it was hard to feel removed from active fighting. At this time, some of the most violent and well-documented protests against the war were happening stateside. It was a turbulent time for all.

PERSONAL REFLECTIONS ON THE VIETNAM LETTERS

THESE LETTERS TOOK ON a different tone than the others. Mary continued to dutifully write to Grace, but for the most part, the letters were mundane and unemotional. By this time, Grace was in her elder years. I sense Mary was trying to shield her mother from Mary's life so as not cause worry.

From oral histories, we know Mary experienced at least two close calls with death or injury while in Vietnam, yet neither of these events are mentioned in her letters. In one case, Mary was dining on the rooftop restaurant of her billet. and a sniper fired at the diners. The back of Mary's calf was hit by a spent bullet, causing no real physical damage. Mary reported that an officer at a nearby table retrieved the bullet and gave it to her saying, "Here

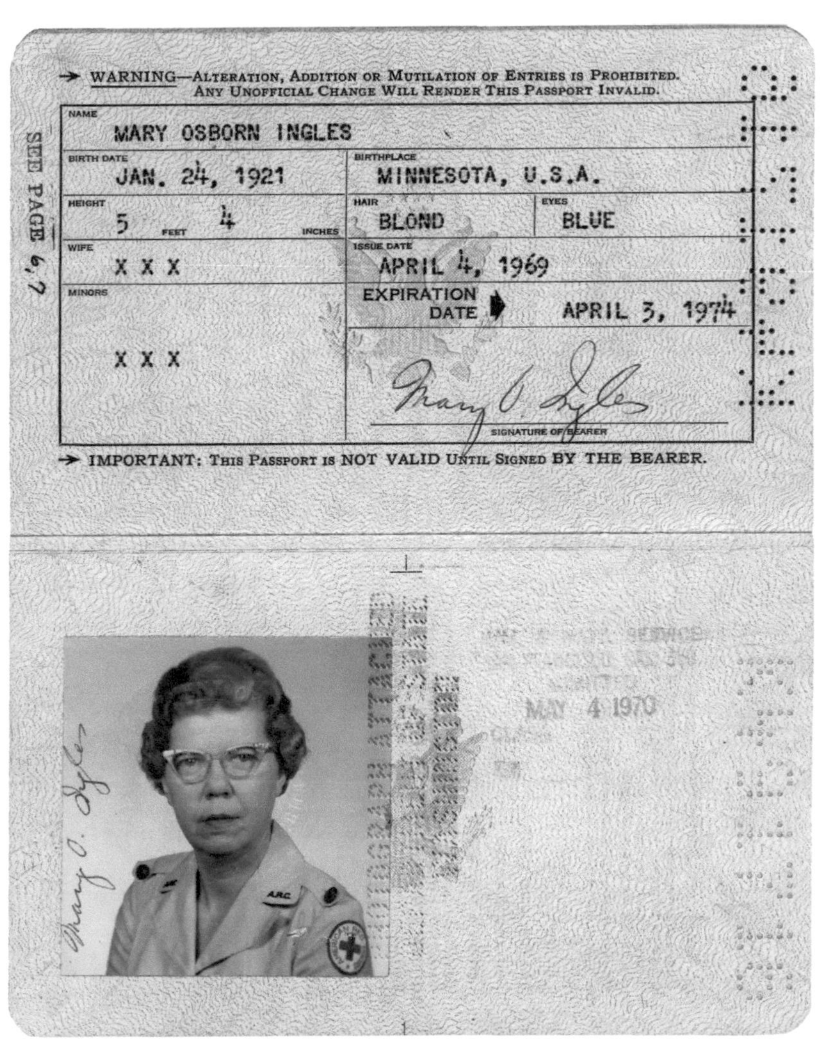

MARY'S PASSPORT (1969 – 1974)

ma'am. Today is your lucky day." Another time Mary reported standing at a bus stop waiting for the bus to go from the hospital to her billet when a soldier waiting with her yelled, "RUN." She did so without hesitation. Seconds later, a hand grenade destroyed the bus stop. The soldier had seen someone driving by pull the pin and loft a hand grenade into the bus stop. Had he not seen the action and had Mary not responded so quickly, her life could easily have ended that day.

Today, events like these would be recognized as life-changing traumas. In the late 60s and early 70s, they were just things that happened over there. When Mary went to Vietnam, she was already pretty formidable. By the time she returned, she was a force to be reckoned with.

THE WORK AND THE LIFE

AS IN PREVIOUS LETTERS, Mary recounted details about her work and her living situation. She often included a comment of "don't worry about me" when she outlined some of the hardships she encountered. Her letters provide insight into the job of the ARC and life in Saigon during the war.

All the following excerpts are from letters written in Saigon unless otherwise noted.

Postcard written while en route
from San Francisco to Saigon
Wed, May 7, 1969

Dear Mother—Apparently, we have skipped May 6 or at least will have by the time we reach Saigon. We had to make an unscheduled stop on Guam to refuel. Something about head winds. It was 4:00 AM Guam time and we were only there an hour, so couldn't see anything but the rather stark terminal. To that point we had 13 hrs flying time: 5 to Hawaii, 8 to Guam. Supposed to be 3 to Clark and 2 ½ to Saigon. Will mail this at Clark. Have slept

some, but it is a grind. I have kept my watch on S.F. time, but even so am confused. My watch says 1:00AM and it is beginning to get light. Have been in dark up to now. Love, Mary

* * *

Postcard written while en route
Wed, May 7, 1969

Dear Mother—We land in Saigon in 10 minutes. It will be about 9:30AM May 7. Temperatures just around 88°. We have been en route almost 22 hrs—18 hrs flying time. Nothing to see at Clark. 66 miles from Manila—rather barren looking. I am fine, but look forward to a bath, bed and change of clothes. Have been in these for over 36 hours. Love, Mary

* * *

Wed, May 7, 1969

Well, I am here and it is hot. But I guess I'll get used to it. I got the VIP treatment this morning. Penny, Mr. Higgins (he is ARC Director of Operations) and a Mr. Young met me. They whisked me through customs, currency exchange, etc. Then brought me into Saigon to the billeting office. I am billeted temporarily in something called The Ambassador. It is reminiscent of the Osaka Hotel in Tokyo only less so. There are 3 beds and one is being occupied by an ARC girl who arrived a few hours after I did. There is an air conditioner which helps a bit although the building is hardly built to get maximum benefit from any unit.

I had a shower and went to bed. I was awakened at 4:00 to let my roommate in but went back to bed and slept until

MARY EN ROUTE TO A HOSPITAL VISIT

7:00 when Penny came. She took us to the Rex—about 2 blocks—for a drink in her room and dinner. I am back now—10:00 PM—and will go to sleep again.

I will be able to move to the Rex next week. Her room was not bad at all and the air conditioner there was effective.

Tomorrow Penny is tied up in the AM with the Vietnamese Red Cross. She will pick us up at noon to go to the office. We will have to go across the street to another billet for breakfast at 8:00.

All is well, and I may write you again in the AM. For now, I am ready for some more sleep.

* * *

Thurs, May 8, 1969

I am at the office and have a little time to kill. This has been a rather ambulating day. I slept well from 10:00 until 2:00 AM—then was awake until 4:00—back to sleep for a couple of more hours. I am told that everyone wakes up around 2:00 for the first week or so because this is [the] corresponding time to wake up time at home.

Nancy Stone (my temporary roommate) and I went across the street to another BOQ for breakfast. We were free for the morning and stayed in our room. I unpacked (sort of) and wrote a couple of letters. At noon, Penny came for us and we had lunch at the Rex. Then stopped by the PX for soap powder, Kleenex, etc. and came to the office. I have been thru various Personnel activities—forms for ID cards, ration cards, etc., etc. Will have further orientation in the next few days.

It is really beastly hot. Even where there is air conditioning I drip constantly. I'll probably get better acclimated soon, but everyone is saying that this is the worst time of the year. The rainy season is about to start, I understand.

I am determined not to complain about the heat, so won't mention it any more than I can help.

I am meeting a lot of people. All very cordial and welcoming. When I get them sorted out, I'll write you about them, so you'll know to whom I am referring.

* * *

Fri, May 9, 1969

. . . I had the maid wash 2 uniforms today and she did them nicely. When I get into the Rex, I will pay the maid about $10 a month and she will do all of my laundry. Since this is a transient billet, you pay by the piece. So far I have done my own underwear each night. I didn't want to let it accumulate. There is only cold water—actually it is tepid.

. . . We went to the bank today and they charged me a 25 cent fee to cash a $50 personal check. I need to find out if there is any other way to get checks cashed. If not, I may have to change my salary allotment and have more money sent to me over here. This is just one of those things that I wasn't properly informed about in the States.

* * *

Sat, May 10, 1969

. . . Getting things done over here is complicated and time consuming. Today one of the men in Personnel Services took four of us to get our membership cards for the Officers Open Mess. It sounds simple, but transportation is scarce, so we had to combine the trip with four other stops and it took two hours driving around in the heat. When I got back, one of the girls from one of the hospitals had just called that she was at the airport returning from leave. Penny asked me to go meet her. The airport is only 5 minutes from the office.

The office has a total of 4 vehicles assigned—a pick-up truck which has seats and can carry about 8, a station wagon, a sedan, and a carry-all. We also have 3 Vietnamese drivers. Periodically, for reasons I don't quite understand, none of the drivers show up. Two of the men in the office have driver's licenses, but transportation gets very tight. All of the vehicles are very ancient, poorly maintained and dirty. This again is something I don't understand—that is, why the military has so many ancient, poorly maintained vehicles over here. It is not that the ARC is assigned the dregs; you see any number of similar vintage and condition. Anyway, when we have all of our drivers, they take us all home from work at 5:00. So far, I haven't ridden the so-called "work buses" but will start next week. This will mean leaving the hotel at 6:15 in the morning.

While talking about driving—I have been many places in the world, but I have never seen anything to compare with the congested traffic here. Millions of motorbikes, pedicabs, bicycles, small cars, trucks of all sizes etc. etc. It has to be seen to be believed. Each drive is an adventure. Where they all come from and where they are going, I can't imagine. I am told there are estimated 2 million people in Saigon now and 5 or 6 years ago there were only about 40,000.

It was probably a very attractive city at one time. Now it is run down, jam crowded, dirty and noisy.

. . . Two new staff arrived this evening from the States, so I'll probably have to make connections with them tomorrow. One part of the job is that we take all staff coming thru Saigon out to dinner etc. and look after them. With someone coming and going all the time this is going to be an almost daily affair. I can see that one does not have much free time here. At the moment there is a 10:00 PM curfew for Americans, so at least everyone goes to bed early. You have to if you are going to be up at 5:00 or 5:30 every day.

* * *

Sun, May 11, 1969

As you will see from the enclosure, there is an Episcopal Church here, and I took my first taxi ride to go to the 11:00 service this morning. It is really not far from my billet, about 8 blocks, but it is too hot to walk anywhere. With the help of one of the Vietnamese girls at the hotel, I managed to convey to the taxi driver where I wanted to go.

The church is of stucco construction—very open with ceiling fans, so not too uncomfortable. The priest is an attractive young Britisher with the British sense of humor. The service was so very comforting. He had more congregational participation than usual. Lay readers read the lesson. They have a small choir who did quite well. There were about 40 people altogether. The sermon was very good. He speaks well.

I introduced myself to the priest and his wife after church. They served cold fruit punch on the church porch, and I met several people. One couple engaged in some sort of missionary work—I didn't quite understand what— drove me back to the hotel. I filled out a card as I planned to continue to go. So at least I have found my "church home" for the next year.

After church, I went across the street for lunch. One of the ARC men was there, so I had company. I was glad to discover that they have a snack bar at that billet—it is called Brinks—as well as at the Rex where you can get sandwiches. The dining rooms are field ration messes, and

BULLETIN FROM ST. CHRISTOPHER'S CHURCH

the food is so heavy. If I had known about the snack bar sooner, I would have been glad to just get a sandwich at noon. The hotel I am in at present has no food facilities, so I had to go to Brinks for breakfast this AM too. They served an hour later on Sunday, 6:30 to 8:30 instead of 5:30 to 7:30 on the weekends.

. . . I slept better last night, woke up at 2:00, but was able to go back to sleep and didn't get up until 7:30. This evening, Penny and I are taking two new staff to dinner. They arrived from the States late yesterday. In the meantime, I am content to stay in my room where it is relatively comfortable. These rooms have very high ceilings—are large and not at all sealed. So a window air conditioner can only do so much cooling. But it helps and I'm not knocking it. I would be dead without it. Some of the billets where the secretaries stay are not air conditioned, and I pity them.

* * *

Mon, May 12, 1969

. . . Today, for the first time, I caught the work bus at 6:15. One of the ARC men was on it, so I was guided through the process. I had a fairly long conference with Penny today, the first time we have really talked. There are five new arrivals going through orientation and I am participating in that. Part of it today included going across town to get some field clothing issued and visit one of the PX's. The latter have a very odd assortment of stock, and I can foresee many problems from time to time. The best one I have seen so far was the Air Force one at Tan Son Nhat. It isn't far from the office, but you have to have transportation. I hope I can get over there again soon. In fact, you need transportation to get to any of the PX, so there is going to take planning and foresight I can see.

Speaking of field clothing—Penny says she has never had hers on, and Charlotte has worn hers only once on a field visit. However, you have to have it just in case.

. . . I have a real nice little maid here who speaks some English. She just came and brought me a bottle of cold water. None of the city water is potable so we are provided with bottles of drinking water in old whiskey bottles. She apparently keeps some in a refrigerator somewhere and when she knows I am here, she brings me a cold bottle. She also does my laundry and quite well too. Since this is a transient billet, I pay her by the piece. When I get to the Rex, I will pay a flat monthly rate.

* * *

Sat, May 17, 1969

I stayed at the office this afternoon, although I didn't have to. It was something to do, gave me a chance to read up on some of the files, and was relatively cool. There really isn't anything to do in your off-duty here. It is too hot to go out in the streets even if I wanted to, which I don't. I'll have to get lined up on some reading. So far, I have been reading paperbacks, which are all I have been able to get my hands on. There is Special Service library somewhere, but I haven't been able to figure out where. Tomorrow I'll go to church and in the evening Penny and I will take a new girl out to dinner. Penny reviewed this project with me today. It is one for which we will share the cost. It is worth it though, because you certainly need some looking after when you first arrive.

. . . Since I'm going to be in my present room apparently for three or four more weeks, I will start today carrying the packages down. I have been assured that I will not be given any roommates, which is a blessing. Another

ARC girl—assigned to Personnel Service—will be in the same building when she arrives this weekend, so I'll have at least another woman around. When I get to the PX I'll get some liquor and knick-knacks so I can have people in for drinks or something. You have to have transportation to get to any of the PX, so you have to plan ahead and grab your chances.

* * *

Undated

. . . Next week Penny and I are responsible for covering the office from 7:00 AM to 7:00 PM. Monday, we will do it together, so she can show me the ropes, then we will alternate the rest of the week. This apparently comes up about once a month. As I have said before, there is really nothing to do outside of work, so it is just as well to have long hours.

I think I have written you that getting to the Rex seems somewhat remote. I should have known better than to count on one week. Yesterday I talked to the Sgt. in charge of this building and he said he would try to get me a refrigerator. That would be a real boom. I put some cakes and ginger ale in the community one in the hall and they promptly disappeared. Actually with a few amenities such as that and some better furniture I could be a lot worse off than I am here at the Ambassador. The billeting officer promised our Director of Personnel that he would not give me anymore roommates as long as I am at the Ambassador. I have a GS-14 rating [government service rating] which is equivalent to a Lt Col which is some help.

. . . My little maid here is very good and accommodating and does a pretty good laundry job. So I can't complain about her. She even speaks a little English, which is more than most Vietnamese do.

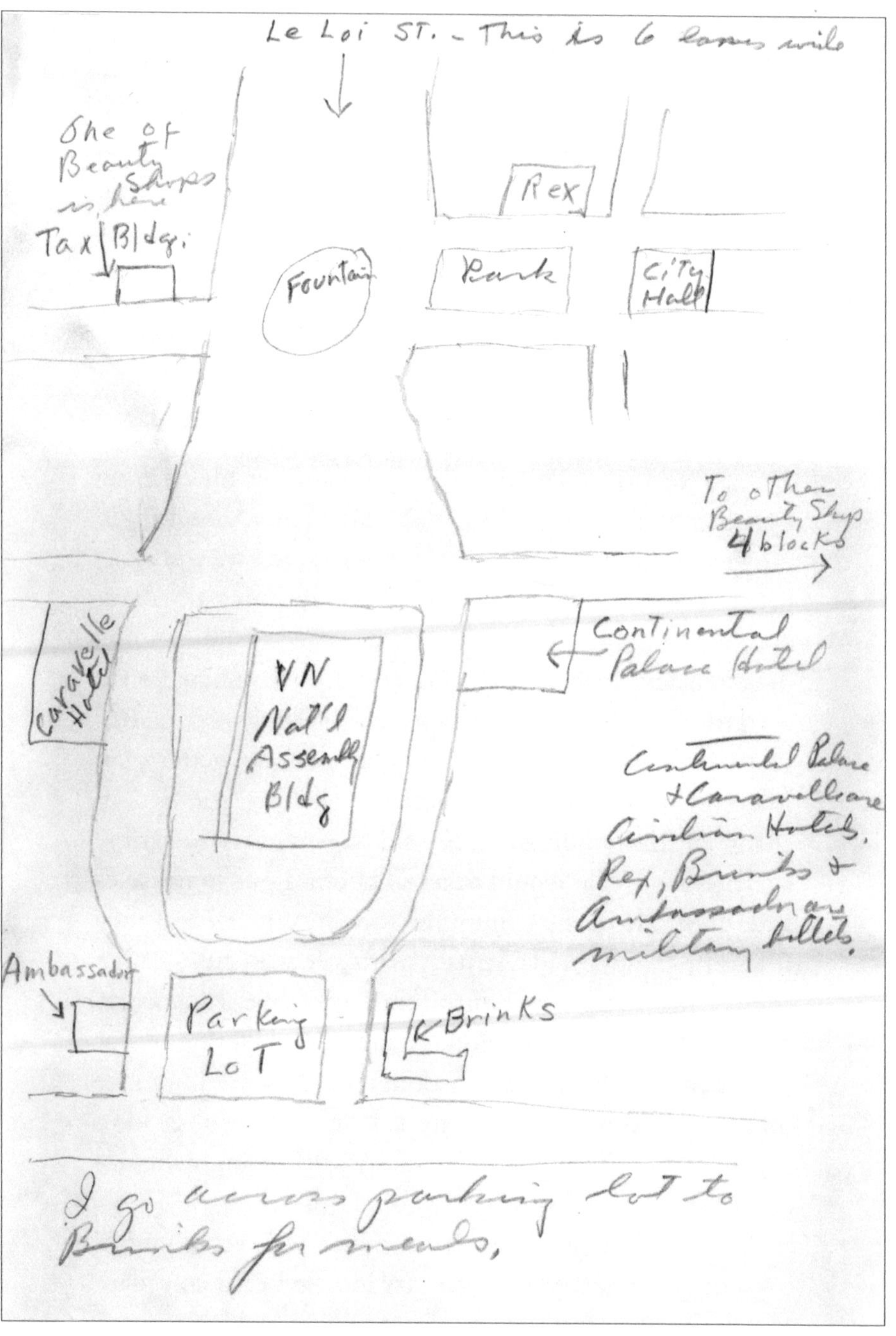

MAP OF SAIGON WHERE MARY LIVED AND WORKED

* * *

Wed, 21 May, 1969

. . . I have had a fairly busy day with one thing or another. One of our girls from the hospital is going home on emergency leave due to the death of her brother. I met her when she flew into Saigon this afternoon. She can't get out to the States until tomorrow, so we had to arrange billeting. This evening Penny and I had her to dinner at the Rex and I am just back from that. Looking after our approximately 60 girls is a major part of my job.

Written by Grace Ingles: *Who could do a better job of "looking after our girls" than our Mary? She is so calm and steady but so likable and "easy" with people. I know she constantly "comforts and sustains" and she is so fun besides.*

* * *

Thurs, May 22, 1969

. . . For Daddy's information, as near as I can figure out, there are two so-called field forces in Viet Nam. They seem to correspond to an Army as we knew it in WW II. They are commanded by Lt Gens. There are also four corps over here divided on geographic areas. I believe the corps each come under one of the Field Forces, but I'm not really sure of the chain of command.

. . . One of the biggest drawbacks to this particular place is the odor of bad drains, which is all pervasive. Perhaps you could find a deodorizer to send me. The spray type wouldn't do much good, but something of an Air Wick type might help. They may have some newer kind which operates on that principle, but if not, Airwick might do.

* * *

Fri, May 23, 1969

. . . I had a chance to go to another PX today, and was able to get a large can of hairspray. The cosmetics etc. are reserved for the American female personnel, but only one of each item per customer. This is to prevent the GI's from buying up the stock for their Vietnamese girlfriends. So, if you haven't already sent the hairspray, you can hold off on one can. You might go ahead and send one when you get it, as the availability is obviously a sometime thing.

* * *

Sat, May 24, 1969

. . . There is a small snack bar across the street at Brinks and I went over there for a sandwich and an iced tea after the hair. I'm glad I like iced tea because it is served automatically with lunch and dinner at all the messes. It is a good solution as the tea covers the taste of the water, all of which has been treated to purify it.

. . . Just so you will know the location of some of the places I mentioned, I am enclosing a rough sketch. It will give you an idea anyway. You can see that things are pretty close together. I can't put the church on this map as it is off in another direction—actually, only about 6 or 8 blocks. Walking anywhere is a further problem as there are few sidewalks and the ones they have are very broken up and rough.

* * *

Mon, May 26, 1969

. . . Now to fill you in on the billeting situation here, I was offered an opportunity to move into a double room at the Rex, which I would share with Betty Hopper when she gets here. She is the other Assistant Director due on or about June 15. However, the room was located across from the Snack Bar kitchen next to the Men's Room, and only a few feet from the bar where they have nightly movies or rock'n'roll band. The room was very small—hardly big enough for one. The alternative was to stay on here for an indefinite period—also with the possibility of having to share this with Betty.

Well, after weighing the pros and cons, I decided to stay here. They have promised to get me a refrigerator, and another wardrobe and will move out the third bed. There are two rooms here, so if I have to share at least there would be some semblance of privacy. You can see from the sketch I sent yesterday that I am not far from the Rex.

Now that the decision is made I will really unpack and do some furniture rearranging as soon as they move the extra bed out. I think I may send to Sears for some cheap curtains and bedspreads to brighten the place up. It can be made more livable with a little effort.

I've really been getting exercise the past two days. The elevators have been out of order at Rex, Brinks and here. Yesterday, I walked down six flights here (138 steps), up five flights at the Rex, down five flights at the Rex, up six flights here. This AM down six flights here, up seven flights at Brinks for breakfast and back down again. Tonight, fortunately the Brinks' elevator was working so I could ride up and down to get dinner. I did that as soon as I got back from work without cleaning up or changing. So, I only had to climb the six flights here once. Now I know why I had to pass a physical before coming over here.

This week, Penny and I are alternating the duty, which means staying in the office until 6:00. We both stayed tonight so she could show me the routine. I'll stay Tuesday and Thursday. They have a different roster for weekend duty which is 12:00 to 6:00 on Saturday and 7:00 to 6:00 on Sunday. I'll get that, too, in due course. We do have a car to bring us home, which is a help. Actually they set up transportation to take all the staff home every day, so I only ride the bus in the AM.

Looking again at your letters—Yes, the Rex is the higher ranking billet. Supposedly only colonels. My rating of GS14 equivalent entitles me to be there, but of course I'm outranked by any real colonels. Generals live in air-conditioned trailers in an area near MACV [Military Assistance Command Vietnam] Hqs. Gen Abrams and his deputy Gen Rosson have an elaborate setup, of course.

. . . I'm getting busier at work and feeling more useful. Each chore takes me a long time as I have to do much research and background reading, but I am learning all the time.

* * *

Wed, May 28, 1969

. . . Monday we received word that effective July 1, we will get a 5½% pay raise. I don't know where the money is coming from, but I do think ARC is doing its best to keep up with inflation. We have had a raise almost every year. This is a sizable one and will mean for me an increase of $23.50 every two weeks in my base salary. It will also mean more tax deductions and we will probably have to submit an amended federal income tax estimate, won't we, Daddy?

I appreciate Daddy trying to bolster my bank balance by putting my share of the Lincoln income into my checking account. I really don't want it there and as soon as I get the deposit slip from the Chase Bank confirming the deposit, I'll send the check to you made out to Perpetual to deposit it there. What I would like Daddy to do is to put a page in the notebook he keeps for me and list all the Lincoln deposits. I will put them in my savings account for the moment. I have plans for that money and I would like him to keep a record of how much it is.

He asked for the address of the branch of the Chase Bank where my account is. I thought I had left that with him and my account number, but here it is again:

Chase Manhattan Bank
33 East 23rd St.
New York, NY 10010.
My account number is 0-210-0002-002-1-021332

Thank you, Daddy, for sending the photostat of the statement from the storage co. As soon as I hear from them and get a receipt for the payment I made, I will have all I need to clear the sub advance I received from ARC and to start the process of getting reimbursed for monthly storage payments.

* * *

Fri, May 30, 1969

Happy Buddha's birthday! You may have read that the VC declared a 48 [hour] ceasefire in honor of Buddha's birthday. All it has meant for us is that we have been in what is called a Grey Alert. This merely means that we can go about our business but stay off the streets as much as possible and out of all Vietnamese stores, markets, etcetera. So as so far as I know, there hasn't been any particular incidents in Saigon, but the alert was a precaution as the VC are not very good about observing ceasefires. The alert will end at noon tomorrow. I only mention it as a news item, and not to create any concern, because there isn't any as far as I am concerned.

Tonight, when I got home, I found they had moved in another chest of drawers. I can use it, and, of course, should I get a roommate it would be necessary. The Sgt. told me tonight he has another wardrobe lined up and will have it next week. He didn't mention the refrigerator and neither did I. I didn't want to "bug" him as I know he is doing his best for me, and I am sure you get further by being nice and appreciative, not demanding.

* * *

Tues, Jun 3, 1969

My foot lockers were delivered today and I have been getting them unpacked—at least partially. I really don't think I made too many mistakes in what I brought. I was glad to get some of the things. I put the bedspread—the green, yellow and blue plaid one I used in Germany—on the bed in my "sitting room" and it sure improves the looks. I was also glad to get some of the extra towels and things like double plugs and extension cords. I will have to finish the job another night, but really need the second wardrobe which has not yet been produced.

One of our cars was [in] an accident today and another is in the shop, so for the first time I had to come home on the bus. It was a bit complicated as you have to take two buses and it took over an hour. At least I know how to do it now.

* * *

Tues, Jun 10, 1969

. . . This was just another busy day at work. So many of the administrative aspects of the job are hodge-podge over here. It takes some hours to ferret out how to handle each piece of paper. Our staff are so inexperienced that they don't know procedures and anyway they seem to do everything in a different way than any of us are used to in the States.

* * *

Fri, Jun 13, 1969

I don't think I told you that I got my first hardship allowance check from ARC. It was for the 31 day period ending June 6. The gross amount was $139.50 ($4.50 a day). From this was withheld $44.11 for federal income tax and $6.70 for social security. Net amount was $88.69. When we do my amended estimate, this additional income will have to be figured in. They are not withholding Va income tax from this. I understand that when I get my W-2 it will include this added income. I hope I have made this clear, but if not let me know. In other words, the amended estimate for both federal and Va tax will have to show the salary increase which I will start getting June 5th, and $4.50 per day starting May 5.

I might add that $44.11 seems like a lot to withhold for income tax, but maybe they are taking into account that this allowance is added on top of my other salary. If you need it, I can figure out from the check stubs the exact total salary and withholding for the year. At least I can after July 18th when I get my first check reflecting the salary increase.

* * *

Sat, Jun 14, 1969

. . . Well, as I expected, Betty Hopper has been assigned to my room. She arrived today. Although I would, of course, prefer to be alone, I think it will work out OK. She is a real easy-going cheery soul and I don't think we'll grate. It may not be forever as one or the other of us may get a single later on. At any rate, there is no use making it a problem, because it is the way things are going to be.

. . . I had to leave the office this AM before the mail came, which was a disappointment as I am sure there was some from you. I had to go to the airport to meet Betty and another one of our hospital girls who arrived on the same plane and then into town to get them billeted, etc. I still haven't been told if I am to go to the airport tomorrow to meet Miss Betterly. I guess Penny will give me the yea or nay tonight. I hope nay as she gets in at 12:30 and it would mean I would have to miss church.

* * *

Tues, Jun 17, 1969

. . . This was a busy day with Jane Betterly's visit and tomorrow will be equally so. At noon we had a lovely lunch at the General's mess with the MACV Surgeon General and two members of his staff. I really enjoyed it and the officers were all delightful and charming. It is a little hard to get used to having the high-ranking officers younger than I am, or at least no older.

Tomorrow, eight of our hospital field directors are coming in for lunch and a meeting. I am glad for a chance to meet some of the staff. I'm going to ask Jane Betterly to call you when she gets back, which will be the end of June. At least you can have word from someone who has seen me recently.

I learned today that Joan Matthews is going to replace Penny. Joan is an Assistant director in Western area and will be promoted. I met her first 20 years ago when we were both at the same ARC course in San Antonio. I saw her briefly when I came thru S. F. en route over here. She's about my age and a real nice girl, so I think it will be good to have her here.

* * *

Sat, Jun 21, 1969

. . . After deciding that we would keep our beds in separate rooms, we came home a couple of days ago to find that they had been moved into the larger room together. So we are trying this arrangement to see how it goes. It was really our own fault, as we had told Sgt. Thompson we thought we would like the beds in one room. When we changed our minds, we forgot to tell him.

Last night, Betty and I had dinner with Jane Betterly and Penny and they left this morning for Thailand. Jane returns to the US from there, stopping in Hawaii en route. She has said she will call you when she gets back to Washington. Penny will be back here next Sat. So I am acting director and I hope nothing horrendous comes up this next week.

* * *

Tues, Jun 24, 1969

. . . Yes, our "suite at the Ambassador" sounds great, but I wouldn't dream of sending you pictures. It is really not that bad, but it is far from luxurious. With our various rearranging things, we have got it fairly livable and the things we have ordered from Sears will help. More than anything, it needs a paint job. If you find the "solid" Air Wick, do send it. If not, send another bottle in the next mail. I keep the one I have open all the time and it won't last forever. In one way, it is a good thing that both Betty and I smoke, as the smell of smoke sort of overcomes the other.

* * *

Thurs, Jun 26, 1969

. . . I don't think I have mentioned anything about the trial and tribulations of telephone communication over here. It is reminiscent of Korea. I am always glad if I can get a GI operator as they are so helpful to a woman. The Vietnamese women operators take great pleasure in telling you the circuits are busy. You scream your head off when you do finally get thru and then are likely to get cut off mid-sentence. Well, I expected this, so I'm not surprised, but I do hope the direct dial will be an improvement.

* * *

Tues, Jul 1, 1969

Sorry I gave you a short shift with a postcard last night. As I think I told you, we went out to dinner with one of our staff, so the evening got used up. We had two girls go home yesterday—resigning without completing their tours. We have one coming in tomorrow that we are going to send home because she has gotten herself all messed up with a married man. So it goes. I guess you can't have 60 women over here without all sorts of problems.

* * *

Wed, Jul 2, 1969

Another news-less day. My big excitement today was to go to the dispensary to get a follow up plague shot I needed, and a walk to the small PX near the office between rain showers to get a few needed items.

This afternoon Betty and I had a good session with Penny which helped a lot in clarifying our roles and determining individual and mutual responsibilities. We needed it, as Betty and I have been floundering a little bit.

Next week I'm going to visit the two hospitals at Long Binh—about 20 minutes from here. I will go on a bus but will probably stay out there over 3 nights rather than try to commute. I will really be glad to go as the office routine is getting a bit stifling.

* * *

Fri, Jul 4, 1969

. . . We have had 24 brand new Clubmobile girls in this week. They are an attractive, enthusiastic group—all between 21 and 24. They had a rough trip getting here, delayed 24 hours at [undecipherable] and then taking a circuitous route via Anchorage, Japan and Clark. But they are young, and are bouncing right back. They are at Hqrs. until Monday and then will scatter to their various units. One dividend was that an air-conditioned bus has been assigned to cart them around while in Saigon and Betty and I rode downtown with them in comfort this evening.

* * *

Sun, Jul 6, 1969

. . . I go tomorrow morning to Long Binh on the bus, leaving at 9:00. It is only a 45-minute trip. I'll stay over Monday night and come back Tuesday afternoon. As it turns out, I am glad I had this trip scheduled. On Tuesday the first contingent of 9th Division troops who are being pulled out, are having a parade and ceremonies at Tan Son Nhut. ARC was asked to serve coffee when the men arrive prior to the ceremonies. Betty got stuck with the job of organizing that, and I am glad to be out of it. We are drawing in the volunteers who serve at the 3rd Field Hospital here in Saigon. They are our only group of volunteers in Vietnam and were recruited from Embassy wives and other American women over here with husbands in various private businesses.

* * *

Tues, Jul 8, 1969

. . . Betty seemed to have maneuvered the coffee and doughnuts for the departing troops and I gather it went OK. Wonder if it was on TV and if the ARC wasn't evident?

. . . My getting into the Rex is sort of a moot question. I haven't inquired in several weeks. I don't know whether to push or not. Three people I know have moved out of there because their air conditioners had conked out and there were no replacements. I really don't know what to do about it all, so do nothing. I'm OK for the time being and the trouble of moving might not be worth it. I can even rise above the smells—they are at their worst when it rains but will welcome the Airwick when it comes.

* * *

Sun, Jul 13, 1969

Well, I'm back in Saigon and very happy to be in my own little nook for a few days. The more I see where other staff have to live, the more satisfied I am with my "suite at The Ambassador."

The things I ordered from Sears came just before I left and I have just finished hanging the curtains, shower curtain and putting on the bedspread. The curtains and bedspread were supposed to be "lemon yellow" but turned out to be a pretty orange color. However, they are bright and clean and I think improve the looks of things. I also ordered some wood grain contact paper to cover the tops of my chest of drawers and small tables. I'll have to get Betty to help me with that project. But you can see I'm trying to make the place more livable.

. . . I also want to embroider on my beauty parlor experience in Nha Trang. It was a fairly large shop, but no other Americans there and no English spoken by anyone. You sit up straight and the girl shampoos your hair with just shampoo—no water. She really scrubbed it too. Then you go over to the basin where the rinsing takes place. It was really a very good shampoo. They take you out from under the dryer when your hair is not quite dry and as the man combs it, a girl holds a hair dryer over each wave. This technique is definitely not for my hair kind, but I am managing to hold it on my head with hair spray. I took my own comb and brush because they use the same ones on everyone's no washing in between. Well, it is all part of life's experience. Come to think of it, I have surely had my hair done in strange places—Korea, Japan, Hong Kong, Germany, Egypt, Greece and now Vietnam to mention only a few.

* * *

Mon, Jul 14, 1969

. . . Apropos to your remark about the anxious mothers of the 24 Clubmobile girls. I doubt that the mothers are more detached. It's just that they can't exert any real control over the younger generation and it is probably just as well for the relationship that they don't try.

. . . I have weekend duty this coming weekend. That means being the only one on duty for the entire Hqrs from noon to six Saturday and 8:00 to 6:00 Sunday. If no emergencies pop up, I should be able to get my field visit reports written up. Anyway with that extra duty coming up, I don't feel guilty about taking off a morning to get a permanent. Penny is real good about such things. She recognizes that we work long hours, and we are completely free to take some time off when we need it to attend to personal things. I like being treated like a responsible adult, which I think I am.

* * *

Fri, Jul 18, 1969

. . . For Daddy's info, I guess I had better start with business.

1. I received the deposit slip for the dividends he deposited totaling $110.21. I've enclosed a check for that amount made out to Perpetual so he can deposit it in my savings account.
2. I got my first check today, representing the pay raise which went into effect July 4th. The gross increase is from $427.46 biweekly to $450.98 biweekly. Federal tax withholding was increased from $80.78 biweekly to $87.36 biweekly. There was no change in the VA tax withholding, which

remained at $12.99 biweekly I netted $14.46 biweekly. If Daddy feels that an amended estimate is in order for federal tax, I'll take time to figure out precisely what I'll be paid this year and how much will be withheld.

. . . The army does provide screens, but doors are left open, screens get holes in them and the mosquitoes do get in. I got most chewed up at night in my room in Nha Trang because the windows didn't fit tight. Insects just have to be endured, and I am conscientious about taking malaria pills every week. I'll try the insect repellent if you send it. Actually, I seldom get bitten in Saigon, but living conditions on field trips are more problematic. On the trip I just got back from, I had a cot in the Chief Nurse's room. That room was air conditioned so I was luckier than the rest of the girls. The Chief Nurse was a lovely person and very cordial. But housing is very tight everywhere, so you just take whatever bed is made available to you.

. . . Betty is due back tonight—was due in at 6:00. It is now 7:30, so she must have been delayed. Traveling around here is certainly difficult. I won't dwell on it, other than to say that each trip completed is an achievement. However, as you go along you add to your little tricks and bits of information as to how to maneuver. There are many flights and connections that aren't "published" so to speak. You just have to hear about them from others and try your luck. I have a specific trip set up for next Thursday-Friday but nothing definite beyond that. Will probably try to get one or two more in before Penny goes on leave August 11th.

* * *

Tues, Jul 22, 1969

. . . I did get my hair done and it looks better, at least for the moment. He managed to get it set without such a frizzy look. Regardless, I am glad to have it shorter and with some curl in it, even if it is a bit frizzy.

I took a taxi as far as the civilian taxis are allowed to go. Then I hitched a ride in a Jeep driven by a friendly young Puerto Rican Warrant Officer. The whole complex where our office is has a perimeter of several miles beyond which no civilian vehicles can go. This is one of the reasons we mostly try to travel via the military buses. Well, being a woman in an ARC uniform is a help as you can usually get picked up without too much trouble.

* * *

Mon, Jul 28, 1969

. . . Betty left this AM for a week in the Da Nang Area. We have two hospitals there and she also hopes to make connections with one or both of the hospital ships. We have two ARC staff on both the *Sanctuary* and the *Repose*. She should be back sometime over the weekend.

* * *

Sun, Aug 3, 1969

. . . Penny was at the office when I called and greeted me with the news that we all have to go to a reception at 6:00 tonight at the Vietnamese Red Cross—a command performance. With unwashed hair and a strong desire to relax a bit, there is nothing I would rather do less—but "duty calls" anyway. I have had a few hours to wash a mound of underwear, read my mail and write to you.

. . . I'm glad you are "steadier" about my being in Vietnam. Actually the worst part of it is the separation from you and Daddy. I have sort of gotten used to it all so that the things that bothered me at first just don't anymore. Having it cooler as it has been since the rainy season started is a big help. The biggest help, of course, is the "lull in the war." While this creates some staff morale problems in that they aren't busy enough, everyone is grateful that fewer people are being hurt and that there is less tension. So, just go on being "steady." I could omit details of my trips, but I think you are interested. But, I don't want you agonizing over them. "Oh that poor child etc." It is just all part of the game and a very unique experience.

* * *

Wed, Aug 6, 1969

Well, the big news tonight is that I am moving into the Rex on Friday. If I hadn't gotten the Rex, I would have been upset by the way it was handled. The military is turning the Ambassador back into a transient billet. Only all the permanent residents were handed orders today to move out within 48 hours to the new billet assigned to them. No one was consulted as to their druthers. Fortunately, I have been on the waiting list for the Rex for 3 months, so that is what I got. I went by to see the room tonight and it is pretty good. It is a single room, quite large, with bath. Air conditioned, good size closet, refrigerator, bed, desk, bookcase, chest of drawers, 4 chairs and 2 small tables. It is on the 4th floor, same floor as Penny. The only drawback is that the only window opens into the corridor! It is as dark as a pocket. However, I am seldom in my room in the daytime, so it won't matter too much. There is both a field ration mess, and a steakhouse at the Rex, so I can get food right in the building.

I've spent most of the evening packing. It is really amazing how much stuff I have accumulated in a short time. I'll finish the packing tomorrow night, and our supply man will come with his truck to move us on Friday AM. It will give me the weekend to get settled.

Betty is moving to a place called The Hergert which she wanted. It is downtown but not as well located as the Rex. It is small—about 20 people—and she will be the only woman. I wouldn't have cared for it, but she is satisfied.

My curtains won't fit the windows, so Betty is going to take them. She will also take one bedspread. While I am talking about things over here, you asked where Penny, Betty and Joan are from. Penny's home is in Plymouth, Michigan, and she graduated from University of Michigan. Betty is from White Sulphur Springs, W. Va. And Joan is from Moore, Montana. I first knew Joan when we attended the same ARC training class at San Antonio in 1949. You'll remember that was when I met Mary Liz Downing. Joan was one of the four of us who went dude ranching together. She's about my age and a real nice gal. I hadn't seen her again until I had lunch with her and Helen Armstrong in San Francisco on my way over here. She has been assistant director in Western area and is promoted to the Director's job over here.

Written in Grace Ingles's handwriting on the back: *The room with no outside window sounds far from great, but she is alone and can surely be much more comfortable. The idea of having to go out for all meals worried me. Knowing Mary I am sure she often just skipped meals. I'm glad she used better judgment than Betty. But maybe Betty wants to be where the men are. Anyway, I felt this is good news for which I am very grateful.*

* * *

Fri, Aug 8, 1969

Happy Birthday!! I hope you can feel the love I am sending your way, every day, but especially today.

You lost out on a letter last night to my packing chores and a power failure of about 30 minutes duration. Now I am all packed (I hope) and I'm waiting for the man to come with the truck.

You may have heard on the radio that one of the hospitals was extensively hit by sappers and satchel charges. This was the 6th Convalescent Center, our largest hospital. None of the ARC staff were injured, thank God.

* * *

Sat, Aug 9, 1969

. . . I called Ted Thursday AM and we had a brief chat. At that point your news regarding young Ted was later than his. He sounded fine but concerned over the rocket and satchel charge attacks at Nha Trang and Cam Ranh Bay the night before. I am sure you have read about them. The attack at the 6th Convalescent Center was bad—2 dead, 55 wounded—all patients but 4 who were hospital staff. No ARC staff involved, thank God. You probably also heard that there was a terrorist attack in Saigon. I didn't even know about it until I read about it in the paper. It was in a distant section of town from my appointed rounds.

I worked pretty steadily last night at unpacking, but have not done anymore today. I need to finish with the foot lockers. My new room has turned up with two major flaws. The refrigerator doesn't freeze ice and this AM when I went into the bathroom the floor was flooded. Fortunately, it is a little below the level of the room, so the water stayed in the bathroom. I had soggy slippers however.

I left a note about both at the desk. Of course the maid mopped up the floor and hung my slippers and bathroom rug out to dry. But the refrigerator still isn't making ice and I really doubt they did anything about the leak wherever it is in the bathroom. As far as ice is concerned, I have a thermos jug and there is an ice machine on the floor above so I can get ice from that.

The plumbing arrangements in Vietnam are peculiar, to say the least. This afternoon I washed some underwear in my sink. When I let the let the water out it all came up into the bidet, which is adjacent, and then drained off again. I'm glad I found this out before I decided to put extra cleaning supplies etc. in or on the bidet. The shower. is in a corner and measures 2½ feet by 2½ feet. You have to stand straight up and washing the lower part of one's anatomy is a real feat.

Well, all in all, I am better off here than at the Ambassador. At least, so far, there are no unpleasant odors. This noon I went up to the snack bar for a sandwich before going to get my hair done. Incidentally, I am about 3 blocks closer to Jules [the hair salon] than I was. This evening I went up to the Steak House and had a very good rib steak for $1.65. These are the amenities that the Rex has to offer over the Ambassador.

* * *

Mon, Aug 11, 1969

. . . The bridge that blew up that you referred to was between Saigon and Vung Tau. I didn't even know about it until I read about it in the paper. One doesn't travel by road over here for obvious reasons.

. . . It looks like my chances of getting to Thailand on business are pretty slim. We are pulling our worker out of one of the hospitals there which only leaves us with one worker in one hospital there. She is an old timer and doesn't need my help. Penny visited her when she and Jane Betterly were there in June, so it hardly seems likely that I will get a trip there. The present worker goes home in December. If we replace her someone may have to go, but it would probably be Joan. I don't really care as I have no particular interest in Bangkok.

. . . Today they changed all the MPC—something they do periodically to control the gold flow and black market. We had to turn all of our money in and won't get the new back until tomorrow. The mess halls are serving meals on credit, but it is a funny feeling to have no money at all. I do have some piastres (VN [Vietnamese] money) but that never seems like money anyway.

* * *

Tues, Aug 12, 1969

I'm sure you know from the news that the "lull in the war" seems to be over. We didn't get much news actually, but reports by phone from the girls at various hospitals are discouraging. The Navy Hospital at Da Nang took some mortar rounds last night. Again, God was good and no ARC staff or nurses were injured. There is really no point in my not commenting on these things in letters as you get news reports before we do.

We have a lot of staff coming and going this week. Sort of lost two tonight who were to join us for dinner but never showed up. I don't like to feel or act like a mother hen, but I do get concerned.

. . . I didn't see any reason to think Ted will be involved with the "Green Beret" investigation. It did occur supposedly at Nha Trang, but that doesn't put it under Ted's jurisdiction. The command set up over here is peculiar to say the least, but I don't believe Special Forces are in any way under 1st Field Force, which is Ted's outfit.

* * *

Sat, Aug 16, 1969

. . . No, this room does not smell, thank goodness. I guess they have different types of drains. In fact, the plumbing here is much more modern. Don't worry about the "window into the corridor." It is not barred, but I do hope [to] have both the non-functioning refrigerator and a bookcase in front of it. I have to put my mind to rearranging the furniture and I have to do something about the drapes. The ones up are really undesirable—kind of blotchy, pink and blue print which looks like all the colors ran together when they washed, if they ever were. I do have a small outside window in the bathroom. So if I crane my neck and look up, I can see a little daylight.

But I am not complaining. This is so much better than what I had and I'm happy to be here and to be alone.

* * *

Sun, Aug 17, 1969

. . . In case you wonder how I can tell whether it is raining or not—I stand up on the toilet seat and peek out the little window in the bathroom. I woke up in the night— very hot—and realized the air conditioner had gone off. I was relieved to find out there was a power failure—lights weren't working either. I was terrified that the air conditioner had conked out. Anyway, the power came back on in a little while, so all is well. All of the air conditioning units are ancient ones and get such continuous use. If they

breakdown, parts aren't available nor are replacement units. I turn mine off every day when I go to work in order to rest and conserve it (I hope).

* * *

Mon, Aug 18, 1969

. . . I can't really describe my room too well. It is good size, about 15' by 15'. The bath is about 5' by 6'. I have a built-in double door (sliding) closet with an enclosed space above where I keep my suitcases. The floors are tile—squares of green, yellow and gray. Two walls are painted yellow, two green. The walls are very dirty and water stained. The furniture is very scroungy—worn and quite soiled. But it could be a lot worse. Penny and I consulted last night and came up with a scheme for rearranging the furniture. I'll get Don Boyette one night soon to help me with shoving it around. I haven't put up the posters yet as I wanted to get the furniture settled first.

We had a power failure last night, all over Saigon, from 7:00–10:00. There wasn't much one could do by candlelight. Fortunately, it was on by bedtime so the air conditioning could function. This morning there was no water but they got that fixed sometime during the day. We are dependent on the city utilities, which are questionable at best. The water is not potable, so we have a jerry can of potable water in each bathroom from which the maid fills empty liquor bottles in the fridge and bathroom. There is no shortage of liquor bottles over here.

Well, you asked, and so there it is. None of this is reported in terms of a complaint. I am relatively comfortable—much more so than the vast majority of people in Vietnam.

We had a new staff member in today. I solved the "entertainment" problem by meeting her at the BOQ near where she is staying. We had a couple of drinks and an early dinner and then I took a cab home. I went right from the office, so was in uniform, but it was a lot less complicated than trying to get her downtown and back. Betty is away on field trip for two days, so I am having to cope with all these things alone. Therefore, I'm doing what is easiest for me. I'll have to do something similar 2 more nights this week.

* * *

Wed, Aug 20, 1969

. . . I made a little progress on solving some of the minor problems in my room. I got the hotel supervisor (Sgt) on the phone today. He admitted that he was well aware the refrigerator didn't work. He has no replacements, but I am "on the list" to have a functioning one moved in when some other room becomes vacant. He confessed that I was the present victim of just such a switch. He did remove my nonfunctioning floor lamp—it was an enormous wooden Vietnamese job—and replaced it with a very nice looking table lamp—Stateside model. Of course, the switch doesn't work, but I can easily turn it on and off by pulling the plug. Anyway, I am pleased to have it—it looks nice and makes a good reading lamp. I haven't had anymore "flooding" problems. I about decided the other was my fault for not being careful to keep the shower curtain inside. I think I'm going to like the way I have rearranged the furniture.

* * *

Sat, Aug 23, 1969

Joan Matthews arrived today and I met her at the plane together with Jack Higgins, our Director of Operations, and Ernie Rose, Director of Personnel. Because she has a GS15 equivalent rating (equal to Col.) she was given the "distinguished visitor" treatment—self and luggage first off the plane, use of air conditioned trailer while someone else attended to the immigration, customs and currency exchange procedures. No getting in lines, etc. I went with her to her billet and got her settled. I have arranged transportation to bring her here tonight to have dinner with Betty and me. We'll figure out a plan for tomorrow. I know Joan is an Episcopalian, so she may want to go to church.

Mary Bowers, a hospital field director whom I have known over the years, arrives tomorrow, so I'll have to figure her into the plan too, somehow.

* * *

Sat, Aug 30, 1969

. . . Yes, I'm glad I have a "normal" life to return to. On the other hand, this is part of my "life" too. I don't say that I am too thrilled by this part, but there is a certain satisfaction in finding out that I can "cope." It is amazing how one adjusts to the nuisances and inconveniences. I don't mean I don't complain about them. I do. But it is just all part of the game, I guess.

* * *

Tues, Sep 2, 1969

. . . One of the light bulbs in the wall fixture burned out last night and I left a note at the desk to have it replaced. I was very surprised tonight to find that not only had they replaced that one, but also put a bulb in the closet. So now I have a dry closet. I really hadn't worried too much about that because the air conditioner (when it works) keeps the air from being too damp.

On the negative side, we had no water in the building where our offices are today. That was a real handicap. When we couldn't stand it any longer, we went two blocks away to use the ladies' room and the Special Services Club. Joan was the most miserable as she is having the "new arrival's" bout with diarrhea.

* * *

Wed, Sep 10, 1969

This won't be much of a letter because it is being written by candlelight. The power is out at the Rex, at least the 110 which presents a few complications like no elevators etc. The air conditioners are on 220 so mine is working. Actually, it has been relatively cool today—much rain, so I don't really need the air conditioning. Anyway to save my eyes, I won't try to reread and answer the letter I had from you yesterday.

. . . Well, the air conditioner just quit. At this moment, I guess I really have no recourse but to go to bed, although it is isn't 8:00 yet.

5 minutes later—the lights came on, but still no air conditioner. Now I guess I can fall back and regroup and try to answer your last letter.

. . . Well, the air conditioner just came back on. So maybe all systems are go. Let's hope so.

. . . As handicapping as it is to be having to constantly scramble for transportation, I am grateful that I do not have to drive in Saigon. At 5:00 PM I get on a bus, shut my eyes to what is going on in the streets, and eventually

get deposited at the Rex. This comment is apropos of you mentioning not worrying about me driving in a downpour.

* * *

Mon, Oct 13, 1969

. . . We have had a couple of difficult staff problems the past 2 weeks. One girl we are sending home because she just couldn't take it over here. The other has gotten messed up with an enlisted man and the CEO has demanded she be removed from the hospital. I had to handle the first one, and Betty is off trying to cope with the second. We have averaged about 2 resignations a month since I have been here, mostly because of "romance." I know I am of the old school, but I find it hard to accept that people can't fulfill a commitment of one year. I could sympathize with the one I had to handle as she was 54 years old and should never have been sent over in the first place. But these younger ones— with their whole lives ahead—should be able to postpone their own desires for a few months, it seems to me. Well, I have blown off enough, but I do get discouraged with the young who are so self-centered. On the other hand, we have some wonderful ones who carry on under the most difficult conditions and I am really proud of them.

* * *

Wed, Oct 15, 1969

. . . We had 3 new staff members to dinner tonight. Such bright, attractive young girls. It was a refreshing shot in the arm—much needed.

* * *

Sun, Oct 19, 1969

It's 1:30 on a hot Sunday afternoon and my air conditioner just went off. The air conditioners are run on 220 and frequently go off without our losing the 110 power for lights. My particular one seems to be on a faulty line as it blows a fuse or something when others don't. It always happens on Sunday or at night when I can't get anyone to fix it. All I can do is hope that it is a general power failure, which they will fix because it's not just my machine. I'll be without it for the night. Sorry to complain. But it does seem a bit much.

* * *

Sun, Oct 26, 1969

. . . All of the electricity went off in the Rex—and surrounding areas—at 8:30 this morning and is still not back on. (It is now 2:30.) Fortunately, it's relatively cool outside. I have the door open into the hall and the small window in the bathroom. I have moved the chair into the bathroom so get the cross breeze. I have to sit in the bathroom because this is the only outside light. At least since it is a general power failure, I'm sure they're working on it and maybe it will be fixed before dark. Last Sun., when it was just my air conditioner that was out, there was no hope of getting it fixed. It seems mean to have some light problems on Sunday—the one day I'm free to relax in my room.

* * *

Tues, Oct 28, 1969

. . . We have been having a series of real hard rains every night—thunderstorms, almost cloud bursts. Night before last, lightning hit the main power line to the area where our office is. Consequently, yesterday we had no electricity at all and since the water pumps are electric, no water in the building. Ugh.

* * *

Tues Eve, Oct 28, 1969

. . . They finally got the power back on in the office today. Think I wrote you that the main cable was struck by lightning 2 nights ago. The best thing was that the electric pump could also work so that we have water again in the building. The building our offices are in has been condemned as structurally unsound, so we may have to move. Oh, joy!

I had my hair done this AM. I took a taxi to outside the gate. Civilian taxis can't go nearer than about 1½ miles to our office. I only had to wait about 5 minutes before a friendly Col. in his staff car picked me up and deposited me at the office. Over here you meet a lot of nice people by hitchhiking.

* * *

Sat, Nov 22, 1969

. . . You enclose the clipping about the attack at An Khe. We do not have ARC staff assigned to the 17th Field Hospital. There was an SRAO [Supplemental Recreational Activities Overseas] unit there who are billeted with the nurses. No nurses or ARC staff were hurt. One of the girls got a bit hysterical and had to be sedated. In other words, the news report was inaccurate. Sorry I didn't mention it sooner, but I didn't think about its making the papers. It was in Stars and Stripes, but the account was more accurate.

We may have to staff that hospital again. We had a girl there until last spring when it was turned into an exclusively POW hospital. Now, it is being reverted to a hospital for U.S. military.

* * *

Mon, Nov 24, 1969

. . . I don't think I can explain Betty's decision to extend to you, since you don't know her, but it didn't surprise me in the least. She has great enthusiasm for whatever she is doing and feels she is just beginning to get her teeth into the job here. She has unusual ability to rise above physical discomforts and to see the best side of everything. So, for her, the decision is the right one—but not one I could make.

* * *

Mon, Dec 8, 1969

. . . Above is a squib about yours truly, which was in 1942 Classmates of the Alumni Quarterly. I wrote them last spring when I changed my address so they did get the facts straight.

* * *

Wed, Dec 10, 1969

. . . No, you shouldn't have known about my 25th anniversary in the ARC. The actual date has no meaning to me either. Since I have "broken service," the 25 is arrived at by adding all the bits and pieces. Two months in San Antonio Chapter, 2 years and nine months at National during the war, and then 22 straight since October 47 when I went back to work in N.Y.

* * *

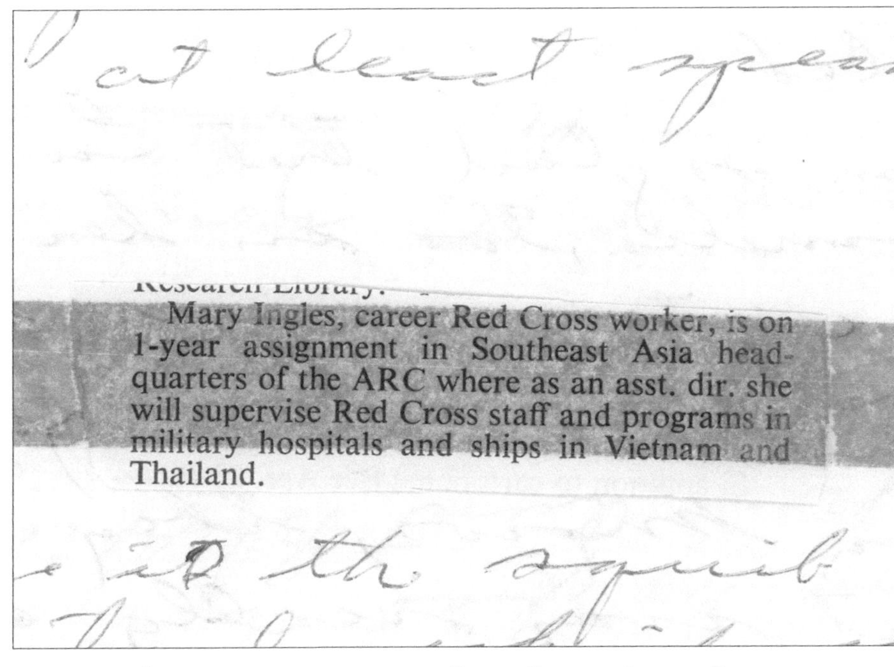

MARY'S JOB DESCRIPTION FROM HER SMITH COLLEGE ALUMNI QUARTERLY

Sat, Dec 13, 1969

. . . When I got back to my room [from dinner], I found a broad stream of water running down the wall and collecting on the floor. I routed the Sgt out and they found that the trouble was coming from the latrine upstairs. They eventually got that fixed—at least they stopped the flood into my room. But all of this took until nearly midnight.

. . . When I came back this PM from getting my hair done there were ambulances and MP's in front of the Rex and they wouldn't let anyone in. It seems one of the kitchen help (Vietnamese) had fallen down the freight elevator shaft (six stories). They finally let "residents" in and I went right to my room so I don't know the full story. The consensus seems to be that he had been killed.

* * *

Wed, Dec 17, 1969

. . . We had an interesting experience today. Gen Smith, J-1 at MACV Hqs. arranged a MACV briefing for the ARC Hqs. staff. We went to Hqs. and after a brief tour and coffee were taken to a briefing room. Representatives of J-2, J-3 and Pacification gave us excellent briefings with slides, charts, etc. on what is going on over here. It was most informative and clarifying. Then we all went to the command mess where about 8 Maj Gens and Brig Gens hosted us to drinks and a delicious lunch. My luncheon partner was Gen Clements, class of '40. I felt it was quite a compliment to ARC to have so much pains taken for us and so many high-ranking officers turn out for us.

* * *

Sun, Dec 21, 1969

I didn't get a letter written yesterday, sorry. The staff Christmas party Friday evening was OK. We had it in the courtyard of the Continental Palace, which was gaily decorated [with] colored lights. The dinner was only mediocre considering we had paid the equivalent of $9 apiece. Prices here are really terrible. Last night Joan and I went out to dinner. I had onion soup, fried shrimp and salad, and we split a small bottle of wine and it came to $10.00 apiece.

* * *

Fri, Jan 9,1970

Back in Saigon, safe and sound, but, as always had rather tiring trip. I had to check in at the airport at Nha Trang at 10:30. The flight left at 12:00. It made one stop en route and we finally got to Saigon at 2:45. I was able to ride in the flight deck. It was a C130—which is always more comfortable. I called the office for transportation, but none was available. So I finally took a bus part of the way and thumbed a ride in a Jeep for the final lap. Got to the office about 3:45. No lunch, of course, except a sweet roll I picked up at the airport at Tan Son Nhat. I didn't tell you this to upset you, but just a little "vignette" of what wears one out over here.

When I got home tonight, there was a sign in the lobby that the water would be off from 10:00 PM until at least noon tomorrow. So I have taken an early shower and I'm at least clean. They had the maids fill our waste baskets with water and I have a 5 gallon Jerry can also, so I guess I can manage to get the toilet flushed in the morning. At least we had advance warning. It is something to do with connecting new pipelines or some such.

* * *

Sun, Feb 1, 1970

. . . The story on the bomb in the Rex Theater was [in] all the news reports yesterday, so I'm sure you heard about it. I hope you didn't let it give you an anxious few days until you got my letter that I was OK.

The big Vietnamese holiday of Tet (Lunar New Year), is from February 5–8. I'm really lucky that my trip to Australia comes right at this time. All of the Vietnamese are on holiday for the period and transportation etc. is going to be a problem. There will be no maid service, laundry, beauty shops closed etc., etc. I honestly did not know all of this when I applied for R&R but I just lucked out.

* * *

Mon, Feb 2, 1970

I had real good mail today, but don't know that I can stay awake long enough tonight to really answer it.

February is a bad month as we have about 20 staff coming and going. This means having someone to dinner almost every night, plus the time with them in the office for either orientation or "exit" interviewing. Tonight was no exception—three in, two out. Tonight we had one to dinner. She is a gal who was admitted to the hospital 2 days after she arrived. She was discharged to duty today and will not have to be evacuated, thank goodness. We'll pick up on her orientation tomorrow and get her off to her hospital on Wednesday.

* * *

Figuring out staffing requirements was a complicated and unpredictable part of Mary's job. Troop withdrawals and increases changed frequently and impacted the appropriate levels of staffing, which had to be determined months in advance.

Saigon

Fri, July 4, 1969

. . . We are all speculating about the effect of troop withdrawals on our program. The present lull is welcome, of course, but at the same time some of the staff are restless because they haven't enough to do. They live in such confinement that the only thing that saves them is to be real busy.

* * *

Chu Lai

Tues, Sep 16, 1969

. . . As always, I feel even more cut off than usual from the world news when I am on a trip. I never see a paper and seldom hear news broadcast. I did hear that Nixon has announced 35,000 troop withdrawal by December. So much of this is on "paper" that it really doesn't make a lot of difference.

* * *

Saigon

Wed, Oct 1, 1969

This is proving to be an unusually busy week. So many decisions to be made about staff. The effects of the troop withdrawals are being felt. One hospital is being closed, another reduced in size. I'm going to be an expert in closing hospitals, dispensing of property, etc. before I leave here.

* * *

Saigon

Tues, Oct 7, 1969

. . . These are trying days as we are under a lot of pressure to reduce staff and yet fear to cut ourselves too thin in case the whole thing blows wide open. We try to juggle around and pray we are doing the right thing. We can't get any "hard" information from the military on plans for hospitals because they honestly don't know. There are a myriad of "contingency" plans, but who knows which one will be used?

Well, one just lives it day by day. At least I won't have to get up tomorrow until 7:00—a real treat when I normally get up at 5:00.

* * *

Despite spending almost every day at a hospital, Mary rarely wrote about the cases. However, she did share some examples of the tragedies of war in the fall of 1969. The first was a patient Mary encountered when visiting a hospital in Da Nang. The second involved an ARC worker in Saigon.

Da Nang

Mon, Sep 22, 1969

. . . One sad note was that the father of one of their patients flew over from the States at his own expense, which is unusual to say the least. The patient is only 19 and the father only 37. The boy is horribly wounded and it is very doubtful he will live. Our staff have been very much involved in the case, of course. Once the hospital staff accepted the fact that the father was coming, they have been very nice to him. He is staying in the officers' quarter, eating in the mess. They even outfitted him with some fatigues when his luggage went astray for a couple of days. In the US and even in Germany and Japan, we were set up to take care of relatives, but everything is complicated over here. This is the third case I have known of where a parent or parents of patients came to Vietnam.

* * *

Saigon

Fri, Oct 4, 1969

I don't know if I did write anymore about the patient I mentioned whose father came over. Anyway, the boy died, but his father was with him for about five days and was there when he died. The military came through and cut the necessary red tape to let the father fly home with the body.

The father expressed much gratitude to Red Cross and the girls certainly went all out. I saw them just before I left and they were both completely wrung out emotionally.

* * *

Saigon

Tues, Sep 30, 1969

. . . We have had a distressing several days and they aren't over yet. One of the Clubmobile girls was in a jeep accident, suffered head injuries, is critically ill and is not expected to live. She's in the hospital which is the neurosurgical center so is getting the best of care. But the outlook is grim. Her poor family!!

* * *

Saigon

Wed, Oct 1, 1969

. . . The SRAO girl I mentioned in my letter yesterday is still alive—but barely—really only because of the machines and other extraordinary measures the medical profession has devised to keep the body technically alive. The agony of her family in the States is too terrible to contemplate.

Well, I shouldn't burden you with the sad situation, but it has cast a pall over things.

* * *

Saigon

Thurs, Oct 2, 1969

. . . The SRAO girl I wrote you about died this morning. Joan is off on a field visit, so I got involved in all the plans for handling the myriad of arrangements connected with it. We would like to keep it out of the press, but of course haven't been able to, so you may read about it. This is the first instance in which an ARC woman has died over here. It was not the result of hostile action, but that doesn't really help her family any, poor souls.

* * *

Saigon

Mon, Oct 6, 1969

I enclosed the very small notice that appeared in Stars and Stripes about our poor little ARC girl who died. We were relieved that it didn't get more publicity. I wonder if there has been anything in the US papers about it. Joan went to the memorial service for her yesterday. She said it was tastefully handled and the Chapel was crowded. A good number of ARC, of course, but a very large turnout of military personnel. We felt it was a tribute not only to Hannah, but to the Red Cross generally.

* * *

Saigon

Mon, Oct 13, 1969

. . . I had your letter of 4 October. Just to set the record straight, our young Red Cross girl was not killed when the Jeep hit a mine. As a matter of fact, she was on the way to a party. The jeep made a sharp turn and she fell out, landing on her head. Jeeps don't come with safety belts and people can fall out of them easily. Among others, our sympathy has gone out to the young man who was driving. He wasn't at fault. Nor was she—no drinking, etc. Just one of those tragic mishaps. Anyway, I'm glad if there has been minimal publicity at home.

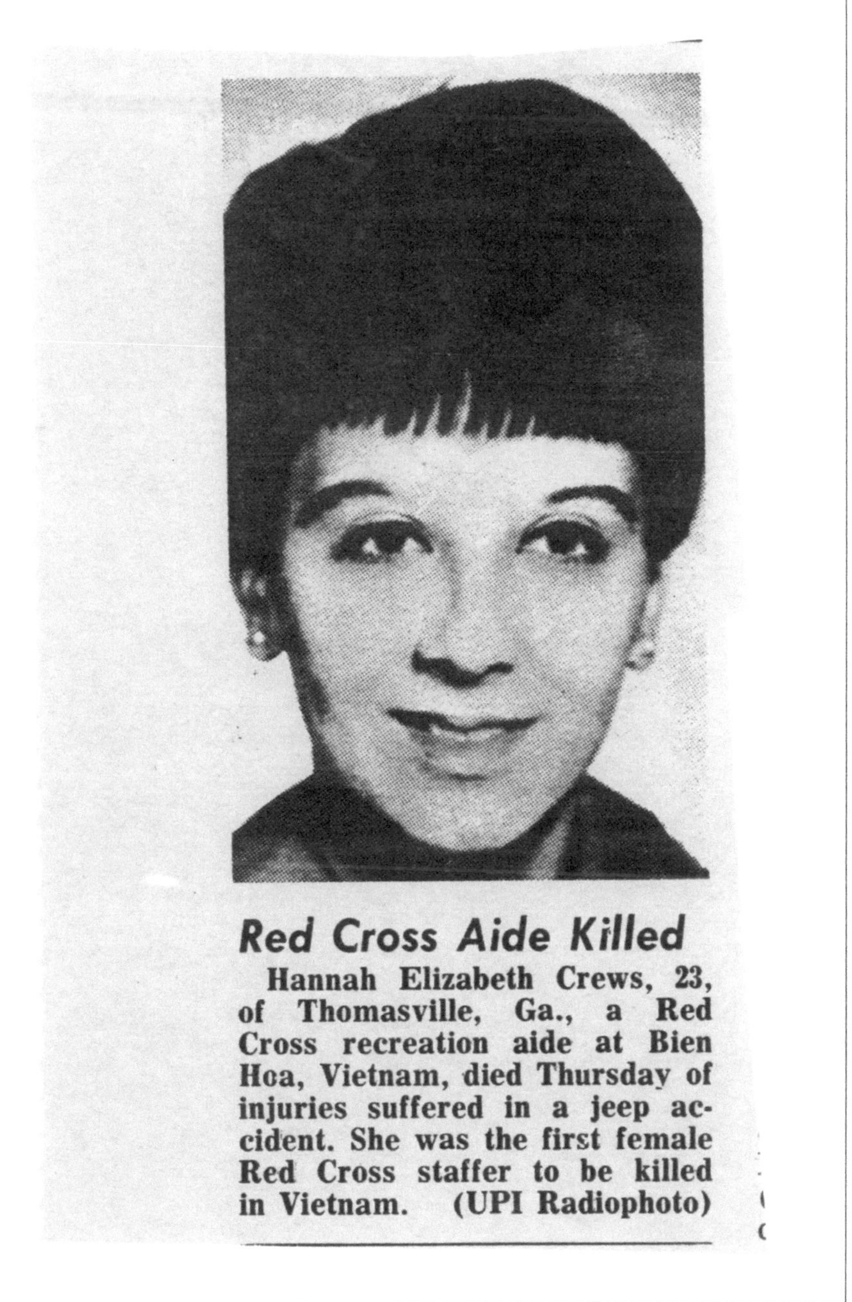

DEATH NOTICE OF HANNAH ELIZABETH CREWS

DEPARTMENT OF THE ARMY
HEADQUARTERS AREA COMMAND
HOTEL PEX B.O.Q., SIAGON
APO 96243

SUBJECT: Courtesy Letter　　　　　　　　23 October 1969

Attention All Occupants

Gentlemen,
　　　Pleased be advised that the Undersigned has Officially assumed the duties of "Hotel-Supervisor" of this establishment; effective the 22d of October.

　　　Therefore, with your permission, I'd like very much to take this opportunity to respectfully inform you, of my serious intentions of serving your needs both by our routine regulations and personally.

　　　Please permit me to interject here in my letter, that I can not but personally express that serious consideration is honestly due Senior-grade Officers and Senior-grade Officers of our close and friendly Allies.

　　　I personally feel that Air-conditioners and Refrigerators are not a "luxury" (as some individuals will joke about) but are an absolute "necessity" especially in this area of the world; and this Siagon climate. Truthfully how can any Senior Officer, who is exhausted because of the lack of sleep, be expected to perform his many, many duties and balance carefully his heavy responsibilities; and make paramont correct decisions which more times than not, must be made immediately; decisions which may directly or indirectly affect the lives of the hundreds of thousands of our Free World Forces; when his body and mind are honestly just too-tired simply because he could not sleep the previous night because of the heat. Refrigerators, I feel are a close "second" in this climate, where the body demands a continuous supply of cool liquids.

　　　As I shall show you personally any possible extra considerations I respectfully request that you in turn as an individual be please grant me your consideration in the form of "patience" and endure with me during periods of time where I may be handicaped because of not receiving my requests for supplies (i.e. Light-bulbs, etc.) or during a period where I am attempting to "bend" a Regulation or Hotel Policy, trying to aid you.

　　　I'm certain that you can understand that there is no military duties, which would prepare the average "Field-Soldier" for this job as your "Hotel-Supervisor"......However there is one advantage which is in your favor......and it's simply this:　I'm on Your-side!

Respectfully forwarded,
I am,

JOSEPH-EDOUARD GAUDREAU
Staff/Sergeant　US Army
Rex Hotel-Supervisor

Dis.
　1 Ea Ind.
　1 Off.Open Mess BB.

SGT GAUDREAU'S LETTER

* * *

Amidst the tragedies and hardships, there were those who tried to create an atmosphere of levity. The letter from the new billet supervisor was an example of one attempt to interject some humor into the daily struggles.

> Saigon
> Sun, Oct 26, 1969
> . . . I enclosed the letter we all received from the new Sgt. who has just taken over as hotel supervisor. I think it is a scream and you just know he labored over it. Guess I'll have to tackle him about a refrigerator and trying to find out why my air conditioner shorts out all the time. He sort of asked for it, didn't he?

Subject: Courtesy Letter

23 October 1969

Attention All Occupants.
Gentlemen,

Please be advised that the Undersigned has Officially assumed the duties of "Hotel Supervisor" of this establishment; effective 22d of October.

Therefore, with your permission, I'd like very much to take this opportunity to respectfully inform you, of my serious intentions of serving your needs both by our routine regulations and personally.

Please permit me to interject here in my letter, that I cannot but personally express that serious consideration is honestly due Senior-grade officers and Senior-grade officers of our close and friendly Allies.

I personally feel that Air conditioners and Refrigerators are not a "luxury" (as some individuals will joke about) but are an absolute "necessity," especially in this area of the world; and this Saigon climate. Truthfully, how any Senior Officer, who is exhausted because of the lack of sleep, be expected to perform his many, many duties and balance carefully his heavy responsibilities; and make paramount correct decisions which more times than not, must be made immediately; decisions which may directly or indirectly affect the lives of hundreds of thousands of our Free World Forces; when his body and mind are honestly just too tired simply because he could not sleep the previous night because of the heat. Refrigerators, I feel, are a close "second" in this climate where the body demands a continuous supply of cool liquids.

As I shall show you personally any possible extra considerations, I respectfully request that you in turn as an individual please grant me your consideration in the form of "patience" and endure with me during periods of time when I may be handicapped because of not receiving my requests for supplies (i.e. light bulbs, etc.) or during a period where I attempt to "bend" a Regulation or Hotel Policy, trying to aid you.

I'm certain that you can understand that there is no military duties, which would prepare the average "Field-Soldier" for this job as your "Hotel Supervisor." However, there is one advantage which is in your favor . . . and it's simply this: I'm on Your Side!

Respectfully forwarded.
I am.
Signature
Joseph Edward Gaudreau
Staff/Sergeant US Army
Rex Hotel supervisor

Dis.

1 Ea Ind.

1 Off. Open Mess BB

* * *

Unfortunately, the higher ups did not seem to share Sgt. Gaudreau's sense of humor. He was replaced in less than a month. However, he did accomplish at least one important task: he managed to get Mary a working refrigerator.

Saigon
Mon, Nov 24, 1969

The enclosed was in our rooms tonight. We figure, poor Sgt Gaudreau hung himself by his letters. Probably offended some of the high ranking occupants who have no sense of humor. We will miss his letters, and also his service efforts to try and help us. But at least I have him to thank for a functioning refrigerator. I guess Sgt Howe got the wind, as his note is certainly restrained. [Sgt. Howe's letter did not survive.]

* * *

About halfway through her tour, Mary received news about her next assignment.

Saigon
Sun, Jan 11, 1970

. . . I do have something to tell you that I wish I didn't. When I got back from the Philippines, there was a letter from National Headquarters advising that I would be assigned to the Southeastern Area Hqs in Atlanta when I returned home. Elaine Lynch, who is in Southeast Area is to replace me here. To say that I was upset is an understatement, but I could not say I was surprised. I knew there was no vacancy in Eastern Area and that my future assignment would depend on who was to replace me here.

I went back through channels reminding them of the written request in my file before I came to Vietnam that I'd be reassigned in Washington area for personal reasons. I requested that I'd be considered for vacancies in other services either in Eastern Area or National Headquarters. I also said that if I went to Atlanta, I would like to be considered for transfer back to Eastern area when the first vacancy occurred.

Well, all that really didn't do any good because they came back again saying there was no present vacancies; would I please go to Atlanta; and that if any future home emergencies came up, they would do what they could about a transfer.

So you see, I really have no alternative except to quit, and I don't think I should do that, do you?

I tried to look on the positives. It could have been Saint Louis or San Francisco, and at least Atlanta is the nearest to Washington. I can get home for weekends now and then; you and Daddy can come to Atlanta now and then; and there will be the telephone. There's no use kidding ourselves that it will be as wonderful as when I was in Alexandria was [or] that it is what any of us wanted.

This was the possibility that upset me the most when I was asked to come over here. It was not this year away, but the almost certainty that I couldn't return to Alexandria. I didn't say too much about this to you at the time, but I'm sure you understood that it might happen.

I haven't had a chance to work out plans in my mind yet. I will have some leave at home when I return, but I will also want to save a little for a visit later in the year. If I had known about this, I wouldn't have squandered 5 days of leave in P. I., but saved it for later use.

Well, it's a blow to all of us, but we can all adjust to it as we have to so many other things in the past. The job there will be the same as the one I had in Alexandria. Penny is the Director there, so that is a plus. People speak well of Atlanta as a place to live. The cost of living should be a little less than in Washington.

Well, there is no use belaboring this further at this point. You will need some time to readjust your thinking. I have already had a month. I didn't write you sooner for two reasons. 1. I didn't want to ruin your Christmas. 2. I waited to see what, if anything would come of my "protest."

I am so sorry.

* * *

Saigon
Sat, Jan 24, 1970

. . . I had a very nice letter from Penny. I had written her at the time I was "protesting" National regarding going to Atlanta. I wanted her to know that my objections were not personal as far as she was concerned, in case she had heard about it through someone else. Anyway, she couldn't have been nicer and more understanding and assured me that if I did end up in Atlanta, she would be very happy to have me on her staff. You know she didn't want to go to Atlanta either. She wanted to go back to San Francisco. She went on Disaster as soon as she got home and did not actually get to Atlanta until after the first of the year. She was in the throes of apartment hunting and said she would share her research with me. She said there are many lovely apartments, but the ones she looked [at and] liked most were $200.00 and up. She is looking for a 2 bedroom apartment. I had been toying with 2 bedrooms myself but at those prices, I guess I'll settle for one bedroom again. You and Daddy will just have to stay at a motel when you come. What I really would like is one [in] which the second bedroom is like a den. I would then put my hide-a-bed in it to serve as extra sleeping space, and get a new sofa for my living room. Well, all of that is for the future.

One thing I have been thinking about is a car, which of course I must have. I suppose the sensible thing would be to get it in Wash. so I could load it up when I go South. But that raises the questions of having to license it in D.C. or Va. and then again in Georgia and possibly paying two state taxes on it. Daddy might do some research on that if he wants to. The only drivers license I have at the moment is Virginia.

I also don't know what kind of car I want. Since I anticipate doing some long distance driving. I will want an 8 cylinder car. I like the Ford Fairlane I took to Germany so much, so maybe I should get another. I'll have to have one with an air conditioner if I'm going to be in the South. Again if Daddy wants to collect up some literature for me, I would be happy to peruse it. You can order cars through the PX for delivery anywhere in the U.S. but I'm a little leery of that. I may make some inquiries however, if I get a chance.

I have no objection to Atlanta as a place. Everyone speaks highly of it, and I am sure it is a good place to live. Probably far superior to the Washington area under present conditions. We all know that the one objection is those 650 miles from you.

* * *

The Hospital Visits

Mary was at the height of her career when posted to Vietnam. She was an assistant director, responsible for supervision of Red Cross staff and programs in military hospitals and ships in Vietnam and Thailand. These responsibilities required her to travel extensively throughout the country. She wrote lengthy descriptions of how she got from point A to point B. It was never a straightforward journey. Because she was the big wig, her visits were significant events at the hospitals, and she often wrote about the reception she received upon arrival.

Saigon
Thurs, May 29, 1969
. . . Tomorrow is a holiday, but they aren't much observed over here, so I'll be working as usual. I am getting more and more into the work and it is good to feel you are being useful. Penny is talking about having me make a couple of quick trips out to some of the nearby hospitals next week. I'm anxious to go as I need to know the staff, see the hospitals and understand more of what is going on. These trips would be round trip by bus—about 45 mins each way—and no overnights. If I'm going I have to do so before Miss Betterly arrives on June 15th, because Penny will take off with her for a couple of weeks and I'll have to hold down the fort.

* * *

Saigon
Tues, Jun 3, 1969
. . . I must warn you to be prepared for gaps in mail. I am taking my first field trip tomorrow and will be away two nights. I'll try to write a postcard, but don't know what the mail service will be once I get out of Saigon. One of the hospitals is being deactivated and I have to go help the two girls close out their operation, dispose of property, etc. Now don't start worrying. It's part of my job and I'll be able to do it better once I get to know the staff and see the hospitals.

* * *

Postcard written Wed, June 4, 1969

Dear Mother, I'll try to mail this tomorrow, although the girls say mail only goes in and out about 3 times a week. I had an interesting trip getting here, and will write you all about it when I get back to Saigon. This is a very quiet area—so much so that the hospital is being deactivated. Two real nice young girls here whom we are transferring. All is well. Love, Mary.

* * *

Tuy Hoa

Fri, Jun 6, 1969

I mailed you a postcard yesterday, but heaven knows if you'll ever get it. At the moment I am sitting in the airport at a place called Tuy Hoa (pronounced "tooey waa") waiting for a flight back to Saigon. There are only four flights a day in and out of here, but they still make you check in two hours before flight time.

I flew up here Wednesday on a C130, sitting in a bucket seat. There were three AF Sgts, me and about 100 Koreans on the flight. All the Koreans had been eating kimchi, of course, and the smells took me right back to my Korea days. The plane made three stops en route, so at least you could get off briefly and stretch, but the whole thing took four hours.

The ARC field director met me at the airport and took me in an open Jeep to the hospital—about 5 miles. The hospital is located right on the beach in deep sand. The wind blows all the time, so the dust and dirt is something. My poor hair looks like something I have never seen before.

We have two nice young girls at the hospital, and I think they were real glad to see me and took good care of me. I had a room in Nurse's Qtrs [quarters]—quite adequate. No air conditioning, of course, but the girls borrowed a fan for me and at night it was comfortable. Pretty hot in the daytime. The buildings are what they call tropical huts—screened around top of wall with tin roof. There was a latrine and shower next door, shared by 6 people.

The hospital is closing down at this location and will be moving. They have only about 20 patients now and soon will have none. All of the personnel are being reassigned to other hospitals all over VN [Vietnam]. Our two girls are too. One leaves today and the other on or about June 21st.

The big job here was to go over all the property and mark out plans for what is to be done about it. The plans have been made, but it leaves a lot of work for Marva Mitchell, the HFD [hospital field director], to accomplish in the next couple of weeks. She doesn't seem fazed by it and the hospital staff are being cooperative.

Wednesday night the girls took me to a party one of the chopper units was having in the little club they have fixed up. They had cooked a Mexican dinner—tacos and beans. Since I hadn't had any lunch—was en route and no place to eat—it tasted real good. They were a real nice bunch of young men and I do admire the way a group in this situation always seem to go ahead and make do, fix things up as best as they can and have fun.

Last night, Marva and I went to the outdoor movie at the hospital. Saw a James Bond picture. We carried over aluminum chairs and set them in the sand to watch.

Except for the physical lay out this wasn't really a very typical hospital to visit. It has a real dead feeling because of the closing down and with no patients, the staff had nothing to do. Everyone was restless and anxious for orders and to move on.

Well, I think I accomplished what I was sent to do. I will be happy to get back to Saigon and get really cleaned up and get my hair done. I'll also be glad to get the mail, which I am sure is waiting for me. With all its drawbacks I am surely more comfortable in Saigon than the girls in the hospitals.

* * *

Postcard written Evening Fri, June 6, 1969

Dear Mother. Well, I made it back and my room surely looked good to me. It was an all day project as the plane I was booked on never came—too windy to land. So I finally managed to talk my way on the Korean flight again, and after three stops finally got to Tan Son Nhut. I had a bit of a struggle getting transportation to the hotel, but finally succeeded. Have bathed and washed clothes. Now for bed!! Mary.

* * *

Saigon

Sat, Jun 7, 1969

. . . Before I launch into answering [your letters], I had better finish up my saga of my trip yesterday. Shortly after I finished the letter I wrote from the airport, they announced that the plane I was booked on couldn't land at Tuy Hoa because of high winds. The only other flight out that day was the return flight of the "Kimchi Local" on which I had come up. At Tuy Hoa they were allotted so many bookings clear thru to Saigon and they were all taken unless someone didn't show up. They could book me as far as Nha Trang— about halfway. I called Nha Trang to see about booking from there on. No space—if I got to Nha Trang, I could try

for standby space. I had been talking to the AF Sgt behind the desk who was trying to help me. The check in time for those with reservations was 1:15. At 1:10 he slipped over and moved the clock up 5 minutes. Then tapped the Korean who had the list on the shoulder and pointed to the clock. So, he scratched off a name and put mine on the Saigon list.

The plane finally took off after 3:00. Two stops, 3 hours later, accompanied by at least 100 kimchi smelling Koreans, I finally arrived in Saigon. It took me nearly an hour of phone calls before I managed to get a car to take me to the Ambassador—finally getting home at 7:30. I had a break then. I was too tired and dirty to go out to eat, but I ran into one of the ARC men. He went over to the snack bar and brought a sandwich and a can of orange soda up to my room.

I have not recounted all this to upset you, but just to keep you posted on my adventures. I amuse myself along the way by thinking about how Jean Gross [a family friend] just wouldn't believe this. One of the things that makes it tolerable is that all of the servicemen are so nice to you. The AE Sgt., the little Army Pfc who carried my bag and told me all about the R&R in Hawaii with his wife from which he had just returned—they were together for their eight-month anniversary and her birthday.

* * *

Saigon

Tues, Jul 8, 1969

. . . As you know, I have been on a field visit to Long Binh for two days. I went down on the bus Monday AM. I intended to take the 9:00 AM bus—got there at 8:45 to have the door slammed in my face and about 20 others because the bus was full. So I had to sit in the sun for an hour and take the 10:00 bus. The bus at least was air conditioned and the trip only took about 45 minutes. The field director met me at the bus stop and took me to the hospital in a jeep. The visit [was] relatively uncomplicated. The quarters where I stayed are a bit elemental, but they do have inside plumbing—16 people using two showers and two potties, but you manage. I only had to endure for one night, so wouldn't dare complain. No air conditioning of course and lots of mosquitoes. It was cool enough that I could keep a sheet over me to avoid excessive bites.

Things at that hospital seem to be going relatively well. We have one sour apple in the bunch. A 55 year old who should never have been sent overseas in the first place and isn't about to make the best of it. The other three are under 30, good kids with positive attitude, but old lugubrious is wearing them down. You want to hit her over the head, but at the same time you can't drive her over the edge and have to give her some TLC and hope she'll make it. She is the girl who roomed with me my first few days here, and I wondered then how she would ever adjust—and she hasn't.

Last night the staff took me to a Chinese restaurant on the base for dinner. It was very nice and we had a real good dinner.

I came back this afternoon on the 3:00 PM bus. Took two more buses to get downtown in Saigon and was in my room by 4:45, just ahead of a downpour.

* * *

Postcard written Fri, July 11, 1969

Still in Nha Trang. This has been a hectic visit. Many problems, but the visit was timely because I was able to get some things redirected. I had dinner with Ted Wednesday and will again tonight. I would be able to go back tomorrow but can't get a flight. I am ready to leave and I'm sorry I committed myself to the weekend. I am on the track of a beauty parlor and hope I can find it tomorrow. Will write again when I'm back in Saigon. Love, Mary.

* * *

Saigon
Sun, Jul 13, 1969

. . . My trip back today was one of the best I have taken so far. I had to check in at 6:30. One of the ARC men picked me up (and another ARC man returning to Saigon) and took us to the terminal. After checking in we had time to dash to the mess for a quick breakfast. We took off at 7:30. The plane was a Caribou which carries about 20 passengers. Since it was early, it wasn't hot. The flight was smooth and the plane had windows so we could see out. We only flew at 8500 feet, and the flight took 1½ hours. Bucket seats of course, but really quite painless. When we got here we called the duty worker at the office and he sent a car to take us to our billets. So I was in my room by 10:30.

* * *

Saigon
Fri, Jul 18, 1969

This will be a quick note before I go off to work. My 2 day trip to Long Binh went OK. Biggest problem there is that the girls are restless. There really isn't quite enough work to keep them busy and the confinements of their daily life bear in on them. This is true everywhere, but when they are real busy on the job, they can take it better.

* * *

Saigon

Sat, Jul 25, 1969

. . . I am back home in Saigon and found good mail which I will answer later in this letter. First, though, I'll bring you up to date on my doings. I have been on a visit to the hospital located at Cu Chi, which is located at Hqs of the 25th Division. The only way to get there is by chopper. On Thursday I went to what is called Hotel #3—the Chopper Terminal at Tan Son Nhut AB [Airforce Base] in Saigon. Getting on a flight is all rather informal. You just tell them where you want to go and when a flight is going—if they have room—you get on. After a couple of hours wait, I finally got on a flight—on a chopper called "Harvey" and off we went. It has open sides and you fasten your seat belt put a scarf over your head and hang on like grim death. Once we took off, the flight only took about 15 minutes. It's an experience to say the least. Once I got to Cu Chi, I called the girls at the hospital and they picked me up in a Jeep.

The area is pretty primitive, but they have the hospital area fixed up pretty well by now. Most of the hospitals over here are basically complexes of Quonset huts, but at this one, all of the wards are air conditioned. They had just completed and turned on the air conditioning in the nurses' quarters the day before I arrived. The first night I slept under a blanket, but the second night the air conditioner had conked out so it was a hot night. I can't complain as I was only there two nights, but the others are stuck with it.

Overall, the visit was OK. We have four nice youngsters there—the oldest 26—and they are doing a good job. The patient load is down—thanks to the "lull" In the war—and they are a bit restless because there is not enough

to do. Yet they feel guilty for voicing such a complaint. At the moment, this is a real problem over here. None of us want a big patient load, but when the staff aren't busy, they feel unneeded and the discomforts and the dissatisfactions assume a greater importance. It's a diabolical dilemma.

Anyway, they turned on such entertainment for me as the place had to offer. The first evening we went to their hospital club for charcoal broiled hamburgers. The second night to a "Chinese" restaurant concession on the base.

This morning, they got me to the chopper pad at 7:30 for a flight at 8:00. I am sure the pilot wasn't a day over 19 but he welcomed me aboard graciously. After we were airborne, he informed me that he couldn't land at Hotel #3 in Saigon because of heavy clouds. Would I like to go back to Cu Chi or go to Long Binh? I opted for the latter as I knew they had buses into Saigon. So he put me down there and let me off. I trudged about half a mile to the Hqs of the 20th Aviation Bn. They kindly provided a driver and Jeep to take me to the USARV [US Army, Vietnam] Hqs where the bus terminal is. I just missed the 9:00 bus to Saigon, so went to the ARC Field Director's office to wait until the 11:00 bus. I was at the bus stop at 10:30 and a sedan driven by a young EM pulled up and asked if I was going to Saigon. He filled his car up with me and four other GI's and delivered me at the office at 11:30.

So you see, one does manage one way or another. Being a woman and in uniform is a great advantage. You always get courteous treatment and the best that is available. It is really kind of fun and each trip is an adventure.

. . . I have another trip planned for next week—leave Tuesday afternoon, come back Friday AM. Two hospitals involved. So get yourself steeled for another mail gap. After that, I'll stay put about three months. I'll be glad, and so will you.

* * *

Saigon

Mon, Jul 28, 1969

. . . I have something a bit different coming up. Later this week I have a visit scheduled to our hospital in Vung Tau. This is also the main base of the Australian forces in Viet Nam and there is an Australian Army Hospital there with some Australian Red Cross personnel assigned. Today our hospital field director called to see if I could stay over Saturday as the Australians are having reception Saturday evening for a visiting Australian Red Cross official. So I have juggled my schedule and will do just that. Vung Tau is a resort area and supposed to be very nice, so it should be a little break. The end result is that I will start my trip Wednesday instead of Tuesday. I am going to another hospital first before going to the Vung Tau Thursday afternoon. A further end result is that you may be in for an even longer gap in mail, but I'll do the best I can on that score.

* * *

Vung Tau

Sat, Aug 2, 1969

I am at Vung Tau and it is a real monsoon day. It has been pouring since early morning. It is now 10:30 AM— but it does seem to be clearing a little, so maybe we'll be better later.

I mailed a letter to you from the hospital at Binh Thuy, but have no idea how long it will take to reach you. I had the usual frustrating time with transportation getting from there to here. I got to the air terminal at 1:00, ostensibly to take a 3:00 flight. The flight finally left at 5:00—a Caribou plane. For the 4 hours I was there in that crummy terminal I had to stand as there was no place to sit down. For a little while a nice young sailor let me share half of his duffel bag on the floor. He had been there six hours waiting. The flight itself, once I did get it, took about 40 minutes and was uneventful.

Ellen Lewis, the hospital field director and the man who is the field director for this area, met me in a jeep. All of the hospital staff live in a "villa" about 3 miles from the hospital. A 2½ ton truck runs a shuttle back and forth. The villa is 3 stories and has large rooms with private baths. I have a room to myself—sparsely furnished but adequate.

After a shower, Ellen took me over to the nearby Officers' Club for dinner. At 8:00 Alicia Harper, the recreation worker, had a little party in her room for the two ARC men and one of the Australian Red Cross girls.

Yesterday I spent at the hospital—the business part of my visit. Last night, the two girls and 2 ARC men took me to the "Grand Hotel"—a civilian establishment—for a very good dinner.

Today, Ellen had planned to take me downtown to get my hair done, but the weather makes that questionable. I got up at 9:00 and using a combination of hot plates etc. Ellen fixed me some scrambled eggs and coffee.

These are two darling girls here—both by coincidence from Natchez, Ms. They had not actually known each other before although they know most of the same people at home. Alicia is a few years older than Ellen which, of course, put her in a different "crowd" at home. Anyway, they love each other and work beautifully together, and are completely a part of the hospital family.

Vung Tau—like Nha Trang—is a resort town and a very quiet area war wise, so the staff here lead a much less restricted life than in a lot of places. The army uses this for an "in-country "R&R Center, sending some men down for three days to "play" a little.

I expect to have my usual transportation struggle tomorrow. The flight Ellen had booked me on has been cancelled, so I'll have to take my chances on getting something else.

. . . This evening we go to the Australian Red Cross reception. I'm going to use a little time now to start writing my reports. It will put me that much ahead when I get back if I can get some of it done.

* * *

Saigon

Sun, Aug 3, 1969

Well, I'm back in Saigon OK, but no trip ever seems to go without its delays and frustrations.

I got up this morning at 5:00 as the FD from the post was to pick me up at 5:30 to be at the air terminal at 5:45. Alicia Harper, one of the American Red Cross girls, came pattering into the lobby of the billet at 5:25 with a cup of coffee and a glass of juice for me before I took off. It was a good thing she was there because the FD overslept and didn't come. Alicia got on the phone and got me some transportation, but I got to the airport too late to get booked on the 7:30 flight. I did get manifested on the 10:30 flight. I walked over to the hospital—it isn't very far—and had breakfast in the mess hall. Then went back to the terminal in the hopes I might get on an earlier, unscheduled flight. No luck on that and the flight I finally got on was an Australian flight—a C7A—US calls them Caribous and the Australians call them Wallabies.

They landed at the civilian air terminal at Tan Son Nhut instead of the military terminal. I had my usual struggle getting transportation. I called the office, but our cars were out. I finally managed to get a military taxi, but it took a lot of phone calls and a firm refusal on my part to take "no" for an answer. Anyway, I got to the Ambassador about 12:30. While I still had my clothes on I went over to Brinks and had lunch.

. . . Before I start to answer the letters, I'll go back and finish up with my time at Vung Lau. I wrote you Saturday AM. In the afternoon, the nice young assistant field director from the base came with a Jeep and took Ellen and me on a tour of Vung Lau. After the torrential rain in the morning, it was a good thing we were in a jeep as the roads in some places were axle deep in water and almost washed out. The setting is really beautiful—lovely beaches, wooded hills, etc. The town itself is run down as is every place over here, and there is so much filth and abject poverty.

When we got back, the Australians had called and said we were to wear civilian clothes instead of going in uniforms. The FD had managed to get a station wagon to take us to the Australian compound. The reception was in their officers' club, which wasn't great but about like most of the clubs people have been able to put together over here. It was quite informal—drinks and hors d'oeuvres. The Australians are very cordial and charming and it was most pleasant. The two Australian Red Cross girls showed me their "Red Cross center" at the hospital. They operate a recreation program for the patients very similar to ours. They do not have a casework program such as ours. It was a very pleasant experience. When we left, we stopped in at the American Officers' Club for a pizza. So all in all it was a nice visit and a little change.

* * *

In September, Mary spent ten days traveling to different hospitals around the country.

Chu Lai
Mon, Sep 15, 1969

I'm at a place called Chu Lai where we have two hospitals. One of them is temporarily without a staff member—it is a one worker station and is covered by the staff from the other temporarily. So in a sense I am visiting two hospitals and will be here through Wednesday. This hospital has a lovely location—on a sort of cliff overlooking the China Sea. That is about the best that can be said for it as it is pretty makeshift and run down looking. Not many comforts but they do have inside plumbing in the nurses' quarters—but only for the last two months. I have a decent enough room to stay in. It was pretty hot during the day, but relatively cool tonight.

My trip up was time consuming but went relatively well. The military taxi picked me up at 6:00 and I had to check in before 6:55. I flew to Da Nang where I had a 2½ hour wait until I got another plane to here. Got here about 2:00. Both planes were C-130s and I was invited to sit in the flight deck, which is relatively cool and comfortable.

I see I have used the word "relatively" several times. I guess all things are relative, which really means they could be, and often are, a lot worse.

The girls are cordial and I think, happy to see me. They entertained me at their little club. Like so many places the club is a "self-help" project, but they have done real well and it is air conditioned. A group of the nurses are engaged in painting and laying floor tile in the latrine area. It is really wonderful how people turn to and fix up what they have. I take my hat off to them. I only have to

stay a couple days, but they are stuck here and are not letting it get them down.

Well, I don't know when you'll get any letters I write from upcountry, but I'll keep writing and mailing and hoping.

* * *

Chu Lai
Tues, Sep 16, 1969

Another "day at the sea." This hospital at Chu Lai is located on a bluff overlooking the South China Sea. Both days have been clear and sunny, quite warm actually, but there is a sea breeze which is a big help. The hospital itself is pretty ramshackled, the most "unimproved" one I have visited. Air conditioners are sitting in crates, generators partially installed but a "stop" has been put on all improvements. This is pretty typical of the state of things over here. No one knows what the future holds so many plans are at a standstill.

Today we spent a good part of the day at another smaller hospital near here, where we are planning to assign one staff member in October. By contrast, it is practically new—almost completely air conditioned and wonderful morale among the staff. I have never received such a royal welcome. CO, Executive and Chief Nurse at the door to meet me, a coffee attendant by nearly all the offices, and nurses to meet me. They're so anxious to have a Red Cross worker, have built a Red Cross building, and showed me around with such pride in what they have accomplished. So much of the work over here is done by self-help. The nurses and doctors scrounge materials, put up walls and ceilings, paint, lay tile—whatever they can think of to improve things. Of course, they are very proud of their accomplishments, and rightfully so. The girl we are assigning over at the othcr hospital is lucky because she is so wanted and will be given so much support.

George Jessel is coming tomorrow to put in a show here at the hospital. He is not one of my favorites, but I guess you take what you get over here.

This evening, we went over to the American Division Club and had drinks and sandwiches with the ARC men and the Clubmobile girls in this area. When we came back we sat for a while outside the hospital club looking at the fishing boats and enjoying the good sea breeze. A lovely setting but marred by three choppers bringing in casualties while we sat there. I can't get used to that, and I hope I never do.

I'll be here through tomorrow. This is longer than I usually stay in one place, but I did have two hospitals to look into.

* * *

Chu Lai

Wed, Sep 17, 1969

. . . This was a big day here. George Jessel came with a show. I only watched part of it and to me it was pretty sad. He is 71 and looked all of it and much too old to be here. The big excitement was that Gen. Abrams flew up to present him a citation as this was his last stop on his present trip. This little hospital was really rocked to be the site of such an important visit.

It has stayed cold and really been quite comfortable, which is a big help. I had the mamasan wash a couple of my uniforms today. They are pretty sad and I can see why the girls here wear fatigues rather than trying to wear our regular uniforms.

* * *

Phu Bai

Thurs, Sep18, 1969

Well, all of today was involved in getting here. Through a "friend," the girls at the 91st had set up a chopper flight, supposedly to leave Chu Lai at 8:30 and come all the way here, with a stop at Da Nang. I finally got started at 10:00 and got to Da Nang about 11:00. There, the chain broke as the chopper wasn't going any further. I asked around and learned the 142nd Trans Co had a flight coming at 2:00. The members of that company were most cordial, made me at home, in their office, etc. Come lunchtime, a cute young warrant officer pilot took me to lunch at their mess. He even found a latrine for me to use and stood guard while I did so. Then it started to rain, so the plane couldn't take off. Finally, at 4:00, it cleared enough for us to go. They dropped me off at an unknown (to me) chopper pad. Again, I was able to get a lift by Jeep and get to the hospital at 5:00.

The rain didn't hold off long and it has been pouring for hours. This is monsoon season up here and it is the real McCoy. This is a very primitive hospital and knee deep in mud.

I am in a room with two double deck bunks. It has an air conditioner and is normally used for a sleeping room for nurses on night duty. I have to go about 100 yards to a latrine, but it does have inside plumbing.

Our lone ARC worker was very glad to see me and we had dinner at the mess and a pleasant evening at the club. Then she had a call that two of the Red Cross Clubmobile girls had gotten stranded here trying to get back to Da Nang. So I'm about to get two roommates. Never a dull moment.

I am supposed to leave here tomorrow at 3:00 to go back to Da Nang, but who knows what tomorrow will bring?

These are not horror stories to make you say "poor Mary." It's just all part of the game. I, at least, don't have to stay up here indefinitely and live day after day in the mud and wet.

I will have to stop as my roommates should be arriving momentarily. It's quite a life!

* * *

Da Nang
Fri, Sep 19, 1969

The saga over the last 24 hours is rain. Never have I experienced such a continuous downpour under more adverse conditions. Poor Phu Bai—a mud hole and a quagmire. I have slogged about, thoroughly wet ever since last night. This has been no series of showers—just rain coming down in sheets.

I mailed a letter today written last night telling you about the two little drowned rats of Clubmobile girls we gave sanctuary to. Ah youth!! They slept like the dead and were up and off at 7:00—in an open Jeep in the downpour. We never heard from them again and have to assume they got a flight out.

I completed my visit and got to the airport at 2:30. I left at 4:00 on a Marine C-47 for Da Nang. Although it was also raining here, it was like stepping into another world. I am staying at the Navy hospital and the Navy always takes care of itself. The quarters are extremely nice, air conditioned with all modern conveniences including washers and dryers. I have a mass of dirty clothes and will do a big laundry over the weekend. The HFD picked me up and we had dinner at the mess—linen tablecloths and napkins no less. After a shower and a change, she and her steady beau took me to the very elegant officer's club—Filipino band

and much gayety. I even danced one dance with a sweet young Marine captain.

Now I'm ready to hit the hay. Tomorrow I hope to spend the day on the hospital ship *Sanctuary*, which is due in sometime tonight. I have to call them in the AM on the ship to shore phone to see if it is OK.

I'll be staying in these nice quarters all week and will make a visit here and also to the Army hospital in this area. Also expect to be able to visit the *Repose* later in the week. It is a pretty arduous schedule, but if I can get it all done, I will feel I have accomplished a lot.

I am fine and seem to keep going well. I am hoping to maneuver some way to get my hair done as it is in very bad shape. Getting it thoroughly wet a couple of times hasn't helped.

* * *

Da Nang
Sun, Sep 21, 1969

This is really an oasis in the desert. By that I mean these extremely comfortable nurses' quarters at the Naval Hospital and Da Nang. You have to hand it to the Navy—they take care of their staff. The quarters are air conditioned, very clean, washers and dryers, ironing boards and steam irons, a comfortable lounge with complete supply of China, refrigerator, stove, everything to fix breakfast or a light snack.

I got up at about 8:00, had some breakfast, and now have a load of laundry in the washer. Will move it to the dryer soon and will iron the uniforms. I am not very good in that department, but I'll manage and, at least, will have some clean clothes. This afternoon I am borrowing some curlers, shampoo and a hair dryer from one of the girls and will wash my hair. It is in deplorable condition, so you can see my plans for today are to try and get really cleaned up.

I had a very good day yesterday. I called the *Sanctuary* on the radio about 8:00 and made plan to go out for the day. The staff here arranged transportation for me to the boat landing. I took a 10:00 launch out to the ship—it took about 30 minutes. It was a nice sunny day which all contributed to the occasion.

The two girls on the ship are just darling and welcomed me warmly. In fact, I was received most cordially by all the staff. I toured the ship, met the CO and the Chief Nurse. We had lunch in the wardroom, linen tablecloths and napkins, waited on by Filipino mess stewards. We talked business until 4:00.

The ship is a beautiful hospital. The CO said he had enough qualified medical staff to staff a first-rate medical school. They just lack nothing needed to care for patients. They received their patients by chopper directly from the "battlefield." Our two girls have made a wonderful place for themselves and are very much a part of the ship. It's a good assignment, but the obvious drawbacks are the need for them to share a small cabin and office, the isolation from other ARC staff, and the confinement.

At 4:00, a gang of ranking officers and nurses were coming ashore for a party in honor of the ship's executive officer who was leaving. They invited me to come along as our two girls were included. We came ashore by launch and went to a very nice Navy Officers' club. It was a gay party—wine with dinner—an ear-splitting floor show. A Navy captain who is deputy commander of the shore activity joined us. He was kind enough to send me back to the nurses' quarters here when the rest of the gang left to get the launch back to the ship. I was invited to stay overnight

at the ship, but declined as I was all settled in here.

So, it was a good day yesterday—very different, interesting and fun. I am grateful too for this day to relax and recharge my batteries. I think I'll try to work on some of my reports this afternoon.

Tomorrow I plan to visit the Army hospital here and Tuesday I hope to visit the *Repose*. The two ships alternate—one is always "on station" up north to receive casualties and the other is in Da Nang. Three days alternating schedule.

I talked to the office yesterday and again heard how much mail was awaiting me. I sure wish I could get my hands on it. I have written nearly every day on this trip, but have no idea how the letters have been reaching you. I hope they are dribbling in in some kind of order. I'll continue to keep them coming.

* * *

Da Nang
Mon, Sep 22, 1969

This has been another very pleasant day. I spent it at the 95th Evacuation Hospital, which is the Army hospital in this area. I am always impressed by the esprit-de-corps at these hospitals. Each one is sure it is the best, and there is such pride in showing their place off to you. The one today has nice facilities by Army standards. They are building a new building for the Red Cross. We have had only two girls there, but are adding a third next week.

. . . Tomorrow, I hope to get aboard the *Repose* (hospital ship) which is due in tonight. We have had another clear, sunny day today and I hope it holds through tomorrow at least.

I had a very good day yesterday. I did laundry and did

not have to iron the uniforms as one of the mamasans did that for me. After lunch I washed my hair. I borrowed curlers and a dryer from one of the girls and it turned out amazingly well. I got one field visit report written and read some. In the evening, I went to the club and saw a movie—"Buona Sera, Mrs. Campbell." Silly, but amusing. Anyway, with a relaxing day and an opportunity to get clean, I feel quite rejuvenated and up to another busy week. If I can get the *Repose* out of the way tomorrow, I'll spend Wednesday and Thursday making my official visits here at the Naval Hospital and go back to Saigon Friday.

As difficult as some aspects of these trips are, it is really the meat of the job and give me a pick-up. I am sure that the letters I have written along the way sound more "alive" than most I write from Saigon. Of course, the most help-ful thing about this trip has been having these comfortable quarters to stay in this week.

* * *

Da Nang
Tues, Sep 23, 1969

This has been another interesting day. Again, I went to sea—aboard the USS *Repose.* This time it was a beauti-ful sunny day again, so the harbor was calm and the ship steady. Again, we have two grand girls on the ship. In gen-eral, however, the atmosphere wasn't as "happy" as aboard the *Sanctuary*—largely I felt because of the personalities of the CO of the ship and the CO of the hospital. They were very candid to me however, and we had a beautifully served lunch in the Captain's private dining room—just the three of us, the two captains and the ship's Executive Officer.

I came back to the launch at 5:00 with one of our girls and a group of officers. They invited me to have dinner at one of the officers' clubs—a different one from the last time. A doctor and nurse from the Naval Hospital were in the group so we got transportation together back to the hospital. Tomorrow and Thursday I will make my official visit here and have booked myself on a flight back to Saigon on Friday AM.

* * *

Da Nang
Wed, Sep 24, 1969

Another busy day! I spent today and will also spend tomorrow making my official visit to the Naval Hospital. This is one of the largest hospitals over here with the most complex program. It is not a "pulling together" staff so there are problems to try to smooth over and work out.

As far as I am concerned, the staff have been cordial, but have also let me alone after duty hours to go my own way, which I have appreciated.

Tomorrow evening the whole staff will be going out to dinner with me, including the two girls from the 95th Evac Hosp. Consequently, I may not get a letter written.

Needless to say, I am so anxious now to get back to Saigon and my mail. It has been hard being without mail for two weeks. I hope all the letters I have written you on the road have gotten through in fairly quick order.

* * *

Da Nang
Thurs, Sep 25, 1969

Well, I seem to have figured this out just right, as I have exactly one envelope left for this is my last letter "on the road." And I am ready to go "home to Saigon." I have stood up real well, but it has been a busy two weeks. I dread having to write up all the reports, but I'll get them done in due course.

Tonight, three of the girls from here and the two gals from the 95th congregated for dinner at one of the clubs. It is located on a really lovely beach and there was a full moon. I had lobster, which was very good. I think it is about the first time I have had it over here.

Well, this is sure, but it will wind up the trip. Next time I write, I'll have some letters to answer.

* * *

The rest of Mary's hospital visits were limited to shorter trips.

Saigon
Thurs, Oct 30, 1969

I am back from my quick trip to Binh Thuy. It was really a very pleasant jaunt. The weather was relatively cool and I had no particular flight complications. In fact, coming back today I was able to get on an unscheduled cargo flight—not in the flight deck—and got back sooner than I expected. We have had 2 workers down there, but the hospital had reduced in size so we pulled out one, leaving only the recreation worker. My mission was to give her some "instant" training in casework and administrative. She's a real good girl and will cope.

* * *

Saigon
Fri, Nov 7, 1969

Six months ago today I arrived in Vietnam, so it is downhill from here on out.

I got back this evening from my trip to Pleiku. It was a relatively uncomplicated trip, but I am tired, nonetheless. The biggest surprise was that it was delightfully cool there. It is in the mountains, the air was fresh and non humid and I slept both nights under a blanket. The bad side was that yesterday they admitted 63 casualties to this one small hospital. Even had to send some on immediately to other hospitals as all 4 operating rooms were going and they couldn't handle them. It looks like the "lull" is over. It is just heartbreaking.

So the fact that my air conditioner isn't working tonight doesn't seem very important.

* * *

Cam Ranh Bay
Mon, Jan 19, 1970

I'm at Cam Ranh Bay at the 6th Convalescent Center. Two old friends—Mary Bowers, HFD and Marty Howe, Recreation Supervisor—are here. Both are old-timers, so the place is in good shape. Such a relief after struggling with so many inexperienced people. This is a big place—1300 beds, about 700 patients at the moment. It is just what the name implies—patients are sent here from other hospitals for reconditioning before going back to duty. It is located right on the beach—sand everywhere and blowing today as there was a strong wind—it is sunny and cool. The girls live in trailers and I am staying in a small room in the one shared by Mary Bowers and the Chief Nurse.

I flew up this morning—a good trip, riding in the flight deck! I'll be here through tomorrow and then I'll visit the Air Force Hospital a few miles from here—also at Cam Ranh Bay.

I had a letter from you this AM when I was briefly at the office. Also enclosed was the nice letter from John and Karen.

The girls are giving a party for me tonight, so I haven't time for more now.

* * *

Cam Ranh Bay
Tues, Jan 20, 1970

This visit is about over and I'll go over to the Air Force Hospital tomorrow. Today wasn't as nice weather wise—rain on and off.

. . . The girls had a very nice party last night. Twelve people, which was about maximum for a trailer. The mess officer sent over a tray of deviled eggs and fixings for tacos, which the girls fixed and served.

There are no problems here. Mary and Marty are old hands and have the situation well and smoothly organized. There are 5 staff here plus a part-time secretary who divides her time between here and the Air Force Hospital.

* * *

Cam Banh Bay
Wed, Jan 21, 1970

Well, I made the move from the Army to the Air Force today. Mary Bowers drove me over this AM. Helen Whiltner, who is HFD here was with me for a short time at Wiesbaden, although I haven't seen her since.

The contrast between the Army and the Air Force is very noticeable. As usual, the Air Force gives priority to creature comforts, and the hospital is well set up and looks almost "Stateside." All the women are billeted in a compound about 6 blocks from the hospital. I am in a transient room with 2 beds, so I may acquire a roommate while I'm here. It is air conditioned, has a refrigerator and is very nice. They have a large central latrine, but it is only a few steps away from my room.

The weather today was sunny and cool. Again there are no real problems here. Four good girls and a part-time secretary.

This evening the girls are having a "cookout" in my honor. I will be here all day tomorrow and have booked a flight back to Saigon on Friday morning. So, all goes well.

* * *

SOCIALIZING AND TRAVELING

MARY WROTE IN AN early letter that "this is not a 'sociable' war." Unlike Korea, when almost every letter included information about KTs or a dance, there were far fewer references to socializing other than taking new staff to dinner when they arrived. Travel had to be done "out of country" and Mary did a trip to Manila, Philippines, and one to Sydney, Australia.

Saigon
Sat, May 10, 1969

. . . Last night, one of the girls who has just spent a year on the Hospital Ship *Sanctuary* was here en route home. Penny had us to her room for a drink then we had dinner at an excellent French restaurant a block from the Rex. I had a filet of turbot almondine and it tasted wonderful after the mess hall food I had been eating. I understand that there are a number of good, safe restaurants which is a nice diversion.

Tonight, there is a farewell party for two of the Hospital staff who are leaving and I understand some of us will go to another restaurant afterwards for dinner.

* * *

Saigon

Sun, May 11, 1969

. . . Last night I went to a KT party at the Rex for two people who are leaving. One of them is Charlotte Lagg, the Assistant Director/recreation in our service. At 7:30, six of us, including Penny, Charlotte and Mr. Higgins, the ARC Director of Operations, went to the Caravelle Hotel for dinner. This is the number one civilian hotel here. Very plush. We had an excellent dinner. I had lobster. With the 10:00 PM curfew, all parties break up early!

* * *

Saigon

Mon, May 12, 1969

. . . I told you about going to dinner Saturday night at the Hotel Caravelle. Today I settled up my part of the bill and it came to $14.00 for my dinner! The glass of wine cost $2.30. So I think I have had my first and last meal at the Caravelle. Those are New York prices, and it just isn't worth it.

* * *

Saigon

Sun, May 18, 1969

. . . At 6:00, went over to the Rex and Penny and I and two of the ARC men had drinks and dinner. Home by 9:30 and I went right to bed. I slept through until 6:00 and then back to sleep again until eight. One of the best sleeps I have had.

At 9:00 I met Penny and the same two men at the Continental Palace for breakfast. This is one of the old civilian hotels here and they have a tree shaded courtyard where we had breakfast. I left them there at 10:30 and took a taxi to church. This Sunday we used the Anglican prayer book—Morning Prayer. A nice service and more people than last Sunday. The priest is quite a good preacher. After church I chatted with a couple of WAVE officers and then walked home. It is only about 5 blocks, but walking anywhere is not a pleasure. There are no real sidewalks and, of course, the heat.

* * *

Saigon

Undated

First page missing

. . . This is not a "sociable" war—no travel except on official business, no leaves allowed by the military "in-country." The latter is a much used expression. One talks about how long one has been "in-country," where one is assigned "in-country" etc. While I'm here, I will be entitled to an R&R—5 days—and one leave—also five days. Both have to be taken out-of-country. Australia is so popular for R&R that no one gets to go before being eight or nine months "in-country." You can't apply for R&R until you have been "in-country" three months. Then you list your preferences and your name goes into a pot with everyone else. Military get priority, of course. I really haven't given it much thought. My ardor on Australia cooled when I found out it was a 14-hour flight each way. Having just completed an 18-hour flight, that is not very inviting. Well, we'll see.

If you go on leave, you have to pay all of your own expenses—airfare, etc.—and make all your own hotel arrangements etc.

* * *

Saigon

Fri, Jun 13, 1969

. . . I have social engagements for every night through Wednesday, so my letter writing time may be a bit limited. Tomorrow night there is a big farewell party for Glenn Ferges who is "second in command" ARC wise and goes home next week. They have lined up part of the roof at Brinks and are going to have steaks. Don't ask me how they come by steaks as we don't have commissary privileges. Apparently, someone has an inside track somewhere.

* * *

Saigon

Sat, Jul 25, 1969

. . . Betty and I went over to Brinks for lunch and then I went and had my hair done. Betty and Penny were going to the Vietnamese Opera this evening with Mr. Higgins, the ARC Director of Operations. They had a ticket for me, but I opted out. I wanted a nice quiet evening alone, and I can't imagine two hours of caterwauling of Vietnamese opera.

. . . Tomorrow evening we are having a "hail and farewell" for coming and going ARC Hqs staff. It is to be on The Brinks roof again and I hope it doesn't rain as it did last time. Not much chance that it won't however, as it rains every evening. If not oftener.

* * *

Saigon

Mon, Jul 28, 1969

. . . I had dinner tonight with a darling girl who is on her way home after 18 months here. She is from Eastern area and I knew her in the States. Her name is Judy Scales and Ethel knows her if you should call Ethel. She is resigning when she gets home to marry a doctor she met over here. I sure wish ARC could hang on to some of these fine young women but you can't wish them anything but happiness if they have found the right man for themselves.

* * *

Saigon

Sun, Aug 10, 1969

I've had a quiet day but was grateful for it. My only outing was to go to church. I liked Chaplain Pennel even less than I did the last time. He just isn't my cup of tea. I had a sandwich at noon at the Snack Bar upstairs and dinner this evening at the mess—also upstairs. I had dinner with Don Boyette. Here's the ARC field director. At the field office for Saigon. He's a very nice young man and a great friend of Mary Howell's. His room is just around the corner from mine. He came in and lifted the footlocker out of the middle of the room into the corner, so the room looks fairly organized.

* * *

Saigon

Sat, Aug 16, 1969

… One of my neighbors here at the Rex is Don Boyette, one of the Red Cross field directors here in Saigon. He's a nice person, a little younger than I am and a confirmed bachelor type. I haven't known him before, but we have many ARC friends in common. Anyway, he stopped by for a drink last night and then took me out to dinner at the Mayfair—a nice French restaurant. It was a pleasant evening and a little change. That was one of the reasons I didn't get a letter written last night.

* * *

Saigon

Fri, Oct 17, 1969

… I had such a nice evening. Meredith Clores who has just completed a year aboard the *Repose* and is here clearing to go home. Joan and I took her to dine at Kamunihkos. She's a lovely girl and so interested in everything. This is her first time in Saigon. She has been to the Philippines several times—the ship goes there for 10 days every 90 days—and has given me lots of good dope on things to do and see there. It has gotten me quite enthused about my leave. She was so thrilled because the ship's captain gave her the Red Cross ensign flown by the ship as a farewell gift. Wasn't that nice?

* * *

Saigon

Sat, Dec 13, 1969

Sorry I didn't get more than a pc off last night, but I'm sure you are glad when I have a bit of social life.

Joan and I had invited 2 of our favorite men from the office to come down for drinks and dinner. One is Joe Cerniglia who is the director of SMI [sergeant major instructor] (the male FDs) and the other is Ernie Rose, Director of Personnel. Joe is going to the Philippines next week and wanted to see my dresses as he wants to get some for his wife. This really precipitated the whole thing. Unfortunately, Joan is down with a bad cold or flu or something, but Betty came and the four of us had a very pleasant evening. We had dinner at the steakhouse upstairs.

* * *

Saigon

Tues, Dec 16, 1969

… I tracked down and called Bruce Nichols (M's friend from East Lansing) and invited him to escort me to Christmas Eve services at St Christopher's. I'll admit that I had the ulterior motive of wanting a safe escort to be out on the streets of Saigon at 11:30 at night. He seemed very happy to go. I asked him if we would have any problem if we were out after curfew and he said, "Not if you were with me." He is Exec. of the MP Battalion here in Saigon, so I think that is a happy solution for both of us. I asked him to come early for drinks and dinner and I really felt he was glad to have a plan for Christmas Eve, so I didn't feel that I was imposing. At least he was very, very nice. He said he had had 2 letters from Catharine and was apologetic that he hadn't had time to answer them. I told him M had sent me a picture of his children and wife which I will give him.

Back to Sunday and my lunch with the Counsells. I waited after church until they were ready to go. They had invited six people (Joan was one, but was sick with a cold and cancelled out). I drove with them to their house, balancing Sarah Jean in her car crib on my knees. The other guests were a girl who works for USAID [US Agency for International Development] and has been in Saigon for 6 (!!) years, and AF Sgt, a young man who works for OICC [officer in charge of construction] (whatever that is) and a Chinese boy from Hong Kong who is connected with Asian Christian Services. They had a very nice apartment and everything was so well done. While Mrs C took the baby upstairs to feed and bed-down, Mr. C served us drinks. Then we moved to the dining room and a beautifully set table—white tablecloth, flowers, etc—for a lunch of chicken Curry with all the doo-dads. I'm not wild about Curry, but this wasn't bad and I ate it. We had ice cream with pineapple sauce for dessert, then adjoined to the living room for coffee and liqueurs. They had two Vietnamese servants who had prepared the meal and waited on the table. Among other things, I learned that Mr C had been in Southeast Asia for quite a few years—in Singapore before Saigon—has been here about two years. He studied at Cambridge, and one of his classmates was named Patermoster. Counsell and Patermoster could hardly have followed any vocation but the priesthood could they?

Apparently, they have groups for lunch every Sunday. He said they realized that people in Saigon work such long hours that they rarely have an opportunity to meet people outside their own group of working associates (how true!). For this reason, they feel their luncheons provide this opportunity—also how true and how thoughtful of them. It was a nice change for me and I did appreciate it. I'll have to figure out some way to reciprocate. I can't even write a bread and butter [letter; one expressing thanks] as I don't know how to mail anything through the local postage. Maybe I can "hand deliver" a note to them on Sunday.

* * *

Saigon
Christmas morning 1969

Well, this has been and is being a strange Christmas but really the saving grace is that it doesn't seem at all like Christmas. I'll go back and talk about yesterday first.

I went in the morning to get a permanent and got out to the office at 10:30. I found that Joan had gone to the doctor and had been sent home. She had a cold for over a week and now has a virus infection and bronchitis. She really feels lousy. Betty was just waiting until I got there, as she has also been sick and was nauseated. So, she went home. It really didn't matter as there was really nothing to do. We had a couple of calls from hospitals and I was glad I was there to talk to the girls.

At 2:00 we had a party for 9 Vietnamese who work for Hqs.—gave them gifts and had ice cream and fresh fruit. We had it on the roof of our building. The Vietnamese presented presents also—a lovely plant, a Vietnamese doll and a decorated cake. Everyone left at 4:00.

I looked in on Joan who feels awful, but there wasn't a lot I could do for her. I got bathed and dressed and at 6:00 Don Boyette, the RC field director who is my neighbor and his roommate Bob Hillerud (Lt. Col AF) came by. Don had received a package from Mary Howell and Virginia McKenna which they had sent us jointly. We opened it together, all sorts of fancy cocktail foods—cheese, smoked oysters, cans of meat balls, etc. Don is going to leave Fri, but when he gets back we will give a party to use up the food. I gave the men a couple of drinks and they left at 7 when Bruce and his Lt Larry Phinney arrived. After drinks we went upstairs for a steak dinner.

Bruce announced when he got there that he didn't think we would be able to go to church because of the mobs in the streets. There were several peace demonstrations in progress, including one by Americans!! in front of the Catholic cathedral. When we went upstairs, we could see down into the plaza by the Rex and the nearest thing I can liken it to is Times Square on New Year's Eve. There were at least 100,000 people jamming the area. No trouble—just walking and milling around. I wouldn't have gone out in that for anything, and Bruce was obviously relieved when I said so. We had a very pleasant time together. Bruce is a comfortable old-shoe type of person and Larry is a sweet little boy from South Carolina with perfect Southern manners. They left about 9:30, anxious, I felt, to be on their jobs as MP's. I pray there is no real trouble but in my little cave I wouldn't know.

After they left, I decided it would be good time for me to open my Christmas presents and I managed to do it calmly and without any emotion. Your box was just wonderful with all the things I had asked for and more. The KT napkins with my initials; 6!! pair of stockings; the travel alarm clock with "times around the world"; the Christmas towel; compact and lipstick; and the little things—jar of Maxim, gum, Kleenex, filters and lighter.

Martha's, John and Audrey's and Nene's boxes were more or less the same type. Many little packages, all useful and thoughtful. I will be writing each of them, of course. Cornelia sent me Nora Loft's, "The Lost Queen," and Martha, a book by C. P. Snow, so I have some good reading ahead.

I received yesterday the package from Margot which Daddy sent on. It is a cross stitched luncheon set—cloth and napkins. She wrote me that she had gotten it in Spain and had sent it to you for my next apartment. Unfortunately, I did not know this in time to let you know not to forward it. However, I put it in the footlocker to bring home.

Originally, Betty and I had planned to split office coverage today—she in the AM, me in the PM. When she was sick yesterday, it looked like I would be the only one on my feet. However, she called me at 5:00 AM, said she was feeling better and was going out, so I went back to bed and didn't get up until 9:00. I'm writing this now and will dress shortly and start wending my way office-ward. Will check on Joan too. Betty has invited me to dinner at her billet tonight and I guess I'll go.

* * *

Saigon
Sun, Feb 1, 1970

. . . Last evening Don and I had our party and it was highly successful. We had 15 people and they really went for the conglomeration of food we set forth, using combined donations received from various sources. We had smoked oysters, smoked shrimp, sardines, black olives, several kinds of cheese, deviled ham, crackers, etc. With people living scattered all over the city, it is always an undertaking to get people together. But they seem to enjoy it when the opportunity is presented.

* * *

One notable highlight in Mary's social life was when longtime family friend Ted Harvey was stationed in Vietnam. Mary did see Ted on a few occasions. Ted was like a brother to Mary, and from her letters you get the sense that visits with him provided some of the few moments of relaxation that Mary enjoyed.

Saigon

Thurs, May 22, 1969

. . . Of course, the biggest news for me in your letters was the news that Ted Hervey is coming over here. I'm sorry for him, Nene and the children, but, selfishly, I can't think of anyone I would rather see over here. As near as I can figure out from your letter, he will be G-1 with 1st Field Force which has Hqrs at Nha Trang. That is a fair piece from Saigon, but we do have a hospital there which I will be visiting in due course. Also, I am sure he will come thru Saigon en route and may be here off and on on official business. Be sure to get from Nene his exact address and the location and let me know. Tell him our ARC Hqrs are located in the MACV Annex, and my office phone is MACV 3053 or 4018. I hope to be in permanent billets before he arrives so I can send you my phone number before then.

* * *

Saigon

Wed, Jun 25, 1969

. . . I am really looking for a contact from Ted as I believe you wrote he was leaving US on June 25th. He would arrive here on Friday if that is so. I certainly hope he has to spend a few days in Saigon en route to Nha Trang. If he should be here over the weekend, maybe I can take him to Saint Christopher's.

* * *

Saigon

Thurs, Jun 26, 1969

I got an indirect word from Ted Harvey today. The ARC field director at Nha Trang called in and said Col. Harvey wanted his phone number passed to me. So apparently he is here, but didn't pass through Saigon. At the moment, the phone system is being partially converted to direct dial, which will eventually mean better service (we hope). For these couple of weeks, however, we are undergoing "operation minimize." All this to explain that long distance calls are severely limited, so I don't know if I can call Ted or he call me. Well, we'll see, and I'll let you know when we communicate.

* * *

Saigon

Thurs, Jul 3, 1969

My big news today was that Ted Harvey called me at 7:00 AM from Nha Trang. He said he had been trying to get through for days unsuccessfully and had written me a letter which he could now tear up. We had a nice visit and he sounded fine. He had made a couple of visits to the units—4th Division, etc. He said in his job he would really have no reason to come to Saigon, so hoped he would see me in Nha Trang. I didn't know it when I was talking to him, but I'm going to Nha Trang next week—probably Wednesday. When I was talking to the hospital field director about plans, I asked her to call Ted and tell him when I would be there. He said that his and Nene's trip was wonderful and he seems to be getting settled.

* * *

Saigon
Sun, Jul 8, 1969

. . . I expect to take off again tomorrow afternoon for Nha Trang, which will mean another gap in letters I fear. I'll come back Friday afternoon or Saturday AM. I asked Edna Fecht, the hospital field director, to get word to Ted that I was coming. I talked to her Monday AM and she said she had done so. I sure hope he won't have to be away. I liked Cecil's idea and will enjoy relaying it to Ted.

Written at the bottom of the letter in Grace Ingles's handwriting:
Martha, I just talked to Nene. Ted wrote that he had gotten the "transient general's room" at the hotel for Mary. Good old Ted! At least she will have her own "pottie" there. It will mean a lot to both Ted and Mary to get together.
Cecil was so outraged at Mary's having a roommate she said, "It would be better if she and Ted were rooming together. They at least like each other." I wrote that to Mary and she is referring to that.

* * *

Nha Trang
Wed, Jul 9, 1969

Well, here I am in Nha Trang and thanks to Ted and being taken care of like a queen. When I got to the office this AM there was a message that he had called to tell me that he arranged for me to stay in the VIP billet—the King Duy Tan Hotel. When Edna met me, she said Ted wanted me to have dinner with him. I haven't been able to reach him—he was at a briefing—but I left a message with his Sgt that I was here. He lives in the same hotel, so he will show up in due course. I have a nice air conditioned room with private bath. Not the Ritz, but by Vietnam standards the best I have been in since I arrived.

Among the messages Ted left for me was to be sure to bring a swimming suit—the beach is beautiful. Since he had talked to Penny—and charmed her I am sure—she said why didn't I stay up there until Sunday instead of coming back Friday. So I went back to the Ambassador and got the bathing suit, some shorts and a few more clothes and I will stay until Sunday. I don't know how much free time Ted will have, but Edna seems glad to have me. So I am getting a little in country R&R.

The flight up was interesting. I had the horrible 2 hour hot wait at Tan Son Nhut. However, on the plane I was invited to sit in the flight deck. It was air conditioned and once we took off it was fine. The flight engineer—a Sgt—chatted with me and pointed out all the sights we flew over. Of course we had a grand view. While you're in back you see nothing.

I've had a shower and am partially dressed. Mr. Higgins, the ARC field director—who also lives here—is going to meet me at 7:00 AM, take me to breakfast and then to the hospital. The ARC at the hospital have a carry-all assigned to them which Edna drives, so transportation is no real problem.

I'm going to figure out a way to get my hair done Friday or Saturday. It sure needs it already. My head perspires so that my hair just gets gummy in about 3 days.

I'll leave this open and add more after I have seen Ted. Nha Trang is referred to as the Riviera of VN. It was a favorite resort of the French and it is right on the beach—the Chinese sea. There was a nice sea breeze blowing this afternoon when I arrived, but now it is raining.

Well, Ted showed up and he looks great. He has gone to clean up, and then we'll go to dinner. I'll close this so I can get it in the mail, but I'll be writing more in the next day or so.

In Grace Ingles's handwriting at the end of the letter: *Needless to say, this letter has made us so happy. Bless Ted and Penny and the Good Lord Himself for this little break that has been given her.*

Ted, is G1 up there for that particular army force, so has authority and being Ted is looking out for Mary. They enjoy each other and are good friends and I see this as a break for Ted too.

* * *

Saigon

Sun, Jul 13, 1969

. . . Before I answer your letters, I'll fill in a few details from the Nha Trang. Of course, seeing Ted was the highlight and we spent three evenings together. I think he's fine, although finding the frustrations of the whole setup over here trying. He works long hours but at noon every day, he spends ½ hour on the beach, right across the hotel which is so good for him. He has a nice large room, air conditioned, so is living comfortably. Of course we are completely relaxed together and both enjoyed being able to chat about our respective families. I put in there details because I am sure Nene will want to hear them.

* * *

Saigon

Mon, Jul 28, 1969

. . . Sorry if I left out a few details about my visit with Ted, but glad he wrote Nene and she filled you in. I must call him one of these days. The main deterrent is that I have to call him at his office and from mine, and that is never too conducive to a chat.

* * *

Saigon

Sat, Dec 13, 1969

. . . This morning I picked up the phone and called Ted at 7:00 AM. I hadn't had any contact with him in months. He sounded fine. Said he was going to Hawaii 24 January. He was very impressed with the "Luther Miller Tribute." I told him I hoped to get to Nang Chang in early January before he goes to Hawaii. He said he had sent you a Christmas card. I urged him to manufacture a reason to come to Saigon and preferably over a weekend so we could go to Saint Christophers together.

* * *

Nha Trang

Thurs, Jan 8, 1970

I only got a p.c. off last night, but will try to do better now.

My trip up went relatively smoothly and I was able to ride in the flight deck of the C130—a vast improvement over the bucket seat in the back. I got here about 1:00 and our HFD, Lucy Fuller, met me. I spent the afternoon at the hospital and Lucy brought me to the hotel. I had called Ted in the meantime and made plans with him for the evening. I had to get myself moved three times as the first two rooms had out of order plumbing. The one I ended up in had no blanket or pillowcase, but Ted eventually procured both for me.

Ted came about 7:30 and took me to the Command Mess for dinner—we had a real good lobster. We then came back to his room for drinks. We had a real good visit. He showed me pictures of the family and some of his

Christmas cards, including yours. I think he looks well and seems fine.

As luck would have it, he had to go to Saigon today, the first time he has been there. After my day at the hospital, Lucy brought me to the hotel and waited while I changed. We then went to a promotion party for a couple of the nurses and then to the officers' club at the Air Base for dinner.

When I got back to the hotel about 9:00 there was a note in my box from Ted saying he was back and to call him at the mess. I tried, but they said he wasn't there, so I left a note in his box saying I was in my room and imagine he'll be along soon.

This AM I was able to get breakfast here at the hotel and Ted sent his car at 7:30 to take me to the hospital. It is a real asset for me to have him easing my way. Not to mention our nice visit.

I am leaving tomorrow at noon—I have to check in at the air base at 10:30.

The weather is very cool, much cooler than Saigon. It rained off and on yesterday, but today is just cloudy. I have wished for a sweater today, believe it or not.

* * *

Saigon
Fri, Jan 9, 1970

. . . I enclose the sweet note from Ted I found under my door this morning. That bit about "changing shoulder pads" is not to be mentioned to anyone. There is a possibility that he will change jobs for the rest of his tour, but it isn't definite and he hasn't told Nene. We had about an hour together last night after I wrote you. He really poured out some of his frustrations in his present job. I think it

did him good as he could talk to me as he couldn't to anyone else over here, and probably not even Nene. We also had a good talk about how he sees his career, which I'll tell you about someday. Too much to try to write. Anyway it is always good to be with him—good for both of us—because we have so much in common that we can really let our hair down. He needs his R&R and a little time with Nene and I'm so glad they will both have it.

His comment re whiskey sour mix. I have so much more ahead than I'll ever use that I took him a package as a little "presents." The article on "Saigon" was in December 29 Newsweek, which I gave him.—the title: "The worst city in the world."

* * *

9 Jan 70

Dear Mary,

Your visit was fun and I appreciated it. I hope you enjoyed it as much as I did.

What a coincidence that at the same time you came here I went to Saigon! It seems like the pattern of this whole stupid war.

Thank you for the whiskey sour mix—12 of them. They should keep things a little in a rosy glow for a period of time at least through Tet.

Thank Gracie for all her support to Nene. She wouldn't have made it without Gracie to lean upon. Give my best to Hal. I'm glad he has retired for the 2nd time. I know he will be anxious for something to do, but knowing Hal, that won't be hard to find.

Mary, hope to see you again before long. I finished the article on Saigon and am a little depressed by it.

Come again soon. Maybe if I change old shoulder

patches I'll have reason to visit Saigon more frequently. Good luck. Hope to see you before too long, Ted.

* * *

Saigon

Fri, Feb 13, 1970

Ted, bless his heart, called me this afternoon to check if I was back OK [after returning from Sydney], and what a kind of trip I had had, etc. I think he must have marked it on his calendar to call today. It was so sweet of him and I sure appreciate it. He is "sweating out" word on his stateside assignment. Said he had listed a preference for whatever Army it is that has headquarters in Atlanta. Now, wouldn't that be something?

* * *

Mary did have two opportunities to travel abroad while in Vietnam. She went to the Philippines and to Australia. She traveled alone on both trips.

When Mary was about two years old, the family was stationed in Manilla, Philippines. Her younger brother, John, was born there on December 1, 1922. She had seen pictures from that time and had heard many stories about life there but didn't have any memories of it.

Saigon

Thurs, Oct 16, 1969

. . . Today I more or less settled on my leave plans. At least, I have applied for Philippine and Australian visas and gotten some dope on the flight schedules. Tentatively, I will go to the Philippines on Nov 29 and come back Dec 8. Pan Am has 2 flights a week in each direction—RT fare $167.00. I will apply for R&R to Australia the end of Jan

or the 1st of February. I'll be getting more dope and details later and will keep you advised. Pan Am will make hotel reservations for me in the P. I. [Philippine Islands] if I go when scheduled. I would be in the P. I. on John's birthday. Coincidence. Yes?

* * *

Saigon

Sat, Oct 25, 1969

. . . I received your letter of 20 October today. I think I have written you that I have made my reservations for the Philippines. One of the reasons I want to go is because I have heard it talked about all my life. I guess in a way it is a "sentimental journey," even though I have no personal remembrance of it. I am sure Daddy has a lot of questions about my plans, but I really don't have many and we'll have to make them as I go along. I have the airline reservations to and from and have requested hotel reservations for when I arrive. I sort of plan three or four days in Manilla and then the Baguio. I think I'll try to arrange to be driven to B. so as to see the countryside.

* * *

Manila, Philippines

Fri, Nov 28, 1969

Well, here I am in Manila. Getting off in Saigon was rather hectic—not really, I guess, but just a lot of waiting in line for immigration, customs, money exchange, etc. and that airport is so crowded, run-down and dirty. Anyway, I did get a ride to the airport and was early so had time for all the line waiting.

Once on the plane, I was in the lap of luxury. After all my junketing around in Vietnam, I had almost forgotten what a commercial jet looks like. The plane was going clear on to San Francisco and Los Angeles via Guam and Honolulu. It was not fully loaded, but full enough. They served a very good lunch and I had a glass of sherry first. The flight to Manila was only 2 hrs and 10 minutes. Weather was good at Manila airport, I went through the formalities very easily. A representative from the hotel met me at the airport. He had my name and was looking for me. He put me into a car from the hotel. I hadn't changed any money so didn't pay for it, but it will probably show up on my bill.

This hotel, I find, has recently changed its name to the Savoy. I think it means that it is no longer under the Sheraton umbrella. Anyway, I have had a lovely "studio" room on the 7th floor. With big bath (yes, a tub) and all the nice little touches. I got here about 2:30 and have stayed here enjoying it. The room has a balcony and looks right out over Manila Bay.

I have been on the phone lining up a few things. I called Kay Gilbride, the ARC gal at Sangley Point and she couldn't have been nicer or more helpful. She suggested I call USO [United Service Organizations] about tours as they are just as good and cheaper than the commercial tours. She also gave me a lot of other hints, including info that she can arrange a car for me through Special Services to drive me to Baguio, for $1.00 an hour—it's about 6-8 hours by car. I think I'll contact her again about that when I get my overall plans laid out. I am now trying to call the USO to see about taking a city tour in the AM. It is always a good way to get the lay of the land in a strange city.

The weather here is very pleasant, low 80s I would

judge, and there is a nice breeze off the water. The room is air conditioned but it was almost too cold, so I have opened the door onto the balcony.

In a little while I'm going to take a long, hot tub bath. Then we'll have an early dinner and call it a day. It is a nice feeling not to have to push oneself or do anything I don't want to.

On first impression, Manila is very much an American city. I am sure you wouldn't recognize it, but it looks clean and prosperous. Such a contrast to Saigon and of course the signs are mostly in English and everyone I have come in contact with speaks English.

Well, I guess that will do for the first installment. I'll mail it when I go to dinner.

Written on the back in Grace Ingles's writing: *Martha. This made me so happy. Save this and other letters I'll send on about her trip. All is well here. Love, Mother.*

* * *

Manila
Sat, Nov 29, 1969
I've managed to have a rather full day, but not too busy.

I got up about 7:15 and had breakfast in my room—on the balcony, actually. At 8:30 I started calling about tours. Actually, I couldn't find one that had any other customers but finally arranged for a private car and driver through the USO for 20 Pesos for the morning (about $5). The car was a Japanese make—Toyota—but air conditioned and comfortable. The driver spoke good English—almost everyone here does—and he knew his way about. We went to places you would remember. The Intramuros, San Augustin Church, Fort Santiago, Santo Tomas, Malacanang Palace,

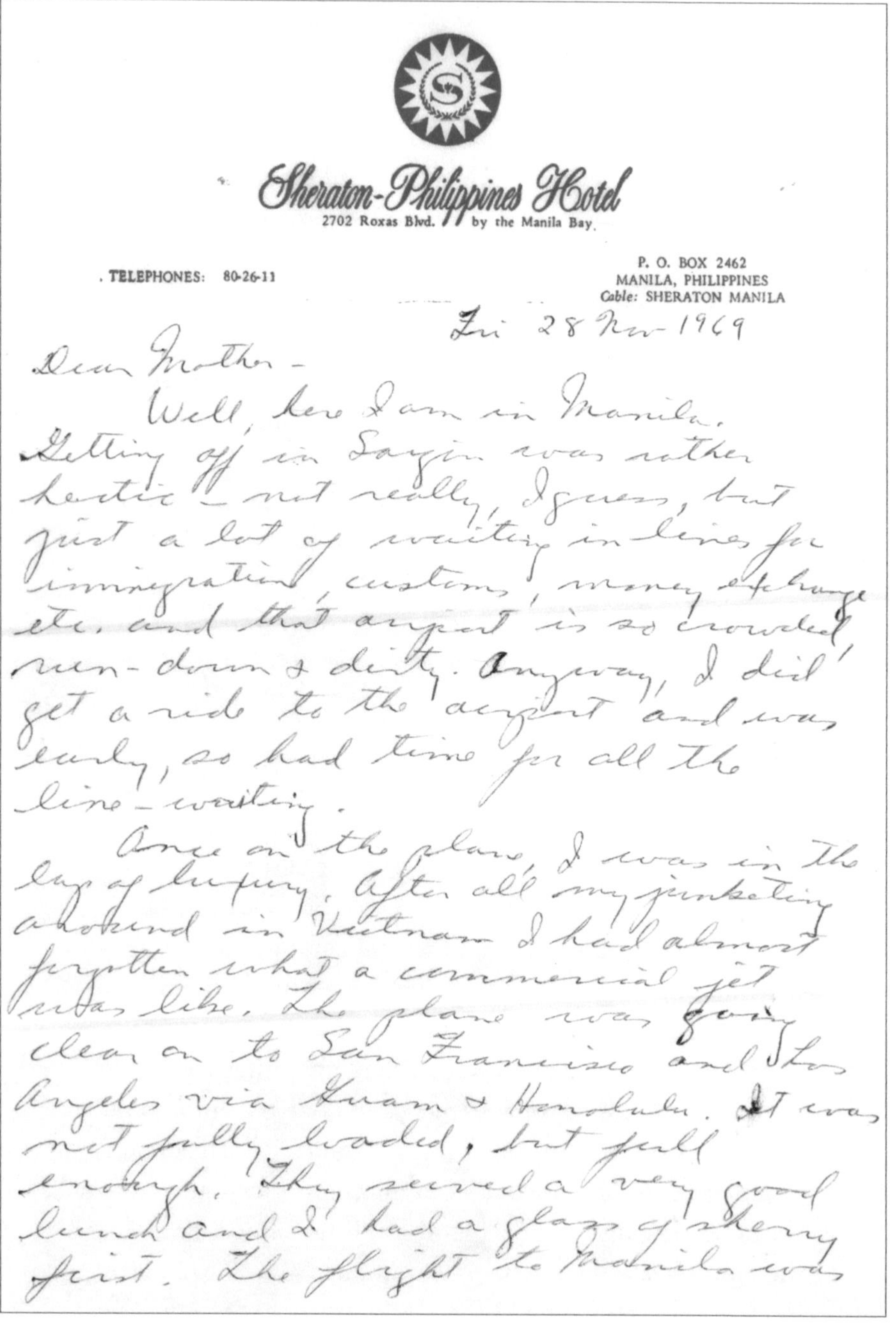

Sheraton-Philippines Hotel
2702 Roxas Blvd. by the Manila Bay.

TELEPHONES: 80-26-11

P. O. BOX 2462
MANILA, PHILIPPINES
Cable: SHERATON MANILA

Fri 28 Nov 1969

Dear Mother –

Well, here I am in Manila. Getting off in Saigon was rather hectic – not really, I guess, but just a lot of waiting in lines for immigration, customs, money exchange etc. and that airport is so crowded, run-down & dirty. Anyway, I did get a ride to the airport and was early, so had time for all the line-waiting.

Once on the plane, I was in the lap of luxury. After all my junketing around in Vietnam I had almost forgotten what a commercial jet was like. The plane was going clean on to San Francisco and Los Angeles via Guam & Honolulu. It was not fully loaded, but full enough. They served a very good lunch and I had a glass of sherry first. The flight to Manila was

LETTER ON STATIONARY FROM SHERATON-PHILIPPINES HOTEL, MANILA

etc. Between World War II and an earthquake in 1968, there isn't much left of the old part of the city. The cathedral was totally destroyed but has been re-built. I tried to picture the city as you remember it, but it is difficult. There's so much new building. We drove through the Escolta Shopping Center—just a busy downtown section. A whole new skyscraper city has been built at Makati.

I had him take me to Fort McKinley (it is now called Fort Bonifacio). The American War Memorial Cemetery is there and it is beautiful. I found Jimmy Rumbough's grave and took pictures of it and of the cemetery. You will have to let me know if I should write Polly about this visit and send her pictures. I noted that he died on Dec. 3, 1944—almost exactly 25 years ago. I particularly wanted to make the visit for Polly's sake but now I'm unsure that it would be right to tell her.

The post is now a Philippine Army post, but I didn't really see anything that would make me think it looks the way you remember it.

We got back at noon and I had him drop me at the Old Manila Hotel. On the outside, at least, I am sure that it looks the same and I took a picture of it for you. The USO is located there and I went in for information. I made arrangements to take an all day tour tomorrow by boat to Corregidor [Island]. I also picked up my ticket for the performances this afternoon of Philippine folk dancing by the Bayanihan Dancers at the Philippine Women's University.

I had lunch at the Manila Hotel and then came back to my room and took a nap. At 4:15 I took a cab to the university for the folk dancing. It was very colorful and gay and I was glad to see it.

I have had my dinner in a Chinese restaurant here in the hotel and here I am.

There are about 5 restaurants here in the hotel. Last

night I went to the Grill Room. Last night I went down to the bar for a drink before dinner but that was pretty grim when one is alone. So tonight I ordered a drink in my room before I went down to dinner. I didn't bring a bottle with me because of the weight of carrying it.

Mon when I can talk to Kay Gilbride again (the ARC Field Director at Sangley Point) I am going to come to grips with making plans to go to Baguio if she can get me a car at the military rate. The driver I had today quoted me a price of 350 pesos—almost $90.00—which is ridiculous. I can fly there round trip for 55 pesos—about $16.00.

I have a tentative arrangement with the USO for a trip on Monday to Tagaytay. This is where Taal Lake and the volcanoes are. That is 20 pesos if another person goes. I would have to pay 40 pesos if I go alone, but I might do it.

I haven't gotten into any shopping. The one thing I want to get is one of or two cotton dresses with the lovely embroidery on it. The driver took me to a shop today, but I know from experience that one doesn't pay at the shops the tourist guides take you to. I have the name of a shop— well recommended—which gives a military discount. I'll probably go there Tuesday if I go to Baguio. I'll probably go Wednesday and come back Friday or Saturday.

So you can see I'm keeping busy and trying to see what I can see.

I have a good bed and a nice room and slept well. I am really enjoying the luxury of comfortable living.

Well, I guess this finishes chapter two. I have to be at the Army-Navy Club at 7:30 in the morning for the tour to Corregidor. I imagine the Army-Navy Club is one of your old haunts.

* * *

Manila

Sun, Nov 30, 1969

Well, this has been a long day. I had my breakfast at 6:15 and was at the Army-Navy Club at 7:30. Actually, I just stuck my nose in there to ask directions to the boat landing. The club looked very elegant and well kept. I am not sure if it's still a US bastion—probably not.

The boat landing was just beyond it and the boat was a good size one and quite well equipped with comfortable vinyl covered benches and tables on a covered deck. Thank goodness it was comfortable because it turned out to be a 12 hour trip. I hadn't understood this and didn't take anything to read. It was a nice day, weatherwise—some overcast but sunny part of the time. The water was smooth. We left at 8:00 and after three hours reached Limbones—across the Bay from Corregidor. Another thing I didn't know in advance was that we stopped for three hours for swimming on a lovely beach. I didn't go ashore because I had no beach clothes. The method of getting ashore was on a raft towed by a motorboat.

They served a buffet lunch on board. Not very good. After lunch, I lay down on one of the benches and slept a little. I was the only passenger who stayed aboard. We left there at 2 and went to Corregidor about 45 minutes away. There they had several small buses which took us on an hour and a half tour of the islands. Of course, everything of the old post and the fortifications are destroyed and in ruins. I could imagine how it once must have been well and solidly built and real old army. The big green batteries etc. made me think of Fort Hancock and the Cocheris although I don't know that they were ever actually stationed at Corregidor. All the defenses planned for a sea attack and no good at all against the air.

At "Topside" there is a new and elaborate Pacific

War Memorial not just in honor of Corregidor and the Philippines, but of the Total War in the Pacific. It was built by the US and only finished about 2 years ago. It cost a lot of money and I wonder how many will ever see it. Corregidor is hardly what one would consider accessible even to Manila.

We left there at 5:00 and finally got back to Manila at 8:00. They didn't serve another meal. But I had some beer and some other people shared some cheese and crackers with me. A lot of people on board who knew the [undecipherable] had brought great hampers of food. There were a fair number of Americans, but mostly Filipinos. I would judge there were about 100 altogether.

Well, I had a day out in the fresh air and there was lovely scenery to look at, but I must admit I was lonesome and bored a good bit of the time, but I'm glad I went and saw Corregidor. We did not go to the Bataan Peninsula but of course could see it a good part of the day—all day, I guess.

I didn't want to dress and go out again when I finally got back to the hotel, so ordered some supper in my room. Now I've had a bath and washed clothes and here I am.

Tomorrow I will check with USO on the Tagaytay tour and will also see what I can do re: plans for Baguio. Now I am for bed and should sleep after all that fresh air.

* * *

Manila

Mon, Dec 1, 1969

Today turned out to be a holiday—National Heroes Day—so maybe John is one of their national heroes. Anyway, I gave him some special thoughts.

Actually, what it meant to me is that I wasn't able to finalize any of my plans for going to Baguio—car, hotel or air flight back. Everything seemed to be closed. However, I have feelers out. Kay Gilbride will call me tomorrow as to yea or nay on the car, the hotel tour desk will see about a hotel reservation, and the airline ticket office should be open.

I had made arrangements with USO for a tour of Tagaytay today. There was a little mixed up about the time on that, but finally a car and a driver picked me up at 11:30. It was about an hour's drive, which I thoroughly enjoyed—seeing some of the countryside—rice fields, coconut plantations with bananas, papayas and pineapples growing under them, carabao, and some nipa huts. Not a lot of the latter two as it is pretty civilized, but enough to get a few pictures to remind you of the Philippines you knew when you see them.

At Tagaytay was a lodge with a circular dining room overlooking Lake Taal and the Taal Volcano. The latter has been erupting recently and was belching smoke and you could hear the rumblings. It was a lovely view and we were about 2500 feet above sea level. They served a buffet lunch which was adequate. I must say that I have really had no good food here. I've eaten at three different restaurants here in the hotel and none were very good. There are undoubtedly better restaurants in the city, but I don't dare venture out at night.

On the way back, we stopped in Las Pinas to see the famous bamboo organ in the church there. You may have seen it in your day as it is just outside of Manila.

It was a pretty day, although a bit hazy and I really enjoyed the drive in a nice air conditioned car. The guide was pleasant and since I was alone, stopped whenever I wanted to take a picture.

I learned from him that about three blocks from my hotel is the US Embassy compound with PX and APO.

I walked over there when I got back—mainly wanted to buy some film—but everything was closed because of the holiday. I did get a Stars and Stripes and shall go again tomorrow. Will mail this letter there as it will be cheaper and maybe faster. I have mailed a letter every day so far, so hope you have been getting them.

I have no particular plans for tomorrow. I'll have to work on my plans for Baguio, and I guess I should do some shopping. I also will get my hair done if it needs it.

I may try another hotel when I get back. Kay suggested the Hotel Filippinas, which is closer to town and less expensive. I'll look it over tomorrow. This hotel is actually in Pasay and it is a 10 minute cab ride into town. Taxis are about the only thing that is cheap here. It only costs about $0.50 to go downtown.

I don't think I have mentioned that there are two shells of Japanese submarines left on the beach near the hotel. I guess they left them there as sort of a reminder.

I enclose a couple of clippings from the local paper that I thought might interest Daddy. They have just had an election here—reelected President Marcos, so mostly the papers are full of that.

Well, I can't think about anything else tonight. I am fine, am getting rest, and enjoying being comfortable, but I am getting a bit tired of my own company. Meals are the worst, but I eat early to get it over with. In my room I read. I brought several books with me—which is what I do anyway in my spare time.

PS I have a TV but the offerings are years old US shows.

* * *

Manila
Tues, Dec 2, 1969

I am going down shortly to get my hair done, but will write this now so I can mail it then.

This has been a rather frustrating day, battling against Philippine inefficiency, but I think I have things straightened out for now.

I called Kay Gilbride this AM and she had done her part. She had arranged for and paid for a car to drive me to Baguio tomorrow. $15—and I have mailed her a check. The car is to pick me up at 6:00 AM. She said the early departure was necessary to get ahead of the traffic. She estimated an 8 hour drive.

I tried to contact the hotel travel desk to see if the girl had confirmed my hotel reservation, only to find that for some reason she didn't come to work today. So I got on the phone myself and do have a room at the Pines Hotel Baguio. Then I contacted the Philippine Airline office here in the hotel—which she was also supposed to do. I found that the only reservation I could get back to Manila on Fri was a plane leaving Beguile at 7:00 AM and nothing on Sat, so my time up there will be pretty short, but it was the best I could do.

I walked over to the Embassy Compound and did mail a letter to you, but the PX had no film. All this took a couple of hours.

I then took a taxi to Lesoro's, the shop recommended to me by several people. I got a little carried away there, I guess, but I ordered 5 dresses. They are all dripped dry cotton with embroidery and are being made to my measurements in different styles. I got them in blue, pink, grey, aqua, and yellow. Since they only cost $10 apiece, I haven't really spent a lot of money. The embroidery is the same color as the dress—is not all over but is different designs.

You'll probably have visions of something garish and awful, but they are not. I also got one for Joan at her request. They would have been ready this afternoon, but I told them I would pick them up on Friday. If they turn out at all well I'll have a nice summer wardrobe for the rest of my time overseas and next summer.

They had beautiful sports shirts, but remembering how the ones I got before for Daddy never really fit, I didn't get him one.

I looked at other things they had—wood carvings, mother of pearl stuff, etc. but didn't find anything I wanted. I bought some film—quite expensive—and had my glasses adjusted at the optical shop. Then I went to the Hotel Filippinas to have lunch and look it over. I wasn't too impressed, so I have decided to come back here for the rest of my stay. I really don't know what I'll do those last three days, as I have about done all the things that interest me. But I'll fill the time somehow. At least I am getting a rest.

It was pretty hot and humid today when I was out, but my room is very comfortable. I'm getting a lot of mileage out of the lovely robe Jean sent.

I'll mail you a letter or two from Baguio, but they will probably take a long time to go out.

* * *

Baguio City, Philippines
Wed, Dec 3, 1969

Well, here I am at Baguio. I got up at 5:00 and ate a roll I had brought up from the dining room last night as it was too early for room service. I checked out of the hotel and the driver was waiting for me with an air conditioned 1969 Ambassador. His name was Oscar and he was a good driver. Also he didn't talk except to answer my questions.

We stopped at 7:00 at a place Kay had told me about and I had a coffee and a roll.

The drive took less time than had been predicted—5 hours. It was very slow going through many of the villages. One cannot really call it "back country" as things are generally very civilized. The last part, of course, was up the mountain road. Although all the roads are paved, many are in pretty poor condition, especially the last part. I couldn't help but think what the driver must have been like, what the drive must have been like when you used to make it, as I doubt there was even a pretense of paved roads then.

It has been a pretty day and I really enjoyed the drive.

I am a bit disappointed in my room, but it is OK. It is small, on the back and doesn't have much of a view. The air is fresh and I have the window open. I have a shower but no tub.

Lunch will be served at 12:00 and I'll be ready. I started this while waiting. I'll add more later.

Now I am waiting until it is time to go to dinner. The lunch was very good, one of the best meals I have had. I had potato soup and broiled prawns.

After lunch I took a walk, although one doesn't walk far in a mountain town—too much up and down. Then I read for a while in the lobby. There isn't a comfortable chair in my room. I had a good nap and a bath and here I am.

I have arranged tomorrow for a car and driver to show me the sights. I don't know just what they are, but presume the driver will. I am told there is a village near here where the Igorots [indigenous people] do the wood carving. Also there is a weaving school and a silver school. I think I'll have him take me to Camp John Hay which is where I presume you used to stay. It is a military recreation area, but they are having some sort of conclave there so I can't get in.

The mountains are lovely and it is a pleasure to just look at them.

Guess I may as well mail this when I go down to eat, even though it may be slow getting on its way.

* * *

Baguio City, Philippines
Thurs, Dec 4, 1969

I had my brief touch with glamour today when I had a very close up view of Mrs. Ymelda [*sic*] Marcos, First Lady of the Philippines. I never did find out why she was in Baguio today, but as I was coming out of the dining room, she and her party were walking through the lobby. She was really beautiful, quite tall—lovely skin. She was dressed in bright red gold trimmed pantsuit. Several of the ladies in her party were also in pantsuits, so this apparently was the uniform of the day. They just had an election here, and President Marcos was the first man to be reelected president of the Philippines.

I had arranged for a car this morning and spent the morning touring Baguio. We visited the Easter weaving school, founded by the Anglican missionaries; the St. Louis Silver School where they train boys to do silver filigree work; a wood carving place and drove all over the town and surrounding countryside. We drove through Camp John Hay and it was really beautiful. They have a gorgeous golf course there—all up and downhill. I am sure this is where you used to come although I imagine it was more primitive in your day.

The scenery, of course, everywhere, is beautiful and I enjoy the clear mountain air. I didn't buy anything, much to the disappointment of my driver. I am not a buyer as

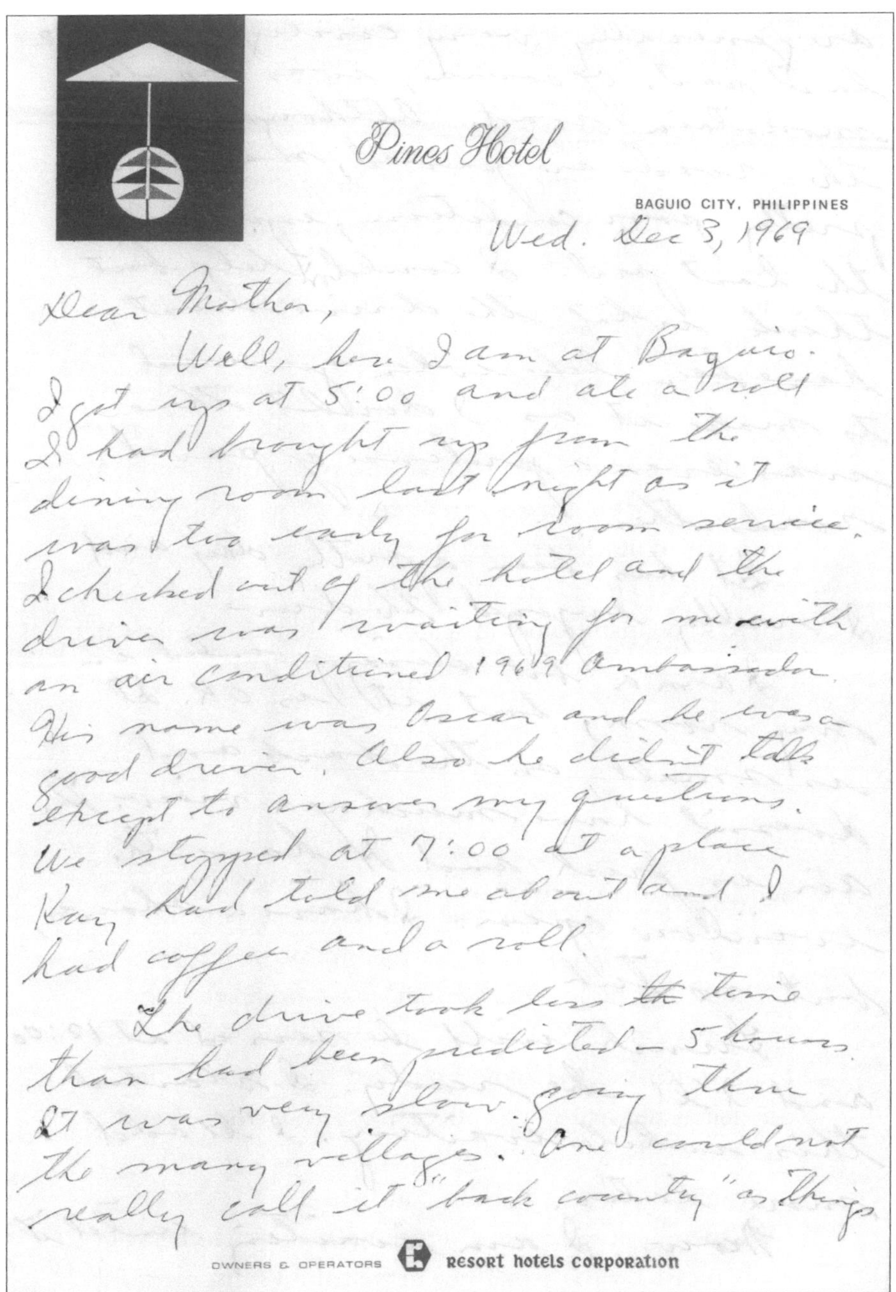

LETTER ON STATIONARY FROM PINES HOTEL, BAGUIO

you know, and I didn't see anything I wanted for me or anyone else.

Anyway, one morning exhausted the sights pretty well. I spent the afternoon reading and sleeping. Whatever else, I am certainly getting a good rest out of this trip. I must admit that time hangs pretty heavy, and, as much as I dislike going back to Vietnam, I won't be sorry to have something to do again.

I saw in the paper that the movie "True Grit" is playing in Manila, so I think I will go see it over the weekend.

I have to be up early in the morning as my plane leaves at 7:00. It is ironic that with all the time in the world, I have had to get up so early so often to get transportation.

I mailed one letter here this morning, but will mail this in Manila as I'm sure it will go out faster. I'll be glad when I have some mail from you again. Well, I guess that does it for today.

* * *

Manila

Fri, Dec 5, 1969

Well, I'm back in Manila—in fact, back in the very same room. I had an early start as my plane left Baguio at 7:00. The flight was uneventful—a prop jet plane—and took about 45 minutes. They served us breakfast en route which was welcome. I checked back into the hotel, unpacked and had some coffee. I got a cab, stopped at the APO to mail a letter to you and at the shoe repair to leave my camera case that had come unstitched.

I then went to Lesoro's to pick up my new clothes. I'm really pleased with them. They fit well and I think are most attractive. I wish you could see them. You will eventually, of course. But by then they will have been worn and washed.

In fact, I wore one down to dinner tonight.

I went to the Manila Hilton for lunch. Sort of a waste of money, but something different to do this afternoon. I took a nap, went back to get my camera case and then had dinner in the Japanese restaurant in this hotel. I've now eaten in all the hotel's restaurants except the elegant one cum nightclub. None are too great, although I did enjoy the tempura I had tonight.

So here I am, about ready for bed. I still have it in mind to see "True Grit" tomorrow and will get my hair done. Beyond that, I have no plans.

Well, at least tomorrow I won't have to set an alarm clock. Can't think of anything else to write.

* * *

Manila

Sat, Dec 6, 1969

Well, have managed to fill up another day. I got up in a leisurely fashion and found that the first showing of "True Grit" was at 11:15. So I hied me thither by cab, stopping to mail letter to you. I enjoyed the picture. It followed the book exactly which was good, as it really couldn't have improved on it.

I got back to the hotel at 2:00 and had lunch. At 4:00 I had my hair done. Now I've had my dinner and here I am.

I really haven't a clue as to what I'll do tomorrow. There is an Episcopal Church, but it is way out in suburb called Forbes Park near Ft McKinley. I could take a taxi out but don't know how I would get back as it isn't a neighborhood where taxis would be cruising. So I'll have to see how adventuresome I feel or how strongly I have faith that some Christian soul would bring me back into town. Episcopalians are really not noted for their friendliness, you know.

In Martha's Christmas box were two books which I brought along. I have been doggedly plowing through "The Cloister and the Hearth" by Charles Reed. At least it is long.

I guess my letters have sounded sort of bleak and bored. Well, this hasn't been the most exciting trip I've ever taken, but I've had a lot of rest and a change and a taste of most comfortable living conditions. So, I don't feel that the time and money has been wasted. As much as I dislike Vietnam, I really won't be sorry to get back to where I have work to do. So, I guess this is a plus.

* * *

Saigon
Mon, Dec 8, 1969

Well, I am back in good old "Hondaville." The best part about getting back was to get your mail. Joan had brought home and left in my room letters written through 30 Nov. and she says there is more at the office which she will bring this evening. Before I launch into answering letters, however, I'll fill you in with the end of my trip.

I had a completely feckless day yesterday. Had lunch in my room, but did get dressed and go down for dinner. I read, slept and watched some TV. Not very exciting, but relaxing and undemanding.

This AM I was up early, had breakfast in my room, and was at the airport at 7:15. The trip was uneventful—same nice jet plane, a snack and good service. As usual getting from the airport to the Rex was the most trying part. The office did send a car, but I had to wait about an hour for it and it was hot. I realized that I was only really hot once or twice the whole time I was in the Philippines. Everyplace

I went was air conditioned—Baguio naturally so—and the car trips were in air conditioned cars.

Well anyway, I finally got to the Rex about 12:15 and Praise the Lord, my room air conditioner is working. I had forgotten how noisy it is, but as long as it works, I don't care.

* * *

Responding to questions Grace had written after receiving Mary's letters from the Philippines, Mary provided more details about her trip.

Saigon
Wed, Dec 10, 1969

. . . I received your letter of 5 December today and was glad the "in between" letters from P. I. had caught up to you. Think I'll take time now to "comment on your comments" re: P. I. while it is still fairly fresh in my mind.

You said you wondered how I knew Jimmy R. was in the cemetery at Fort McKinley. I didn't know for sure, but I did know he was buried overseas, so I figured this is where it had to be. Whether Polly ever knows it or not, I felt I wanted to make the visit on her behalf. Did I write you that on one wall of the Chapel, in mosaic, is a slightly abbreviated form of the Collect for Peace from Morning prayer, and in the other that lovely prayer (p. 594) "O Lord support us all the day long, etc." I have a brochure about the place for Polly if you tell me to send it.

I'm sure I told you that Corregidor is all gone to ruins, but with my knowledge of Army posts it was not difficult to visualize how it used to be. An era of Army life that is no more, but one I, at least, had enough contact with to feel nostalgic about. I always have a feeling of homecoming when I go onto a post.

Yes, they did the dance with the bamboo poles. It was,

overall, a very gay and colorful performance. You had mentioned Peilar Lim, but I really didn't feel that I wanted to go up that lane and I realized you didn't expect me to.

I could have gotten you some more monogrammed pillowcases if you had wanted them. I suppose I should have gotten some table linens for myself. I really don't have any, but I just couldn't seem to get myself steamed up about that. You know how hard it is for me to shop for anything and the dresses were the only thing I could get myself worked up to do. I'm glad I did as I am really happy with them.

About Lake Taal and the volcano. My vantage point was a mountain top overlooking it. A far cry from the primitive conditions you describe from your visit. It has erupted periodically through the years, so the shape and configuration etc. has undoubtedly greatly changed. In fact, before I left there were several articles in the paper that another major eruption was expected momentarily and they were starting to evacuate people in the immediate area.

I remembered you, your passion for mango, but this wasn't the season. I saw many mango trees laden with unripe fruit. The prawns were excellent, as was the "native" lobster (lobster tails, actually) which I had a couple of times. I also had some lapu lapu (fish) one night, a rather ordinary whitefish I found. I also tried "adobo" supposedly a typical Philippine dish. Sort of a stew of pork and chicken over rice. Both pork and chicken were stringy and tough. Not a success.

I really didn't see any geckos, but they abound in Vietnam—there is always at least one in my room—so I probably wouldn't have noticed them.

Well, I guess that covers the P. I. until I get some more comments from you in next letters.

* * *

With the Philippines trip behind her, Mary began to focus on Australia.

Saigon
Fri, Dec 26, 1969

. . . I got confirmation today of my R&R in Australia for 5 Feb. We get six nights away, so I shall be back 11 Feb. We get free transportation on R&R which is a big savings. That is why I wanted to save my R&R for this trip. Also the time away is not charged to our annual leave.

* * *

Saigon
Sun, Jan 25, 1970

. . . I'm beginning to get a bit excited about Australia—thanks in part to the things Audrey sent and also to have it getting closer. Between now and then, we are going to be awfully busy with staff coming and going. For some reason, there is an unusually heavy turnover in February. Anyway. It is going to mean entertaining people for dinner almost every night. That may interfere with my letter writing, but I will do my best.

* * *

Sydney, Australia
Fri, Feb 6, 1970

Well, it proved to be quite an undertaking getting here, but I made it, and am more than comfortable in this lovely hotel.

The Vietnamese holiday of Tet started yesterday, which meant that all the Vietnamese were off. To get transportation to Tan Son Nhut I had to go over at 4:00, although I didn't need to check in until 6:30. They do try to give the women special treatment, but the facilities are pretty lacking. They have a small lounge which is air conditioned, and they process the women and Cols there, so we don't have to wait in lines with the G.I.s. There were 2 older, sort of burnt out women—civilian employees—and a young nurse and myself. The nurse, Dottie Blick and I sort of stuck together and ignored the other two.

I had a lousy meal at the mess at 5:00 and just sat until they finally put us on the bus for the plane at 5:00 [*sic*]. The plane was a nice big DC-9 operated by World Airlines, and was, of course, fully loaded. I got myself an aisle seat, my preference for long haul. We finally took off at 10:00. It was an 8 hour, nonstop flight. They fed us dinner about midnight and breakfast at 5:00 AM. I slept some in short snatches, but it was a long night.

We arrived at 8:00 AM Sydney time (2 hours ahead of Saigon time). The R&R people met us and really whisked us through customs formalities. The men were put on buses, but they had a station wagon for the four women.

They took us to the R&R Center where we had to wait about an hour for our briefing, but still it was quite well organized. They arranged our hotel reservations, changed our money, etc. We finally got to the hotel by taxi at 11.

I have a lovely room—twin beds with lovely "circular" bathroom and tub (!) and nice view of the so-called Garden Court.

By the time I got here, I had been in the same clothes for 30 hours and was just pooped. I took a lovely hot bath, washed my underwear, sent my uniform out to be laundered, and ordered a sandwich and iced tea from room service. I called the beauty parlor and made an appointment

for 3:30. Then I went to bed and slept for 2 ½ hours.

After getting my hair done I really felt clean from top to bottom. My little nurse friend called me at 5:00 and I invited her up for a drink. I got smart this trip and brought some bourbon with me. We then went down to an elegant dining room and had a wonderful dinner—broiled lobster tail, fresh vegetables and salad.

So, here I am writing you and will head to bed very shortly. Tomorrow I will tackle finding out about tours etc. But today I just had to get cleaned up and rested.

This hotel is really elegant—the biggest, newest and best in Sydney. We get a special R&R rate so I am only paying $13.50 a day. Dinner only came to a little over $7.00. Actually that is Australian dollars and $1.00 Australian equals about $0.87 US, so it is really more. Anyway, it is close enough to make figuring the money easy.

This was a lovely day weatherwise—temperatures in the high 70s and quite windy but clear. The hotel is centrally air conditioned and the beauty shop and dining room were too cold. I have turned the thermostat down in my room so I'm just right.

* * *

Sydney
Sat, Feb 7, 1970

I've had a fairly full day. The weather was delightful, sunny in the high 70s. I had breakfast in my room and then walked about three blocks to the tourist Bureau where I bought a ticket for a morning bus tour. It was very little of the city itself, but mostly into the suburbs and along the beaches. With a little concentration one can understand the language and the guide was very pleasant. I enjoyed seeing how the people live. Much attention to yards and gardens, and lovely flowers everywhere. Australia is famous for its beaches, and they were quite something. The harbor is magnificent and we saw it from many angles and views.

We got back about 12:30 and had lunch in the hotel coffee shop. The concierge, at my request, got me a seat for a 5:00 PM performance of a show called "Come Laughing Home" which someone had recommended.

I took a nap and a bath and then cabbed to the theater. It was in a suburb and a very unpretentious place—actually "little theatre" almost. It was a "theater in the round," very small. The performance was adequate; the actors did well but the show about a lower class British family was only mildly entertaining.

Getting a cab back was a problem, but on the advice of a fellow theater goer, I walked about 4 blocks to a suburb railroad station and eventually got a cab from there. After a drink in my room, I again went to the coffee shop for some supper and here I am.

There is an elegant "ball" going on in the hotel. People in tuxedos and long dresses—very glamorous.

Actually, though, I have never seen such short skirts as are prevalent here. Maybe I have been away from the US too long, but this is really unbelievable. I feel tacky and old fashioned not that I could ever go to the lengths—or lack thereof that—one sees here.

Tomorrow I plan to go to church in the morning. Thru the R&R center I have made a booking for an afternoon boat tour of the harbor. Sunday in Sydney is pretty dead—nothing is open or moving, but the above plans should fill up the day all right. I hope the weather holds good.

This is a comfortable place to be. One feels at home, sort of. As always when I travel alone, I wish I had someone to talk to and share with.

I haven't seen my little nurse friend today. She had made contact with "friend of friends" and was invited out today. Another nurse from Vietnam is joining her tomorrow so she will be taken care of well.

I'm having a good rest so far and enjoying Australia.

* * *

Sydney
Sun, Feb 8, 1970

Well, the weather turned sour on me today, so I couldn't carry out the plans I had made.

I did go to church this morning at Saint Andrews Cathedral. Today was the 18th anniversary of the Queen's Accension to the throne and they had a special service. I didn't know it, of course, but there is even a special service in the prayer book to be used on the anniversary of the reigning monarch's accension. Anyway, it was a lovely service with special music, including the philharmonic orchestra. I was very glad I went.

The Cathedral itself was not much, sort of gloomy, made of native sandstone.

It wasn't raining when I went, but it was when I came out. I had planned on taking a harbor cruise this afternoon, but the weather was against it. Sydney on Sunday is pretty dead even. Most of the movie theaters are closed. I found that one was open showing "Sweet Charity" with Shirley MacLaine. I went but left at intermission as I didn't care for it.

This evening I had a good dinner at the only one of the 6 hotel restaurants which is open on Sunday.

Tomorrow I have a tour in mind if the weather is decent. I heard the forecast on TV tonight and it sounds OK. There's a TV in my room and tonight I saw an old

Carol Burnett show with Bing Crosby and Ella Fitzgerald as guests. I hope the weather turns for the better, as the rain is a real hardship.

* * *

Sydney
Mon, Feb 9, 1970

I'll write this before dinner as I am going to the theater tonight. I have a ticket for "Fiddler on the Roof," which, believe it or not, I have never seen.

I have had a very nice day. The weather was beautiful—sunny, about 80° and a nice breeze. I went on a cruise of Sydney Harbor under the auspices of the R&R Center. It was a lovely boat—54 feet long and there were only about 15 people on the trip. This is a fabulous harbor—one of the finest landlocked harbors in the world, I'm sure. Many coves and bays etc. We left at 10:30 and cruised about, stopping about 30 minutes at one place for those who wanted to swim. Then we docked at an island where we had a wonderful lunch of broiled steaks, baked potato salad and watermelon. They carried the food along in the boat and the crew cooked it. They even had a young man along who played the guitar and sang for us.

After lunch, we did some more cruising and got back at 3:30. The price of the day, including lunch was $10.00 which was well worth it. They also serve drinks of all kinds, but no one had too much. I enjoyed myself, but was particularly happy for the young G.I.s along to have such a pleasant healthy day out in the air and the sun.

Before I went, I arranged for my theater seat through the hotel. I also went to an optician and got my glasses adjusted. I think they are better.

Tomorrow, I plan to go on another R&R trip, which is out into the country and includes a visit to a koala bear and kangaroo sanctuary. Judging from today's outing, it will be well organized and pleasant.

I am going down shortly for an early dinner. If the weather stays good my last two days here should be fine.

* * *

Sydney
Tues, Feb 10, 1970

I think I wrote you last night before dinner. Anyway, I very much enjoyed "Fiddler on the Roof." Have you ever seen it? It was a very good musical score and I thought the company did very well.

I've had another full day out in the open air. In fact, as a result of today and yesterday, I have a very sunburned face. Today was sold as a "Bush Barbque" by the R&R Center. We started out on a bus—about 40 of us—and after some sightseeing ended up in an open field where a man put on a demonstration of boomerang throwing. I bought authentic boomerangs to send to Johnny and Paul, but will have to wait until I get home to show them how. Not that I know how after only one demonstration.

We then went to a place [where] we boarded a boat for about 1½ hour trip up the Hawkesbury River. At our destination were some very pleasant Australian ladies who had a lovely lunch ready—steaks, etc. The same guitarist-singer as yesterday was along.

After lunch we boarded the boat for a ways where we rejoined our bus. We then went to a wildlife sanctuary where we could see and pet kangaroos and koala bears. Much picture taking of course. Finally, a bus ride back to the city, getting back at 6:00.

I was too done in to go out, so had dinner in my room.

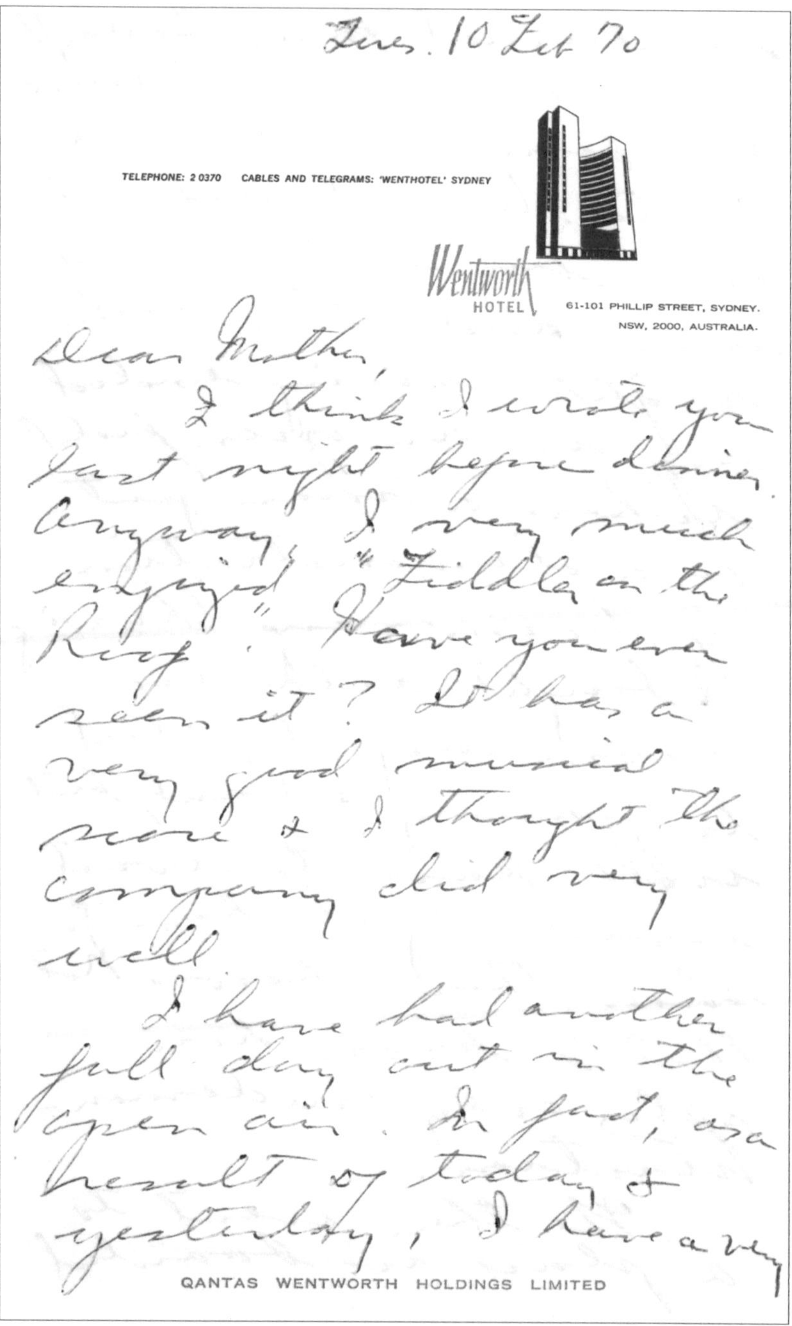

LETTER ON STATIONARY FROM WENTWORTH HOTEL, SYDNEY

These trips that I have taken advantage of the past two days are, of course, really planned for the serviccmen on R&R. But they are so nice—cute hostesses along, etc.—and the boys are well behaved and have such a good time. They serve all kinds of drinks on the boats but I have yet to see anyone over-indulge.

Tomorrow is my last day. I am about sight-seeing and tripped out. I think I will do a little shopping, get my hair done and maybe go to a show. I ordered koala bears (stuffed) for Betsy and Catharine today. They will be shipped from here, and probably take two months to get there.

Well, I guess this does it for tonight. Forgot to say that the weather was beautiful today—crystal clear and top temperature about 80. People here complain of the heat, but I don't.

* * *

Sydney
Thurs, Feb 12, 1970

As usual I'm ready well ahead of time, so will dash off a short letter. This is the day I leave and a bus is supposed to pick me up at 9:00.

Yesterday was a nice day weather wise. I felt I had had enough of tours, so I slept late and then made myself go shopping. I didn't see anything I wanted to buy, but did get a small gift for Daddy. The department stores are about on par with Kanns [a Washington, DC, department store] of 20 years ago. Crowded, poorly laid up and things sort of piled on counters. They do have several arcades of little shops, but not particularly nice ones.

I came back to the hotel coffee shop for lunch and then took a nap. I had my hair done at 3:00 and at 6:00 went down for a real nice dinner in the most elegant dining room.

One thing I looked for but didn't find were some more of those eyeglass tissues—"Sight Savers." I guess I'll have to ask Daddy to send me a couple of more packages.

I don't know exactly when we take off today, but we are due to arrive in Saigon at 5:50 Saigon time. Time here is 2 hours ahead of that. I am glad the flight is a daytime one, as you don't start out tired already and I can get a sleep tonight.

I have enjoyed being here even though there wasn't time to see more of Australia than Sydney. It was a nice thought that I only have 2½ more months to go.

I have read the paper every day, but it is very provincial. I couldn't find any world news so feel completely out of touch. I'll also be very glad to get back to some mail.

I'll write you tonight so you'll know that I'm back.

* * *

News from Home

Maybe because Mary was avoiding writing about her own life, the lives of the family back home took on more prominence in these final letters than during previous tours. Mary and Grace seemed to have a very active exchange about all of Mary's nieces and nephews. It was interesting for me to realize that, although I didn't really know much about Mary while she was away in Vietnam, she knew quite a bit about me, my brothers, and my cousins. I suspect that the details about the family were a way for her to escape for a few moments from her everyday stresses. And it was nice to see that some of the animosity that Mary demonstrated toward her sister-in-law, my mother, in earlier letters had softened. I have to think this reflects that my grandmother, Grace, had reversed her initial negative views toward my mother.

All the following excerpts were written from Saigon unless otherwise noted.

Undated

. . . I was particularly glad to know that Frank had given Daddy a clean bill of health and he was off the special medication. I know he will feel better generally because of that.

. . . I'm glad you gave Andy [Primrose] the go ahead to have your jacket relined. I wasn't aware it needed it, but it is undoubtedly time.

I'm relieved that you are liking Josie better and do pray she continues to work out. You need the help and maybe you can stop fencing with one another and work out a good relationship.

I'm sorry I let Audrey's birthday slip by. I guess it is tomorrow. My only excuse is that I really don't know what day it is out here.

I'd loved the editorial on Saint Christopher. Since our church here is Saint C's I think I'll give it to our minister. I know I wrote you yesterday about going to church, but did I say we used the Anglican prayer book? Seems he does that the third Sunday of each month.

* * *

Thurs, May 22, 1969

. . . I hope Daddy will see the Feyereisens at West Point. It was sweet of them to send you an invitation to young Paul's graduation. I am glad he made it and I know it wasn't easy for him.

How too bad that Marge Griffin's luncheon for Audrey coincided with your Garden Club luncheon! You don't get that many invitations to luncheons that you would enjoy and it was mean that you couldn't go to both.

* * * .

Mon, May 26, 1969

. . . Don't hesitate to send clippings you think I might be interested in. At best the Stars and Stripes is pretty sketchy, and I have trouble getting one so only see one every day or so. I try to catch the news on the radio, but all in all I am pretty out of touch with what is going on in the world.

You told me about going to Doctor McIntyre and I gathered you liked him, but you didn't say whether he changed your prescription or not and if it has helped. So, what happened?

I am glad Audrey's birthday party went well. You said she was wearing a wiglet. Did it cover all of her hair or just something added to the top? What color is it? I know you will enjoy your luncheon with her and her friends.

. . . I am always glad when you have your Garden Club outings. You always enjoy them and you need the outside contacts and stimulation.

I'm glad that Daddy has heard from the trust company regarding Helen's affairs. It has kept him stirred up and uneasy for two months. Actually, it is less than three months since Helen died, and I guess lawyers and trustees aren't geared to moving fast on anything.

* * *

Wed, May 28, 1969

. . . Catharine's letters to each of you were sweet. A bit effusive perhaps, but sincere. And you do both have such a lovely relationship with her.

* * *

Saigon
Thurs, May 29, 1969

. . . I'm so glad you had a nice visit with Johnny and Paul. They are sweet children.

. . . If Stephen won't live in the dorm, I wonder about the fraternity house. But maybe that is something seniors don't do either.

* * *

Sat, May 31, 1969

. . . Had a nice letter from Audrey sending some puzzles and a copy of a picture of me. I think I'll send it on to Martha, as you said you had one.

* * *

Thurs, Jun 12, 1969

. . . I am very pleased that Ted got the Legion of Merit. It was wonderful that Nene and the children could be there. Cornelia ran true to form, of course. Be sure to get Ted's address for me before he leaves Washington.

* * *

Tues, Jun 17, 1969

. . . I'm delighted that you are again telephone chairman for the Garden Club. It is a perfect job for you—one you can do and handle so efficiently and gracefully.

Am glad Betsy is OK. Kids are amazing—scare you to death, but bounce right back.

* * *

Sat, Jun 21, 1969

I had a darling letter from Paul which I will send you after I have answered it. He typed it and quite well too. He is such a love.

* * *

Tues, Jun 24, 1969

The visit of Catharine's houseguests seems to have gone very well and I know it pleased them both. I am so glad Martha went ahead with her trip to Ann Arbor, mainly because it gave her a good visit with John Robert. Wasn't he sweet to the girls, and Stephen too. They love Catharine good and are so good to her. I am sure her friends were thrilled with the attentions of two "college men."

* * *

Thurs, Jul 3, 1969

. . . I think the idea of a Garden Club tour to Williamsburg by bus sounds good. It is something you would both enjoy. And, as you say, you wouldn't have to tour every garden. I hope it works out.

I thought Martha's letter, which you sent, was real good. I'm so happy she's having a chance to have some "good close visits" with Stephen. She won't have him very much longer. For her to say, "I'm very, very fortunate in my children. I believe they, all three, really love me" is just wonderful.

. . . I am glad Daddy went to see Paul's team win the "pennant," even if Paul scarcely got in the game. As you say, John and Audrey really put out to give those children the support and love they need.

* * *

Tues, Jul 8, 1969

. . . I am always glad when you can spend a little time with John, Audrey and the children. As a matter of fact, you probably see them just about the right amount of time. The visits [are] always welcome and meaningful, and no feeling of overdoneness on either side.

I can sympathize with Betsy's hair problems. Being afflicted with straight fine hair, I know the hopelessness of it all.

* * *

Mon, Jul 14, 1969

. . . I'm glad Martha's weekend at the lake seems to have gone well. It sounds like a nice place and I envy them the cool weather, need for fireplaces, etc.

Wasn't Stephen wonderful to just take off and go up to see Catharine when he read her letter? Catharine is so fortunate in her brothers and they are so good to her. She certainly will miss Stephen as he is the one she turns to whenever she has a problem. I don't imagine it hurt Catharine any with her "cool" cabin mates to have such a good looking brother show up on the scene.

* * *

Fri, Jul 18, 1969

. . . I'm always glad when Martha has a chance to see John Robert. Although Catharine has been a bit upset this summer, I think Martha sounds pretty good again, better than she did a few weeks ago. I do think these last few weeks with Stephen will always mean a lot to her. I haven't

THE INGLES CHILDREN, BETSY, JOHNNY, AND PAUL, IN 1969

yet gotten the letter about Stephen's plans, but will be interested. He acts pretty wild, but basically he is a sensible and sensitive boy. He'll do all right.

. . . Daddy's plan to take John and the boys to the Army-AF game sounds good. All will enjoy it. I hope he writes The Thayer [Hotel] now for a reservation as they are bound to be jammed that particular weekend.

* * *

Sat, Jul 25, 1969

. . . I had read in the paper that PEPCO was having a power crisis due to the heat wave, and I prayed you wouldn't have to do without your air conditioning. Your last card said it had rained, so I hope the crisis is over.

* * *

Mon, Jul 28, 1969

. . . I'm delighted that your luncheon with Audrey, Nene and Cecil went so well. Not that I doubted it would.

* * *

Vung Tau
Sat, Aug 2, 1969

. . . I am enclosing a check for Paul's birthday, which I will appreciate you giving to Audrey. I should have gotten it off sooner. It will probably be late now and I will wait to mail this until I get back to Saigon.

* * *

Sun, Aug 3, 1969

. . . I had to ask Betty what "decoupage" is, and am still not sure I understand it. Anyway, it does sound like something that would be right up Catharine's alley.

When I hear that Stephen has finally graduated, I will send him a graduation present. He hasn't seemed to put much time in on this last course but I imagine he passed.

. . . Your news about Aunt Florence is so sad. There is some comfort in knowing that they have good nurses etc. I know how hard it is for you to write to her and how it breaks your heart to know the condition she is in.

. . . I am very pleased with Daddy's birthday present for you. I know you will enjoy the new color TV. That old one was "all right" but not a good picture. I hope you will dispose of it as you also have the little one I had in my bedroom as a reserve if needed. So "enjoy" your new color set.

* * *

Mon, Aug 11, 1969

. . . The picture of Martha was real good, but I can't say much for me in the group picture. At least it was nice to have one of us all together. John referred to "our trip and vacation at Bedford Springs" and you said they would be away August 10 to 21. However, I am very vague as to where they are going on "the trip." More college shopping perhaps?

I appreciate Daddy's writing me from N. Y. I know it was a real effort for him to write long hand. I do hope he will get an electric typewriter. Couldn't we all give it to him for Christmas even if he gets it now?

. . . I'm so glad you're enjoying your birthday TV. You can get your achy knees up and still not miss anything you want to see.

JOHNNY'S SENIOR PORTRAIT

CATHARINE AND JOHN ROBERT

* * *

Sat, Aug 16, 1969

. . . I'm so glad Stephen called. His "unfinished" letter was sweet. He does love you both and feels close to you. Both of the boys have given Martha some real moments of pleasure and support this summer. They both love and understand her, and she should be very grateful for that.

* * *

Sun, Aug 17, 1969

. . . Speaking of Christmas (ugh), I believe I am going to ask you and/or Audrey to take on the chore of picking out a Christmas card for me. I'll never be able to get any here. You know my tastes, and I know I would be satisfied with whatever you pick out. I believe you can get a discount by ordering in September. I would need about 125 and would like to have them printed with "Mary O Ingles." I don't care about price, although I wouldn't want to shoot the moon. Do you suppose you could do this for me?

* * *

Wed, Aug 20, 1969

. . . John Robert's letter was such a pleasant surprise. I figured he was with you last night and know you all enjoyed it. We are so lucky that those boys feel like they do about us and come to see us because they want to. I'll be so interested to hear all about it. If John Robert gave you his address in Eustis, please send it to me.

* * *

Fri, Aug 22, 1969

. . . I'm glad the Ingles trip seems to be going so well. They should be home by now, and I know you'll be glad to have them back.

John is going about this college business in a typical John Ingles fashion. Nothing precipitous, careful investigation, considering all angles etc. In all of this, I haven't had any idea what course of study Johnny is considering. Obviously not engineering. After their last trip, the most important reactions seemed to be the size of the gymnasium and the conditions of the golf course.

* * *

Sat, Aug 30, 1969

. . . John and Audrey do have a nice "family" life with the children. I sometimes wonder though, if they ought not to encourage the boys to branch out more. They are lovely boys, but have been so protected and restricted that they aren't getting much chance to mature.

* * *

Mon, Sep 8, 1969

I enclosed Stephen's darling, but lonesome, homesick letter. I was so touched that he would write me at such great length. You will probably want to share it with Martha, but ask her to send it back to you to keep for me. I am sure things started to pick up for him as soon as he got on the job and got busy. I sure hope he had more than the $50.00 I sent him to live on for two weeks.

. . . I am so glad you were able to find my Christmas

cards at "one sitting" and I know I will like them. The price is real good. Please let me know the total cost. You were so good to take on the project for me and I don't intend to let you pay for them. I do plan to write a "mimeo" letter. I may have to send it to Daddy to have reproduced for me. Maybe I can do it at the office—we have a mimeo machine, but I don't know if I can use it for something personal.

I'm glad you and Audrey could have a "day out" together along with the project. I know you both enjoyed it.

. . . Well, I'm rundown again, but happy tonight especially after receiving Stephen's letter. I treasure my relationship with those two boys. I have really had all the gravy there—no real responsibility but to indulge and spoil them and love them and to be loved in return. I've been very lucky and I am particularly grateful to Martha for letting me share them.

* * *

Wed, Sep 10, 1969

. . . Betsy is sure a chip off her Daddy—hard headed and determined. The main difference is that John never makes a fuss. He just calmly goes ahead and does what he wants to do. I side with Audrey on the parakeet bit. In my lonely old age, I may come to a parakeet or canary, but birds as pets have no appeal to me at this stage.

* * *

Fri, Sep 12, 1969

. . . I enclosed Catharine's sweet letter. I held it until I had answered it, which I did last night.

. . . Well, at least we can be pleased that John shot a 75

CATHARINE'S SENIOR PORTRAIT

at golf. I hope he did as well in the finals. He must have really been hot, as I don't think that is his normal game.

* * *

Sun, Sep 28, 1969

. . . I had a nice letter from John Ingles yesterday telling me about the study and the children. Their plans for the study sounded so good and I know it will be a welcome addition.

. . . Apropos of your comment about Catharine calling her brothers "my boys." I remember when they all arrived at Fort MacArthur and we met them at the airport. Catharine was 18 months old. Anyway, the boys climbed happily into my car and M and C got into yours. When C realized the boys weren't with her, she started to carry on—"My boys! My boys!" Do you remember?

* * *

Tues, Sep 30, 1969

. . . I am glad to know you had your flu shots before Frank went off on his trip. I hope you had no adverse reactions. What a comfort it is to have him looking after you.

. . . I'm so glad Daddy had a happy evening at [the] RCA do. It sounds like quite a bash and I'm happy he was part of it.

* * *

Tues, Oct 7, 1969

. . . I'm very glad to know that Daddy made a move about his retirement from the RCA boards. The decision has been bothering him for so long. I know he will miss it, but it is so much better for action to be taken on his initiative.

* * *

Mon, Dec 8, 1969

. . . And thinking of Daddy I guess the most momentous news was his resignation from the RCA boards. I know he has been planning on it, but it is still a wrench for him I'm sure. I'm so proud of the way he handled it—with head high and flags flying. Not many men have had two complete, highly successful careers in one lifetime. He should be very proud, as we are all so very proud of him, I have a feeling that the consultant contract will be renewed as well as it should be. He refers to it as "the end of an era," but as you say, it has been a good era and is largely responsible for you being able to live as comfortably as you are.

. . . I am glad the Schrader's trip to Pennsylvania went well. M seems to "fall in love" with every college she visits. I am sure there are many lovely small colleges, but as you say, it is Catharine who is going to college, not M.

. . . Your Thanksgiving Day sounded so nice. I am always happy when John can go to church with you and I know you are. The new room sounds lovely and I do hope Mr. Roulsen will find time to do his bit before Christmas. It doesn't sound as if it would take him long, so maybe he can work it in between other jobs.

* * *

Wed, Dec 10, 1969

. . . How wonderful of Stephen to call you. I am sure he paid for the call too. And grand that he will be home for Christmas. That will just make Christmas for Martha and Catharine and for Stephen too. And I'll be happy, too, in my thoughts about them.

* * *

Fri, Dec 26, 1969

I have been thinking of you especially today on your anniversary and was happy to know of the nice plans John and Audrey had made for it. However, I heard on the radio tonight that there was a "snow emergency" in Washington so I guess that knocked out the plans. I couldn't be sure of the date so at least I hope it didn't prevent you getting together on Christmas. It wouldn't be the first Christmas that snow has messed up [plans] for you, however

* * *

Sun, Jan 25, 1970

. . . I received all the Australian literature Audrey sent. I am going to write her when I finish this letter.

* * *

Mon, Mar 30, 1970

. . . I'm glad that Betsy has finally gone back to school. She needs to pick up her routine again and be less the center of attention. [Spring of 1970, I had knee surgery. I was hospitalized for over a week and not able to go to school for some time after I was released from the hospital.]

* * *

The engagement, wedding plans and wedding of Mary's eldest nephew, John Robert Schrader, to Karen Palmer received a lot of airtime in the letters.

Sat, Aug 16, 1969

. . . Well, now to turn to your letters. Of course, the biggest piece of news is about John and Karen. I'm really pleased about that as I think they will be good for each other. They have certainly had a long time to get to know each other. I am sure Karen will be good for John—he needs looking after. She certainly knows by now his failings as well as his many strengths and must feel she can be happy with the whole package. I guess I'll have to write him a letter to East Lansing for Martha to forward, as he leaves for Eustis next week. I hope you get to see him en route. After he gets there it would be no trick for him to zoom up to Washington in the Porsche for a weekend.

* * *

Fri, Aug 22, 1969

. . . Your next letter should tell me about John Robert's visit. I was so interested in the views of meeting the family. The Palmer family sounds real solid and I'm glad the dinner went so well. It was all a bit hectic, but I know it made Martha happy to have John Robert in and out for a few days and to be feeling she was doing something for him.

. . . I hope Karen's aunts will contact you. They sound like nice people.

* * *

Thurs, Sep 11, 1969

. . . I guess there is no reason for John Robert and Karen not to go ahead with their marriage. It comforts me to know Karen has a profession and can find work wherever they are. She could probably get a job at the Army Hospital at Fort Lee as all the hospitals hire civilian nurses. They are under civil service and pay well. I suppose it is old fashioned of me to worry about how they can live on a 2nd Lt's pay. If they aren't worried, why should I be? I wonder if Karen will try to keep her car. If she gets a job, she would undoubtedly need it, but how could they afford to make payments on two cars? Again, it is not my problem.

. . . The question of the wedding present comes to mind. Of course I can always send a check, but would like to know if there are any special projects I might go in on.

. . . I'm returning the clipping of the engagement announcement as you may have another place you want to send it. I will buckle down this weekend and write Martha and John Robert.

* * *

Sat, Sep 27, 1969

. . . Well, back to John Robert and Karen. I suppose they will need things to set up housekeeping, but I don't imagine they'll be any one place for very long. My thought of sending a check was that it might help on necessities not normally considered as wedding presents. I am sure they are going to be strapped financially. John Robert won't get that per diem and mileage once he is married, although he will of course get a qtrs allowance. The per diem and mileage is only because he is a bachelor and there was no room at the BOQ Eustis. Well, anyway, I'll take your advice on the wedding present if you think the casserole is a good idea. It is OK with me. I have no idea where my calling cards are.

* * *

Sun, Sep 28, 1969

. . . I am glad that your shopping forays have been successful. Having the wedding in the offing provided an incentive which is something you and I always need. I hope you did go back and get the pearls. But why don't you let Daddy give them to you for Christmas? He never knows what to get, and these seem like something you really want.

. . . I guess this is the weekend for the three Palmers to come to the football game. I hope the weather was good and that it went well. I think the plan for them to go to Kazoo [Kalamazoo, Michigan] for the shower and arrange for the dinner at the same time sounds good.

* * *

Fri, Oct 4, 1969

. . . I am glad the weekend with the Palmers went so well. I was sure it would. I hope that got some of her anxieties about wedding plans cleared up by talking to Karen.

. . . The pewter idea sounds OK, and I would trust Audrey. If she's getting something in pewter, she might get a corresponding piece from me. Price is no particular object—I would spend anywhere from $30 to $50.

* * *

Tues, Sept 30, 1969

. . . I was interested in John Robert's letter. I was really not surprised at the change in his orders. The others never made any sense in view of his being regular army and his ROTC flight training. Of course I wish he wouldn't fly, but the flight pay will help financially. I do admire his resilience and refusal to let anything throw him. I just hope he leaves the Porsche in a safe place when he goes off to get married.

* * *

Mon, Oct 6, 1969

. . . Of course you will be the best dressed grandmother at the wedding, probably the best dressed woman.

. . . The pewter candlesticks are OK with me if they fit in with something Audrey and John decide to get. The price is no consideration, and I'll leave it to Audrey's judgment as to whether 7½" or 5½" are the best height.

* * *

Fri, Oct 10, 1969

. . . M&C should be in Washington now and I hope you are all enjoying it. Just be sure you get your naps and don't get too tired.

. . . I did receive an invitation to the wedding. I don't suppose it is really necessary, but I will "regret" formally. Just a "protocol" question—I do want to send the kids a check in addition to the candlesticks. Should I send it to John Robert or Karen? And where should I send it?

. . . Yes, I do seem to "bug out" on family weddings. Maybe it's just as well, as I am too prone to express my opinions and complicate things. [Mary was living in Germany in 1952 and missed the wedding of her brother, John Ingles to Audrey Primrose.]

Catharine and Martha Schrader

* * *

Sun, Oct 12, 1969

I have been thinking about M&C being there. I do hope it is a relaxed and happy time for all of you. With the various decisions made about the wedding it ought to be. I think M planned to send C back today and stay on a few days longer by herself.

. . . Since M is getting the candlesticks as my wedding present, I have decided to write John Robert and send him a check. They can use it any way they want, either to help on honeymoon expenses or to buy things they will need in getting settled. I want to write Karen a letter—something I haven't done to date.

* * *

Wed, Oct 15, 1969

. . . I hope you enjoyed John Robert's visit and that he was persuaded to buy a new suit. I sent him some money a few days ago. I said he could use it on the honeymoon or getting settled but wish he would use it to buy a decent suit. It would be sensible to wear his uniform, but I know he needs a good suit, not a six-year-old outdated model, fit or no.

* * *

Fri, Oct 17, 1969

. . . It sounds as if John Robert's visit was a real cheery one for all. He really has the ability to make everyone happy when he is around. He may be a bit impractical and a dreamer, but his good spirits, charm and optimism are wonderful assets. I don't know whether I am glad or sorry that the suit fit. I somehow hate to think about his being

Hal and Grace at the wedding

Hal and Grace with Karen and John Robert Schrader at their wedding

married in a six-year-old suit, even it has been scarcely worn. I wish he would wear his uniform, but I realize that young people these days have such mixed feelings about the war and being a part of it. Maybe it is right for him to at least have his wedding disassociated from it all.

* * *

Tues, Oct 28, 1969

. . . The various notes you sent on from Karen's aunts were so nice. They seem like lovely family and they have certainly all rallied around to help Karen. It is so sad that her mother can't be there, but the aunts are certainly doing all they can to make up for that.

* * *

Thurs, Oct 30, 1969

. . . Today I received your wonderful long letter written in the Detroit airport en route home. I gobbled up every word, and I can't tell you how relieved I was that it all went so well. I have a thousand questions, although you were wonderful about all the details and you will probably fill me in in subsequent letters. I particularly want to know about Steven, how he looked. . . . . Is he happy?

. . . I'm a bit confused about John Robert and Karen from now on. Do they go back to Eustis for a while? If so, where will they live? When do they go to Texas? Where is Fort Walters? These things too, I'm sure you will tell me

I really got quite homesick reading about it and wishing

I could be there. All those people whom I don't know. I'm glad Steven persuaded M. to leave me out of the toasts. It wouldn't have been appropriate when only the immediate family would have been involved. It was a sweet thought, though.

Well, now it is all over and I do pray for John Robert and Karen's happiness. Somehow, I feel confident that they are going to be OK. I'm so glad I had a chance to see them together last Christmas.

I surely hope that I will be sent some of the many pictures which you said were taken. I eagerly await your next letter with further details. Now you can relax and think about it and get rested.

* * *

Mon, Dec 8, 1969
. . . John Robert's picture came and I was so happy to see it. He is so handsome and looked so fit and thin. As I was opening it, I said to myself, "If I know my daddy, he will have enclosed an envelope to mail it back in." And of course, I did know my daddy and he had, complete with stamps yet!

* * *

Fri, Jan 9, 1970
. . . I was so happy to see the three snapshots of the "wedding." I've poured over them with a magnifying glass. I'm eager for more, but realize I may have to wait until I come home. I'll send these back as you requested, but want to keep them a few more days to look at.

* * *

Mon, Jan 12, 1970
. . . Before they go astray, I am returning various pictures. In the picture of Catharine with Pete Palmer, she is almost too beautiful to be believed. How did we ever get such a beauty in our family?

* * *

Cam Ranh Bay
Tues, Jan 20, 1970
. . . This is my first experience in staying in a trailer and I keep thinking of John Robert and Karen. They are really quite comfortable and, of course, [have a] minimum of housekeeping. I do wonder how Karen finds enough to keep herself busy all day.

* * *

Current Events

The Vietnam letters also included more references to events of US politics and the world than previous letters. Mary wrote of following the moon exploration, the "Teddy Kennedy problems" (Chappaquiddick), and Nixon's "de-escalation" attempts. Maybe by the late 60s and early 70s, it was easier and quicker to get news from halfway around the world, so it was natural for Mary to write about such current events. Or maybe they gave her something else to write about instead of revealing the conditions she was enduring.

All the following excerpts are from letters written in Saigon.

Tues, Jun 24, 1969

. . . The paper tonight carried the news of Judy Garland's death. So sad! She had such a lot of talent and such an unhappy life.

* * *

Thurs, Jul 3, 1969

. . . I have enjoyed the many clippings about Prince Charles. I hope you were able to watch the Investiture. I also hope you'll be able to see the new film about the Royal Family.

* * *

Fri, Jul 18, 1969

. . . I too am concerned about the Apollo 11. As of now, things seem to be going OK. I am praying for all of them, especially Mike Collins.

* * *

Tues, Jul 22, 1969

You lost out to "men on the moon" last night. We had dinner with Penny at the Rex last night and then watched the videotape of the astronauts walking on the moon on her TV. The latter doesn't function too well but we could get the general idea.

. . . Well, I just heard that Armstrong and Aldrich have relinked up with the command module, so that is another hurdle passed. I have really felt kind of sorry for Mike Collins having to zoom around alone, missing all the fun, yet being so vital to it all.

* * *

Sat, Jul 25, 1969

. . . The moon trip seems so unreal. I think I wrote you that I had seen some of the TV of the walk on the moon. Last night I saw the TV replay of the landing and the safe arrival on the carrier. The whole concept is so overwhelming that all I find myself thinking is "Thank God they are home."

. . . I really won't comment on the Ted Kennedy mess. The hearing is to be Monday, so we shall see.

* * *

Mon, Jul 28, 1969

. . . That was some storm they had in Alexandria [Virginia] and I am glad I missed it. [I] imagine the chapter and area office were out in force to handle the disaster. I have never understood why ARC doesn't get itself into the news reports because I'm sure they were on the job.

I have read some, but not all, of the Kennedy clippings you sent. So much to wonder about and question. It is so tragic for the girl and the family. I don't think Teddy is coming off very well, but I can't help but feel sorry for the elder Kennedys. Life has surely meted out to them more than their share of sorrow and tragedy.

* * *

Sun, Aug 3, 1969

. . . I'm just not going to fill letters commenting on the Teddy Kennedy fiasco. I have read some, but not all of the clippings you sent. There has been much of it in the papers here too.

When Pat Nixon visited the 24th Evac, she spent about 5 minutes in the Red Cross talking with the staff. They were so thrilled. I'm going to send them the picture and article you sent from The [Washington] Post. I was not visiting there at the time. That was there a couple of weeks ago. I'm including some clippings from the Stars and Stripes about the Nixons' visit.

* * *

Tues, Aug 26, 1969

. . . The Hurricane Camille sounds awful. Many calls today to see if we had any info other than press reports. We don't. We try to discourage requests to try and get reports from Disaster Areas but can appreciate people's anxiety. It will be a tremendous disaster operation for ARC and very costly.

* * *

Tues, Sep 2, 1969

. . . We are actually awaiting what Nixon has to say about further troop withdrawals later this week. We are hard put to know how to project our staff needs which we have to do six months in advance. Our staff requisition for Feb should go in this week.

* * *

Fri, Sep 12, 1969

. . . I thought of you watching the Miss America Pageant, and I'm glad your favorite won. I don't really know what the fascination of the yearly event is. I guess it's

really because the girls are not only beautiful, but seemed to be such fine all around girls.

. . . I just can't comment on the disaster which seems to have befallen the Episcopal Church. I guess it is just one more casualty in the whole impending collapse of what we like to think of as the "American way of life." I may be forced to flee to a mountain top in Bavaria in my old age, as I can't imagine that America will be any place to live 15-20 years from now.

* * *

Tues, Sep 30, 1969

. . . I was so interested in your report on "The Royal Family" and the reviews of it. How I wish we could have watched it together.

* * *

Fri, Oct 4, 1969

. . . I enjoyed the clipping about Mamie, Julie and David [Eisenhower]. Mamie was far from popular with the press when she was in the White House, but the tide of affection has now swung in her direction, and I am glad.

* * *

Sun, Oct 12, 1969

. . . I was interested in the clipping you sent about the televising of the "Forsyth Saga." It is quite a feat. I read the whole saga many years ago and loved it, but I do recall the multiplicity of characters and complexity of relationships and how hard it was to keep it all straight. I wonder if it

ANDREW TULLY

$200,000 Episcopal Donation

Possibly I might learn to live with if not approve the Episcopal Church's $200,000 surrender to a mob of thugs were it not for the apologies mounted by the church. Wisdom would seem to dictate that these confused clergymen go into hiding until the furor blows over.

Instead, a statement signed by the Rt. Rev. William F. Creighton, Bishop of Washington, defends the $200,000 bribe. The surrender, it says, was not in response to threats, and the dough will not come from the church's budget but from a special fund made up of contributions. The money, adds Creighton and Co., will be used to support such movements as the Black Economic Development Conference (BEDC).

Creighton and Co. should muscle in on the shell game racket. At the meeting at which the $200,000 fund was voted, the Rev. Muhammad Kenyatta seized the microphone and employed an impressive collection of obscenities to demand dough. Kenyatta is administrative chairman of BEDC. Thus the Episcopal church committed itself to pay off an outfit which has always advocated violence.

I realize some churchmen today are belatedly overcome by a feeling of guilt over living high off the hog for centuries while the poor went hungry and unsheltered. But if they now seek to make amends for their high living, they should extract the required money from their own pocketbooks, not from the life savings of their flocks.

Moreover, none of these men of the cloth have explained satisfactorily why the payola is going to the black militant groups. Surely, it would be more fitting and practical to funnel the money to such as the NAACP, which for more than a century has fought the black's battle.

Indeed, the Creighton statement admits this, as follows: "We did hear prophecies from white and black deputies that increasing violence would result from the white apathy toward the problems of poverty and racial discrimination. That such prophecies have a factual basis is evident in the rising rate of serious crime."

In short, give a hoodlum money and maybe he'll stop murdering, mugging, burning and looting.

But, just as important, the $200,000 bribe is a crime against the communicants of the Episcopal Church. I suspect a goodly percentage of these people are now wondering whether they can trust their bishops and ministers to spend the church's money wisely and legally. In their place, I would sit down and write a brief letter to my spiritual adviser.

It would inform him in simple English that henceforth I would hand over no more of my hard-earned cash, but would give it to a charity of my choice. I am not interested in playing small loan company to an underground manufactory of Molotov cocktails.

Copyright, Andrew Tully

10 Pacific Stars & Stripes
Wednesday, Oct. 8, 1969

would be harder on TV—if you missed a show, you would never be able to catch up.

* * *

Sun, Oct 26, 1969

. . . I've been reading Time's report on the moratorium and what it is all about. It seemed a calm and sensible evaluation, if not very encouraging. The overseas editions of Time [are] on sale over here and I try to get one every week. It fills in a lot of gaps on the news which I find hard to keep up with.

* * *

Mon, Feb 2, 1970

. . . I had Daddy's letter with his various suggestions regarding TVs, etc. I really can't think about that just now. I'll really have to wait until I find an apartment and see what space I have, etc. I assume I can have [the] little portable back that I gave you. That will give me something to use until I get settled.

I will appreciate his getting me some price info on cars. He can tell from the dope I sent him on the Plymouth as to what equipment I would like. I would like to know about the Ford Fairlane and also the Chevy Nova. I am not interested in a Ford Mustang—they are too uncomfortable to ride in. I might like to know about the Ford Falcon. I want a small car, but I do want 8 cylinders. I have driven 6 cylinders and they scare me. They don't have enough umph to move quickly when you need to pass on the highway or get quickly into a line of traffic, etc. There is only about $100 difference between 6 and an 8. If I'm going to order a car from here, I'll have to do it immediately after I get back

from Australia as you have to order 75 days prior to the delivery date you want.

* * *

Fri, Feb 13, 1970

. . . I was most interested in the price information you sent re: the Plymouth. It convinced me that I will not get involved in any deal from over here. I was suspicious of the whole thing and your figures convinced me. If you can send me some dope regarding Fords and Chevy Novas, I would be interested—for advanced consideration. However, I will not buy a car until I get home. I have some concern about whether I will have to pay double tax if I get a car in Wash. and then take it to Georgia. Also, I would have to register it in both places.

I appreciate your various suggestions about car equipment, etc. Some I will probably take, and some I probably will not. However, since I am not going to order a car from here, these decisions can wait.

* * *

IMPORTANCE OF THE LETTERS

A FINAL STORY ARC THAT spanned all tour locations was how important Grace's letters were to Mary. The letters from her mother—how anxiously they were awaited, how carefully they were read and reread, how speedily they were answered—were a critical part of Mary's overseas assignments. The love and reliance between the two women can clearly be read between the lines.

All the following excerpts are taken from letters written in Saigon unless otherwise noted.

Mrs. Harry C. Ingles

Martha – Keep Mary's
letters and return
them to me sometime.
She was so glad I saved
her letters from Korea and
Germany and had a
wonderful time re-
reading them.
She said "I was surprised
to see how well I wrote".
I feel better now that she
is there, her letters are
always a joy & she is so
good about writing often –

Note from Grace Ingles to Martha Schrader

Undated note from Grace Ingles to Martha Schrader, included with the first letter from Mary: *Martha—Keep Mary's letters and return them to me sometime. She was so glad I saved her letters from Korea and Germany and had a wonderful time re-reading them. She said, "I was surprised to see how well I wrote!" I feel better now that she is there. Her letters are always a joy and she is so good about writing often.*

* * *

Sat, May 10, 1969

I had my first mail from home today—a sweet letter from Daddy which he wrote from the University Club.

* * *

Wed, May 21, 1969

. . . No mail again today, which probably means I'll receive a batch together again.

Written at the bottom of the letter in Grace Ingles's handwriting: *I write and I write and I feel badly when there are two days without mail.*

* * *

Sat, May 24, 1969

I'm not pleased with the way mail seems to arrive over here this week. I had a bunch on Monday, two on Thursday and that is all. It may straighten out of course, but I would like it to come in regularly. I really can't understand it as it is all flown in and there are many flights each day. Well, there's nothing I can do about it except gripe a little. I do hope my letters to you aren't following the same pattern.

* * *

Thurs, May 29, 1969

I'm sorry I complained last week about gaps in mail as it seems to have concerned you. You and Daddy have been simply wonderful about writing and this week I have been getting mail daily. Today, a letter from you written Saturday May 24th and a long letter from Martha. Most of her news you had relayed to me, but I appreciated her writing and will answer her.

* * *

Sat, Jun 7, 1969

. . . You say I'm good about writing, but I have to say the same right back. You and Daddy have been just wonderful, and seldom miss a day. And as to filling my every expressed wish! Today I received the seat cushion for the office and I don't think I wrote about it more than a week ago. It is exactly what I wanted and it fixes me up just fine. Thank you, thank you!

* * *

Tues, Jun 24, 1969

. . . Your letters aren't dull to me. They help me feel close to you. I have been so involved the past three years I know and I am interested in all the little details, even that the sirloin roast turned out well. After all, these were the kind of things we talked about every night.

* * *

Thurs, Jul 3, 1969

. . . Writing you is never a chore. Sometimes I really don't have much to say and feel a little apologetic about how dull the letters are. However, I figure you would rather have a few lines of nothing rather than no letter, so I send them anyway.

* * *

Tues, Jul 8, 1969

. . . OK, I won't apologize anymore for dull letters. I'll just write them and trust you to endure.

* * *

Sun, Aug 3, 1969

. . . Well, I have gone over all your letters and commented on some, but not all, of the highlights. It has been a 2 hour project, but one I've thoroughly enjoyed. I really prefer getting letters one at a time, but no complaints.

* * *

Chu Lai
Wed, Sep 17, 1969

I talked to Joan today and she said I had lots of mail. I sure wish I could get my hands on it, but I'll just have to endure being cut off from the world.

* * *

Fri, Sep 26, 1969

. . . I had lots of mail and it took me over an hour to read it all. I am not going to try to answer it tonight, but it is wonderful to be in touch again. The only thing I was disappointed in was that most recent letter—yours of 20 September—did not mention receiving many letters I wrote and mailed along the way. I did write every day, but of course expected them to be slow in reaching you. They'll get there in due course.

* * *

Sat, Sep 27, 1969

The prospect of answering about 15 letters from you and Daddy at one sitting is a bit overwhelming, but I will start and do the best I can.

* * *

Sun, Sep 28, 1969

. . . Well, what with rereading letters and jotting down comment, I've been at this for over an hour, a most pleasant hour as I feel I have been having sort of a conversation with you.

* * *

Tues, Sep 30, 1969

Tonight I won't palm you off with a postcard, but will try to catch up with all of your letters. Really, you and Daddy are so wonderful about writing that I am sometimes hard put to it to keep up with you.

* * *

Fri, Oct 4, 1969

. . . Now don't start thinking you can't spell anymore. You do fine, and if you guess because you don't want to trudge out a dictionary, I don't mind a bit. Just keep writing. That's all I ask.

* * *

Mon, Oct 20, 1969

. . . Don't worry about "shaky hands." You have had enough on your mind and heart to make them shaky. I can always read your letters, love them, and count on them. So shake if you must, but don't stop writing.

* * *

Tues, Dec 16, 1969

There is so much mail pouring in these days that I find myself getting confused. Isn't that a strange complaint to make? The flood of Christmas cards plus much mail from you, Daddy and Martha is almost too much to keep up with. I'm going to try to bring a little order out of chaos by trying to get caught up with you and you with me.

* * *

Mary's retirement certificate

MARY AND JOHN INGLES DANCING AT THE WEDDING OF BETSY INGLES TO ERIC CHRISTENSEN, 1990

Mary couldn't save the letters written to her due to space constraints. In other postings, she wrote of her monthly ritual to reread the letters before throwing them away. But the fact that her letters were preserved by her mother, and eventually by Mary, indicates how important the correspondence was to her. I think they were a tangible reminder of the deep devotion the two women shared.

The letters from Vietnam end in March of 1970. Mary completed her tour there and returned to the States in the spring of 1970. No one in the family remembers her moving to Atlanta, so she must have been successful in her attempts to be assigned to the Washington, DC, area. Her final assignment for the ARC was creating a policies and procedures manual for the organization, something she was undoubtedly qualified to write given her years of experience and the varied locations she worked in. She retired from the ARC in 1981 and lived in Alexandria, Virginia, the rest of her life. She never returned to Europe or Asia after she left the ARC.

Mary Osborn Ingles passed away on July 27, 2011.

Glossary of Terms

AAA bn	Antiaircraft artillery battalion
AB	Airforce base
AGO card	Adjuntant General's Office card, standard issue military identification card
APO	American Post Office
ARC	American Red Cross
ASCOM	Army Service Command
Ascom City	Large US Army base outside of Seoul, Korea, active between 1945 and 1970
ASTP	Army Specialized Training Program
AWOL	Absent without leave
BMR	Baseline Monitoring Report
Bn	Battalion
BOQ	Bachelor Officers' Quarters
Capt	Captain
CG	Commanding general
Clubmobile girls	ARC staff who worked on frontlines to provide a touch of home, compassion, and comfort to US military
CO	Commanding officer
Col	Colonel
DMZ	Demilitarized zone
EM	Eligible man or eligible men
FD	Field director
FDA	Field director, Asia
FEA	Field Office Eastern Area (ARC acronym)
FO	Field office or field officer
Gen	General
GI	Ground infantry soldier or government issue soldier
Gray Ladies	ARC volunteers who provided services, including letter writing and serving in recreational rooms, at hospitals

GS rating	Government Service rating
HFD	Hospital field director (ARC acronym)
Hqrs, Hqs	Headquarters
Iron Curtain	The division between Soviet influences and Western influences
K14	Military airport in Seoul
KMAG	Korean Military Advisory Group
KT	Cocktail or cocktail party
LCU	Landing Craft Utility, type of boat used to transport troops and equipment
Lt	Lieutenant
Lt Col	Lieutenant colonel
LWOP	Leave without pay
MACV	Military Assistance Command Vietnam
MASH	Mobile Army Surgical Hospital
MATS	Military Air Transport Service
MP	Military police
MPC	Military Payment Certificate
MSC	Military Sealift Command
OEC	Operational Evaluation Command
OICC	Officer in charge of construction
OT	Officer trainee
PX	Post Exchange, a retail store on military bases
Qtrs	Quarters
Quonset huts	Prefabricated semi-circular structures made of corrugated steel
R&R	Rest and recreation or rest and relaxation
ROTC	Reserve Officers' Training Corps
sapper	In the letters, this refers to Viet Cong commando units
satchel	Charge, demolition device, or bomb
SGO	Surgeon General's Office
Sgt	Sergeant
SI list	Seriously ill or injured list
SMH	Service Medical Hospital (ARC acronym)
SMI	Sergeant major instructor
SRAO	Supplemental Recreational Activities Overseas (ARC acronym)
TDY	Temporary duty
The long gray line	The continuum of all West Point cadets and graduates
UNCMAC	United Nations Command Military Armistice Commission
USAID	US Agency for International Development
USARV	US Army, Vietnam
USO	United Service Organizations. The USO provides several different services to those serving in the military and their families. It is particularly known for providing world class entertainment to those posted overseas.
VN	Vietnam
WAC	Women's Army Corps
WAVE	Women Accepted for Volunteer Emergency Service, women's branch of the US Naval Reserve

Acknowledgments

I HAD NO IDEA WHAT I was getting into when I started this project, and had it not been for the help and encouragement of many people, this book would have remained just an idea forever. I want to thank my husband, Eric; my daughter, Grace (who is named for the recipient of these letters); and my son, Carl, for their constant encouragement. I thank them for patiently listening when I complained and for always showing interest in my progress. I also thank my brothers and cousins who helped by providing photos and verifying oral histories. This project has brought me closer to them, and I have learned so much about our shared grandparents. Many thanks go to the numerous friends who gave me hope that this book might be interesting to people outside of our family. I thank my editor, Julie Scandora, for her painstaking work and for allowing all the letter writers to maintain their voice while also being grammatically correct. Finally, "thanks" doesn't seem like a big enough word to give to Melissa Coffman of Book House Publishing. Without her support, suggestions, encouragement, humor, and patience I would never have been able to create *Letters to Grace*. She started as a consultant and has now become a cherished friend.

About the Author

Betsy Ingles Christensen was lucky enough to grow up with all four of her grandparents, including Grace Salisbury Ingles, having an active role in her life. She was also lucky enough to know the joy of receiving personal letters, for her father, John Ingles, was a devoted letter writer. When she became the owner of the family letters, she felt an obligation to liberate the stories held within the pages. Betsy hopes others will enjoy and learn from her family's stories and perhaps pursue the adventure of finding and documenting their stories as well.

She is also the author of two children's books about her blind rescue dog, Randy: *Resilient Randy Finds His Home* and *Resilient Randy Loses His Vision*. For information on those stories, visit her website: ResilientRandy.com.

Betsy lives in the Seattle area with her husband, Eric, and their dog. To her great joy, her children, Grace and Carl, also live in the Pacific Northwest.

9 781967 874057